Sustainable Development Goals Series

The **Sustainable Development Goals Series** is Springer Nature's inaugural cross-imprint book series that addresses and supports the United Nations' seventeen Sustainable Development Goals. The series fosters comprehensive research focused on these global targets and endeavours to address some of society's greatest grand challenges. The SDGs are inherently multidisciplinary, and they bring people working across different fields together and working towards a common goal. In this spirit, the Sustainable Development Goals series is the first at Springer Nature to publish books under both the Springer and Palgrave Macmillan imprints, bringing the strengths of our imprints together.

The Sustainable Development Goals Series is organized into eighteen subseries: one subseries based around each of the seventeen respective Sustainable Development Goals, and an eighteenth subseries, "Connecting the Goals," which serves as a home for volumes addressing multiple goals or studying the SDGs as a whole. Each subseries is guided by an expert Subseries Advisor with years or decades of experience studying and addressing core components of their respective Goal.

The SDG Series has a remit as broad as the SDGs themselves, and contributions are welcome from scientists, academics, policymakers, and researchers working in fields related to any of the seventeen goals. If you are interested in contributing a monograph or curated volume to the series, please contact the Publishers: Zachary Romano [Springer; zachary.romano@springer.com] and Rachael Ballard [Palgrave Macmillan; rachael.ballard@palgrave.com].

Olanike S. Adelakun · Erebi Ndoni
Editors

Reproductive Health and Assisted Reproductive Technologies In Sub-Saharan Africa

Issues and Challenges

palgrave
macmillan

Editors
Olanike S. Adelakun
School of Law
American University of Nigeria
Yola, Adamawa, Nigeria

Erebi Ndoni
School of Law
American University of Nigeria
Yola, Adamawa, Nigeria

ISSN 2523-3084 ISSN 2523-3092 (electronic)
Sustainable Development Goals Series
ISBN 978-981-99-2410-3 ISBN 978-981-99-2411-0 (eBook)
https://doi.org/10.1007/978-981-99-2411-0

Cover illustration: Christian Ohde/Alamy Stock Photo

This Palgrave Macmillan imprint is published by the registered company Springer Nature Singapore Pte Ltd.
The registered company address is: 152 Beach Road, #21-01/04 Gateway East, Singapore 189721, Singapore

To all IRC 20 scholars and all African researchers striving towards "The Africa We Want".

Foreword

Reproductive health is gaining traction in several parts of Africa today despite the traditional, cultural and environmental limitations. The legal and institutional frameworks as well as constitutional imperativeness are *sine qua non* to the development of reproductive health in Africa. This book speaks to the challenges of reproductive health rights, the existing position and the future of reproductive health in the countries of focus.

Reproductive health is an all-encompassing process as it connotes health in all its ramifications including physical, mental, emotional and social balancing of the people and not necessarily absence of illness, disease or infirmity. It is also a concept that is beyond sexual engagement, sexuality or assurance of "satisfying and safe sex life." It connotes freedom, liberty and rights to make informed and enlightened decisions on issues that affect well-being and satisfaction in all its strata.

In this book, from the introductory chapter to the conclusion of the work, the authors navigated the various legal instruments including the 1994 International Conference on Population and Development, Sustainable Development Goals (SDG), the African Union Agenda 2063, the national constitutions and statutory provisions across Africa including Nigeria, Liberia and South Africa. The authors used current data to convey home their points and called attention to the gaps that need to be filled for reproductive health rights to develop in the manner that will galvanise other socio-economic rights to take a pride of place in Africa.

The economic implications of reproductive health, the challenges faced by aged persons and the implications of pandemics on reproductive health were addressed in some of the chapters where the authors adroitly navigated the issues in a way to make reproductive health more acceptable to the continent and ensure that the craving for biological children does not diminish the progress and contributions of reproductive health in Africa. The issues were discussed in a way to assuage the perception and the attachment to cultural idiosyncrasies.

It is important to stress that this work has opened up a new vista in Africa in this area of knowledge and it is now more imperative for African scholars of the social-legal bent to focus their research searchlight on hitherto "dry" areas of law, provide data as well as law reform options with a view to advancing knowledge, not for knowledge's sake, but for the purpose of advancement of the society in all its ramifications.

I congratulate the editors for this feat and commend the authors for the great industry displayed in their various contributions.

This book will go a long way in ensuring that the stereotype of the average African man or woman is changed for the better and reproductive health will be perceived through a different prism. It will assist academics, legal practitioners, policy makers and the generality of the society. This is a welcome addition to our library in a way to open our eyes to this emerging area of law, it is highly recommended.

June 2022

Prof. Wahab Egbewole, SAN; FCArb
University of Ilorin
Ilorin, Nigeria

Acknowledgements

The Editors would like to thank the Law and Society Association (LSA) and International Research Collaborative 20 (IRC 20) for their support that led to the initiative of this book.

The leadership of Professor Abdulwahab Egbewole, SAN in bringing African scholars together is appreciated. The Editors are also grateful to Associate Professor Azubike Onuora-Oguno for chairing the session that births the publication at the 2021 virtual LSA annual meeting.

The kind support of the professional Palgrave is acknowledged. Special thanks to Vishal Daryanomel, Saranya Siva, Lavanya Devgun and the entire editorial team for their editorial support.

The input of Professor Donrich Thaldar, who graciously offered to contribute a chapter, to this book is also acknowledged.

Our profound appreciation also goes to our families for their understanding, love and support through every phase of this project.

Contents

Notes on Contributors

Ibrahim Banaru Abubakar is a senior registrar in family medicine at Ahmadu Bello University Teaching Hospital in Zaria, Nigeria. He has a specialist background in sexual and reproductive health and rights, earning a MHSc and M.Phil. with an unwavering commitment to health policy research and advocacy. Originally trained in the sciences, his master's degree in health economics ignited his interest in multidisciplinary research approaches focused on health equity and sustainable development. He serves on a number of thematic working groups, including the Nigerian Economic Summit Group's Health Policy Commission and the Nigeria National Development Planning Committee post-2020.

Olanike S. Adelakun, LL.D is a lecturer at the School of Law, American University of Nigeria. Olanike specialises in women's rights, child protection, sexual and gender-based violence, reproductive health rights and sexual harassment, all withing the field of international family law. Olanike is one of the coordinators of IRC 20; she is also the coordinator of the UNFPA funded capacity building course on gender-based violence in emergencies since 2019. Olanike consults for the government, United Nations entities, INGOs and CSOs in her field of engagement. Her research and consultation have led to a series of scholarly publications, development of curriculum and training modules, advocacy toolkits, policy briefs and judicial opinions. Olanike is an alumnus of the Hague Academy of International law and also an active member of several professional bodies including the Nigerian Bar Association, International Federation of Women Lawyers, Law and Society Association, African Network of Constitutional Lawyers and International Society of Family Lawyers, to mention a few.

Folakemi O. Ajagunna, Ph.D., is a Lecturer in the Department of Private and Property Law, Faculty of Law, University of Ibadan, Nigeria. She is also a Staff Clinician at the University of Ibadan Women's Law Clinic. Her research interests include reproductive and sexual health law, public health law and Clinical Legal Education. She is passionate about research on emerging legal, social and ethical issues in assisted reproductive technologies in Nigeria. She teaches Reproductive Health Law, Land Law and Equity and Trusts at the University of Ibadan.

Adetokunbo Alase is a doctoral candidate at the School of Law, Western Sydney University Australia. His research investigates the environmental dispute resolution from the mining sector perspective and the implication of adaptive governance on remediation of harm or disaster. Prior to his candidature at WSU, Adetokunbo was a Law lecturer at Lead City University, Ibadan Nigeria.

Anne Alase is a medical practitioner who has worked in mental health and with other vulnerable populations. After years of practice in Nigeria, Anne now practices Psychiatry in the United Kingdom where she continues to support women to achieve their goals. On quiet days, she spends time with her twin boys who keep her on her feet. The future for Anne will involve continued exploration of the intersections between law and psychiatry with the aim of finding common grounds that can lead to a better world.

Veronica Fynn Bruey, Ph.D., is a multi-award winner academic-advocate. Holding six academic degrees, she has researched, taught, consulted and presented at conferences in over 30 countries. She's authored five books, several book chapters and journal articles. She is the editor-in-chief of the *Journal of Internal Displacement*; co-lead Displaced Peoples Collaborative Research Network; lead of Disrupting Patriarchy and Masculinity in Africa International Research Collaborative; president of the International Association for the Study of Forced Migration, and Co-Chair, Africa Interest Group, American Society of International Law. She is an Action Canada Fellow and assistant professor of Legal Studies at Athabasca University. Veronica is a born and bred Indigenous Liberian war survivor.

Somterimam Paul Dogara had her early education in the Federal Government Primary School, Wuka and Girls' High School, Gindiri, Plateau State. She holds a B.Sc. degree honours and M.Sc., both in Anatomy, from the University of Maiduguri and the University of Lagos respectively. She is currently a Lecturer in the Public Health department of the Taraba State University, Jalingo.

Aliki Edgcumbe is a doctoral research fellow at the University of KwaZulu-Natal (UKZN). She acquired her Bachelor of Laws (LL.B.) from UKZN in 2007 and completed a Master of Laws (LL.M.) at UKZN in 2021, specialising in child care and protection law. Her dissertation focused on the case of *AB v Minister of Social Development*, where she scrutinised the genetic-link requirement in surrogate motherhood agreements as contained in section 294 of the Children's Act and explored the use of psychological evidence in constitutional litigation.

Harsha Gihwala is a Research Officer at the GHJRU (UCT). Her areas of interest include access to justice for victims of sexual and gender-based violence, crimino-legal research and the development of law and policy that best serves those who have experienced incidences of violence against women. Before joining the GHJRU, she fulfilled her practical vocational training at the Women's Legal Centre, a feminist public interest legal centre. Harsha holds an LL.B. from the University of Cape Town, and is currently completing an LL.M. specialising in Criminology, Law and Society, with a dissertation focusing on rape sentencing cases in South Africa.

Grace Titilayo Kolawole-Amao has been teaching and carrying out research in the field of law at Bowen University, Iwo, Nigeria since January 2011. She holds a Bachelor of Laws (LL.B.) degree from the University of Ibadan, Nigeria, a Barrister-at-Law (B.L.) degree from the Nigerian Law School, a Master of Laws (LL.M.) degree from the University of Ibadan, Nigeria, a Master of Philosophy (M.Phil.) degree in Law from Obafemi Awolowo University, Nigeria and Doctor of Philosophy (Ph.D.) degree in Law from the Obafemi Awolowo University, Nigeria. Her research interests are Criminal Law, Reproductive Health Law and Human Rights Law.

Paul Dogara Manga is a medical doctor and the current Director of Health Services at the American University of Nigeria (AUN) Health Center Yola. A graduate of the University of with an MBBS. He also has a Diploma in Disaster Management from the Adamawa State Polytechnic Yola and a Post Graduate Certification in Ultrasound, from New Delhi, India. Paul is currently studying towards a Master's degree in Public Health at the Texila American University. He is a trained gender-based violence in emergencies specialist with keen interest in reproductive health. He is also a certified sonologist.

Erebi Ndoni, Ph.D. is an Assistant Professor at the American University of Nigeria. The central premise of her research is the achievement of sustainable development which has fostered a long-standing interest on thematic areas that cut across this goal such as Gender Studies, Disability Rights, Natural Resources, International Trade and Social Responsibility. Erebi is licensed to practice law in Nigeria and also a qualified Solicitor of England and Wales. Erebi engages in projects and community services that focus on promoting gender equality and the protection of women's rights. She is one of the Co-ordinators of IRC 20. She has also consulted on several gender-related projects for some United Nations Organizations including the United Nations Populations Fund (UNFPA) and the United Nations Entity for Gender Equality and the Empowerment of Women (UN WOMEN) in developing and facilitating course, training s and advocacy materials on Sexual and Gender-Based Violence (SGBV), Gender-Based Violence in Emergencies (GBViE) and Ending Violence Against Women and Girls (EVAWG). Some of her professional affiliations include the Nigerian Bar Association, International Federation of Women Lawyers, the Society of International Economic Lawyers and the African International Economic Lawyers Network.

Dorcas Odunaike, Ph.D., is an Associate Professor at the School of Law and Security Studies, Babcock University, Ogun State where she teaches at the undergraduate and graduate levels. Her area of expertise covers Commercial Law, Family Law and Intellectual Property Law and she has published extensively in those areas of the law. She is a recipient of the Australian Leadership Award Fellowship, 2012 and has served as Legal Adviser to many organizations. She is also an active member of many professional bodies, including the Nigerian Bar Association, the Nigerian Association of Law Teachers and Nigerian Association of Adventist Lawyers.

Amarachi Chizaram Okonkoh is a lecturer at the Babcock University School of Law and Security Studies, Ogun State, Nigeria. Her area of expertise is Health Law, Reproductive Health Law and the intersection of Intellectual Property and Health Law. She provides legal advisory to organisations within the health space and is an advocate for health reform and the strengthening of access to essential healthcare through the law. She is passionate about influencing the development of an ART specific law in Nigeria through research and advocacy.

Bolanle Maryanne Oyekan, LL.B. (OOU), LL.M. (Unilag), is a qualified Legal Practitioner and Corporate Governance expert in Nigeria. She is a Ph.D. candidate at the University of Ottawa, Ontario, Canada, and a member of the Open African Innovation Research Network and New and Emerging Researchers Network with interests in Health Law Technology, Policy and Ethics. Her current research is in Regulating Assisted Reproductive Technology practice in Africa. She is a recipient of many scholarships including the 2021 Special-Merit Scholarship for Graduate Students at the Faculty of Law, University of Ottawa, Ontario, Canada, and the 2021 Audrey J. Boyce Graduate Law Scholarship.

Bonginkosi Shozi, Ph.D., is currently a postdoctoral research scholar at the Institute for Practical Ethics, at the University of California San Diego. He is also an Honorary Research Fellow at UKZN's School of Law, affiliated with the Health Law and Ethics Research Interest Group. Dr Shozi conducts research on the legal, ethical and human rights implications of novel health-related technologies from an African perspective. This includes genetic technologies—such as CRISPR—as well as assisted reproductive technologies, and pharmaceutical products.

Nasreen Solomons is an admitted attorney of the High Court of South Africa and a Research Officer at the Gender, Health and Justice Research Unit (UCT). Her research areas include Sexual and Reproductive Justice, Public Health, and access to justice for underserved communities. Nasreen previously worked as an attorney at the Women's Legal Centre leading its SRHR programme, and fulfilled her practical vocational training at the Legal Resources Centre. Nasreen holds a B.A. in English, History and Philosophy; an Honours degree in Historical Studies; and an LL.B. from UCT; and is currently completing an LL.M. by dissertation, focusing on Refugee Law.

Donrich Thaldar, Ph.D., is a professor of law at the University of KwaZulu-Natal, Durban, South Africa. His research interests are biolaw and bioethics, with a focus on genomics research and new reproductive technologies. He also has a private law practice, where he focuses on strategic litigation in biolaw. He served as legal counsel in several landmark cases in biolaw in South Africa, including the country's first physician-assisted dying test case, its first case of posthumous conception, and its first case that considered the validity of a known sperm donor agreement.

Abbreviations

ACHPR	African Charter on Human and Peoples' Right
ART	Assisted Reproductive Technologies
CABICOL	Catholic Bishop Conference of Liberia
CEDAW	Convention on the Elimination of all forms of Discrimination Against Women
CESCR	Committee on Economic, Social and Cultural Rights
CFRN	Constitution of the Federal Republic of Nigeria
CRPD	Convention on the Rights of Persons with Disabilities
CTOPA	Choice on Termination of Pregnancy Act
D&E	Dilation and Evacuation
DNA	Deoxyribonucleic Acid
ECOWAS	Economic Committee of West African States
ET	Embryo Transfer
EVAWG	Ending Violence Against Women and Girls
GBViE	Gender-Based Violence in Emergencies
GDP	Gross Domestic Product
GIFT	Gamete Intra Fallopian Transfer
HIV	Human Immuno-Deficiency Virus
HPA	Health Professions Act
HPCSA	Health Professions Council of South Africa
ICCPR	International Covenant on Civil and Political Rights
ICMART	International Committee for Monitoring Assisted Reproductive Technology
ICPD	International Conference on Population and Development
ICSI	Intra Cytoplasmic Sperm Injection
ICT	Information Communication Technology

IHRL	International Human Rights Law
IUI	Intra Uterine Insemination
IVF	*In Vitro* Fertilization
LGA	Local Government Area
MVA	Manual Vacuum Aspiration
NHA	National Health Act
NMA	Nigerian Medical Association
OP-ICESCR	International Covenant on Economic, Social and Cultural Rights
PGD	Preimplantation Genetic Diagnosis
PGT	Preimplantation Genetic Testing
PoA	Program of Action
PWD	Persons with Disabilities
RBA	Rights-Based Approach
RH	Reproductive Health
RHR	Reproductive Health Rights
SDG	Sustainable Development Goals
SEA	Sexual Exploitation and Abuse
SGBV	Sexual and Gender-Based Violence
SMA	Self-Managed Abortion
SOGON	Society for Obstetrics and Gynaecology of Nigeria
SRH	Sexual and Reproductive Health
SRHR	Sexual and Reproductive Health and Rights
UDHR	Universal Declaration of Human Rights
UNFPA	United Nations Populations Fund
UNICEF	United Nations International Children's Emergency Fund
UN WOMEN	United Nations Entity for Gender Equality and the Empowerment of Women
VAPPA	Violence Against Persons Prohibition Act
WHO	World Health Organization
WWD	Women with Disabilities
ZIFT	Zygote Intra Fallopian Transfer

List of Figures

List of Tables

PART I

Reproductive Rights

CHAPTER 1

Introduction—Reproductive Health Rights and Reproductive Technologies in Africa

Olanike S. Adelakun and Erebi Ndoni

The International Conference on Population and Development (ICPD) held in 1994 marked a hallmark of change as reproductive capacity was translated from an object of population control to the tenets of empowerment and autonomy in relation to sexual and reproductive health and reproductive rights. Reproductive rights connotes the ability to have a satisfying and safe sex life, the capability to reproduce and the autonomy to do so.[1] This implies not just access to information regarding reproductive health but also access to services and regulations within the ambit of the law. This also influences the right to make decisions related to reproduction devoid of discrimination, coercion and violence as entrenched in human rights treaties.

[1] 7.2 ICPD Programme of Action.

O. S. Adelakun (✉) · E. Ndoni
American University of Nigeria, Yola, Adamawa, Nigeria
e-mail: nikegolden@yahoo.com

O. S. Adelakun and E. Ndoni (eds.), *Reproductive Health and Assisted Reproductive Technologies In Sub-Saharan Africa*, Sustainable Development Goals Series,
https://doi.org/10.1007/978-981-99-2411-0_1

In 2013, the African Union adopted Agenda 2063 as a master plan for sustainable development and economic growth in Africa.[2] One of the aspirations of Agenda 2063 is the establishment of an Africa where human rights are respected.[3] Furthermore, goal 3 of aspiration 1 is to promote healthy and well-nourished citizens by broadening access to quality healthcare services, especially for women and girls. Similarly, one of the targets of Goal 3 of the Sustainable Development Goals on Good Health and Well-being is to ensure universal access to reproductive healthcare services. It is therefore imperative that reproductive health rights be considered, in the African continent, to determine the extent to which these rights are statutorily guaranteed in Africa.

Regulatory frameworks for becoming parents in sub-Saharan Africa have focused on adoption and fosterage without taking into consideration that in sub-Saharan Africa, the importance attached to having a biological child cannot be overemphasised and an adopted child cannot take the place of a biological child. Thus, many infertile persons across Africa take extreme measures and 'cut corners' to achieve the dream of becoming biological parents. The lack of regulation of some of these measures has opened up the opportunity to exploit vulnerable stakeholders such as surrogate mothers, gamete donors and commissioning parents.

While reproductive rights in terms of population reduction have gained much attention in sub-Saharan Africa, little attention has been paid to the reproductive rights to conceive and choose the mode of conception from a fertility perspective within the continent. Furthermore, most literature in the area of reproductive health in sub-Saharan Africa focuses on family planning, the right of access to contraceptives and mortality rate. The utilisation of assisted reproductive technologies (ARTs) is rapidly increasing in sub-Saharan Africa, therefore transforming the region into a novel frontier for reproductive tourism. Additionally, the gradual recognition of same-sex marriage and association in some parts of Africa has necessitated the need to explore ART as a means for same-sex couples and partners to achieve the desire of becoming biological parents. It is therefore essential that regulation is put in place to avoid abuse and exploitation.

[2] African Union, 'Agenda 2063: The Africa We Want' <https://au.int/en/agenda2063/overview> accessed 18 June 2022.

[3] Aspiration 3 Agenda 2063.

This edited volume explores different aspects of reproductive rights and ART in sub-Saharan Africa. The distinction of this edited volume emanates from its examination of reproductive rights from the perspective of the right to conceive and options to become parents for infertile persons and persons who could not conceive without the utilisation of ART.

Some of the chapters in this volume were proposed and accepted for the Law and Society Association (LSA) Annual Meeting held virtually under the International Research Collaborative (IRC) 20 in 2021 that was held virtually due to the Covid-19 pandemic. The chapters in this volume were expanded through a general call for contributions in the area of ART in Africa.

The book's introductory and current chapter by Olanike S Adelakun and Erebi Ndoni, both of School of Law, American University of Nigeria, provide a background to the subject of ART in Africa and give a summary of the aspects covered in the remaining eleven chapters of the book.

In the second chapter of the book, Olanike S. Adelakun, a law lecturer at the American University of Nigeria, Somterimam Paul Dogara, a lecturer of public health at Taraba State University and Dogara Manga Paul, a medical director at the American University of Nigeria, explore the awareness of reproductive health rights among married women in the Adamawa State of Nigeria and compared the result to similar studies carried out in different parts of Nigeria. Adelakun, Paul and Paul posit that a combination of factors such as lack of awareness, cultural norms and patriarchy influence the right to reproductive autonomy. Data retrieved through the study revealed that the level of awareness of reproductive rights and reproductive autonomy is low in the region and when compared with other studies across Nigeria, there is a need for strategies to create more awareness on reproductive rights in Nigeria. They concluded on the need to replicate the study across Nigeria and Africa.

Ibrahim Banaru Abubakar, of Ahmadu Bello University Teaching Hospital, in the next chapter considers the sexual and reproductive health and rights of senior citizens through the prism of human rights. Ibrahim argues that despite the enormity of the ageing population and its projected increase in Africa, there has been neglect in terms of policy in this regard. This neglect attributed to socio-cultural norms is reflected through societal beliefs which can be overcome by sensitisation.

Ibrahim concludes the chapter by positing that senior citizens, as rights-holders, are entitled to the protection and promotion of their sexual and reproductive health rights.

In her chapter, Erebi Ndoni, an Assistant Professor at American University of Nigeria, brings to the fore the discourse on another set of vulnerable people in society as she examines the reproductive health rights of persons with disabilities in Nigeria. Erebi's chapter highlights the importance of inclusion as the world strives towards the attainment of the sustainable development goals. Her evaluation of the laws indicates gaps in certain legal provisions and certain cultural norms which impinge on the reproductive rights of persons with disabilities. She therefore makes recommendations on the domestication of certain provisions of the Convention on the Rights of Persons with Disabilities (CRPD) in order to effectively promote the reproductive health rights of persons with disabilities in Nigeria and across Africa.

In examining the provision of safe and legal abortion services through the utilisation of telemedicine during the Covid-19 pandemic in South Africa, Nasreen Solomons and Harsha Gihwala, who are both research officers at the Gender Health and Justice Research Unit, University of Cape Town, explore the importance of access to reproductive health services in emergency situations. Solomons and Gihwala discuss how the use of telemedicine was adopted to remotely provide healthcare in the peak of the Covid-19 pandemic in South Africa. The authors explored how telemedicine was limited during this period to exclude sexual and reproductive health services, especially abortion services which the authors argue would have been instrumental in reducing the burden of the healthcare system. 4 chapters on facets of abortion = good, but that's a third of the book!

Adetokunbo Alase, Doctoral Candidate of School of Law, Western Sydney University, Australia, and Anne Alase, a Specialty Doctor at Norfolk and Suffolk Foundation Trust, United Kingdom, in Chapter 6, engaged in a discussion of how the Covid-19 pandemic impacts on the reproductive health norms in West Africa. Alase and Alase argued that despite the fact that reproductive health rights are a human right, it was negatively affected during the lockdown period occasioned by the pandemic and this caused a setback in the progress made thus far in West Africa in promoting and protecting the reproductive health rights of women. The authors propose a systematic interplay of normative rules and informal guidelines in protecting and promoting the reproductive health right of women in times of emergencies. Using selected Post Covid-19 Economic Recovery Plans or Documents within West Africa, the authors maintain that African nations can build on adaptive governance literature to ensure effective reproductive rights measures in times of emergencies.

Veronica Fynn Bruey, Assistant Professor of law at Athabasca University, takes us through reproductive health rights in Liberia by specifically evaluating cases of abortion. Liberia ranks among one of the highest in terms of maternal mortality which is mostly attributed to unsafe abortion. Bruey showcases the lack of reproductive autonomy in Liberia on the premise that a woman's choice to abort a pregnancy is restrained by law. Adopting the rights-based approach and feminist legal theory analysis, Bruey examines the effect of (il)legal and (un)safe abortion on girls' and women's reproductive rights in Liberia. She concludes that post-war reconstruction needs, coupled with the effect of the Ebola Virus and Covid-19 pandemic crisis, emphasise the importance of the reproductive health rights of women now more than ever.

Grace Titilayo Kolawole-Amao, a senior lecturer at Bowen University, Nigeria, writes on reproductive health rights and regulation of assisted reproductive technologies in Nigeria. Grace emphasises the importance of reproduction and the need for persons to have the autonomy to make reproductive decisions. She examined the impact of infertility on the inability of some persons to have biological children and takes us through the relief that ART has brought to infertile persons. Grace further identified the various forms of ART practices available to become biological parents in Nigeria and in examining the legal and regulatory framework for ART in Nigeria, Grace comes to the conclusion that there is dire need to regulate the ART industry in Nigeria.

Bonginkosi Shozi, affiliated to both Institute for Practical Ethics, University of California and University of KwaZulu-Natal as well as Aliki Edgcumbe and Donrich Thaldar, both of School of Law, University of KwaZulu-Natal, South Africa, in their chapter, analyse the contemporary developments in the regulation of ART in South Africa. Drawing on the Constitutional Court's decision in *AB v Minister of Social Development*,[4] the authors examined reproductive health rights from the constitutional and judicial approach. Shozi, Edgcumbe and Thaldar engaged in the analysis of the legal framework for the regulation of ART in South Africa

[4] *AB v Minister of Social Development* 2017 (3) SA 570 (CC).

by identifying the core and permissive statutes and policies. The authors examined the position and rights of gamete donors and examined the regulation of surrogacy, genetic testing and other forms of medically assisted reproduction in South Africa. The authors posit that the understanding of reproductive health rights should transform and develop in the light of new frontiers in ART practice such as heritable human genome editing and non-invasive pre-natal testing.

In Chapter 10, Folakemi O. Ajagunna, a lecturer and staff clinician at the Faculty of Law, University of Ibadan, writes on the issue of informed consent and ethical considerations in ART in Nigeria. Ajagunna notes that the right to informed consent cannot be detached from a patient's right to reproductive autonomy. Adopting a socio-legal research methodology, Ajagunna engaged in vitro fertility (IVF) doctors, embryologists and women seeking IVF services in Nigeria to determine if the existing Guidelines on informed consent in medical practice are indeed adhered to in IVF treatments in Nigeria. Ajagunna discovered that while there are existing Guidelines to ensure that informed consent of patients is obtained in ART treatments, the reverse is the case in actual practice. Ajagunna thus recommended for additional medical rules and a legal framework to regulate ART practice in Nigeria to promote and protect the rights of parties to informed consent in ART treatments in Nigeria.

Amarachi Chizaram Okonkoh, a law lecturer, and Dorcas Odunaike, an Associate Professor of law, both at Babcock University School of Law and Security Studies, take up the issue of contract for gestational services by examining the legal status and enforceability of surrogate motherhood agreements in Nigeria. Okonkoh and Odunaike examine the extent to which established contract principles may be invoked in determining the validity and enforceability of surrogate motherhood agreements and the rights and obligations of contracting parties in Nigeria. The authors analysed the landmark case of *Re Olatunde*[5] to determine the different approaches to enforcing a surrogate motherhood agreement in Nigeria. Okonkoh and Odunaike raise concerns about the uncertainty and risk of conflicting decisions that may arise in Nigeria on the enforceability of surrogate motherhood agreements due to the lack of regulation of ART practice. The authors therefore emphasise the need for a regulatory framework for surrogacy contracts in Nigeria.

[5] *Re Olatunde* DHC /50/CS/2021 (Unreported) filed on 28 September 2021 in the Rivers State High Court, judgment was delivered on 29 November 2021.

In the concluding chapter of the book, Bolanle Maryanne Oyekan, a Doctoral student of the Faculty of Law, University of Ottawa, examines the role of data collection in developing effective legal framework for the practice of ART in sub-Saharan Africa by using Nigeria as a case study. Oyekan explores the role of the African Regional Registry in ART data collection by examining Nigeria as a participating country. She emphasises the importance of data collection for effective monitoring and quality control of ART services, especially with the proliferation of the ART industry by private fertility practitioners. Oyekan's analysis pays attention to the narratives of data collection and monitoring and how these fit into the effective legal regime of ART in Nigeria.

CHAPTER 2

Awareness of Reproductive Health Rights Among Married Women of Childbearing Age in Nigeria

Olanike S. Adelakun, Somterimam Paul Dogara, and Paul Dogara Manga

2.1 Introduction

Right to reproductive health, remains a socio-economic and non-justiciable right in many African countries, including Nigeria. Section 17 of the Constitution of the Federal Republic of Nigeria (CFRN), 1999 (As amended) implores the state to direct its policies towards safeguarding the

O. S. Adelakun (✉) · P. D. Manga
American University of Nigeria, Yola, Nigeria
e-mail: olanike.adelakun@aun.edu.ng; nikegolden@yahoo.com

S. P. Dogara
Taraba State University, Jalingo, Nigeria

O. S. Adelakun
School of Law, New York University, New York, United States

O. S. Adelakun and E. Ndoni (eds.), *Reproductive Health and Assisted Reproductive Technologies In Sub-Saharan Africa*, Sustainable Development Goals Series,
https://doi.org/10.1007/978-981-99-2411-0_2

health, safety and welfare of all persons in employment as well as to ensure adequate health and medical facilities for every person. Despite efforts by various stakeholders to ensure that the right to health is moved to the realm of fundamental human rights in the CFRN, being a right that has a direct bearing on the realisation of the right to life,[1] these efforts have been met with resistance and still remains non-justiciable in Nigeria.[2] Currently, section 6(6) of the CFRN ousts the courts' jurisdiction to entertain matters on the socio-economic rights recognised under the directive principles of state policy contained in Chapter 2, among which is the right and access to healthcare services. In fact, the Supreme Court in Nigeria held in the case of *Abacha v Fawehinmi*[3] that despite domesticating the African Charter on Human and People's Rights (African Charter), its provisions are subject to the CFRN and any contradictory provision of the African Charter is null and goes to no effect.

However, in the past years, due to the global commitment to the Sustainable Development Goals (SDGs) and the regional commitment towards the Agenda 2063 which both aim to achieve good health, well-being and well-nourished citizens,[4] right to reproductive healthcare in Africa has received attention. Due to the high pregnancy-related complications and maternal mortality rate in Africa, emphasis of reproductive healthcare has been more on fertility care and control compared to infertility treatments. To this end, several African governments have directed their policies towards contraceptives, family planning and reducing maternal mortality to the barest minimum but these reproductive health services remain largely unmet in Africa, including Nigeria.[5] While several studies have been conducted on the gaps in meeting reproductive health

[1] AKA Kolawole "The Right to Life and the Right to Health: Any Nexus?" (2010) 2(5) *OIDA International Journal of Sustainable Development* 99.

[2] O Nnamuchi "Kleptocracy and Its Many Faces: The Challenges of Justiciability of the Right to Health Care in Nigeria" (2008) 52(1) *Journal of African Law* 2.

[3] (2000) 6 NWLR [pt.] 2.

[4] See SDG 3 and Goal 3 of Aspiration 1 of Agenda 2063.

[5] MA Ayanore, M Pavlova and W Groot "Unmet Reproductive Health Needs Among Women in Some West African Countries: A Systematic Review of Outcome Measures and Determinants" (2015) 13(5) *Reproductive Health* 8.

needs,[6] factors responsible for the low realisation of the right to reproductive healthcare,[7] reproductive health literacy,[8] consent related issues in accessing reproductive healthcare and services as well as reproductive rights awareness among adolescents in Nigeria,[9] few studies have investigated the awareness and perception of the reproductive rights among women of childbearing age in Nigeria.

This chapter investigates the level of awareness and the perception of women of childbearing age on reproductive health rights (RHR) in Nigeria. Fresh data was collected in Adamawa, Nigeria and the findings were compared with existing similar studies in Nigeria. The study finds a correlation between the level of RHR awareness, and the progress made thus far in realising the right to reproductive health in northern Nigeria.

2.2 Literature Review

2.2.1 Reproductive Health and Rights

Reproductive health has been defined to be the ability of an individual to 'have a satisfying and safe sex life, access to safe, effective, affordable and acceptable methods of family planning based on informed choice and dignity that ensures the prevention of and treatment of sexually transmitted infections such as the prevention and care of HIV/AIDS.'[10] RHR refer to the freedom that people enjoy to make reproductive health choices concerning if, when and how to have children, the number of

[6] DT Esan and KK Babajidda "The Perception of Parents of High School Students About Adolescent Sexual and Reproductive Needs in Nigeria: A Qualitative Study" (2021) 2 *Public Health in Practice* 1.

[7] O Olomola and F Ajagunna "Knowledge and Access to Reproductive Health Rights Among Adolescents in Ibadan, Nigeria" (2020) 28(3) *African Journal of International and Comparative Law* 401.

[8] H Vaisanen et al. "Sexual and Reproductive Health Literacy, Misoprostol Knowledge and Use of Medication Abortion in Lagos State, Nigeria: A Mixed Methods Study" (2021) 52(2) *Studies in Family Planning* 217.

[9] EA Envuladu, K Massar and J de Wit "Adolescents' Sexual and Reproductive Healthcare-Seeking Behaviour and Service Utilisation in Plateau State, Nigeria" (2022) 10 *Healthcare* 1.

[10] Olomola and Ajagunna (2020) 403.

children, decision as to family planning and decisions related to termination of pregnancy.[11] It has also been described as the basic right that individuals have to decide freely and responsibly and to have information that will aid such free decision.[12] This right has been often described synonymously with reproductive autonomy. While RHR is the human right that enables a person to assert sexuality and reproduction, reproductive autonomy is the end result of RHR which gives a person the freedom to express and realise the reproductive right.[13] Thus, it is not farfetched that both terms are interrelated and cannot be completely detached from each other in order to achieve reproductive justice. RHR apply to both men and women but this chapter focuses on the RHR of women of childbearing age. Thus, reference will be made to reproductive health and RHR of women in this chapter.

Attention was drawn to the RHR of women at the global level after the 1994 International Conference on Population Development (ICPD) Program of Action in Cairo[14] where advocacy for the reproductive right and autonomy for women was made. The right and ability of women to make reproductive health decisions have been impeded by social context and gender inequality which is deep-rooted in many societies and pronounced in Africa. However, to achieve economic, social and sustainable development, women's autonomy cannot be overlooked as a result of which SDG 5 emphasises gender equality by advocating for 'universal access to sexual and reproductive health and reproductive rights.'[15]

[11] EKM Darteh, KS Dickson and DT Doku "Women's Reproductive Health Decision-Making: A Multi-Country Analysis of Demographic and Health Surveys in Sub-Saharan Africa" (2019) *PLOS One* 2.

[12] Olomola and Ajagunna (2020) 403.

[13] RJ Cook "International Human Rights and Women's Reproductive Health" (1993) 24(2) *Studies in Family Planning* 79.

[14] United Nations Population Fund *Programme of Action: Adopted at the International Conference on Population and Development, Cairo 5–13 September 1994* (New York: United Nations Population Fund 2004).

[15] SDG 5.6—United Nations "Transforming Our World: The 2030 Agenda for Sustainable Development" (2015).

2.2.2 *Legal Recognition and Protection of Reproductive Health Rights*

Although international human rights instruments did not deal with reproductive rights directly, there are provisions in some international instruments from which reproductive rights can be inferred. Article 3 of the Universal Declaration of Human Rights (UDHR), 1948 provides for the human right to life, liberty and security of all persons. A similar provision on the right to life can be found in Article 6(1) of the International Covenant on Civil and Political Rights (ICCPR), 1966. The right to life has been described as male-oriented since the right has been criticised to be narrowly interpreted to ignore women's reality because it did not pay attention to the death of women that may occur from pregnancy-related complications or from childbirth.[16] Furthermore, Article 9 of the ICCPR provides for the right to liberty and security of human persons. This right can be interpreted to recognise the reproductive choice of women on the basis of protection of the life and health of women. Thus, where national laws and cultural norms are permissive to restrict access of women to reproductive health services such as when the reproductive choices of women are dependent on their partners, this can be said to be a violation of the right to liberty and security of those affected.

Article 23 of the ICCPR also recognises the right to marry and found a family. This can be extended to a recognition of the right to procreate by deciding on when, how and the number of children to have, including the spacing of children. Again, lack of access to reproductive health services such as family planning, contraceptives, pregnancy-related treatments and infertility treatments can be hinged on this right. A lot of factors have threatened the right to find a family in Africa such as infectious diseases which increase the infertility rate as well as maternal mortality rate.[17] Article 17 of the ICCPR protects the right to privacy and family life which is quite related to the right to found a family but differs because it protects persons against arbitrary and unlawful interference with privacy, correspondence, home or family and offers protection from unlawful attacks on a person's honour and reputation. This echoes Article 12 of the UDHR.

[16] Cook (1993) 79.

[17] A Germain et al (eds) *Reproductive Tract Infections: Global Impact and Priorities for Women's Reproductive Health* (New York: Plenum Press 1992).

The Convention on the Elimination of all forms of Discrimination Against Women (CEDAW), 1979, enjoins state parties to repeal all national laws that discriminate against women.[18] Article 19 of the ICCPR as well as Article 19 of the UDHR recognises the right to seek, receive and impart information. This is directly related to the right to information on reproductive health. Articles 14(b) and 16(e) of CEDAW specifically require state parties to ensure that women have the right to information and counselling on health and family planning. Thus, women will only have access to reproductive health services only when they are aware of the services, where they are offered, how, when and at what cost.

All these rights recognised by international instruments are also recognised by the African Charter on Human and Peoples' Rights, (African Charter), 1981. Article 16 of the African Charter specifically recognises the right to enjoy the best attainable state of physical and mental health. This has been said to include the right to access family planning services.[19] More particularly, the Protocol to the African Charter on the Rights of Women in Africa (Maputo Protocol), 2003 recognises the health and reproductive rights of women. Article 14 of the Maputo Protocol provides for the rights of women to control their fertility, to choose whether to have children, the number and the spacing of children, right to choose the method of contraception, protection from HIV/AIDs, right to information on the health status of the woman and her partner and the right to education on family planning.

Nigeria is a signatory to all the international and regional instruments examined and has ratified them. In pursuant to section 12 of the CFRN which requires every treaty to be domesticated into national law before it can have effect, the instruments, except CEDAW and Maputo Protocol have been domesticated in Nigeria. Although the CEDAW and Maputo Protocol have not been domesticated, the Violence Against Persons Prohibition Act (VAPPA) was enacted in 2015 and protects persons against every form of violence. While lack of access to RHR information cannot be said to be an act of violence in itself, the lack of information could promote an environment of violence as a result of which the VAPPA

[18] Article 2(g) of CEDAW.

[19] J Gebhard and D Trimino "Reproductive Rights, International Regulation" in A Peters and R Wolfrum (eds) *The Max Planck Encyclopedia of Public International Law* (Oxford: Oxford University Press 2008) <www.mpepil.com> accessed 21 November 2021.

can be invoked. It therefore suffices that there is a legal platform to create awareness on the RHR of women in Nigeria.

2.2.3 Knowledge and Awareness of Reproductive Health Rights

A study by Ogunlayi to assess the awareness of sexual and reproductive rights among adolescents in South-West Nigeria reveals that many students at the secondary school level attribute sexual and reproductive rights to childbearing and while they have heard about sexual and reproductive rights, many do not know the contents of the said rights neither were they aware of their reproductive health.[20] A similar study carried out by Adeokun et al. in Northern Nigeria shows a very low level of awareness of reproductive health among adolescent boys and girls such as low knowledge of safe menstrual period, the possibility of getting pregnant at first coitus and sexually transmitted diseases.[21] The deficiency is a cause for concern because the study revealed that about 40% of the adolescent participants were in a relationship and sexually active despite the perceptions of the traditional and religious norms of the Northern region of Nigeria.[22] About 84% of participants in the study were eager to learn about reproductive health issues and require information.[23]

A study to investigate the knowledge of the use of family planning methods among women of reproductive age in Bauchi state of Nigeria shows that the majority of participants got information about family planning on radio and television campaigns.[24] The study further shows that out of the 9 family planning methods promoted, participants were only aware of the use of injectables and condoms.[25] Awareness of RHR is

[20] MA Ogunlayi "An Assessment of the Awareness of Sexual and Reproductive Rights among Adolescents in South Western Nigeria" (2005) 9(1) *African Journal of Reproductive Health* 105.

[21] LA Adeokun, et al "Sexual and Reproductive Health Knowledge, Behaviour and Education Needs of In-School Adolescents in Northern Nigeria" (2009) 13(4) *African Journal of Reproductive Health* 46.

[22] *Ibid.*

[23] Adeokun et al (2009) 46.

[24] CE Asogwa "Knowledge and Use of Family Planning Methods Among Women of Reproductive Age in Bauchi State, Nigeria Exposed to 'Get it Together' Media Campaign" (2018) 16(3) *Gender and Behaviour* 12009.

[25] *Ibid.*

important in order to improve the ability to seek and obtain reproductive health information which may assist a woman and her family in making informed decisions on childbirth and spacing.[26] Such decisions on reproductive health thus have an impact on the overall health of a woman.

2.2.4 Impediments to Realising Reproductive Health Rights in Nigeria

Scholars have attributed the low level of RHR awareness and realisation to cultural and religious norms which brings about a perception that discussion and information seeking on sexual-related matters is a taboo.[27] Furthermore, several discriminatory cultural rites that are practised in several Nigerian communities such as female genital mutilation, compulsory ingestion of herbal concoctions during pregnancies, widow rites and so on, hinder the realisation of reproductive rights of women. These practices are linked to the patriarchal system of African societies which has suppressed women's rights for ages. This is irrespective of the fundamental right against discrimination as guaranteed by section 42 of the CFRN.

Furthermore, the disparity in economic opportunities that places women at a disadvantage in terms of unequal access and opportunities to work and earnings compared to their male counterparts puts women at an economic disadvantage. Economic disadvantage reduces a woman's ability to effectively access reproductive healthcare service, especially in cases where such services are expensive and beyond the economic capacity of the woman. Thus, ineffective RHR cannot be completely detached from developmental challenges.[28]

[26] OA Moronkola, MM Ojediran and A Amosun "Reproductive Health Knowledge, Beliefs and Determinants of Contraceptives Use Among Women Attending Family Planning Clinics in Ibadan, Nigeria" (2006) 6(3) *African Health Sciences* 156.

[27] L Akhirome-Omonfuegbe "A Critical Appraisal of Women's Reproductive Rights in Nigeria" (2019) 10(1–2) *Afe Babalola University Journal of Sustainable Development Law and Policy* 275.

[28] Akhirome-Omonfuegbe (2019) 276.

Although RHR is gradually gaining recognition and promotion in Africa,[29] including Nigeria, there is a lot to be done to effectively realise this right. The government needs to take a proactive step to ensure access to quality and affordable reproductive healthcare services in Nigeria.

This study investigates the level of awareness of RHR and information-seeking behaviours of women in Adamawa state.

2.3 Methodology

A stratified sampling technique was used to select the study population. 150 women attending antenatal care across 2 public and 1 private healthcare facilities in Yola South and Yola North Local Government Areas (LGAs) were recruited for the study. Simple random sampling was used to select participants in order to eliminate bias. Participants were recruited from April 2020 through December 2020. The healthcare facilities visited offer fertility reproductive healthcare services such as family planning, antenatal and postnatal healthcare services and childbirth delivery services.

2.3.1 *Study Participants*

Women attending the healthcare facilities for antenatal and postnatal care were approached by the investigators at the reception areas and were invited to participate in the study. A total of 150 women from age 13 and above were selected to participate in the study. 52% of the women have post-secondary education, 31.3% have secondary education, 14% have primary education while 2.7% have no formal education.

2.3.2 *Study Design and Data Collection*

The researchers developed a paper-based questionnaire for the purpose of the study. The items of the questionnaire were divided into two sections with the first section focusing on women's socio-economic and family characteristics while the second section focused on knowledge and perception about reproductive rights, autonomy and decisions. The socio-economic and family characteristics section consisted of 18 items to determine the age, educational level, number of children and items

[29] O Ayanleye "Women and Reproductive Health Rights in Nigeria" (2014) 6(5) *OIDA International Journal of Sustainable Development* 127.

to determine the level of ease to discuss reproductive health issues with parents and spouses/partners. The second section consists of 20 items. The answers in both sections were coded from ranges of 1–6 and the lower the score, the higher the level of knowledge about RHR. The instrument was translated into Hausa and Fulfulde.

One health researcher assessed the instrument for validity and it was piloted on 5 women of childbearing age but not from the study sample. The pilot study population did not encounter any problem with the questionnaire and no changes were made to the data collection instrument.

Some participants completed the questionnaire themselves while some were assisted by the two co-investigators who read the contents to the participants in Hausa or Fulfulde, depending on the preference of the participants. The responses were translated into English language.

2.3.3 Ethical Consideration

The study protocol (PRO-20-04-04) was approved by the American University of Nigeria Institutional Review Board (AUN-20-04-04). The Medical Directors of the healthcare facilities granted permission to conduct the study in the facilities but were not part of the survey. Informed consent for the study was obtained from every participant with confidentiality ensured during the survey.

2.3.4 Data Processing and Analysis

The data was analysed using a thematic analysis approach by grouping the main themes together. The questionnaires were checked for completeness and were assigned serial numbers for identification. Open-ended questions were grouped according to their similarities and coded. The data was input into a Microsoft Excel pivot table to facilitate sorting and data management. Coding was verified by randomly comparing the coded questionnaires with the spreadsheet input for accuracy after which inconsistencies were resolved. The questions were analysed using frequencies and percentages.

2.4 Result

Table 2.1 presents the socio-demographic characteristics of 150 women who participated in the research. The age bracket with the highest number of respondents is 26–35 years with 62 (41.3%) respondents. There were 129 (86%) respondents who were married, 13 (8.6%) single, 4 (2.7%) each of divorced and widowed, respectively. Regarding the number of children, 33 (22%) of the respondents did not have a child at the time of data collection, 30 (20%) have two children while 12 (7.9%) have four children. Only 4 (2.7%) of the respondents did not have any formal education. The majority of the respondents 47 (31.3%) have up to secondary education, while 10 (6.7%) have a postgraduate degree. The respondents were mainly of two religious groups, 83 (55.3%) are Christians and 67 (44.7%) are Muslims. No participants from other religions participated in the study. About all participants held their religious faith as very important, only 7 (4.7%) thought of religion as being simply important.

Table 2.2 shows respondents' attitude to reproductive health matters. 96 (64%) and 114 (76%) of respondents indicated that they do not live in the same household as their father and mother respectively. All of the married respondents said that they live in the same household with their husbands. 62 (41.3%) and 90 (60%) of the respondents said they find it very easy to discuss important issues with their father and mother, respectively. However, 124 (82.7%) and 68 (45.4%) will never discuss sex-related matters with their father and mother respectively. While 21 (14%) find it easy to discuss important issues with their husband, 60 (40%) find it difficult and 39 (26%) find it very difficult to do so. 100 (66.7%) of respondents say they discuss sex-related issues with their husbands often, whereas 36 (24%) do so occasionally with 14 (9.3%) saying they never discuss such issues.

Figure 2.1 above presents respondents' knowledge of RHR. While 112 (74.7%) of the respondents indicated that they know the meaning of RHR, 38 (25.3%) did not know what RHR means. On the other hand, 89 (59.3%) have received a form of information on RHR while 61 (40.7%) never received information on RHR.

Table 2.3 above shows the respondents' decisions on reproductive health issues. On the number of children to have, 85 (56.7) of the respondents made a mutual decision with their spouse, 30 (20%) say decisions are made solely by their husbands, 27 (18%) of the respondents make the

Table 2.1
Socio-demographic data of respondents

Socio-demographic characteristics	*Frequency*	*Percentage (%)*
Age (Grouped)		
13–17	3	2
18–25	48	32
26–35	62	41.3
36–45	30	20
Above 45	7	4.7
Marital status		
Single	13	8.6
Married	129	86
Divorced	4	2.7
Widowed	4	2.7
Prefer not to say	0	0
Number of children		
None	33	22
One	25	16.7
Two	30	20
Three	25	16.7
Four	12	7.9
Five and above	25	16.7
Educational level		
No formal education	4	2.7
Primary	21	14
Secondary	47	31.3
Diploma/OND	35	23.3
University	33	22
Postgraduate	10	6.7
Religion		
Christianity	83	55.3
Islam	67	44.7
None	0	0
Other	0	0
Importance of religion		
Very important	143	95.3
Important	7	4.7
Not important	0	0

decision themselves, while relatives decisions make up 5.3% of the respondents. As regards the spacing of children, the decision made by both partners is 83 (55.3%), with 0% contribution from relatives. Regarding the decision to use family planning, 81 (54%) respondents made joint

Table 2.2 Attitude of respondents towards reproductive health matters

Variable	*Frequency*	*Percentage (%)*
Does your father live in the same household with you?		
Yes	54	36
No	96	64
Does your mother live in the same household with you?		
Yes	36	24
No	114	76
Does your husband live in the same household with you?		
Yes	129	86
No	21	14
How easy is it to discuss important things with your father?		
Very easy	62	41.3
Easy	45	30
Average	14	9.3
Difficult	16	10.7
Very difficult	5	3.3
Do not see him	8	5.4
How easy is it to discuss important things with your mother?		
Very easy	90	60
Easy	43	28.7
Average	5	3.3
Difficult	5	3.3
Very difficult	4	2.7
Do not see her	3	2
How easy is it to discuss important things with your husband?		
Very easy	21	14
Easy	12	8
Average	8	5.3
Difficult	60	40
Very difficult	39	26
Do not see him	10	6.7
Have you ever discussed sex-related matters with your father? If YES Often or occasionally?		
Often	11	7.3
Occasionally	15	10
Never	124	82.7
Have you ever discussed sex-related matters with your mother? If YES Often or occasionally?		

(continued)

Table 2.2 (continued)

Variable	*Frequency*	*Percentage (%)*
Often	41	7.3
Occasionally	41	10
Never	68	82.7
Have you ever discussed sex-related matters with your husband? If YES Often or occasionally?		
Often	100	66.7
Occasionally	36	24
Never	14	9.3

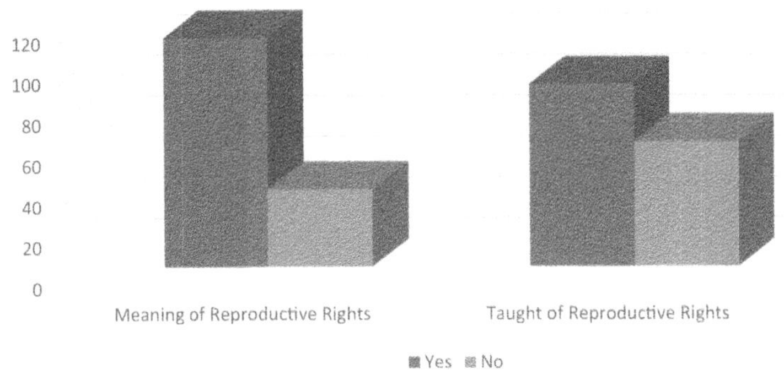

Fig. 2.1 Respondents' knowledge on reproductive health rights

decisions with their spouse, 36 (24%) respondents made decisions alone and 29 (24%) say their husbands make the decision. On the family planning method to use, 61 (40.7%) make joint decisions with their spouse, 21 (14%) say the husband decides and 12 (8%) say the decision is made by the husband's relatives.

The reproductive information-seeking behaviour of respondents is presented above as Fig. 2.2. While 60 (40%) of the respondents indicated they receive information on contraception, pregnancy, abortion and sexually transmitted diseases from a health facility, 90 (60%) say they did not get such information. 104 (69.3%) make enquiries by asking questions, 41 (27%) do not ask questions. 64 (42.7%) of respondents affirmed

Table 2.3 Reproductive health decisions

Variable	*Frequency*	*Percentage (%)*
Who decides the number of children that you should have?		
Me	27	18
My husband	30	20
Both my husband and I	85	56.7
My relatives	2	1.3
My husband's relatives	6	4
Who decides the spacing between your children?		
Me	25	16.7
My husband	27	18
Both my husband and I	83	55.3
My relatives	0	0
My husband's relatives	0	0
It is not decided. It is whenever I get pregnant	15	10
Have you ever used family planning?		
Yes	60	40
No	90	60
Who decides whether you need to use family planning?		
Me	36	24
My husband	29	19.3
My husband and I	81	54
My relatives	1	0.7
My husband's relatives	0	0
My doctor	3	2
Who chose the family planning method that you used?		
Me	42	28
My husband	21	14
My husband and I	61	40.7
My relatives	5	3.3
My husband's relatives	12	8
My doctor	9	6
Would you consider to use family planning in future?		
Yes	110	73.3
No	40	26.7
Do you do anything to prevent pregnancy apart from family planning?		
Yes	99	66
No	51	34

(continued)

Table 2.3 (continued)

Variable	*Frequency*	*Percentage (%)*
What do you do to prevent pregnancy?		
Condom	27	18
Withdrawal	25	16.7
Safe period	44	29.3
Others	54	36
Whose decision is it to use this method?		
My decision	49	32.7
My husband's decision	28	18.7
Joint decision	73	48.6

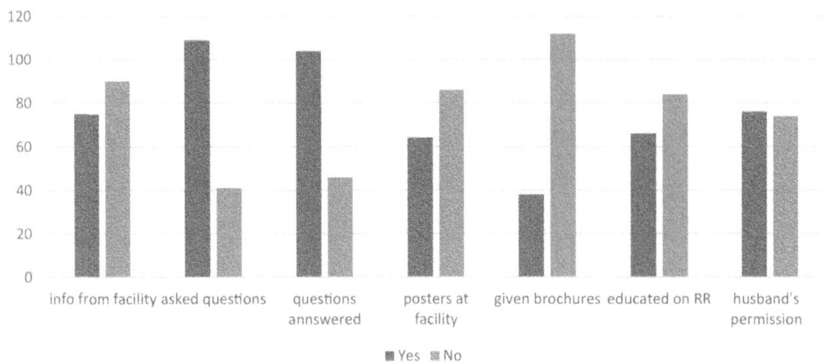

Fig. 2.2 Reproductive information seeking behaviour

that they have seen posters on RHR in the facility they visited, while 86 (57.3%) indicated they did not see such posters. 38 (25.3%) have been given brochures on RHR, whereas 112 (74.7%) have not been given any brochures in the facility they visited. 66 (44%) respondents showed that they have had education on RHR, with 84 (56%) saying otherwise. When asked if the doctor ever asked them to obtain the husband's consent before the doctor could provide reproductive health services or information on reproductive health and rights, 76 (50.7%) answered in the affirmative while 74 (49.3%) answered in the negative.

2.5 Discussion

The realisation of RHR among women of childbearing age is largely dependent on the level of awareness of the rights among the women themselves. This study was carried out to evaluate the level of awareness of RHR among women of childbearing age in Adamawa state with a view to compare the findings with other parts of Nigeria and replicate the study across the country and across Africa. Our study revealed that socio-demographic factors influence the awareness of RHR among women of childbearing age. Majority of the participants (74.7%) know what RHR means while 25.3% of them do not understand what RHR means. Most of the respondents that lack knowledge about RHR either lack formal education or possess only primary school education. This is an indication that education plays an important role in understanding RHR as it applies to women of reproductive age.[30] Despite the high number of participants with knowledge of RHR, only 59.3% of the respondents have received information on RHR. It is therefore possible that the knowledge held by some of the participants on RHR may not be accurate.

The study found that a higher percentage of the respondents displayed a reluctant attitude to discuss sex and reproductive matters with their parents. Although a higher percentage of the respondents, 40% and 20% found it difficult and extremely difficult respectively to discuss important issues with their husbands, most of these respondents (66.7%) discuss sex-related issues with their husbands. This shows a tradition of reluctance on the part of parents to discuss sex and RHR related matters in Nigerian households as supported by earlier findings.[31]

The essence of a woman's awareness of RHR is mainly to uphold and assert her reproductive autonomy but the findings in this study reveal that only 18% of the participants exercise reproductive autonomy on the number of children to have while only 24% of the respondents exercise reproductive autonomy on the spacing of their children. A higher

[30] SR Psaki et al "Causal Effects of Education on Sexual and Reproductive Health in Low and Middle-Income Countries: A Systematic Review and Meta-Analysis" (2019) *SSM Population Health* 18 https://doi.org/10.1016/j.ssmph.2019.100386; AN Odo et al "Predictors of Young People's Use of Sexual and Reproductive Health Services in Nigeria: A Mixed-Method Approach" (2021) 21(37) *BMC Public Health* 7.

[31] Esan and Babajidda (2021) 6; MA Olubayo-Fatiregun "The Parental Attitude towards Adolescent Sexual Behaviour in Akoko-Edo and Estako-West Local Government Areas, Edo State, Nigeria" (2012) 2(6) *World Journal of Education* 30.

percentage of the participants agree that the decision in respect of the number of children to have and the spacing is a joint decision between the spouses. However, in some instances (20%), the sole decision on the number of children to have is made by the husband while the relatives decide in 5.3% of the study population. While the husbands of 18% of the respondents makes the sole decision in terms of spacing of children, relatives have no say in this regard. 10% of the participants do not make any decision on spacing their children; they decide to have children whenever they get pregnant. Furthermore, it is only in the case of 28% of the respondents that the respondents get to exercise reproductive autonomy on the choice of family planning. The joint decision by spouses is made in 40.7% of cases while the husband, relatives and doctor decide for the women in other cases. Furthermore, 50.7% of the participants confirmed that their doctors require their husbands' consent before providing reproductive health services and information to them. This finding supports earlier findings of the need of spousal consent and approval before accessing reproductive health services in Nigeria.[32] This finding shows that some women in Yola metropolis still experience difficulty in exercising their RHR. This can be attributed to cultural norms that impede the enforcement and realisation of RHR in Nigeria as established by Akhirome-Omonfuegbe[33] as well as gender stereotype and patriarchy which deprives the woman of the right to reproductive autonomy in a marriage.[34] Thus the submission of the African woman to her husband in marriage cannot be completely ignored in advocating for the RHR of a woman in Nigeria.[35] It is rather unfortunate that the doctors, who should understand the principle of informed consent, decide the choice of family planning for 6% of the respondents. A justification for this, considering the percentage of the population affected, maybe that the lack of formal education and lack of access to RHR information impedes the ability of the affected population to fully comprehend the nature and effectiveness of reproductive health services.

[32] OA Makinde and AM Adebayo "Knowledge and Perception of Sexual and Reproductive Rights Among Married Women in Nigeria" (2020) 28(1) *Sexual and Reproductive Health Matters* 288.

[33] Akhirome-Omonfuegbe (2019) 275.

[34] Makinde and Adebayo (2020) 288.

[35] OS Yusuff "Reproductive Rights and Reproductive Choice of Yoruba Women in Southwestern Nigeria" (2020) 6(1) *Advanced Journal of Social Science* 149.

Additionally, there is a cause for concern for doctors, who should support in the realisation of RHR, to require spousal consent before making reproductive health services available to women. It is therefore important to educate medical personnel on the importance of reproductive autonomy. Considering the conservative nature of the northern region of Nigeria, the need to seek consent of the husband in providing reproductive health services and information has been attributed to religious, factors, cultural norms, level of education of the women and family structure (several family structures grant the husband all decision-making powers as the head of the household.[36]

In relation to the RHR information-seeking behaviour of the participants, although the majority of participants did not get direct information on RHR from a health facility, they ask questions to acquire information as needed. However, more than half of the participants (57.3%) have seen posters on RHR at health facilities where they visited. Also, very few of the participants (25.3%) have received brochures on RHR in the past while others have never received such brochures.

2.6 Limitations

This study was conducted in Adamawa which makes it impracticable to generalise the findings to the whole of Nigeria. Though similar studies in Nigeria were compared with this study, fresh data could not be collected across Nigeria due to financial constraints.

2.7 Conclusion

This study investigates the level of awareness of RHR among women of childbearing age in Adamawa State, Nigeria. It was found that socio-demographic factors such as education and age influence the level of awareness of women on RHR. The study further finds that cultural factors such as patriarchy, gender stereotype and traditional norms contribute to the impediment to effectively realise the RHR of women in these LGAs. The study finds that when compared with other parts of Nigeria, there is a discrepancy in the level RHR among married women across Nigeria.

[36] HM Schwandt et al "'Doctors Are In the Best Position to Know...' The Perceived Medicalization of Contraceptive Method Choice in Ibadan and Kaduna" (2016) 99(8) *Patient Education and Counseling* 1404.

2.8 Recommendations

In order to further realise the RHR of women, it is pertinent to intensify the creation of awareness on the reproductive rights of women to effectively seek and use reproductive health services based on the informed consent of the women themselves. Furthermore, programs that target the inclusion of men in knowledge awareness should be intensified so that men in the communities can be empowered to protect and advance RHR of women.

Funding The authors received no funding for this research.

Conflicting Interests

The authors declare no conflicting interests.

Bibliography

Adeokun, L.A. et al. "Sexual and Reproductive Health Knowledge, Behaviour and Education Needs of In-School Adolescents in Northern Nigeria" (2009) 13(4) *African Journal of Reproductive Health* 37–49.

Akhirome-Omonfuegbe, L. "A Critical Appraisal of Women's Reproductive Rights in Nigeria" (2019) 10(1–2) *Afe Babalola University Journal of Sustainable Development Law and Policy* 257–280.

Asogwa, C. E. "Knowledge and use of family planning methods among Women of Reproductive Age in Bauchi State, Nigeria Exposed to 'Get it Together' Media Campaign" (2018) 16(3) *Gender and Behaviour* 12004–12012.

Ayanleye, O. "Women and Reproductive Health Rights in Nigeria" (2014) 6(5) *OIDA International Journal of Sustainable Development* 127–140.

Ayanore, M.A. Pavlova, M. & Groot, W. "Unmet Reproductive Health Needs Among Women in Some West African Countries: A Systematic Review of Outcome Measures and Determinants" (2015) 13(5) *Reproductive Health* 1–10.

Cook, R.J. "International Human Rights and Women's Reproductive Health" (1993) 24(2) *Studies in Family Planning* 73–86.

Darteh, E.K.M., Dickson, K.S. & Doku, D.T. "Women's Reproductive Health Decision-Making: A Multi-Country Analysis of Demographic and Health Surveys in Sub-Saharan Africa" (2019) *PLOS One* 1–12.

Envuladu, E.A., Massar, K. & de Wit, J. "Adolescents' Sexual and Reproductive Healthcare-Seeking Behaviour and Service Utilisation in Plateau State, Nigeria" (2022) 10 *Healthcare* 1–10.

Esan, D.T. & Babajidda, K.K. "The Perception of Parents of High School Students About Adolescent Sexual and Reproductive Needs in Nigeria: A Qualitative Study" (2021) 2 *Public Health in Practice* 1–7.

Gebhard, J. & Trimino, D. "Reproductive Rights, International Regulation" in A Peters and R Wolfrum (eds) *The Max Planck Encyclopedia of Public International Law* (Oxford: Oxford University Press 2008) <www.mpepil.com> accessed 21 November 2021.

Germain, A. et al. (eds). *Reproductive Tract Infections: Global Impact and Priorities for Women's Reproductive Health* (New York: Plenum Press 1992).

Kolawole, A.K.A. "The Right to Life and the Right to Health: Any Nexus?" (2010) 2(5) OIDA *International Journal of Sustainable Development* 95–106.

Makinde, O.A. & Adebayo, A.M. "Knowledge and Perception of Sexual and Reproductive Rights Among Married Women in Nigeria" (2020) 28(1) Sexual and Reproductive Health Matters 2877–2290.

Moronkola, O.A., Ojediran, M.M. & Amosun, A. "Reproductive Health Knowledge, Beliefs and Determinants of Contraceptives Use Among Women Attending Family Planning Clinics in Ibadan, Nigeria" (2006) 6(3) *African Health Sciences* 155–159.

Nnamuchi, O. "Kleptocracy and Its Many Faces: The Challenges of Justiciability of the Right to Health Care in Nigeria" (2008) 52(1) *Journal of African Law* 1–42.

Odo, A.N. et al. "Predictors of Young People's Use of Sexual and Reproductive Health Services in Nigeria: A Mixed-Method Approach" (2021) 21(37) *BMC Public Health* 1–8.

Ogunlayi, M.A. "An Assessment of the Awareness of Sexual and Reproductive Rights Among Adolescents in South Western Nigeria" (2005) 9(1) *African Journal of Reproductive Health* 99–112.

Olomola, O. & Ajagunna, F. "Knowledge and Access to Reproductive Health Rights Among Adolescents in Ibadan, Nigeria" (2020) 28(3) *African Journal of International and Comparative Law* 401–417.

Olubayo-Fatiregun, M.A. "The Parental Attitude towards Adolescent Sexual Behaviour in Akoko-Edo and Estako-West Local Government Areas, Edo State, Nigeria" (2012) 2(6) *World Journal of Education* 24–31.

Psaki, S.R. et al. "Causal Effects of Education on Sexual and Reproductive Health in Low and Middle-Income Countries: A Systematic Review and Meta-Analysis" (2019) *SSM Population Health* 1–23. https://doi.org/10.1016/j.ssmph.2019.100386.

Schwandt, H.M. et al. "'Doctors are in the Best Position to Know...' The Perceived Medicalization of Contraceptive Method Choice in Ibadan and Kaduna" (2016) 99(8) *Patient Education and Counseling* 14000–11405.

United Nations Population Fund. *Programme of Action: Adopted at the International Conference on Population and Development, Cairo 5–13 September 1994* (New York: United Nations Population Fund 2004).

Vaisanen, H. et al. "Sexual and Reproductive Health Literacy, Misoprostol Knowledge and Use of Medication Abortion in Lagos State, Nigeria: A Mixed Methods Study" (2021) 52(2) *Studies in Family Planning* 217–237.

Yusuff, O.S. "Reproductive Rights and Reproductive Choice of Yoruba Women in Southwestern Nigeria" (2020) 6(1) *Advanced Journal of Social Science* 138–151.

CHAPTER 3

A Human Rights-Based Perspective to Sexual and Reproductive Health and Rights of African Senior Citizens

Ibrahim Banaru Abubakar

3.1 Introduction

It is established that the world population is not only ageing but ageing rapidly, with the unprecedented challenges of an ageing population.[1] According to United Nations Population Fund (UNFPA) data,[2] there was an estimated 205 million people aged 60 and over worldwide in 1950, a

[1] World Health Organisation, 'Ageing' <https://www.who.int/health-topics/ageing#tab=tab_2> accessed 30 November 2021.

[2] United Nations Population Fund, *Ageing in the Twenty-First Century: A Celebration and A Challenge* (UNFPA 2012).

I. B. Abubakar (✉)
Ahmadu Bello University Teaching Hospital, Zaria, Nigeria
e-mail: drimbanaru@gmail.com

O. S. Adelakun and E. Ndoni (eds.), *Reproductive Health and Assisted Reproductive Technologies In Sub-Saharan Africa*,
Sustainable Development Goals Series,
https://doi.org/10.1007/978-981-99-2411-0_3

figure that has more than doubled to 1 billion in 2019.[3] Ageing was hitherto mostly seen as an issue in developed countries. However, growing evidence suggests that low and middle-income countries will host over 80% of the older population by 2050.[4] In Africa, there were about 69 million people aged 60 and above, in 2017 with a statistical projection that by 2050 the number will rise sharply, up to 226 million.[5]

Recognising that when added years are predominated by significant declines in physical and mental health, it brings negative implications for both the older person and society, the international community has adopted several strategies aimed at the well-being of older people. This includes the Vienna International Plan of Action on Ageing, adopted in 1982, which resulted in commitments to direct policies, legislation, and programmes to address the quality of life and well-being of the elderly.[6]

A second global consensus plan on ageing came in 2002, the Madrid International Plan of Action on Ageing, which was more comprehensive, looking at a rights-based approach to policies on older people.[7] Despite these global initiatives, policy and programmatic actions were mostly geared towards physical health, non-communicable diseases and mental health, with sexual and reproductive health left in the background.

The sexual and reproductive health and rights (SRHR) reality of older people is characterised by discrimination based on the perceived misconception that older people are "asexual".[8] Thus, their SRHR issues are pegged as "taboo" by individuals and societies.[9] In many clear and unclear ways, ageing and sexual desirability are depicted as mutually exclusive, and individuals and societies hold little interest in letting older people's SRHR issues be on the agenda. Even in the science community, it is an area less

[3] WHO (n 1).

[4] World Health Organisation, 'Ageing and Health' <https://www.who.int/news-room/fact-sheets/detail/ageing-and-health> accessed 30 November 2021.

[5] United Nations, *World Population Ageing* (UN 2017).

[6] United Nations, *Vienna International Plan of Action on Aging* (UN 1983).

[7] United Nations, *Political Declaration and Madrid International Plan of Action on Ageing* (UN 2002).

[8] Aboderin Isabella, 'Sexual and Reproductive Health and Rights of Older Men and Women: Addressing a Policy Blind Spot' (2014) 22(44) Reproductive Health Matters <https://pubmed.ncbi.nlm.nih.gov/25555775/> accessed 28 November 2021.

[9] Ibid.

researched and not topical in policy dialogue.[10] This lack of attention to older people's SRHR is rife despite growing advocacy for the lifecycle approach to health. The lifecycle approach to health includes sexual and reproductive health and it elucidates providing services throughout the life of an individual.[11]

From the biological point of view, ageing results from the complex impacts of the accumulation of various molecules and cellular damage over time. Ageing is not linear and is impacted by social and environmental factors. There are several conditions of interest to the SRHR of older people.[12] Thus healthy ageing is a matter of preventive strategies initiated from childhood and throughout the life course.

Due to a decline in hormonal factors such as oestrogen and progesterone around the time of menopause, older women may experience a remarkable decline in overall ovarian function, resulting in some physical and mental changes. The constellation of signs and symptoms around menopause could include poor energy, irritability, and mood changes, as well as a decline in sexual drive.[13] Older men also experience some changes with age, but not as conspicuous as those of women. The changes come from a decline in testosterone hormone levels, with a gradual decline in semen production, and some form of erectile dysfunction.[14] As earlier stated, social and environmental factors could accelerate ageing, as it is with non-communicable diseases and the many medications that older people use.

The body of evidence shows that most men and women remain sexually active at old age and, like the non-linear ageing pattern, some do not report being affected by any form of sexual dysfunction. Being sexually active means their risk of sexually transmitted infections, including

[10] International Planned Parenthood Federation, IPPF 'IMAP Statement on Sexual and Reproductive Health and Rights of the Ageing Population,' (February 2018) <https://www.ippf.org/sites/default/files/2018-03/IMAP%20Statement%20-%20SRHR%20of%20the%20ageing%20population.pdf> accessed 30 November 2021.

[11] Ibid., 4.

[12] WHO (n. 4).

[13] Banke-Thomas Aduragbemi, '"Leaving No One Behind" Also Includes Taking the Elderly Along Concerning Their Sexual and Reproductive Health and Rights: A New Focus for Reproductive Health" (2020) Reproductive Health.

[14] Ibid.

Human Immuno-deficiency Virus (HIV), is substantial and the incidence may well be increasing in coming years.[15]

3.2 The Marginalisation of Older People in the Sexual and Reproductive Health Discourse

In 2013, the world welcomed the international conference on human rights, tagged "ICPD Beyond 2014 International Conference on Human Rights", which was held in Noordwijk, the Netherlands. The conference identified older people as one of the key marginalised groups in the provision and access to SRHR. The conference echoed a set agenda on the sexual and reproductive rights of older people as contained in relevant international instruments, including the Convention on the Elimination of All Forms of Discrimination Against Women (CEDAW).[16]

In a more elaborate sense, the conference drew conclusions on older people, emphasising age as a potential determinant of inequality, thus calling for deliberate and concerted efforts by governments to ensure the sexual and reproductive rights of older people, ensuring not only quality and access but mechanisms for accountability.[17] Long-standing and recurring discrimination against older people in sexual and reproductive rights is typically based on misconceptions that lead to social constructs associating old age with perceived asexuality, as well as taboos surrounding sexuality and sexual life in the elderly.

The human rights conference framing of older people as marginalised groups as far as SRHR is concerned is so apparent when one engages with health research in SRHR and finds a clear lacuna in the body of evidence on the sexual and reproductive concerns of the elderly. Important global surveys such as the Global Reproductive Health Survey and country-level representative studies such as the Demographic and Health Survey fall short of addressing the demographics of the elderly.

Older people find it even more challenging to access healthcare. The poor decisions as to health-seeking behaviour are because elderly people do not have adequate information about their sexual and reproductive

[15] IPPF (n 10).

[16] United Nations Population Fund, *ICPD Beyond 2014: High-level Global Commitments* (UNFPA 2014).

[17] Ibid., 35.

health and are locked in the stereotypical belief of society that they do not have sexual desires. Furthermore, even those with the foresight to seek medical attention face challenges. Barriers to accessing healthcare services are attributable to a lack of the capacity to pay for services and the absence of health insurance coverage.[18] The apparent disparity in access to healthcare between men and women can be traced to the gender-based discrimination faced by women, such as lower socioeconomic status and a lack of education. Negative stereotyping about ageing is pervasive and is also seen in healthcare settings where the peculiar needs of the aged are not considered.[19] Person-centred care, on the other hand, would have health professionals seeing the elderly in a contextually appropriate manner and giving due consideration to the elderly person's informed choices as to the benefit of science.

Whereas research indicates a heightened risk of STIs, including HIV, among the elderly, healthcare professionals often exhibit a capacity gap as regards sexual and reproductive health in geriatric age groups, making access particularly hard for older people. Many health promotion strategies, such as HIV screening programmes, exclude older people, and the prevention information available is not tailored in ways that are acceptable to and appropriate for older people.[20]

3.3 Legal Framework Available for Protecting the Sexual and Reproductive Rights of African Older Persons

Bearing in mind the ageing population in Africa, the peculiarities and needs of senior citizens, the African Union, leveraging on the extant provisions of Article 66 of the African Charter on Human and Peoples' Rights (the African Charter), adopted a Protocol to the African Charter on the Rights of Older Persons (Older Persons' Protocol) in January 2016.

The Older Persons' Protocol in Articles 4 and 5, aims to promote and protect the rights of the aged and guarantee a social system that encourages their full participation and contribution to society. The Older

[18] IPPF (n. 10).

[19] Ibid.

[20] IPPF (n. 10).

Persons' Protocol enjoins state parties to enact legislation that ensures the recognition of older people in decision-making as regards their well-being without undue interference, and to make a deliberate effort to guarantee older people are able to express opinions and exercise franchise in social and political life.

In terms of access to health, the Older Persons' Protocol encourages state parties to guarantee older people's rights to health tailored to their specific needs, as well as to provide older people with medical health insurance and to promote the study of gerontology and geriatrics in health personnel training.[21] This instrument seeks to alleviate the prejudices inherent in our social constructs that regard the elderly as tired and retired individuals who make no significant contribution to society and whose needs and rights, including sexual and reproductive rights, are insignificant.

Domesticating the Older Persons' Protocol will offer Africa more research on the sexual and reproductive health of older people. For instance, the major health survey in African countries, the Demographic and Health Survey, focuses on sexual and reproductive research on people younger than 49 years of age,[22] excluding the elderly population, thereby creating a huge knowledge gap on the peculiar needs and problems of those above the age of 49 years and well into old age. Ratifying the Protocol will make amends in this regard and add to the body of knowledge, the peculiar needs of older men and women as regards sexuality and reproduction; the key systemic and socio-cultural barriers faced by elderly people in accessing services for sexual and reproductive health; and the structural inequalities that exist within the elderly population in matters relating to sexual and reproductive health and rights with the aim of making evidence-based policies.

Accepting that the Older Persons' Protocol will enhance the protection of older people against social and sexual abuse, research has shown that some women report sexual abuse in old age. This protocol, when implemented, will enhance other relevant international and regional treaties that protect women against sexual abuse as provided for in Article 8 of

[21] Protocol to the African Charter on the Rights of Older Persons, a15.

[22] National Population Commission & ICF International, Nigeria *Demographic and Health Survey 2013* (NPC 2014).

the Older Persons' Protocol that "States Parties shall prohibit and criminalise harmful traditional practices directed at the elderly, as well as take all necessary steps to eliminate harmful traditional practices, including witchcraft accusations, that endanger the welfare, health, life, and dignity of the elderly, particularly elderly women". This provision contained in Article 8 is also very crucial in taming harmful traditional practices of ascribing infertility to the alleged witchcraft of older women[23]; the blame for having difficulty conceiving or giving birth is put on the mother-in-law. They accuse them of using witchcraft either to destroy or block their wombs. The Protocol brings renewed public enlightenment and based on the impetus of the protocol will, in my opinion, greatly reduce this misconception.

The Protocol to the African Charter on the Rights of Older Persons will reduce the proliferation of taboos against the sexuality of the elderly. Article 3 of the Protocol to the African Charter on the Rights of Older Persons obliges state parties to pave the way for the elimination of stereotypical social constructs marginalising older people and take measures in correction where there are established sources of discrimination or stigmatisation. Putting these measures in place will help to eliminate biases resulting from social constructs that deny older people's sexual rights, give them substantive equality, and make society more responsive to their needs.

On 10 December 2008, on the occasion of the observance of International Human Rights Day and coinciding with the 60th anniversary of the Universal Declaration of Human Rights, the United Nations adopted the Optional Protocol to the International Covenant on Economic, Social, and Cultural Rights (OP-ICESCR). This adoption is in follow-up to enduring advocacy on the increasing concern and needs for recognition of the rights of individuals to equality before the law and the opportunity to bring before adjudicating body complaints in their individual capacities.

The protocol affords individuals or groups of individuals the right to put forward complaints before the United Nations Committee on Economic, Social, and Cultural Rights (CESCR) when they believe their

[23] Friday Eboiyehi, 'Convicted Without Evidence: Elderly Women and Witchcraft Accusations in Contemporary Nigeria' (2017) 18(14) Journal of International Women's Studies 247.

rights under the ICESCR have been violated by their state, a party to the covenant, and having exhausted all available local means of remedy.[24]

Article 12 of the ICESCR urges state parties to guarantee the rights of everyone to the highest attainable standard of health. However, owing to growing disparities and constant indignation and violations of sexual and reproductive rights, the CESCR put forward a general comment guiding state parties on the promotion and protection of sexual and reproductive rights, focusing on various barriers militating against the full realisation and enjoyment of these rights. The CESCR emphasises the interrelation between sexual and reproductive rights and other inherent rights central to the covenant, including education and non-discrimination, which have been subjects of concern, especially for vulnerable and marginalised groups like women.[25]

The CESCR mentions four fulcrum elements central to realising rights to sexual and reproductive health; availability, accessibility, affordability and acceptability.[26] Through modalities advised by the committee, including adequate training and retraining of healthcare personnel, ensuring and providing access to healthcare facilities, and the provision of accurate and adequate education on sexual and reproductive health, state parties, through the commentary, are enjoined to maximise available resources and mitigate discrimination against certain quarters due to their vulnerability and being in the minority. Some core obligations expected of state parties include the elimination of laws and policies that undermine or criminalise certain groups or individuals' access to sexual and reproductive health in terms of facilities, services, and information; facilitating access to sexual and reproductive health services of a qualitative standard; making laws against gender-targeted violence, including female genital cutting and forced marriages, and seeing to their enforcement; ensuring, without any form of discrimination, adequate and accurate comprehensive sexuality education; ensuring the provision of basic and essential medical supplies for sexual and reproductive health services; and lastly, ensuring access to remedies and redress for any violations of the rights to sexual and reproductive health.

[24] OP-ICESCR a2,3.

[25] United Nations, 'General Comment No. 22 (2016) On the Right to Sexual and Reproductive Health (Article 12 of the International Covenant on Economic, Social, and Cultural Rights),' (UN 2016).

[26] Ibid., 5.

Assenting the OP-ICESCR is an impetus to achieving justiciability of socioeconomic rights, especially sexual and reproductive rights. The OP-ICESCR offers an opportunity for African countries to strengthen domestic socioeconomic rights laws. Article 3 of the OP-ICESR, which provides for the admissibility of complaints before the Committee, clearly stipulates that, as a requirement for a complaint to be entertained by the Committee, the complainant is obliged to have exhausted all available local remedies before reaching the Committee. Underlying the obligation to exercise and exhaust domestic remedies is a huge opportunity for the state to provide the holistic means to redress and address violations of rights. Going by the practice of human rights, remedies must be available domestically in an adequate measure to ameliorate the harm suffered by the violation of rights. This envisions States making deliberate attempts to make enabling laws in this regard.

The OP-ICESCR will offer an alternative trajectory to alleviating poverty as an impediment to realising sexual and reproductive rights. Socioeconomic inequalities are the primary drivers of the HIV and AIDS pandemic. As earlier established, access to healthcare is largely determined by the capacity to pay.

Making a case for the OP-ICESCR, the UN High Commissioner for Human Rights, Louise Arbour, said, among others, that assenting the OP-ICESCR,[27] will provide an important platform to expose abuses that are often linked to poverty, discrimination and neglect, and that victims frequently endure in silence and helplessness. It will provide a way for individuals who may otherwise be isolated and powerless to make the international community aware of their situation.

Poverty remains an issue of concern in Africa as it impacts sexual and reproductive rights, and many of the determinants of poverty are avoidable and remediable in the light of the ICESCR because their roots are traceable to marginalisation caused by violations of the ESCR in the form of avoidable exclusion of individuals living in informal settlements and other marginalised groups, discrimination against women or unmarried females on access to certain reproductive health services, corruption and inequitable distribution of services. Through the OP-ICESCR, the people

[27] Unite Nations, 'Top UN Official Hails Adoption of "Missing Piece" in Human Rights Protection' <https://news.un.org/en/story/2008/06/263282-top-un-official-hails-adoption-missing-piece-human-rights-protection> accessed 28 November 2021.

will have the means to hold the government accountable for its obligation to ensure socioeconomic rights relevant to sexual and reproductive rights. This will reasonably create an avenue of systemic thinking and solve the puzzling socioeconomic inequalities militating against the full realisation of sexual and reproductive rights and solidify the foundation of local protection of socioeconomic rights.

The OP-ICESCR will promote awareness of socioeconomic rights. With the accession of the OP-ICESCR per proviso, there is an invaluable window of opportunity to enhance awareness of socioeconomic rights. The optional protocol obliges state parties to widely circulate the ICESCR and the optional protocol, as well as the general commentaries in terms of recommendations of the committee overseeing the ICESCR.[28] This deliberate awareness creation will also invariably promote civil society movements and community engagement in promoting the generality of socioeconomic rights, including reproductive and sexual rights. Countries will also be able to gauge the standards of their domestic provisions against international best practices.

3.4 A Holistic Approach to Realising Older People's Sexual and Reproductive Rights in Africa

3.4.1 *Affirmative Policies, Including Equal Access to Healthcare Services*

The lack of inclusivity for older people in sexual and reproductive health programming is a result of discrimination. A human rights-based approach to affirming older people's rights to SRHR will make societies recognise the inherent socioeconomic, gender-based, and age-related discrimination meted out to elderly people who should have equal rights as younger people. Adoption of effective, inclusive policies will therefore greatly remedy the plight of senior citizens.

Recognising that old age is often associated with poor health, the World Health Organisation (WHO) came up with strategies for health promotion throughout life and the lifecycle approach to health, including

[28] OP-ICESCR, a9.

SRHR.[29] This is also buttressed in the Madrid Plan of Action,[30] which calls for action by state actors to reduce the cumulative effect of factors that increase the risk of disease and consequential dependence in old age and to promote policies that prevent ill health in older people.

The Madrid Plan of Action technical guidance implicitly calls for full legal protection of older people's sexual and reproductive health in line with provisions of international instruments such as Goal 3 of the Global Goals for Sustainable Development (SDGs), which seeks to ensure healthy lives and well-being for all at all ages.[31] Furthermore, the UN human rights council expresses that SDG 3 offers an opportunity for the realisation of older people's health rights.[32] This implies policies enacted by states should be based on up-to-date older persons' sexual and reproductive health needs and informed by reliable disaggregated data, stressing the need to fill the research gap in older persons' SRHR.

Policy regulations and guidelines should also comply with the imperatives of equality between men and women and health as a human right. To this end, laws and policies impeding access to the continuum of sexual and reproductive health must be changed.

There should be explicit policy directions affirmative to seniors' access to the range of sexual and reproductive health services, be they promotive, preventive, or curative, at the right time without incurring financial difficulties. Specifically, such policies will also address gender-related disparities. Legal mechanisms will uphold universal access and bring in accountability. Guaranteeing equal access also entails providing training and retraining for healthcare providers and old people's caretakers to improve the general understanding of seniors' SRHR needs and promoting age-friendly services as a way of improving the demand for services by the seniors.

[29] World Health Organisation, *Multisectoral Action for Life Course Approach to Healthy Ageing: Draft Global Strategy and Plan of Action on Ageing and Health* (WHO 2016).

[30] United Nations (n. 7).

[31] Ibid.

[32] United Nations, 'Report of the Independent Expert on the Enjoyment of all Human Rights by Older Persons' <https://www.un.org/development/desa/ageing/news/2016/09/report-of-the-independent-expert-on-the-enjoyment-of-all-human-rights-by-older-persons/> accessed 30 November 2021.

3.4.2 *Social Safety Nets for the Seniors*

There is a substantial link between poverty and poor health outcomes.[33] User fees at the point of access to sexual and reproductive health constitute a significant barrier to access. Therefore, there is a dire need for deliberate actionable policies that prescribe acceptable social protection levels for senior citizens, including health insurance.

3.4.3 *Involvement of Stakeholders to Generate Awareness and Strengthen the Research Capacity*

The race to the realisation of older people's SRHR will be highly inadequate without the radical inclusion of stakeholders across the vertical and horizontal cross-cutting issues related to seniors' SRHR. Involving and empowering the elderly to be active partners across all levels, from policy framing to programmatic implementation, will improve their overall well-being and, by implication, their acceptance of healthcare services, with better health outcomes. The inclusion of seniors as active participants in the promotion of sexual and reproductive health from an early age has been shown to improve their decisions and choices as they age, which provides better outcomes.

The complementary roles of civil society organisations and community leaders are imperative. Civil society organisations help the cause of SRHR for the elderly by providing information, comprehensive sexuality education, advocacy, policy-influencing research, and strategic litigation. An example in the global space of SRHR for the elderly is HelpAge. HelpAge coordinates a global campaign, the worldwide Age Demands Action campaign. It is a grassroots campaign where older people's initiatives meet with state actors to set the agenda for issues of concern to older people, thereby influencing policy framing.[34]

Traditional leaders, on the other hand, who are the gatekeepers of the communities through which community social constructs thrive, are veritable tools to help in the creation of awareness that is targeted at

[33] World Bank 'Poverty and Health' (2014) <https://www.worldbank.org/en/topic/health/brief/poverty-health> accessed 30 November 2021.

[34] HelpAge International, *AU Policy Framework and Plan of Action on Ageing* (HelpAge) <https://www.un.org/esa/socdev/ageing/documents/implementation/AUFrameworkBook.pdf> accessed 30 November 2021.

deconstructing myths and misconceptions regarding ageing and stopping ageism as a form of discrimination against the elderly and a bane to the realisation of their SRHR. Community mobilisation campaigns offer long-term strategies that seek social change by promoting attitudinal change and shifts in norms and values. Community mobilisation strategies should therefore involve leaders of the communities that exert influence and offer socio-cultural directions to their communities, which is an essential cue to action in making older people safe and ageing gracefully to enjoy the highest attainable standard of health.

The science community is an important ally to share learning and experience in modelling programmes and enriching the body of evidence, from the prevalence of sexual and reproductive health issues in the elderly to evidence-based tools for service delivery, programmatic action as well as monitoring and evaluation. This will entail the recognition of the need to include cohorts of the elderly in sexual and reproductive health surveys and also maintain a mechanism for reviewing programmes and actions to allow for expansive knowledge of the varied and evolving sexual and reproductive health needs of the elderly.

3.5 Conclusion

For African countries to move towards the realisation of the SRHR of the elderly in line with the SDGs, state actors must take the lead by affirming the rights of the elderly. Through effective legislation, state actors can be able to take appropriate actions to stop ageism and all forms of discrimination against the elderly that prevent them from accessing healthcare services and living sound sexual and reproductive health. Aside from quality, senior citizens should be able to afford the services.

State actors should ensure the delivery of comprehensive sex education to empower growing boys and girls with adequate information to be responsible adults of all ages for better health in old age. Active community mobilisation will result in a societal reorientation towards ageing, which will lead to an increase in promoters of healthy ageing and acceptance of older people's sexual and reproductive needs.

Bibliography

Legislation

African Charter on Human and Peoples' Rights (Adopted 27 June 1981, Entered into Force 21 October 1986) (1982) 21 ILM 58 (African Charter).

Convention on the Elimination of All Forms of Discrimination against Women (Adopted 18 December 1979, Entered into Force 3 September 1981) UNTS 1249 4(CEDAW) Art 11.

International Covenant on Economic, Social and Cultural Rights (Adopted 16 December 1966, Entered into Force 3 January 1976) 993 UNTS 4 (ICESCR) Art 12.

Optional Protocol to the International Covenant on Economic, Social, and Cultural Rights (Adopted 10 December 2008, Entered into Force 5 May 2013) 2922 UNTS 2–4 (OP-ICESCR) Art 2, 3 and 9.

Protocol to the African Charter on the Rights of Older Persons (Adopted 31 January 2016).

UN Committee on Economic, Social and Cultural Rights 'General Comment No. 22 on the Right to Sexual and Reproductive Health (Article 12 of the International Covenant on Economic, Social, and Cultural Rights) (2 May 2016) UN Doc E/C.12/GC/22.

Books and Journals

Aboderin Isabella, 'Sexual and Reproductive Health and Rights of Older Men and Women: Addressing a Policy Blind Spot' (2014) 22(44) Reproductive Health Matters <https://pubmed.ncbi.nlm.nih.gov/25555775/> accessed 28 November 2021.

Banke-Thomas Aduragbemi, '"Leaving No One Behind" Also Includes Taking the Elderly Along Concerning Their Sexual and Reproductive Health and Rights: A New Focus for Reproductive Health' (2020) Reproductive Health.

Friday Eboiyehi 'Convicted Without Evidence: Elderly Women and Witchcraft Accusations in Contemporary Nigeria' (2017) 18(14) Journal of international Women's Studies 247.

HelpAge International, AU Policy Framework and Plan of Action on Ageing (HelpAge) <https://www.un.org/esa/socdev/ageing/documents/implementation/AUFrameworkBook.pdf> accessed 30 November 2021.

International Planned Parenthood Federation, IPPF, 'IMAP Statement on Sexual and Reproductive Health and Rights of the Ageing Population,' (February 2018) <https://www.ippf.org/sites/default/files/2018-03/IMAP%20Statement%20-%20SRHR%20of%20the%20ageing%20population.pdf> accessed 30 November 2021.

National Population Commission & ICF International, Nigeria Demographic and Health Survey 2013 (NPC 2014).

United Nations, 'Report of the Independent Expert on the Enjoyment of All Human Rights by Older Persons' <https://www.un.org/development/desa/ageing/news/2016/09/report-of-the-independent-expert-on-the-enjoyment-of-all-human-rights-by-older-persons/> accessed 30 November 2021.

United Nations Population Fund, Ageing in the Twenty-First Century: A Celebration and a Challenge (UNFPA 2012).

United Nations Population Fund, ICPD Beyond 2014: High-level Global Commitments (UNFPA 2014).

United Nations, 'Top UN Official Hails Adoption of "Missing Piece" in Human Rights Protection' <https://news.un.org/en/story/2008/06/263282-top-un-official-hails-adoption-missing-piece-human-rights-protection > accessed 28 November 2021.

United Nations, Political Declaration and Madrid International Plan of Action on Ageing (UN 2002).

United Nations, Vienna International Plan of Action on Aging (UN 1983).

United Nations, World Population Ageing (UN 2017).

World Bank 'Poverty and Health,' (2014) <https://www.worldbank.org/en/topic/health/brief/poverty-health> accessed 30 November 2021.

World Health Organisation, 'Ageing and Health' <https://www.who.int/news-room/fact-sheets/detail/ageing-and-health> accessed 30 November 2021.

World Health Organisation, 'Ageing' <https://www.who.int/health-topics/ageing#tab=tab_2> accessed 30 November 2021.

World Health Organisation, Multisectoral Action for Life Course Approach to Healthy Ageing: Draft Global Strategy and Plan of Action on Ageing and Health (WHO 2016).

CHAPTER 4

Reproductive Health Rights of Persons with Disabilities in Nigeria: A Legal or Cultural Flaw?

Erebi Ndoni

4.1 Introduction

The International Conference on Population and Development (ICPD) in 1994 affirmed that Reproductive Rights (RR)[1] embrace certain human rights and the promotion of these rights should be fundamental.[2] The Programme of Action (PoA) from the conference encapsulates an ambitious agenda for the fulfilment of inclusive development based on the

[1] The terms Reproductive Rights is used in some texts while others utilise Reproductive Health Rights. The specific usage from a text is adopted in this chapter. An explanation of the terms is considered further in the discourse.

[2] Paragraph 7.3 United Nations Report of the International Conference on Population and Development, New York, 1995.

E. Ndoni (✉)
American University of Nigeria, Yola, Nigeria
e-mail: erebi.ndoni@gmail.com

O. S. Adelakun and E. Ndoni (eds.), *Reproductive Health and Assisted Reproductive Technologies In Sub-Saharan Africa*,
Sustainable Development Goals Series,
https://doi.org/10.1007/978-981-99-2411-0_4

tenets of equity and sustainability. The United Nations Convention on the Rights of Persons with Disabilities (CRPD) recognises the reproductive rights of persons with disabilities (PWD). The CRPD highlights the need for State Parties to promote access to sexual and reproductive healthcare services without discrimination and protect the human rights of PWD.[3] The Sustainable Development Goals (SDG) also emphasize disability-inclusive development with the pledge to leave no one behind. To this end, SDG 3 advocates for equal access to sexual and reproductive healthcare services by PWD. SDG 10 aspires to reduce inequalities for persons with mental impairments or psychosocial disabilities. This category of PWD is assumed to be devoid of the civil rights of marriage and procreation which is part of reproductive rights.

The above treaty provisions, conventions and goals notwithstanding, PWD are still marginalised and stigmatised when trying to enforce reproductive rights. It is perceived as a taboo for PWD to express engagement in sexual issues or demand reproductive health rights (RHR).[4] Data from some developing countries indicate that 29% of birth by mothers with disabilities are not attended to by skilled health workers while 22% of married women with disabilities do not have access to family planning services which is part of reproductive health.[5] There is also a lack of information as PWD do not have access to information on RHR whether formally through medical personnel in healthcare facilities or informally through discussion with parents and peers.[6] The report of the ICPD further acknowledged that discriminatory social practice is one of the diverse reasons for the exclusion of many people in the world from the reproductive health agenda.[7] The marginalisation of PWD as to reproductive rights, reproductive healthcare services and associated reproductive health rights is the premise on which this chapter examines the RHR of

[3] Preamble to the Convention, Paragraph (f), CRPD, Article 25 (a) and (d).

[4] T Rugoho and F Maphosa, 'Introduction: Locating Sexual and Reproductive Rights for Adolescents with Disabilities' in T Rugoho and F Maphosa (eds) *Sexual and Reproductive Health of Adolescents with Disabilities* (Palgrave Macmillan, 2021) p 1.

[5] United Nations, 'Realizing the Sustainable Development Goals by, for and with Persons with Disabilities' available https://www.un.org/development/desa/disabilities/envision2030-goal3.html.

[6] Ibid, p 2.

[7] Paragraph 7.3 United Nations Report of the International Conference on Population and Development, New York, 1995.

PWD to ascertain if the challenge is a legal or cultural one. The cultural flaw arises from the intertwining issues of societal stereotypes, cultural prejudices, and beliefs as regards the RHR of PWD.

Nigeria is a developing country with 25 million of its population categorised as living with a disability. However, the specific consideration of the RHR of PWD has only been brought to the fore in recent years despite the recognition of these rights by conventions and treaties of the United Nations.[8] Moreso, physical disabilities seem to be given priority over mental disabilities as evidenced by the provisions of some regulations. Nigeria ratified the CRPD in 2007 and its optional protocol in 2010. It has also ratified a couple of treaties within the African continent like the African Charter on Human and Peoples Rights and the Protocol to the African Charter on Human and Peoples' Rights on the Rights of Women in Africa (Maputo Protocol) which contain related provisions on the rights of PWD and RHR. Furthermore, Nigeria enacted the Discrimination Against Persons with Disabilities (Prohibition) Act in 2018. Yet another regulation is the National Policy on Sexual and Reproductive Health Rights of Persons with Disabilities which was adopted in June 2018. This shows the desire of the country to strengthen legislations and policies on healthcare for PWD which is identified as one of the ways to foster the inclusion of this vulnerable sect towards the achievement of the SDGs.

While it is acknowledged that marginalisation is encountered generally by PWD, women with disabilities (WWD) are more vulnerable and most affected in comparison to their male counterparts based on intersectional discriminatory factors.[9] Article 6 of the CRPD and SDG 5 specifically recognise that WWD are subject to discrimination at different levels. WWD are three times more likely to have unmet healthcare needs when compared to men with disabilities.[10] More so, several cultural factors interface with the reproductive rights of women.[11] The African

[8] R Rothler, 'Disability Rights, Reproductive Technology, and Parenthood: Unrealised Opportunities' 2017 25(50) Reproductive Health Matters p 67.

[9] A Gartrell, K Baesell, and C Becker, 'We Do Not Dare to Love: Women with Disabilities' Sexual and Reproductive Health and Rights in Rural Cambodia' 2017 25(50) Reproductive Health Matters.

[10] United Nations Sustainable Development Goal 5.

[11] O Ayanleye, 'Women and Reproductive Health Rights in Nigeria' 2013 6(5) OIDA International Journal of Sustainable Development.

society is predominantly patriarchal and prejudiced about the autonomy of women.[12] Most women are also quite disadvantaged in terms of economic empowerment as they depend on men who are the heads of households. Since it is evident that social and economic discrimination is meted out on women generally, WWD appear to be more vulnerable. This chapter therefore draws more inferences from the RHR of WWD in its analysis especially as 13 million of the 25 million PWD in Nigeria are of the female gender.[13]

This chapter, therefore, evaluates the RHR of PWD in Nigeria in a bid to determine the extent of the rights and the discriminations encountered by PWD. The aim is to assess whether the discrimination is one based strictly on the lack of enforcement of legal provisions or if cultural factors are also responsible and how these affect the exercise of the rights.

4.2 Reproductive Health, Reproductive Health Rights and Persons with Disabilities

4.2.1 *Reproductive Health*

The ICPD defines reproductive health as 'a state of complete physical, mental and social well-being and not merely the absence of disease, in all matters relating to the reproductive system and its functions and processes'.[14] Reproductive health, therefore, implies that people can have a satisfying and safe sex life and that they can reproduce and have the freedom to decide if, when, and how often to do so. Implicit in this last condition is the right of men and women to be informed and to have access to safe, effective, affordable, and acceptable methods of family planning of their choice, as well as other methods for the regulation of fertility which are not against the law, and the right of access to appropriate healthcare services that will enable women to go safely through pregnancy and childbirth and provide couples with the best chance of having a healthy infant.[15]

[12] Ibid, p 138.

[13] National Policy on Sexual and Reproductive Health and Rights of Persons with Disabilities with emphasis on Women and Girls, June 2018 p i.

[14] United Nations, *Report of the International Conference on Population and Development* (United Nations: New York, 1995).

[15] Ibid, para 7.2.

Braustein and Grown maintain that the above definition of reproductive health by the ICPD gives an incline to the multifaceted nature of the concept comprising biomedical, socio-political, demographic and human rights dimensions.[16] This chapter is focused on the human rights dimension of reproductive health for PWD.

It is important to note, however, that the concept of reproductive health precedes the ICPD and emerged from the women's rights and health movement.[17] This movement had various themes ranging from the abuse of population control to discrimination against women, abortion rights, safe motherhood, forced sterilisation and the exclusion of women from the developmental agenda. The fact that a movement for the rights of women advocated the cause of reproductive health gives an incline to larger discrimination against the women folk. This lends credence to the resolve of this chapter to draw more inferences on the effect of reproductive health rights on women.

The definition of reproductive health being determined, reproductive healthcare refers to 'the constellation of methods, techniques, and services that contribute to reproductive health and well-being by preventing and solving reproductive health problems'.[18] Thus all methods and mechanisms employed to ensure reproductive health by healthcare professionals would be classified as reproductive healthcare.

4.2.2 *Reproductive Health Rights and Reproductive Rights*

The concept of reproductive health rights spans the life cycle of the human being and is centred on needs and development. It connotes the ability of people to have satisfying and safe sexual life, the capability to reproduce and autonomy to decide the frequency of reproduction.[19]

[16] Elissa Braustein and Caren Grown, 'Reproductive Health, Trade Liberalization and Development' in C Grown, E Braunstean and A Malhotra (eds) *Trading Women's Health and Rights? Trade Liberalization and Reproductive Health in Developing Economies* (Zed Books: New York, London, 2006) p 6.

[17] MJ Roseman and L Reichenbach, 'Global Reproductive Health and Rights: Reflecting on ICPD' in *Reproductive Health and Human Rights: The Way Forward* (University of Pennsylvania Press: Philadelphia, 2009) p 7.

[18] Ibid.

[19] United Nations Population Fund, *Reproductive Rights Are Human Rights: A Handbook for National Human Rights Institutions*, 2014 p 18.

Sonia Correa, one of the drivers of the ICPD states that the terms 'reproductive health; and reproductive rights' showcase certain compromises within the global women's health movements.[20] While reproductive health rights in a lot of contexts may mean the conventional maternal and child health policies including family planning; reproductive rights are more political and seek a transformative platform for the redefinition of sexual and reproductive needs. These rights comprise the strings of gender power relations and the right of women to have autonomy as regards childbearing and spacing. Thus, reproductive health is to be achieved through the promotion and protection of reproductive rights.[21]

Reproductive rights entail the recognition of the basic right of individuals in the decision-making process of the number, spacing, and timing of children; having access to the right information (which could include access to technology in cases of assisted reproduction), and the right to attain the highest standard of sexual and reproductive health.[22]

The nexus between both concepts is highlighted by the fact that the reproductive capacity of women is tied to their health and they should have the autonomy to make decisions that would affect their health. Thus, reproductive health will be improved if reproductive rights are promoted. Policymakers are advised to promote reproductive rights in a bid to maximise the benefits of reproductive health.[23] This presumption of autonomy in the exercise of reproductive rights is however the ideal situation and is not always the reality. The exercise of reproductive rights must in essence be devoid of discrimination, coercion, or any form of violence.

The ICPD put forward what was termed the 'Cairo paradigm' which identified a shift of population policy from fertility regulation towards reproductive health, premised on the exercise of reproductive rights and

[20] S Correa, 'From Reproductive Health to Sexual Rights Achievements and Future Challenges' 1997 5(10) Reproductive Health Matters p 5.

[21] MJ Roseman and L Reichenbach, 'Global Reproductive and Health Rights: Reflecting on ICPD' in L Reichenbach and MJ Roseman (eds) *Reproductive Health and Human Rights: The Way Forward* (University of Pennsylvania Press: Philadelphia, 2009) p 9.

[22] Ibid.

[23] J Gammage and R Clark, 'Women's Reproductive Health: The Impact of Three Kinds of Development and Three Kinds of Women Power' 2016 42(1) International Journal of Sociology and Family, 1–14 at p 12.

the empowerment of women.[24] Reproductive rights thus have infused therein tenets of autonomy and decision-making ability. The ICPD PoA recognises the importance of sexual and reproductive health as a precondition for the empowerment of women.[25] The Principles set out in the ICPD PoA are crucial in the drive towards the realisation of the SDGs as regards the sustainability of the world population and development. The instrumentality of reproductive health towards the achievement of economic and social development was systematised in the ICPD. The ICPD was not a conference in isolation but a build-up from other conferences on sustainable development, economic growth and the empowerment of women which had hitherto been hosted around the world.[26]

Having established that reproductive rights are hinged on reproductive health, this paper contends that for WWD reproductive rights have a different connotation to the extent that it transcends access to methods of birth control and freedom of choice as to motherhood. For WWD based on the discriminatory bias as to the legitimacy of their desire and capacity to have children, reproductive rights entail the recognition of the right to bear children in the first place and subsequent assistance in caring for the children.[27] It is opined that the CRPD in addressing reproductive rights adopts a protective medical and gender binary model.[28] Perhaps this classification emanates from the prominent gender identification categories available at the time which does not give room for the discourse in terms of the reproductive rights of other gender categories.

Irrespective of the fact that certain disability conditions do not medically inhibit PWD from giving birth, some countries have instituted some formal and informal barriers like female infertility and male sterility to

[24] Ibid, (n 18).

[25] United Nations Population Fund *Principles of the ICPD* available https://www.unfpa.org/icpd.

[26] The World Conference to Review and Appraise the Achievements of the United Nations decade for Women, Equality, Development and Peace held in Nairobi 1985; the World Summit for Children held in New York in 1990; the United Nations Conference on Environment and Development held in Rio de Janeiro in 1992 amongst others. Ibid.

[27] G Albrecht, D Mitchell, S Synder, J Birkenbach, W Shalick (eds) *Encyclopedia of Disability* (London: Sage Publications, 2006) p 724.

[28] FJ Ruiz, 'The Committee on the Rights of Persons with Disabilities and its Take on Sexuality' 2017 255(50) Reproductive Health Matters, pp 92–103.

inhibit parenthood for PWD.[29] There is the assumption of the incompetence of PWD to care for their children with the requisite emotional and social guidance to thrive in society.[30] This incompetence is given more emphasis for people with mental disabilities especially as the welfare of the children will be on the State's resources.[31] The dependence on State resources and the incompetence of some PWD should not be the sole reason for the lack of exercise of the rights. The description of PWD will be considered below.

4.2.3 Persons with Disabilities

The World Health Organization (WHO) notes that about 1 billion of the world's population currently experience disability.[32] Article 1 of the CRPD defines PWD to include those who have long-term physical, mental, intellectual or sensory impairments which in interaction with various barriers may hinder their full and effective participation in society on an equal basis with others. The preamble of the CRPD recognises that disability is an evolving concept that results from the interaction between persons with impairments and attitudinal and environmental barriers that hinder their full and effective participation on an equal basis with others. This highlights a distinction between impairment and disability as emphasised by some scholars who define impairment in individual and biological terms while disability is defined as a social construct.[33] According to Lennard Davis 'Disability is not so much the lack of a sense or the presence of a physical or mental impairment as it is the reception and construction of that difference'.[34] Thus, while impairments hinder PWD from certain activities, environmental barriers, for instance, emphasize such physical impairments. If a PWD particularly

[29] Ibid, (n 27)3 p 1398.

[30] Ibid, p 1399.

[31] T. Shakespeare, *Disability Rights and Wrongs Revisited* (London and New York: Routledge, 2014) p 21.

[32] World Health Organization, 'Disability' available https://www.who.int/health-topics/disability.

[33] T. Shakespeare, *Disability Rights and Wrongs Revisited* (London and New York: Routledge, 2014) p 21.

[34] L Davis, *Bending over Backwards: Disability, Dismodernism and Other Difficult Positions* (New York: New York University Press, 2002) p 50.

with physical mobility tries to access a building without ramps or doorways suitable for wheelchair access, not only is there disability because of an impairment but the environmental barriers in the building further heighten the disability[35] and, in this case, the PWD has not been treated equally with other persons intending to access the building.

PWD are perceived as being dependent on others and regarded from a standpoint of pity. The process of the negotiations and drafting of the CRPD highlighted the need to protect PWD from compulsory sterilisation in the exercise of reproductive rights.[36] There is also the notion that PWDs are impotent or asexual. PWD are not however perpetually ill because most PWD have normal life expectancies beyond the disabling conditions.[37] Although individual disabilities may differ, generally, PWD want—society especially medical personnel—to perceive them as being whole and they often explore ways of maximising their physical, mental, emotional and reproductive health.[38]

Most advocates of PWD constantly refer to equality in treatment and prohibition of discrimination. Discrimination in this regard refers to any distinction, exclusion, or restriction based on disability that has the purpose or effect of impairing or nullifying the recognition, enjoyment, or exercise, on an equal basis with others, of all human rights and fundamental freedoms in the political, economic, social, cultural, civil or any other field.[39]

The next section considers the legal framework for RHR of PWD in Nigeria.

[35] This was experienced by the by Jordan Steele-John Australia's youngest Senator in 2017 and the first parliament wheel-chair user. He faced the barrier of mobility as the Parliament building was only accessible with stairs. He also obtained injuries on his knuckles due to the narrowness of the hallways and doors. While he had a physical impairment, the structure of the building was an environmental barrier. See LJ Graham (ed) al *Inclusive Education for the 21st Century: Theory, Policy and Practice* (Taylor and Francis, 2019).

[36] Ibid, (n 24).

[37] LI Iezzoni and Bonnie O'Day, *More Than Ramps: A Guide to Improving Healthcare Quality and Access for People with Disabilities* (Oxford University Press: New York, 2006) p 16.

[38] Ibid, (p 16).

[39] CRPD Article 2.

4.3 Legal Provisions for Reproductive Health Rights of Persons with Disabilities in Nigeria

The law is the basic instrument through which the rights of individuals in society can be protected, promoted, and enforced. Legal provisions will guard against discrimination of PWD in the exercise of RHR. This section thus considers international, regional, and national provisions that are relevant to the subject matter of RHR and PWD. Being an evolving discourse in Nigeria, there is a dearth of literature that directly deals—with RHR of PWD in Nigeria—as a result of which the analysis of the provisions of the various laws becomes essential.

RHR are considered fundamental and should be exercised by all categories of persons in society.[40] Thus, basic provisions on human rights will be considered in this section, however, emphasis will be placed on the provisions that specifically relate to RHR and PWD.

Internationally, several treaties lay the foundation for the determination of the rights of human beings. The United Nations Declaration on Human Rights (UDHR) 1948 for instance contains diverse provisions that lay the foundation for these rights. Article 1 UDHR states that all humans are born free and equal in dignity and rights. This entrenches the equality of PWD and those without disabilities implying that there should be no discrimination against PWD. Article 2 of the UDHR further states the entitlement to rights devoid of distinction of any kind. Although the Article does not specifically mention disability, it is presumed that the word 'other' subsumes the disability qualifier. Other rights protected by the UDHR include the right to life[41]; equality before the law devoid of discrimination[42]; and the standard of living adequate for the health and well-being of individuals and families including the entitlement to special care and assistance of motherhood and childhood[43]; which all reflect the protection of the rights of PWD.

The provisions of the CRPD are also anchored on the need to promote, protect and ensure the full and equal enjoyment of all human rights and fundamental freedoms by all persons with disabilities, and to

[40] Ibid, (n 16) i.

[41] UDHR Article 3.

[42] UDHR Article 7.

[43] UDHR Article 25.

promote respect for their inherent dignity. This treaty came into force on the 30th of May 2008 after the 20th ratification. Article 3 of the CRPD stipulates the guiding principles, one of which is the respect for inherent dignity, individual autonomy including the freedom to make one's own choices, and independence of persons. In essence, the dignity of PWD ought to be respected, recognizing their autonomy to make decisions as regards reproduction. Article 4 of the CRPD states the obligations of State Parties to ensure national laws are aligned with the provisions of the convention. Article 4 specifically recognizes reproductive and family planning education and states that the means to aid the exercise of these rights are provided. Article 23 of the CRPD sets out provisions for the respect of family and the home. While stating generally that measures be instituted by State Parties to ensure the elimination of discrimination against PWD in matters relating to marriage, family, parenthood, and relationships; it specifically states that PWD have the right to decide freely and responsibly on the number and spacing of their children and have access to age-appropriate information. Article 23 (c) further states that PWD including children should retain their fertility on an equal basis with others. This implies that compulsory sterilisation is prohibited. The advocacy for the protection of the RHR of PWD also extends to children with disabilities who may be subject to compulsory sterilisation after birth. Subsequently, Article 25 of the CRPD which contains provisions on health stipulates that there shall be no discrimination in the provision of healthcare programmes especially sexual and reproductive health. These diverse provisions reflect that the Convention specifically provides for RHR.

Regionally, the African continent has instruments that support inclusive and sustainable development on the premise of Agenda 2063 which was adopted to strive towards the desired Africa. The aspirations of Agenda 2063 include an improvement in the quality of life of citizens and PWD have been highlighted as one of its priority areas and consequently the health of its citizens which includes RHR by implication.[44] The African Charter on Human and Peoples Rights (ACHPR) lays the foundation for the enjoyment of the rights and freedoms stipulated therein without

[44] Aspiration 1 Goal 3 of Agenda 2063 stipulates the expansion of quality healthcare services particularly for women and girls. Aspiration 3 emphasises respect for human rights which by implication includes RHR and Aspiration 6 foresees an inclusive continent where no one is left behind based on factors that may induce discrimination.

distinction. Article 13(2) of the ACHPR stipulates equal access to public services by citizens in their country. Reproductive health services fall into the category of public services and should be accessed by every citizen including PWD. Article 18(4) specifically protects the rights of PWD stating the right to special measures of protection in keeping with their physical and moral needs.

Specifically, the Protocol to the African Charter on Human and Peoples' Rights on the Rights of Persons with Disabilities in Africa (The Disability Protocol) ensures that the rights of PWD are protected with specific reference to the right to health[45]; right to family[46]; and Article 27 (K) which specifically guarantees the reproductive health rights of WWD enabling the control of fertility and prohibiting sterilisation without their consent all showcase the commitment of the continent to the protection of RHR.

Furthermore, the Protocol to the African Charter on Human and Peoples' Rights on the Rights of Women in Africa (the Maputo Protocol) also specifically provides for the protection of the rights of WWD who are more vulnerable to discrimination as identified above. Article XXIII of the Maputo Protocol provides for the special protection of WWD. Although the provisions do not specifically mention the reproductive rights of WWD it prohibits discrimination based on disabilities of women. This provision can be read jointly with Article XIV which provides specifically for health and reproductive rights. In essence, the reproductive rights of women are guaranteed by the Article and State Parties are obliged to take appropriate measures to provide services related to reproductive rights. Thus, since the Maputo Protocol provides that WWD should not be discriminated against, their reproductive rights are equally guaranteed. The challenge however lies in the content of the two paragraphs of Article XIV which seem to be contradictory. Paragraph 1 states that women can control their fertility and have the right to decide whether to have children, the number of children, and the spacing of the children. However, paragraph 2, highlighting the measures the State should adopt in protecting the reproductive rights of women, provides for the authorisation of medical abortion in cases of sexual assault, rape, incest, and circumstances where the mental and physical health of the mother,

[45] Disability Protocol Article 17.

[46] Disability Protocol Article 26.

life of the mother or foetus is endangered.[47] This qualification of situations when reproductive rights, in terms of abortion, can be exercised implies that the perceived autonomy is a façade. Scholars have justified this erosion of autonomy on the vulnerability of PWD especially those with mental disabilities who require a higher level of external protection.[48] Justice Holmes in Buck v Bell questioned the parental abilities of those with intellectual disabilities justifying sterilisation without their consent on the need to stall unmitigated drains on the welfare resources of the United States.[49] While the United States law has progressed from involuntary sterilisation proceedings to terminating parental rights, regulatory sterilisation is still faced by persons with intellectual disabilities.[50] The primary justification for sterilisation seems justified as one of the outcomes of the exercise of RHR may be procreation and it is paramount that children are protected from harm which may not be the case if they are left in the care of persons with certain types of disabilities for which higher level of protection is necessary. Furthermore, it is arguable that allowing the birth of children conceived under the other circumstances mentioned in the Article such as sexual assault, rape, and incest may be traumatic for the mother. Thus, while it is ok to have authorised medical abortion, the decision should be subject to the parties involved without any form of coercion from medical personnel.

The laudable provisions stated above notwithstanding, it is trite as provided by section 12 of the Constitution of the Federal Republic of Nigeria (CFRN) 1999 (as amended), that these treaties have to be enacted into law in Nigeria or simply put, domesticated. Thus, in considering the implication of the treaty provisions, attention has to be paid to the provisions that have the force of law in Nigeria. The CFRN 1999 in section 17 in furtherance of its social order provides for the equality of rights, adequate medical and health facilities for all persons, and the evolution and promotion of family life which all imply support for the RHR of PWD. Furthermore, chapter IV of the CFRN 1999 stipulates

[47] Article XIV 1 and 2.

[48] Arstein-Kerslake, 'A Gendered Denials: Vulnerability Created by Barriers to Legal Capacity for Women and Disabled Women' 2019 66 International Journal of Law and Psychiatry.

[49] 274 U.S. 200, 207 (1927).

[50] L Francis, 'Maintaining the Legal Status of People with Intellectual Disabilities as Parents: the ADA and the CRPD' 2019 57(1) Family Court Review.

the fundamental human rights, especially the right to life,[51] the right to freedom from discrimination[52] and the right to private and family life[53] relate to the protection of RHR of PWD in one way or the other.

Nigeria ratified the CRPD in 2010. In furtherance of its obligations under the CRPD, the Discrimination Against Persons with Disabilities (Prohibition) Act was passed in 2018. This law was geared towards the full integration of PWD in diverse areas including health-related matters. It suffices to say that RHR is one of the areas that should be covered by the provisions of this legislation as it borders on health. Section 1 of the Act generally prohibits discrimination based on disability which is classified as an offense and stipulates the requisite penalty upon conviction. Part II of the Act provides for accessibility of physical structures especially public buildings which will be constructed with necessary accessibility aids. Hospitals and other primary healthcare facilities which are avenues for the dissemination of information on reproductive health and accessibility of services fall into this category. The provisions in this part, therefore, ensure that PWD can access such buildings. There is further provision for a transitory period of five years to ensure that buildings in existence comply with the accessibility plan of the Act.[54] The provisions clearly state that PWD have equal access like every other citizen and thus should not be discriminated against. Section 21 on free healthcare states the unfettered access of PWD to adequate healthcare without discrimination. However, neither this section nor the provisions in its entirety specifically mention reproductive health as part of the healthcare services.

The National Policy on sexual and reproductive health rights of persons with disabilities with an emphasis on women and girls indicates the commitment of the Nigerian government to provide comprehensive and integrated reproductive health services devoid of discrimination. The framework of the Policy thrives on the rationale that PWD has similar sexual and reproductive health needs as other people in society and as such require the same services but takes into consideration their particular circumstances which make them vulnerable and could deny them access to reproductive health services if not specifically addressed. The Policy aims

[51] CFRN Section 33.

[52] CFRN Section 42.

[53] CFRN Section 37.

[54] CFRN Section 6.

to improve access to quality and rights-based reproductive health services for PWD in Nigeria.

While the Maputo Protocol has been ratified, Nigeria is yet to ratify the Disability Protocol. Furthermore, beyond the process of ratification, is the need for domestication as highlighted above.

However, irrespective of legal provisions, the fact remains that PWD still faces discrimination and their reproductive rights are not exercised in most instances. While the legal provisions identified above do not necessarily discriminate between men with disabilities and WWD, it is obvious that WWD experience more vulnerability to discrimination. The rationale for this is that women actively go through most reproductive stages like pregnancy and childbirth. They are most likely the main recipients of discrimination in terms of RHR. Furthermore, women are affected by the intersectionality of other forms of discrimination where the lack of economic prowess and other gender stereotypes could heighten the bias of the society towards them and worsen the exercise of their RHR. The fact that disability is experienced differently by men and women cannot be over-emphasised and this can largely be attributed to the culture discussed in the next section.

4.4 Cultural Undertone

Culture is used by Anthropologists when reference is made to a group of people who have a similar way of life or thought process.[55] A society thus emanates from a group of people who have a common culture and rules of behaviour.[56] The adoption of treaties and regulations notwithstanding, culture plays a role in the behaviour of people in any society. The culture in Nigeria is deeply influenced by patriarchy, gender stereotypes, religion and superstitious beliefs, among other issues.[57]

Culturally, disability is viewed negatively and with suspicion in most parts of Africa.[58] Traditional African societies describe disability as a limitation in social participation as a result of physical, emotional, or sensory

[55] Frances Raday, 'Culture Religion and Gender' 2003 1(4) International Journal of Constitutional Law, p 664.

[56] Ibid.

[57] M Eskay, VC Onu, JN Igbo, N Obiyo, and L Ugwuanyi, 'Disability Within the African Culture' 2012 US-China Education Review, p 478.

[58] G Albrecht et al., *Encyclopedia of Disability* (Sage Publications, 2006) p 423.

abnormalities which has a spiritual or supernatural undertone.[59] Nigeria being a part of the African continent by implication has some of these cultural practices. Thus, obscene practices attributed to culture are meted on PWD. These practices emanate from superstitious beliefs that disability is not a type of deformity but rather attributed to a deity, witchcraft, misfortune due to incest, possession of an evil spirit, taboo, and other supernatural acts.[60] There is also the belief that disability is a curse and as such, PWD should be ostracised, or they may be serving some form of punishment by their ancestors.[61] It is alleged that PWD especially persons with mental disabilities are kidnapped and killed for rituals.[62] Most of these rituals are executed on the premise of spiritual cleansing of the land since PWD are allegedly serving some form of punishment by their ancestors.[63] If this is the plight of PWD, then obviously most of them will not live long to enjoy or enforce their reproductive rights.

On the flip side, in some communities, disability has some positive intonation as PWD are classified as having some supernatural powers equal to deities.[64] Such communities are however in the minority as the negative perception seems to be the norm. Whatever the perception, the resultant effect is discrimination, stigmatisation, and marginalisation of PWD. This marginalisation commences right from birth and continues to the education stage where children with disabilities attend special schools irrespective of the possibility for inclusive education. This gradually galvanises a lack of capacity by service providers in rendering services and attending to PWD.

This naturally leads to the bias developed in society towards PWD and this is often expressed by healthcare providers when providing reproductive health services to PWD. This increases the daily challenges of

[59] Ibid.

[60] Ibid, (n 46) p 478.

[61] E Etieyibo and O Omiegbe, 'Religion, Culture and Discrimination Against Persons with Disabilities in Nigeria' 2016 5(1) African Journal of Disability, p 4.

[62] Ibid.

[63] Ibid.

[64] Ibid.

isolation, segregation, marginalisation, social restrictions, and discrimination.[65] There is the widespread assumption in society that PWD are asexual, hypersexual, and do not have the capacity for reproduction or are not suitable partners for marital relationships.[66] Studies have shown that the misconception that PWD lack sexuality has automatically excluded them from sex education as students.[67] Irrespective of the type of disability, the similarity in form of prejudice and discrimination experienced remains constant.[68]

Having established that PWD needs to deal with challenges in society, WWD are more vulnerable in terms of discrimination based on the intersectionality of their disability and gender. Manisuli opines that irrespective of the international and national regulations proscribing sex discrimination, the human rights of women are still systematically infringed upon.[69] For instance, WWD in the United States of America irrespective of the abolition of compulsory sterilisation still face barriers in terms of reproductive freedom and are advised by healthcare workers to terminate their pregnancies most times.[70] The focus of healthcare providers, therefore, seems to be control rather than giving WWD the required information to make autonomous decisions. Thus, while the laws stipulate that there is autonomy in making decisions on reproductive health, healthcare providers control the process through consultations and advice given to WWD. Thus, in reality, WWD does not make autonomous decisions as regards RHR. Most times this control is borne out of ignorance and lack of understanding of the special care needs of WWD.[71]

[65] LA Habib 'Women and Disability Don't Mix': Double Discrimination and Disabled Women's Rights' 1995 3(2) Gender and Development.

[66] Renu Addlakha, Janet Price, and Shirin Heidari. 'Disability and Sexuality: Claiming Sexual and Reproductive Rights' 2017 25(50) Reproductive Health Matters, p 4.

[67] X Hunt, M Carew, SH Braathen, L Swartz, C Mussa, and P Rohleder, 'The Sexual and Reproductive Health Rights and Benefit Derived from Sexual and Reproductive Health Services of People with Physical Disabilities in South Africa: Beliefs of Non-Disabled People' 2017 25(50) Reproductive Health Matters, p 68.

[68] R, Addlakha et al. ibid, (n 55).

[69] S Manisuli, 'Culture and the Human Rights of Women in Africa: Between Light and Shadow' 2007 5191 Journal of African Law 39–67 at p 41.

[70] CL Shandra, DP Hogan, and SE Short, 'Planning for Motherhood: Fertility Attitudes, Desires, and Intentions Among Women with Disabilities' 2014 46(4) Perspectives on Sexual and Reproductive Health, p 203.

[71] Ibid, p 204.

Furthermore, other forms of prejudice and bias are meted out against WWD. A study carried out in Cambodia revealed that WWD are not attractive to men as marriage partners based on the presumption of their incapability of reproduction and motherhood.[72] This rubs off on the confidence of the WWD who do not feel attractive either. Asides from the physical component of beauty, WWD are also perceived to be a burden to their spouses, and as such parents withdraw consent when they introduce potential suitors interested in a marriage relationship. The WWD end up in relationships perceived to be beneficial and less burdensome by their parents and marry spouses that the parents believe can shoulder the financial burden of the disability.[73]

The above lends credence to the notion that discrimination against WWD is not peculiar to Nigeria but it is a global challenge with varying degrees. However, such discrimination is more intense in Nigeria because of stereotypical behaviour induced by deep-seated cultural and sometimes diabolical belief systems. Women in Nigeria are especially affected by various factors like religion, poverty, age, and marital status which results in compounded disadvantage.[74] The prevalence of prejudicial customs heightens the intensity of discrimination against women. It is however noteworthy that WWD values the importance of motherhood the same way as their counterparts without disabilities.

4.5 Recommendations

The CRPD emphasised the removal of social barriers to participation and enjoyment of rights in this context reproductive health rights. It is therefore essential that the RHR of PWDs are not just protected but also promoted. State Parties need to take active steps to ensure that healthcare providers have the requisite knowledge and capacity to provide reproductive health services specifically to PWD. Consequently, with the identification of the greater vulnerability of WWD, the sensitisation and capacity building of healthcare service providers on issues of intersectionality regarding the female gender is imperative. This enunciates the fact

[72] A Gatrell, et al., (n 6) p 35.

[73] Ibid.

[74] S Mansuli n58 p 39.

that the reality of RHR transcends the provision of ramps and access to healthcare facilities.

It is also recommended that domestication of the Disability Protocol and the Maputo Protocol be embarked upon. Specific provisions of the CRPD on RHR should be reflected in the Disability Prohibition Act of Nigeria as stated by Article 4 of the CRPD on the alignment of the provisions with national laws. These specific provisions include Article 23 on respect for family and the home, and Article 25 which prohibits discrimination in the provision of healthcare programmes. More than the enactment of laws, a procedure for monitoring and evaluation is necessary to curb discrimination. Finally, the general sensitisation of society cannot be over-emphasised since disability is hinged more on discrimination than the actual impairment.

4.6 Conclusion

This chapter set out to consider the reproductive health rights of PWD in Nigeria. While generally evaluating the rights of PWD, specific inferences were made about WWD judging from the multiple discrimination faced by women and the increase in vulnerability. The legal provisions were considered and this highlighted the applicable framework for the protection of the rights of PWD including WWD. The analysis showcased that although explicit provisions may be required to model after specific international and regional provisions, the pivot of discrimination also has a cultural undertone. Education, sensitisation and capacity building of the populace especially policymakers and healthcare service providers are imperative.

Bibliography

Abu, H. L. Women and Disability Don't Mix: Double Discrimination and Disabled Women's Rights. (1995) *Gender and Development*, 49–53.

Addlakha, R., Price, J., & Heidari, S. Disability and Sexuality: Claiming Sexual and Reproductive Rights. 2017 25(50) *Reproductive Health Matters*, 4–9.

Albrecht, G., Mitchell, D., Snyder, S., Birkenbach, J., & Shalick, W. (Eds.). *Encyclopedia of Disability* (London: Sage Publications 2006).

Arstein-Kerslake, A. Gendered-Denials: Vulnerability Created by Barriers to Legal Capacity for Women and Disabled Women. 2019 (66) *International Journal of Law and Psychiatry*.

Ayanleye, O. A. Women and Reproductive Health Rights in Nigeria. 2013 6(5) *OIDA International Journal of Sustainable Development*, 127–140.

Betsy, H. *Reproductive Rights and Wrongs: The Global Politics of Population Control* (Illinois: Haymarket Books 2016).

Davis, L. J. Bending Over Backwards: Disability, Dismodernism and Other Difficult Positions (New York: New York University Press 2002).

Devine, A., Ignacio, R., Prenter, K., Temminghoff, L., Gill-Atkinson, L., Zayas, J., … Vaughan, C. 'Freedom to go where I want': Improving Access to Sexual and Reporductive Health for Women With Disabilities in Philipinnes. 2017 25(50) *Reproductive Health Matters*, 55–65.

Eskay, M., Onu, V. C., Igbo, J. N., Obiyo, N., & Ugwuanyi, L. Disability Within the African Culture. (2012) *US-China Education Review*, 473–484.

Etieyibo, E., & Omiegbe, O. Religion, Culture and Discrimination against Persons with Disabilities in Nigeria. 2016 5(1) *African Journal of Disability*.

Frances, R.. Culture, Religion and Gender. 2003 1(4) *International Journal of Constitutional Law*, 663–715.

Francis, L. Maintaining the Legal Status of People with Intellectual Disabilities as Parents: the ADA and CRPD. 2019 57(1) *Family Law Review*, 21–36.

Gammage, J., & Clark, R. Women's Reproductive Health: The Impact of Three Kinds of Development and Three Kinds of Women Power. 2016 42(1) *International Journal of Sociology and Family*, 1–14.

Gartrell, A., Baesel, K., & Becker, C. "We do not dare to love": women with disabilities' sexual and reproductive health and rights in rural Cambodia. 2017 (May), 25(50) *Reproductive Health Matters*, 31–42.

Grown, C., Braunstein, E., & Malhotra, A. (2006). *Trading Women's Health and Reproductive Rights? Trade Liberalization and Reproductive Health in Developing Economies* (London, New York: Zed Books).

Hindlin, M. J., & Fatusi, A. O. Adolescent Sexual and Reproductive Health in Developing Countries: An Overview of Trends and Interventions. 2009 35(2) *International Perspectives on Sexual and Reproductive Health*, 58–62.

Hunt, X., Carew, M. T., Braathen, S. H., Swartz, L., Mussa, C., & Rohleder, P. The Sexual and Reproductive Health Rights and Benefit Derived from Sexual and Reproductive Health Services of People with Physical Disabilities in South Africa: Beliefs of Non-Disabled People. 2017 25(50) *Reproductive Health Matters*, 66–79.

Iezzoni, L. I., & O'Day, B. *Beyond Ramps: A Gudie to Improving Health Care Quality and Access for People With Disabilities* (New York: Oxford University Press 2006).

Manisuli, S. Culture and the Human Rights of Women in Africa: Between Light and Shadow. 2007 51(1) *Journal of African Law*, 39–67.

Reichenbach, L., & Roseman, M. J. *Reproductive Health and Human Rights: The Way Forward* (Philadelphia: University of Pennysylvania Press 2009).

Rothler, R. Disability Rights, Reproductive Technology and Parenthood: Unrealised Opportunities. 2017 25(50) *Reproductive Health Matters*, 104–113.

Ruiz, F. J. The Committee on the Rights of Persons with Disabilities and Its Take on Sexuality. 2017 25(50) *Reproductive Health Matters*, 92–103.

Shakespeare, T. *Disability Rights and Wrongs Revisited* (London and New York: Routledge 2014)

Shakespeare, T., Hameed, S., & Kiama, L. Action Not Words. 2019 27(1) *Sexual and Reproductive Health Matters*, 340–342.

Shandra, C. L., Hogan, D. P., & Short, S. E. Planning for Motherhood: Fertility Attitudes, Desires and Intentions Among Women With Disabilities. 2014 46(4) *Perspectives on Sexual and Reproductive Health*, 203–210.

United Nations. *Report of the International Conference on Population and Development* (New York: United Nations 1995).

PART II

Abortion

CHAPTER 5

The Provision of Safe and Legal Abortion Services in South Africa: Expanding Access Through Telemedicine and Lessons Learned During the Covid-19 Pandemic

Nasreen Solomons and Harsha Gihwala

5.1 Introduction

South Africa is lauded for having one of the most progressive abortion laws in the world, having enacted the Choice on Termination of Pregnancy Act (CTOPA/the Act) in 1996, and providing for abortion

N. Solomons (✉) · H. Gihwala
Gender, Health and Justice Research Unit, University of Cape Town, Cape Town, South Africa
e-mail: nasreen.solomons@uct.ac.za

H. Gihwala
e-mail: harsha.gihwala@uct.ac.za

O. S. Adelakun and E. Ndoni (eds.), *Reproductive Health and Assisted Reproductive Technologies In Sub-Saharan Africa*, Sustainable Development Goals Series,
https://doi.org/10.1007/978-981-99-2411-0_5

upon request up to 12 weeks of pregnancy.[1] The enactment of the CTOPA progressed South Africa from a framework of criminalisation to legalisation, committing to equality in access to sexual and reproductive health (SRH) services, particularly abortion services, in the South African healthcare system. The predecessor to the CTOPA, the Abortion and Sterilization Act,[2] only permitted abortion[3] services in certain limited circumstances, which required written certification by two doctors before the procedure could be provided by a third medical practitioner.[4] This presented pregnant persons (inclusive of women, girls, transmen and non-binary individuals)[5] with severely limited grounds to use the service, and to access such within a severely restricted medical environment. Ostensibly, the limited service would have been available to privileged, white persons, pushing all other pregnant persons to the periphery and making them reliant on informal settings to access abortion services.[6]

Though South Africa progressed to provide a right to safe and legal abortion through the CTOPA, which requires the consent of only the pregnant person when accessing this right, the landscape of service provision continues to be severely limited, and barriers to access still exist. These barriers were only exacerbated by the COVID-19 pandemic. Against the backdrop of the context of abortion service provision that pre-dated the pandemic, we discuss the documented, aggravated barriers

[1] Choice on Termination of Pregnancy Act (CTOPA) 92 of 1996, section 2; Marion Stevens 'Sexual and reproductive health and rights: Where is the progress since Beijing?' (2021) 35(2) Agenda 48, 49; Marion Stevens 'Challenges for achieving sexual and reproductive justice in South Africa' (*Sexual and Reproductive Health Matters*, 2 May 2019) <www.srhm.org/news/challenges-for-achieving-sexual-and-reproductive-justice-in-south-africa/> accessed on 31 August 2021; Satang Nabaneh, Marion Stevens, Lucia Berro Pizzarossa 'Let's call "conscientious objection" by its name: Obstruction to care and abortion in South Africa' (OHRH, 24 October 2018) <https://ohrh.law.ox.ac.uk/lets-call-conscientious-objection-by-its-name-obstruction-of-access-to-care-and-abortion-in-south-africa/> accessed on 12 July 2021.

[2] Act 2 of 1975.

[3] The Choice on Termination of Pregnancy Act refers to terminations of pregnancy, however the authors use the term 'abortion' throughout this chapter.

[4] Abortion and Sterilization Act, s 3(1) and 3(2).

[5] The CTOPA refers to 'women' and 'girls', however this chapter uses the term 'pregnant persons' to refer to women, girls, transmen and non-binary individuals.

[6] Susanne M. Klausen *Abortion under apartheid: Nationalism, sexuality and women's reproductive rights in South Africa* (OUP, 2015).

to access and service provision that resulted from the pandemic, and its health and safety measures; the opportunity to expand access through telemedicine; and the implications of the failure to do so.

5.2 Context of Abortion Service Provision in South Africa and COVID-19

5.2.1 The CTOPA and Context of Service Provision

While the CTOPA provides for abortion upon request up to 12 weeks of gestation, with only the consent of the pregnant person seeking the service required for it to be provided, abortion of pregnancies from 13 weeks, in specific circumstances and after consultation with a medical practitioner, may be permitted. For pregnancies between 13 and 20 weeks, abortions are provided in circumstances where the pregnancy poses a risk to the woman's (language of 'woman' is used in the Act) physical or mental health; the foetus would suffer severe physical or mental abnormality; the pregnancy resulted from rape or incest; or the pregnancy would affect the social or economic circumstances of the woman.[7] Abortions provided in this second trimester period require consultation between the pregnant person and a medical practitioner. After the 20th week, abortions are provided in instances where the pregnancy would endanger the woman's life; result in severe malformation of the foetus; or pose a risk of injury to the foetus.[8] In these circumstances, the abortion may only be performed by a medical practitioner after consultation with another medical practitioner, registered nurse or midwife.

The legislation provides for further measures to give effect to the constitutional rights to bodily and psychological integrity; privacy; human dignity; access to information; and access to health services, including reproductive services.[9] It provides that the procedure may only take place with the consent of the pregnant person, which includes minors,[10] thereby recognising the injustices of the past wherein the consent of the pregnant person was not central to the provision of the service,

[7] CTOPA, s 2(1)(b).

[8] CTOPA, s 2(1)(c).

[9] Constitution of the Republic of South Africa 1996, ss 12; 14; 10; 32; 27(1)(a).

[10] CTOPA, s 5(2).

and extending uninhibited access to pregnant persons of all ages. It also requires that pregnant persons seeking an abortion be informed of their rights in terms of the Act; sets out criteria for the designation of health facilities, both public and private, to provide abortion services; provides for non-mandatory and non-directive counselling; and creates offences for the provision of the service outside the circumstances permitted in the Act, and for the prevention of an abortion or obstructing access to a facility.[11]

Though the Act was a marked change from the previous restrictive framework regulating abortion, with abortion-related maternal morbidity and mortality decreasing by 91% between 1997 and 2002,[12] there have since been serious barriers to access documented that have impeded equitable access to, and provision of, these services in South Africa.[13] Some of the main factors listed as bars to pregnant persons safely accessing abortion services in South Africa include: poor training; lack of staff available and willing to offer abortion services; a limited number of facilities that are designated and therefore able to provide abortion services; and a lack of information dissemination about where to access abortion services. These challenges create critically inaccessible circumstances within which to access time-sensitive medical care. MacLeod delineates these barriers at a macro- and micro-level.[14]

[11] CTOPA, ss 6; 3; 4; 10.

[12] Ramprakash Kaswa, Parimalaranie Yogeswaran 'Abortion reforms in South Africa: An overview of the *Choice on Termination of Pregnancy Act*' (2020) 62(1) Part 4 a5240 South African Family Practice <https://doi.org/10.4102/safp.v62i1.5240> accessed on 29 October 2021.

[13] Stevens 'Sexual and reproductive health and rights' (n 2); Jane Freedman, Tamaryn L. Crankshaw, Victoria M. Mutambara 'Sexual and reproductive health of asylum seeking and refugee women in South Africa: Understanding the determinants of vulnerability' (2020) 28(1) Sexual and Reproductive Health Matters 324; Catriona Ida Macleod 'Expanding reproductive justice through a supportability reparative justice framework: The case of abortion in South Africa' (2019) 21(1) Culture, Health and Sexuality 46; Stevens 'Challenges in achieving sexual and reproductive justice in South Africa' (n 2); Amnesty International 'Briefing: Barriers to safe and legal abortion in South Africa' (2017) Amnesty International Publications www.amnesty.org/en/documents/afr53/5423/2017/en/> accessed on 15 October 2021.

[14] MacLeod (n 13) 53.

At the micro-level, when attempting to access abortion services, pregnant persons experience:

- Refusal of the service by providers, or being dissuaded from utilising the service;
- Trained staff unwilling to provide the service or be involved in certain aspects of its provision;
- Stigma and fear of being ostracised for seeking out and using the service.

At the macro-level, the barriers present were:

- Just over half of the designated facilities were functional;
- Less than a third of trained healthcare providers provide the service;
- Delays at facilities, with pregnant persons being made to wait to be provided the service, or told to return at a later date before being provided with any assistance;
- Advertisements for illegal abortions are widely accessible with little to no follow up by the Department of Health (DoH/the Department) or the South African Police Service (SAPS) in relation to these advertisements;
- Lack of information about the rights provided in the CTOPA or where to access services; and
- Limited access to second trimester abortion services.

A 2017 Amnesty International report[15] found that at the time, of the 3880 public health facilities in South Africa only 264 were providing access to abortion services.[16] This meant that just less than 7% of public health facilities in the country were providing access to abortion services. A vast majority of the population rely on public health facilities due to inequality in access, which impacts upon the ability to access services, infrastructure and resources, and which has become ingrained along a public/private divide.

[15] Amnesty International (n 13).

[16] Amnesty International (n 13). This was based on information received by Amnesty International from the National Department of Health on 3 November 2016.

In South Africa, approximately 83% of the country's population is reliant upon public health services, and 16.9% of the population belong to medical aid schemes, which provide easy access to private health care.[17] The South African Human Rights Commission found that South Africa's public health system was 'largely under-resourced in terms of personnel, availability of suitable medication and infrastructure; conditions which are adversely impacting the ability to deliver adequate care to poor people, especially to those in rural areas'.[18] The inequality in healthcare access is tracked across racial lines due to racist laws, policies and practices that were implemented during pre-democratic South Africa, and largely continues to impact poorer, Black, and persons living in rural areas.[19]

Forming part of the 83% of South Africa's population who are making use of public health services are marginalised and vulnerable groups who experience intersecting discrimination. This includes, among others, women and girls, persons with disabilities, internally displaced persons, asylum seekers and refugees, sex workers, and trans and non-binary persons. Access to SRH services, particularly abortion services, follows this pattern of inequitable access to, and provision of, health care and services, which affects a large proportion of the population and disproportionately impacts vulnerable groups.

In a study submitted in 2017 that assessed how access to abortion services could be expanded at a reduced cost by changing the mix of technologies used to provide the service, Lince-Deroche et al. found that both medical and surgical methods were available in the public sector.[20] Manual vacuum aspiration (MVA), however, was the dominant method

[17] Department of Statistics South Africa 'General Household Survey 2019' (Statistical release P0318, 17 December 2020) <www.statssa.gov.za/publications/P0318/P03182019.pdf> accessed on 29 June 2020; Women's Legal Centre, Legal Resources Centre and Sexual and Reproductive Justice Coalition 'Submission to Parliament: National Health Insurance Bill' (November 2019) <http://srjc.org.za/wp-content/uploads/2019/12/2019-11-29-Joint-Submission-NHI-Bill-WLC_LRC_SRJC.pdf> accessed 7 June 2021.

[18] South African Human Rights Commission 'Access to healthcare educational booklet' <www.sahrc.org.za/home/21/files/FINAL%20Access%20to%20Health%20Care%20Educational%20Booklet.pdf> accessed 07 June 2021.

[19] Macleod (n 13) 52.

[20] Naomi Lince-Deroche, Jane Harries et al. 'Doing more for less: Identifying opportunities to expand public sector access to safe abortion in South Africa through budget impact analysis' (2018) 97(2) Contraception 167.

used for first trimester abortions, limiting a large proportion of abortions to clinical settings. Even more, at the time of writing (June 2017), medical abortion (misoprostol and mifepristone) had only been introduced in six of the nine provinces since 2011.[21] Medical abortion was therefore not uniformly, nor widely accessible. The public health sector, which serviced 80% of the population for the period 2016/17, provided only 20% of abortions, leaving many pregnant individuals to either seek services in the private sector, at a cost, or to turn to illegal services. The study further found that of the abortions provided in the first trimester, 30% were provided via medical abortion; and that a quarter of abortion services were performed in the second trimester due to late presentation of pregnant persons and structural barriers to early access, with the main method of abortion in second trimester being dilation and evacuation (D&E).[22]

5.2.2 *The Effects of the Pandemic on Service Provision—Exacerbating Limited and Inequitable Access*

The poor landscape of abortion service provision was compounded by the stresses placed on the South African healthcare system during the pandemic. While the impact of the virus itself tangibly affected the lives of citizens on a global scale, the nature of the impact disproportionately affected marginalised and vulnerable people the world over.[23] In South Africa, the COVID-19 pandemic was classified as a national disaster on 15 March 2020,[24] with the national lockdown commencing on 27 March 2020. It began as a 21-day lockdown, which escalated into a multi-level protocol resulting in the enactment of regulations placing limitations on movement, and interrupting 'normal life' to varying degrees depending

[21] Ibid, 168.

[22] Lince-Deroche et al. (n 20) 173.

[23] Rouzeh Eghtessadi, Zindoga Mukandavire, Farirai Mutenherwa 'Safeguarding gains in the sexual and reproductive health and AIDS response amidst COVID-19: The role of African civil society' (2020) 100 International Journal of Infectious Diseases 286.

[24] Government Notice: Classification of a National Disaster in terms of the Disaster Management Act 57 of 2002 (15 March 2020) <www.gov.za/sites/default/files/gcis_document/202003/43096gon312.pdf> accessed on 2 June 2021.

on the alert level at which the country was placed.[25] The alert level was influenced predominantly by infection rates and the capacity of the healthcare system to carry those rates.

In March and April of 2020, during level 5 of lockdown, the only services available were those deemed to be 'essential services' for the purposes of the regulations made under the Disaster Management Act.[26] Medical and health services were deemed essential, and were therefore accessible during the lockdown period, with regulation 11B of 16 April 2020 permitting people to leave home when seeking 'emergency, life-saving or chronic medical attention'. The language of the regulations therefore created circumstances in which only necessary medical attention could be sought during the period of lockdown.

On 17 April 2020, following confusion and complaints received about the lack of access to services since the start of the lockdown, namely contraceptive and abortion services, a collective of public interest organisations wrote to the Minister of Health. They requested, among other things, an unequivocal statement clarifying that SRH services, given their nature, were essential services that were therefore accessible during the lockdown period; and that the DoH continued to be committed to making SRH services available and accessible, free from violence, discrimination, and stigma.[27] A follow-up letter was sent in May 2020, but the Minister and Department did not respond to the letters sent on this issue.

[25] South African Government 'About COVID-19: About alert system' <www.gov.za/covid-19/about/about-alert-system> accessed on 2 June 2021.

[26] As amended on 16 April 2020.

[27] Women's Legal Centre, Section 27 & Sexual and Reproductive Justice Coalition 'Protecting Safe Access to Sexual and Reproductive Health Services During Covid-19' (17 April 2020) <https://wlce.co.za/2020/06/18/protecting-safe-access-to-sexual-and-reproductive-health-services-during-covid-19-2/> accessed on 15 June 2021.

5.3 Exacerbating Limits to Access: Documented Barriers to Access During the COVID-19 Pandemic

As reported by Doctors Without Borders,[28] a population's SRH needs are often neglected in emergencies. The UNFPA, in a report on the impact of the COVID-19 pandemic on family planning and gender-based violence, estimated that globally, 47 million women in 114 middle- and low-income countries would not have access to contraception, resulting in 7 million unintended pregnancies.[29] The consequences of these pregnancies in an overburdened healthcare system, already experiencing limitations due to the COVID-19 pandemic, included: barriers to pregnancy-related care as a result of health and safety measures in place at facilities; redirecting pregnant persons into informal, unsafe environments to seek abortion care; and mental and physical distress caused by being compelled to continue an unwanted pregnancy.[30] These consequences have long-term, adverse, and fatal effects on the lives of pregnant persons, impacting their rights to bodily autonomy, and mental and physical health outcomes.

Some of the most pressing issues and challenges that arose in relation to SRH care during the COVID-19 pandemic were:

- 'Closure and cuts to sexual and reproductive health services;
- Movement restrictions, including travel bans, lockdowns, and curfews;
- Global supply chain disruptions; and

[28] Doctors Without Borders 'Women and girls face greater dangers during Covid-19 pandemic' (2 July 2020), <www.msf.org.za/news-and-resources/latest-news/women-and-girls-face-greater-dangers-during-covid-19-pandemic> accessed on 31 May 2021.

[29] UNFPA 'Interim Technical Note: Impact of the COVID-19 pandemic on family planning and ending gender-based violence, female genital mutilation and child marriage. Pandemic threatens achievement of the Transformative Results committed to by UNFPA' (27 April 2020) <www.unfpa.org/sites/default/files/resource-pdf/COVID-19_impact_brief_for_UNFPA_24_April_2020_1.pdf> accessed on 1 June 2021.

[30] Jaime Todd-Gher, Payal K. Shah 'Abortion in the context of COVID-19: A human rights imperative' (2020) 28(1) Sexual and Reproductive Health Matters 17.

- A lack of clear public health information and guidance.'[31]

As mentioned above, the beginning of South Africa's lockdown, and in particular the regulations that were promulgated for Alert Level 5,[32] severely limited the free movement of citizens to instances that were essential only. At first, this resulted in much confusion in communities, including among healthcare providers, about which services were considered essential.[33] Doctors Without Borders reported that abortion services in Rustenburg, in the North West Province were initially shut down due to the interpretation that they did not constitute essential health care. At other sites, patients seeking SRH services were turned away as clinics were attending to COVID-19 health concerns only.[34] This meant that access to abortion services, contraceptives, HIV prevention and treatment medication, STI-related interventions and the treatment of cancers of the reproductive system, were denied.

With shortages in contraceptives and abortion medication, and the confinement of persons to their homes, pregnancy rates were predicted to increase.[35] The global impact of the pandemic on the import and export of goods; the implementation of necessary physical distancing measures; and the closure of factories and borders, resulted in the production and movement of reproductive commodities being negatively affected. This, however, was not irregular as South Africa has been reported to routinely experience stock-outs of reproductive health commodities, particularly contraceptives, at public health facilities.

Nandagiri, Coast and Strong discuss how the pandemic exposed and exacerbated existing barriers to abortion service provision and the inequitable impact this had on different vulnerable groups.[36] Notably,

[31] Doctors without Borders (n 28).

[32] Regulations made under the National Disaster Act 57 of 2002, as amended.

[33] Doctors Without Borders (n 28).

[34] Thuthukile Mbatha 'The dreadful effects of lockdown on access to sexual and reproductive health services' Spotlight (31 July 2020), <www.spotlightnsp.co.za/2020/07/31/the-dreadful-effects-of-lockdown-on-access-to-sexual-and-reproductive-health-services/> accessed 2 June 2021.

[35] Rishita Nandagiri, Ernestina Coast and Joe Strong, 'COVID-19 and Abortion: Making structural violence visible' (2020) 46(1) International Perspectives on Sexual and Reproductive Health 83, 83.

[36] Nandagiri (n 35) 83.

pre-existing and entrenched inequities in service provision have equated to structural violence affecting pregnant persons across intersecting axes of identity. Analysing documented barriers through this interpretive framework exposes cumulative institutional violence; acts as a measure to interrogate 'everyday violence' across a trajectory; and helps document structural violence in national and transnational policies.[37] It is thus important to note that the stock-outs of reproductive commodities in South Africa have overwhelmingly affected low-income and indigent communities who rely on the public health system, which includes groups with intersecting vulnerabilities.

Due to measures requiring physical distancing and the limitation of the number of individuals in certain spaces, access to transport was also impacted by the pandemic, thereby creating additional barriers to access to medical services and commodities. With these measures in place, fewer people were able to make use of public transport, which affected people's ability to access services in a timely fashion. As abortion is time-sensitive, this had implications for pregnant persons' ability to seek out and obtain the service in a timely and legal manner. Once access to a facility was secured, limited consultations were being conducted to ensure the health and safety of staff and patients, which led to fewer appointments and longer waiting times. Thus, without an existing appointment, patients were not guaranteed assistance even when they were able to present at a healthcare facility.

Furthermore, the introduction of a curfew meant that the population's movement was predominantly confined to working hours. While many workplaces introduced work-from-home policies where possible, many essential frontline workers had no choice but to attend work daily. At the height of the lockdown, curfew times were extended, and many would not have had sufficient time or leeway to spend hours awaiting care at public health facilities. Additionally, many people were hesitant to move around 'freely' because of the police presence and monitoring of movement, as well as to limit their own exposure and possibility of infection. This was especially true of pregnant persons, who would forego antenatal care appointments to try and prevent infection.[38]

[37] Nandagiri (n 35) 84–85.

[38] Mbatha (n 35). Ronelle Burger et al. 'Examining the unintended health consequences of the COVID-19 pandemic in South Africa' Wave 1: National income dynamics

All the added measures resulting from the pandemic would have required a pregnant person to plan ahead to ensure access to abortion services. To do so would require access to reliable communication services; to understand which public health facilities offered abortion services and when; the option to take time off work, if required, to visit a health facility; access to transport and/or funds for transport; and if a pregnant person were to opt for abortion care in a private health facility, then access to funds for the service. While some of these barriers existed prior to the pandemic, they were only further exacerbated during the pandemic. Once again, these practical obstacles disproportionately affect pregnant individuals who are reliant on the public health system as a result of the financial inaccessibility of the private healthcare system. Sex workers; undocumented migrants; people living in rural communities; persons experiencing intimate partner violence; minors; persons with disabilities; and those who lack housing are all vulnerable groups who have had to navigate the additional and amplified challenges created by the pandemic. Poor service provision, job losses, services that are far and difficult to reach, and often unsympathetic and exclusionary environments are but some of these challenges.[39]

Compounding these challenges in South Africa were already devastatingly high sexual and gender-based violence (SGBV) statistics, which increased during lockdown.[40] Social distancing and limitations on movement resulted in women being confined to a home with their abusive partners, and felt or were unable to leave to seek assistance. Doctors Without Borders further reported that while an increase in sexual violence was reported, there was also a decrease in clinic visits in Rustenburg.[41] Increased screening at entrances to health facilities created an additional barrier to access, as many women would rather opt to forego assistance

study—Coronavirus rapid mobile survey (15 July 2020) 7 <https://cramsurvey.org/wp-content/uploads/2020/12/16.-Examining-the-unintended-consequences-of-the-COVID-19-pandemic-on-public-sector-health-facility-visits-The-first-150-days-2.pdf> accessed on 9 June 2021.

[39] Todd-Gher (n 30) 41.

[40] Amnesty International 'Southern Africa: Homes become dangerous place for women and girls during COVID-19 lockdown' (Amnesty International Publications, February 2021) <www.amnesty.org/en/latest/news/2021/02/southern-africa-homes-become-dangerous-place-for-women-and-girls-during-covid19-lockdown/> accessed on 2 June 2021.

[41] Doctors Without Borders (n 28).

than have to explain to a security guard that they have been raped or required abortion services.[42]

Restricting access to abortion services does not decrease the demand or occurrence thereof, but does result in an increase in unsafe abortions.[43] 50% of abortions in South Africa occur in the informal sector.[44] In a report submitted to the National Department of Health, Pattinson and Fawcus et al. assessed the usage of maternal and reproductive health services in South Africa during the period of 'hard lockdown', using 2019 statistics as the baseline against which to assess data collected in the first (January–March; period before lockdown measures were instituted), second (April–June) and third (July–September) quarters of 2020.[45] The report collected data on the usage and outcome of certain services in the public health sector from the District Health Information System. The reproductive health services were identified by visits for antenatal care, abortion services, contraception, and births.[46] The study found:[47]

- There was a marked decline in the use of abortion and contraceptive services between 2019 and 2020;
- Pregnant women presented later to clinics for antenatal care, but use of services remained steady between 2019 and 2020;
- There were more births in 2020, but there was a decline in numbers during the period of hard lockdown as compared with 2019;
- There was an increase in maternal deaths at the start of lockdown in comparison with the same period in 2019;
- Rural provinces saw increased pressure on public facilities due to women migrating from urban areas, which increased the burden on facilities and areas that were already under-resourced; and

[42] Doctors Without Borders (n 28).

[43] Todd-Gher (n 30).

[44] National Department of Health 'Presentation 2: SRHR Policy and guidelines dissemination' (November 2020) <www.afro.who.int/news/south-africa-national-department-health-who-and-partners-disseminated-new-sexual-and> accessed on 30 October 2021.

[45] R Pattinson, S Fawcus et al. 'The effect of the first wave of Covid-19 on use of maternal and reproductive health services and maternal deaths in South Africa' (2020) 30 O&G Forum 36.

[46] Ibid, 38.

[47] Pattinson et al. (n 45).

- Metropolitan areas were inundated with severe cases of COVID-19, diverting resources that would otherwise handle routine emergencies to the management of COVID-19.

The study concluded that the reduced usage of services in the public health sector could be attributed to reduced access to transport facilities; fear of contracting the virus at public health facilities and while accessing services; and reduced provision of services given the diversion of resources to managing the pandemic.[48]

Lastly, job losses, which disproportionately affected women,[49] had an important and damaging impact on many, resulting in limitations in access to sanitary and reproductive health products. While the impact of the virus was felt the world over, its effects have, and will continue to be, most damaging in countries whose SRH services, and public healthcare systems as a whole, have been historically under-resourced and often inaccessible to the population who it is best positioned to serve.

5.4 Increasing Access to Abortion Services: The Failure to Introduce Use of Telemedicine and Self-Managed Abortion Services

In understanding that pre-existing and exacerbated barriers in the provision of reproductive health services amount to structural violence against pregnant persons, the theoretical prism of reproductive justice is necessary to crafting approaches and measures to improve access to sexual and reproductive health services, and more specifically abortion services. Reproductive justice:

> implies an intersectional analysis that brings to the fore first, the intertwining of individual and social processes, and second, the complex interaction of the inequities that cohere around a range of axes of discrimination (such as race, class, sexual orientation, gender identity, ability,

[48] Pattinson et al. (n 45) 45.

[49] Daniela Casale, Debra Shepherd 'The gendered effects of the Covid-19 crisis and ongoing lockdown in South Africa: Evidence from NIDS-CRAM Waves 1–3' (2021) <https://cramsurvey.org/wp-content/uploads/2021/02/4.-Casale-D.-Shepherd-D.-2021-The-gendered-effects-of-the-Covid-19-crisis-and-ongoing-lockdown-in-South-Africa-Evidence-from-NIDS-CRAM-Waves-1-3.pdf> accessed on 3 June 2021.

> religion, location, language and age). In addition, histories of oppressions (e.g., the history of legislated and social racialised oppression in South Africa) are foregrounded. Actions, services and interventions that promote justice and equity, address historical oppressions and empower stigmatised and vulnerable people are sought.[50]

Macleod and Feltham-King argue that viewing reproductive health through a reproductive justice lens would be a starting point for public health to be better attuned to promoting health and social justice in a comprehensive and multi-faceted manner.[51] The authors go further to advocate for a reparative justice/care approach, which they argue is part of reproductive justice, and which is the need for social repair and support where inequities or injustices occur.[52] In adopting the reproductive justice approach to the injustices inflicted by barriers and challenges to abortion services, we argue that the introduction of telemedicine is a necessary remedy to tackle barriers and injustice, and effect change and positive health outcomes.

South Africa's Department of Health adopted the Telemedicine Programme in 1999, introducing the use of telemedicine in health services in three phases over a 5-year period.[53] Though the need to include telemedicine as a method of access was recognised, the implementation of the programme faced problems, including a 'shortage of healthcare workers in the State sector and their reluctance to take on any additional work. A second factor was the top-down approach and

[50] Macleod (n 13) 47; CI Macleod, T Feltham-King 'Young pregnant women and public health: Introducing a critical reparative justice/care approach using South African case studies' (2020) 30(3) Critical Public Health 319, 320.

[51] MacLeod, Feltham-King (n 50) 320.

[52] Ibid.

[53] A Le Roux 'Telemedicine: A South African legal perspective' (2008) 1 Tydskrif vir die Suid-Afrikaanse Reg. 99, 102; National Department of Health 'eHealth Strategy South Africa' (Department of Health, 2012) 15 <https://www.knowledgehub.org.za/system/files/elibdownloads/2019-07/South%2520Africa%2520eHealth%2520Strategy%25202012-2017.pdf> accessed 30 October 2021.

the lack of capacity and failure to manage change'.[54] The Department developed an updated eHealth strategy, of which telemedicine formed a part, to establish eHealth as an integral part of health care services. 'eHealth' refers to 'the use of information and communication technologies (ICTs) for health to, for example, treat patients, pursue research, educate students, track diseases and monitor public health'.[55] Telemedicine refers to the delivery of health care services at a distance using ICTs.[56] Part of the strategy was the development of a telemedicine strategy and policy for implementation, the purpose of which was to alleviate the low human resources and establish links between established health facilities and rural areas.[57]

Giving effect to its mandate to regulate health care provision in a manner that ensures services are provided by qualified and skilled practitioners to protect patients from potential abuse, and provide guidance for good practice to healthcare practitioners, the Health Professions Council of South Africa (HPCSA) produced the *General Ethical Guidelines for Good Practice in Telemedicine* in 2014. It stipulates that telemedicine is the practice of medicine using electronic communications ***between practitioners*** to enhance service provision.[58] Essentially, telemedicine is provided where a consulting practitioner conducts a physical examination and consultation with a patient, and then passes this information to a servicing healthcare practitioner who will advise and offer services to the patient. The 2014 Guidelines provide guidance around consent, confidentiality, the storage and handling of patient records, and the roles and responsibilities of practitioners. These Guidelines have not been formally amended or updated since their introduction.

[54] National Department of Health (n 53) 15 quoting M Mars and C Seebregts 'Country case study for eHealth: South Africa' (Rockefeller Foundation, 2008) <http://www.ehealth-connection.org/content/country-case-studies> accessed on 28 October 2021.

[55] Ibid, 7.

[56] BA Townsend, RE Scott, M Mars 'The development of ethical guidelines for telemedicine in South Africa' (2019) 12(1) South African Journal of Bioethics and Law 19; Health Professions Council of South Africa General ethical guidelines for good practice in telemedicine (Pretoria, 2014) <https://www.hpcsa.co.za/Uploads/Professional_Practice/Ethics_Booklet.pdf> accessed on 30 October 2021.

[57] Townsend, Scott and Mars (n 56) 5.

[58] Townsend, Scott and Mars (n 56) 5.

Townsend, Scott and Mars note that large aspects of the Guidelines were inappropriate given the advances in technology and medicine, and that they could not offer guidance to allied health professions, such as nurses, as these professions are beyond the purview of the HPCSA's mandate.[59] Even more, in 2020, the authors noted that the Guidelines have not progressed to stay up to date with global advancements in health, technology and guidance.[60]

During the first quarter of 2020, The HPCSA issued an amended advisory regarding the use of telemedicine during the COVID-19 pandemic. The advisory stated that medical practitioners could diagnose, treat and dispense medical advice and treatment remotely.[61] It was applicable during the pandemic only, and preferred, but did not require, that the patient and practitioner have a pre-existing relationship; and encouraged consultations that were in-person where a practitioner believed that a remote consultation would not be in the best interests of the patient.[62] The advisory was to be practised according to the provisions of the 2014 Guidelines, which favour physical examination and consultation, and written consent from the patient, which in the circumstances of the pandemic were impractical and oftentimes unsafe.[63]

The issuing of this advisory provided a unique opportunity for the HPCSA and the Department to ensure that SRH services were available both virtually and physically, which included access to abortion care. This would be necessary under the current implementation of the CTOPA, as the Act criminalises individuals who provide an abortion outside the requirements of the Act.[64] Since the advisory, there have been reports of

[59] Townsend, Scott and Mars (n 56) 19 & 21.

[60] BA Townsend, M Mars and RE Scott 'The HPCSA telemedicine guidance during COVID-19: A review' (2020) 13(2) South African Journal of Bioethics and Law 97, 98.

[61] Health Professions Council of South Africa 'Guidance on the application of telemedicine guidelines during the COVID-19 pandemic' (26 March 2020), as amended on 3 April 2020 in terms of Health Professions Council of South Africa 'The Health Professions Council of South Africa (HPCSA) response to COVID-19 pandemic' <https://www.hpcsa.co.za/Uploads/Events/Announcements/APPLICATION_OF_TELEMEDICINE_GUIDELINES.pdf> accessed on 25 October 2021.

[62] Ibid, 26 March 2020, para (d).

[63] Townsend, Mars and Scott (n 60) 99.

[64] Choice on Termination of Pregnancy Act, section 10 'Offences and penalties'. This section refers to a person who terminates a pregnancy at a facility not designated to

abortion service provision via telemedicine; however, these reports were from the private sector only.[65] There have been no documented cases from the public health sector.

In November 2020, the Department convened the 'Sexual Reproductive Health Rights Policy and Related Guidelines Dissemination' Workshop. During the workshop, the Department introduced a set of Guidelines that speak to the provision of SRH services, of which the *National Clinical Guidelines for Implementation of Choice on Termination of Pregnancy Act* formed part (the 2020 CTOPA Guidelines).[66] The process of developing these Guidelines started before the onset of the pandemic, however, the final stages of its development continued during the pandemic. The 2020 CTOPA Guidelines make no provision for abortion services via telemedicine, nor does it address the process of designating health facilities, which would increase the number of facilities available for physical access to abortion services. It does, however, state that obstruction to care based on conscience is permitted by direct service providers on condition that they refer patients to a facility where they can obtain access. Arguably, these failings of the 2020 CTOPA Guidelines would only serve to impact negatively on access to abortion services given the current context of an already limited landscape of service provision.

There have been clear measures and opportunities through which the Department could take clear and meaningful steps to strengthen SRH

provide abortion services; or a person who is not a registered medical practitioner, nurse or midwife with the prescribed training providing an abortion.

[65] Kathryn Church, Jennifer Gassner, Megan Elliott 'Reproductive health under COVID-19—Challenges of responding in a global crisis' 28(1) Sexual and Reproductive Health Matters 522, 523; Marie Stopes South Africa 'Safe abortion pills: How to access medical services in South Africa during the pandemic' (2020) <https://mariestopes.org.za/safe-abortion-pills-how-to-access-medical-services-during-the-covid19-pandemic/> accessed on 31 May 2021.

[66] National Department of Health 'National clinical guidelines for the implementation of the Choice on Termination of Pregnancy Act' (November 2020) available at <https://www.knowledgehub.org.za/system/files/elibdownloads/2021-03/Termination%20of%20Pregnancy%20Guideline_Final_2021.pdf> accessed on 2 June 2021. The foreword to these guidelines state that despite the enactment of the CTOPA, South Africa still suffers from 'barriers to high-quality legal services... these include poor general provider knowledge on termination of pregnancy, lack of training and mentorship, and the inadequate availability of relevant medicines and equipment.' The purpose of the Guidelines is therefore said to be the standardisation and expansion of service delivery in order to reaffirm 'all citizens' right to comprehensive reproductive health care...'.

services to ensure service provision for the large portion of the population which the public sector serves, and which population is made up of disparate and interrelated marginalised groups. For this reason, though certain measures were introduced by the issuing of the HPCSA's advisory, it is argued that the lack of reliance on the measures, particularly by the public sector, and their formulation only perpetuated inequalities in, and limited access to, SRH services, and further exacerbate the limited landscape of service provision.

The use of telemedicine to provide abortion services would incrementally increase access thereto by guarding against the overburdening of the public healthcare system, particularly during a pandemic, and ensure the safety of patients in line with the necessary national health and safety guidelines that require physical distancing and restrict movement.[67] The use of mifepristone and misoprostol to induce an abortion does not require specific training or specialisation to administer. The World Health Organization (WHO) supports the use of these drugs for abortion through the first 12 weeks of gestation, which have a 95% success rate when used together, and in circumstances where pregnant persons have access to healthcare providers and accurate information.[68] As such, the use of telemedicine would increase early access to abortion services, and decrease the number of pregnant persons needing to present physically at health facilities.

Pizarossa and Skuster have noted that self-managed abortions (SMA) have been successfully managed since the late 1980s, with pregnant persons safely managing their abortions according to their preferred environments and personal needs.[69] The authors define self-managed medical abortion as 'the process that involves the provision of drugs from pharmacies, drug sellers, or online outlets, without a prescription from a clinician, followed by a woman's self-management of the abortion

[67] 'Accessing safe abortion services amid the COVID-19 pandemic' Sexual and Reproductive Health Matters (23 September 2020) <http://www.srhm.org/news/accessing-safe-abortion-services-amid-the-covid-19-pandemic/#_ftn6> accessed on 1 June 2021.

[68] L Berro Pizzarossa, P Skuster, 'Toward Human Rights and evidence-based legal frameworks for (self-managed) abortion: A review of the last decade of legal reform' (2021) 23(1) Health and Human Rights Journal 199, 201; World Health Organisation 'Consolidated Guidelines on self-care interventions for health: Sexual and reproductive health and rights' (WHO, 2019) 67.

[69] Ibid.

process, including care-seeking for any complications'.[70] The introduction of SMA as a method of accessing abortion services de-medicalises abortion service provision, moving it out of the realm of clinical care.

This work has illustrated a preference for SMA as it fosters privacy, autonomy, confidentiality, and non-judgemental support, which cannot often be guaranteed in formal health settings, especially for persons from marginalised groups.[71] As aptly expressed by Assis and Larrea, and which is trite in the South African context:

> Indeed, the case of abortion shows that medicalisation functions as a barrier for an essential healthcare service, both in "normal" and exceptional times. The current moment is ripe for trusting people in their choices and openly embracing the power of self-management.[72]

Moreover, Marie Stopes South Africa, a member of the Marie Stopes International Global Partnership (an organisation providing access to comprehensive SRH services including abortion services) have shown that telemedicine, according to the WHO recommendations, can work in South Africa. The provision of abortion services in South Africa must be extended to include provision via telemedicine. This must be done clearly and with openly communicated guidelines to the public health sector, and the public in general, to increase access to safe abortion services and to remedy the structural barriers that have long plagued the provision of services, and which have been exacerbated by the pandemic.

5.5 The Necessity of Telemedicine and Self-Managed Abortion Services in South Africa

Currently in South Africa, the requirement under the CTOPA that facilities be designated by the Department of Health to be able to perform abortions limits the number of facilities available for pregnant persons to access safe and legal abortions, particularly in rural areas. Aggravating this

[70] Pizzarossa (n 68).

[71] MP Assis and S Larrea 'Why self-managed abortion is so much more than a provisional solution for times of pandemic' (2020) 28(1) Sexual and Reproductive Health Matters 37.

[72] Ibid.

limitation is the occurrence of healthcare providers who refuse to perform abortions on the grounds of conscience. It is an argument that raises conflicting rights of bodily autonomy on the one hand,[73] and freedom of conscience, thought, opinion, belief and religion on the other.[74] Medical practitioners invoke section 15 of the Constitution in order to object to performing abortion services on the basis on conscience.[75] The CTOPA, however, does not provide for the refusal of services on the basis of conscience, but instead criminalises the prevention of a lawful termination or obstruction of access to a facility.

As discussed above, in November 2020, the Department released the CTOPA Guidelines.[76] These 2020 Guidelines have formalised and allow for direct abortion providers to refuse care based on belief. According to the 2020 CTOPA Guidelines, these providers must refer individuals who are seeking abortion services to a colleague or facility that would be able to offer such services. This caveat around referral should, however, be seen in light of the findings of the 2017 Amnesty International report regarding the number of facilities that are, in practice, providing abortion services. As such, it is argued that medical professionals' now-sanctioned ability to refuse to provide abortion services is a barrier to access.

Understanding the role of the Department to produce legislation, policy, and norms and standards around health; and that the purview of the HPCSA is to provide ethical guidance around the provision of health services in South Africa, who is best placed to issue guidance and clarity on the use of telemedicine in the provision of abortion services? Below we discuss the potential avenues through which to provide clear and unequivocal guidance on the use of telemedicine in abortion services.

[73] Section 12 of the Constitution of the Republic of South Africa, 1996.

[74] Section 15 of the Constitution; Jane Harries, Diane Cooper, Anna Strebel et al. 'Conscientious objection and its impact on abortion service provision in South Africa: a qualitative study' (2014) 11 Reproductive Health 1.

[75] Harries, Cooper and Streber (n 74) 1; C Ngwena 'Conscientious objection and legal abortion in South Africa: delineating the parameters' (2003) 28 Journal for Juridical Science 1; Mary Favier, Jamie M.S Greenberg, Marion Stevens 'Safe abortion in South Africa: "We have wonderful laws but we don't have people to implement those laws"' (2018) 143 International Journal of Gynecology and Obstetrics 38.

[76] National Department of Health Guidelines (n 66).

The HPCSA is a statutory body that is established in terms of the Health Professions Act (the HPA).[77] The role of the HPCSA is to, *inter alia*, coordinate the professional boards established under the HPA; practice control over the training, education and registration required for health professions that fall within the ambit of the HPA; ensure that health professionals registered in terms of the HPA respect health users' constitutional rights; investigate complaints against health professionals; determine policy that is in line with national health policy;[78] and determine rules in respect of matters that the council 'considers necessary and expedient' to achieve the objects of the Act, and in line with national health policy by the Minister.[79] The HPCSA regulates 12 professional boards, including the board which registers medical practitioners, clinical associates and medical specialists.

The HPCSA does not regulate registered nurses and/or midwives. This is done by the South African Nursing Council, which was established in terms of the Nursing Act.[80] This is important to note because in terms of the CTOPA, in certain circumstances, abortions may be carried out by, or in consultation with, a registered nurse or midwife. This means that the advisory that was issued by the HPCSA did not apply to all healthcare professionals who are empowered by the CTOPA to perform abortions. Further, the advisory did not expressly mention how the provision of telemedicine and the current requirements for the provision of abortion services in terms of the CTOPA could be merged, given that section 3 of the CTOPA sets out places where a 'termination of pregnancy may take place'. The section stipulates that a termination may only take place at a facility that has met certain criteria.

Without further guidance from the Department having been provided, it is unclear whether the HPCSA unintentionally overlooked the provision of abortion services in the drafting of its advisory; or whether the Department's refusal to clarify the scope of the advisory was indicative

[77] Act 56 of 1974.

[78] According to section 3(c) of the Health Professions Act, this could concern '[...] matters such as finance, education, training, registration, ethics and professional conduct, disciplinary procedure, scope of the professions, interprofessional matters and maintenance of professional competence.'

[79] Sections 3 and 4 of the HPA set out all of the body's powers, objects and functions.

[80] Act 45 of 1944.

of its uncertainty as to whether the advisory did in fact apply to abortion services. It is however our contention that the HPCSA was not best placed to issue an advisory that applied to the provision of abortion services. Further, it is contended that the provision of telemedicine should be regulated by the Department in order to ensure that all practitioners who are able to provide abortion services in terms of the CTOPA do so, that it is done uniformly, and that the provisions of the CTOPA are not infringed in the process.

The provision of abortion services via telemedicine could be regulated by the publishing of regulations, or through the amendment of section 3 of the CTOPA to include telemedicine. While both of these paths could be seen as necessary, the latter approach is a lengthy process.

The publishing of regulations as a means to give effect to telemedicine would require that any such regulations interpret the meaning of the words 'may take place' and 'take place' in section 3 of the CTOPA so as to allow for abortion services to be carried out remotely. The effects of extending the interpretation of this section in regulations would mean that abortion via telemedicine could be available long after the COVID-19 pandemic, and that the provision of these services could finally begin to meet the objectives set out in terms of the Act. Abortion services could be moved out of clinical settings, thereby eliminating the barriers established when providers object to performing the service; pregnant persons could access these time-sensitive services quicker and earlier; pregnant persons would be provided the opportunity to regulate and determine the process of accessing these services in a way that they are most comfortable with; physical access would no longer limit pregnant person's ability to access these services; access to medication abortion would be improved; remote services would prove to be less of a drain on, particularly, the public healthcare system's human, physical and financial resources; and this particular provision of the CTOPA could finally be updated in line with the global advancement of both medicine and service provision within the area of abortion services. As posited by Church et al., implementing self-managed abortion and abortion via telemedicine 'allows for a cost effective, non-judgemental, and private experience which might be particularly beneficial for marginalized communities who have not always felt respected by the formal health system'.[81]

[81] Church et al. (n 65).

5.6 Conclusion

The COVID-19 pandemic presented an opportunity for self-managed abortions and abortion via telemedicine to be made key and sustained parts of abortion service provision in South Africa. These would be notable and necessary steps towards improving access to abortion services, especially in the public healthcare sector in South Africa. The introduction of both abortion services via telemedicine and robust self-managed abortion policy and practice could overcome serious impediments to access that predated the COVID-19 pandemic, whilst continuing efforts to improve the lives of marginalised and vulnerable groups.

While the CTOPA has gone a long way in legalising the provision of abortion in South Africa, in its current form the Act has not ensured the effective provision of these services, particularly for vulnerable and marginalised groups. The issuing of the CTOPA Guidelines by the Department of Health in November 2020 cemented the ongoing untenable tension between the legalised and necessary provision of abortion services on the one hand, and the objection by some medical practitioners to provide these services on the basis of conscience on the other. This effectively limits access for pregnant persons when attempting to access these services. While the advisory issued by the HPCSA may have been a starting point for the provision of SRH services, which includes abortion services via telemedicine, in the absence of clear guidelines and information provided by the Department, the public health sector continues, in practice, not to extend this access to abortion services.

It is therefore both prudent and necessary to ensure that the Act, as well as all regulations, guidelines, and advisories issued in terms of, or that have a direct bearing on, the Act, are in line with the stated purpose and objectives of the CTOPA. In order to ensure that in practice the Act continues to realise the State's '[…] responsibility to provide reproductive health to all, and…to provide safe conditions under which the right of choice can be exercised without fear or harm,'[82] it is proposed that it is necessary for the Department to promulgate regulations that will allow for the provision of abortion services via telemedicine, by interpreting section 3 of the Act so as to include the provision of abortion services beyond clinical settings.

[82] Preamble to the CTOPA.

Without the advancement of the provisions of the Act, or at least the way in which they are interpreted, access to abortion services in South Africa will continue to be hampered. The effects of this will always disproportionately and impermissibly impact on the lives of vulnerable and marginalised groups, and will continue to fly in the face of the stated objectives and purpose of the Act.

Bibliography

Primary Sources

Constitution of the Republic of South Africa, 1996.

Abortion and Sterilization Act of 1975.

Choice on Termination of Pregnancy Act 92 1996.

Disaster Management Act 57 of 2002.

Disaster Management Act, 2002: Regulations issued in terms of section 27(2) GN 318 of 18 March 2020.

Health Professions Act 56 of 1974.

Nursing Act 33 of 2005.

Secondary Sources

Aly J et al. 'Contraception access during the COVID-19 pandemic' (2020) 5(17) *Contraception and Reproductive Medicine* 1.

Amnesty International 'Southern Africa: Homes become dangerous place for women and girls during COVID-19 lockdown' (9 February 2021).

Amnesty International *Briefing: Barriers to safe and legal abortion in South Africa* (Amnesty International Publications, London, 2017).

Assis MP and Larrea S 'Why self-managed abortion is so much more than a provisional solution for times of pandemic' (2020) 28(1) SRHM 37–39.

Burger R et al. 'Examining the unintended health consequences of the COVID-19 pandemic in South Africa' *Wave 1: National income dynamics study—Coronavirus rapid mobile survey* (15 July 2020).

Casale D and Shepherd D 'The gendered effects of the Covid-19 crisis and ongoing lockdown in South Africa: Evidence from NIDS-CRAM Waves 1–3' (2021) <https://cramsurvey.org/wp-content/uploads/2021/02/4.-Casale-D.-Shepherd-D.-2021-The-gendered-effects-of-the-Covid-19-crisis-and-ongoing-lockdown-in-South-Africa-Evidence-from-NIDS-CRAM-Waves-1-3.pdf.

Church K, Gassner J, and Elliott M 'Reproductive health under COVID-19—challenges of responding in a global crisis' (2020) 28(1) *Sexual and Reproductive Health Matters* 522.

Cleary K, 'COVID-19: Pandemic puts pressure on medicine supply' *Spotlight* (June 2020) <https://www.spotlightnsp.co.za/2020/06/02/covid-19-pandemic-puts-pressure-on-medicine-supply/>.

Department of Statistics South Africa 'Public healthcare: How much per person?' (October 2017) <http://www.statssa.gov.za/?p=10548>.

Doctors Without Borders 'Women and girls face greater dangers during Covid-19 pandemic' (2 July 2020) <https://www.msf.org.za/news-and-resources/latest-news/women-and-girls-face-greater-dangers-during-covid-19-pandemic>.

Doctors without Borders 'South Africa: Providing safe abortion care during a national lockdown' (3 July 2020) <https://www.msf.org.za/news-and-resources/patient-and-staff-stories/south-africa-providing-safe-abortion-care-during>.

Eghtessadi E, Mukandavire Z, and Mutenherwa F 'Safeguarding gains in the sexual and reproductive health and AIDS response amidst COVID-19: The role of African civil society' (2020) 100 *International Journal of Infectious Diseases* 286.

Favier M, Greenberg JMS, and Stevens M 'Safe abortion in South Africa: "We have wonderful laws but we don't have people to implement those laws"' (2018) 143 *International Journal of Gynecology and Obstetrics* 38.

Freedman J, Crankshaw TL, and Mutambara VM 'Sexual and reproductive health of asylum seeking and refugee women in South Africa: understanding the determinants of vulnerability' (2020) 28(1) *Sexual and Reproductive Health Matters* 324.

Guttmacher Institute 'Investing in Sexual and Reproductive Health in Southern Africa' (2020) <https://www.guttmacher.org/fact-sheet/investing-sexual-and-reproductive-health-southern-africa>.

Harries J, Cooper D, Strebel A et al. 'Conscientious objection and its impact on abortion service provision in South Africa: A qualitative study' (2014) 11 *Reproductive Health* 1.

Health Professions Council of South Africa *Guidance on the application of telemedicine guidelines during the COVID-19 pandemic* (26 March 2020).

Health Professions Council of South Africa *The Health Professions Council of South Africa (HPCSA) response to COVID-19 pandemic* (3 April 2020).

Health Professions Council of South Africa 'General ethical guidelines for good practice in telemedicine' (Pretoria, 2014) Guidelines for Good Practice in the Health Professions Council.

Jeranji T 'COVID-19: Sex workers say they struggle to access contraception, abortion and other services' *Spotlight* (August 2020) <https://www.spotlightnsp.co.za/2020/08/03/covid-19-sex-workers-say-they-struggle-to-access-contraception-abortion-and-other-services/>.

Kaswa R, Yogeswaran P 'Abortion reforms in South Africa: An overview of the *Choice on Termination of Pregnancy Act*' (2020) 62(1) *South African Family Practice* a5240 <https://doi.org/10.4102/safp.v62i1.5240>.

Klausen SM, *Abortion under apartheid: Nationalism, sexuality and women's reproductive rights in South Africa* (Oxford University Press, 2015).

Le Roux A, 'Telemedicine: A South African legal perspective' (2008) 1 *TSAR* 99.

Lince-Deroche N et al 'Doing more for less: Identifying opportunities to expand public sector access to safe abortion in South Africa through budget impact analysis' (2018) 97 *Contraception* 167–176.

Lokot M, Avakyan Y, 'Intersectionality as a lens to the COVID-19 pandemic: Implications for sexual and reproductive health in development and humanitarian contexts' (2020) 28(1) *Sexual and Reproductive Health Matters* 40.

MacLeod CI, Feltham-King T, 'Young pregnant women and public health: Introducing a critical reparative justice/care approach using South African case studies' (2020) 30(3) *Critical Public Health* 319–329.

MacLeod CI, 'Expanding reproductive justice through a supportability reparative justice framework: the case of abortion in South Africa' (2019) 21(1) *Culture, Health and Sexuality* 46–62.

Mbatha T, Mafuma T 'COVID-19: What the lockdown means for sexual and reproductive health services' *Spotlight* (22 April 2020).

Mbatha T 'The dreadful effects of lockdown on access to sexual and reproductive health services' *Spotlight* (31 July 2020).

Marie Stopes South Africa *Safe abortion pills: How to access medical services in South Africa during the pandemic* (2020) <https://mariestopes.org.za/safe-abortion-pills-how-to-access-medical-services-during-the-covid19-pandemic/>.

Medical Brief 'Birth control stockouts remain a problem in SA' (6 March 2019) <https://www.medicalbrief.co.za/archives/birth-control-stockouts-remain-problem-sa/>.

Nabaneh S, Stevens M, and Pizzarossa LB 'Let's call "conscientious objection" by its name: Obstruction to care and abortion in South Africa' (OHRH, 24 October 2018) <https://ohrh.law.ox.ac.uk/lets-call-conscientious-objection-by-its-name-obstruction-of-access-to-care-and-abortion-in-south-africa/>.

Nandagiri R, Coast E, and Strong J 'COVID-19 and abortion: Making structural violence visible' (2020) 46(1) *International Perspectives on Sexual and Reproductive Health* 83.

National Department of Health *Presentation 2: SRHR Policy and guidelines dissemination* (November 2020).

National Department of Health *National clinical guidelines for the implementation of the Choice on Termination of Pregnancy Act* (November 2020)

<https://www.knowledgehub.org.za/system/files/elibdownloads/2021-03/Termination%20of%20Pregnancy%20Guideline_Final_2021.pdf>.

National Department of Health *eHealth Strategy South Africa* (Department of Health, 2012) <https://www.knowledgehub.org.za/system/files/elibdownloads/2019-07/South%2520eAfrica%2520eHealth%2520Strategy%25202012-2017.pdf>.

Ngwena C 'Conscientious objection and legal abortion in South Africa: Delineating the parameters' (2003) 28 *Journal for Juridical Science* 1.

Parliamentary Monitoring Group 'Police management of COVID-19 lockdown: SAPS briefing; with Minister and Deputy Minister Present' (April 2020) <https://pmg.org.za/page/PolicemanagementofCOVID19lockdownSAPS%20briefing>.

Pattinson R, Fawcus S et al 'The effect of the first wave of Covid-19 on use of maternal and reproductive health services and maternal deaths in South Africa' (2020) 30 *O&G Forum* 36–44.

Pillay N, Manderson L, and Mkhwanazi N 'Conflict and care in sexual and reproductive health services for young mothers in urban South Africa' (2019) 22(4) *Culture, Health and Sexuality* 459.

Pizzarossa LB and Skuster P 'Toward human rights and evidence-based legal frameworks for (self-managed) abortion: A review of the last decade of legal reform' (2021) 23(1) *HHR Journal* 199–212.

Pizzarossa LB and Nandagiri R 'Self-managed abortion: A constellation of actors, a cacophony of laws?' (2021) 29 *Sexual and Reproductive Health Matters* 1.

Provincial Departments of Health (Limpopo, Free State, KwaZulu Natal, Mpumalanga, North West, Northern Cape, and Western Cape) presentations to National Department of Health *Sexual Reproductive Health Rights Policy and Related Guidelines Dissemination Workshop* (9–13 November 2020).

Rural Health Advocacy Project 'Contraceptive Shortages across South Africa' (2018) <http://rhap.org.za/contraceptive-shortages-across-south-africa/>.

Sexual and Reproductive Health Matters *Accessing safe abortion services amid the COVID-19 pandemic* (23 September 2020) <http://www.srhm.org/news/accessing-safe-abortion-services-amid-the-covid-19-pandemic/#_ftn6>.

Sexual and Reproductive Justice Coalition 'Challenges for achieving sexual and reproductive justice in South Africa' <https://srjc.org.za/2019/05/06/challenges-for-achieving-sexual-and-reproductive-justice-in-south-africa/>.

South African Human Rights Commission, *Access to healthcare educational booklet* <https://www.sahrc.org.za/home/21/files/FINAL%20Access%20to%20Health%20Care%20Educational%20Booklet.pdf>.

South African Government 'About alert system' <https://www.gov.za/covid-19/about/about-alert-system>.

Stevens M 'Sexual and reproductive health and rights: Where is the progress since Beijing?' (2021) 35(2) *Agenda* 48–60.

Stevens, M 'Challenges for achieving sexual and reproductive justice in South Africa' (SRHM, 2 May 2019) <http://www.srhm.org/news/challenges-for-achieving-sexual-and-reproductive-justice-in-south-africa/>.

Todd-Gher J and Shah PK 'Abortion in the context of COVID-19: a human rights imperative' (2020) 28(1) *Sexual and Reproductive Health Matters.*

Townsend BA, Mars M, and Scott RE 'The HPCSA's telemedicine guidance during COVID-19: A review' (2020) 13(2) *South African Journal of Bioethics and Law* 97.

Townsend BA, Scott RE, and Mars M 'The development of ethical guidelines for telemedicine in South Africa' (2019) 12(1) *SAJBL* 19.

Trippe K 'Pandemic policing: South Africa's most vulnerable face a sharp increase in police-related brutality' *Atlantic Council* (24 June 2020) <https://www.atlanticcouncil.org/blogs/africasource/pandemic-policing-south-africas-most-vulnerable-face-a-sharp-increase-in-police-related-brutality/>.

UNFPA *Interim Technical Note: Impact of the COVID-19 pandemic on family planning and ending gender-based violence, female genital mutilation and child marriage. Pandemic threatens achievement of the Transformative Results committed to by UNFPA* (2020) <www.unfpa.org/resources/impact-covid-19-pandemicfamily-planning-and-ending-gender-based-violence-femalegenital>.

Women's Legal Centre, Legal Resources Centre and Sexual and Reproductive Justice Coalition *Submission to Parliament: National Health Insurance Bill* (November 2019).

Women's Legal Centre, Legal Resources Centre and Sexual and Reproductive Justice Coalition *Submission to Parliament: National Health Insurance Bill* (November 2019) <http://srjc.org.za/wp-content/uploads/2019/12/2019-11-29-Joint-Submission-NHI-Bill-WLC_LRC_SRJC.pdf>.

Women's Legal Centre, Section 27 & Sexual and Reproductive Justice Coalition Letter to Minister of Health (17 April 2020).

Women's Legal Centre, Section 27 & Sexual and Reproductive Justice Coalition *Follow up letter to Minister of Health* (9 June 2020).

World Health Organisation *Consolidated guideline on self-care interventions for health: Sexual and reproductive health and rights* (Geneva: World Health Organization, 2019).

Van Dyk J 'This popular birth control shot is out of stock for the second year running. Read why' *Mail and Guardian* (1 March 2019) https://mg.co.za/article/2019-03-01-00-birth-control-injection-south-africa-unplanned-pregnancy-tender-delay-bayer/.

CHAPTER 6

Reproductive Health Norms in West Africa: The COVID-19 Experience and a Path for the Future

Adetokunbo Alase and Anne Alase

6.1 Introduction

Women have been subjects of major disasters and emergencies at different times. These unpleasant happenings are mostly experienced during public health crises, civil wars, insurgencies, extractive operations, and climate change impacts. Responses to these dilemmas have always been minuscule and tend to take the form of advocacy, global norm-making, intergovernmental finance/programs, domestic policies, and civil interest participation. From a legal perspective, international law recognizes women's

A. Alase (✉)
Western Sydney University, Penrith, Australia
e-mail: adetokunbo.alase@gmail.com; 19239851@student.westernsydney.edu.au

A. Alase
NHS United Kingdom, London, UK
e-mail: Anne.alase@nhs.net

O. S. Adelakun and E. Ndoni (eds.), *Reproductive Health and Assisted Reproductive Technologies In Sub-Saharan Africa*,
Sustainable Development Goals Series,
https://doi.org/10.1007/978-981-99-2411-0_6

rights, equality of human rights, and eliminating all practices of prejudice against women.[1] Beyond these regimes are the more fascinating legal instruments on women's reproductive health and sustainability in times of gendered exposure. These instruments are the 2003 Maputo Protocol on the Right of Women in Africa[2] and the Sendai Framework for Disaster Risk Reduction.[3] These encapsulate women's autonomous rights to reproductive health, including childbirth and spacing for better participation in economic and political activities.

Despite global initiatives to alter the narrative, the lockdown measures occasioned by the COVID-19 pandemic disclosed the volatility of the gains achieved in the quest to empower women and now threaten the previously recorded achievements. Fundamental threats are more noticeable in emergencies and disasters as they affect women's reproductive health. According to commentators, times like this further expose women to cultural and harmful practices, especially sexual and reproductive health (SRH).[4] It is the assumption that women take on many responsibilities at these times, including childcare, schooling plans, and care jobs, often on a part-time basis. In addition, these uncertain periods expose women to domestic violence, increased sex, unwanted pregnancies, and in some cases, mental health crises. Admittedly, with recorded limited access to health care during the pandemic, the COVID-19 pandemic could among a series of impacts affect the fertility process and cause a baby boom as the "sit down at home" measures led to low productivity and higher financial struggles: leading to an increase in sexual exploitation. For instance, the distribution of goods through the supply chains especially agriculture

[1] Convention on the Elimination of All Forms of Discrimination against Women (adopted 18 December 1979, entered into force 3 September 1981) 1249 UNTS 13 (CEDAW). update footnotes with appropriate punctuation.

[2] Protocol to the African Charter on Human and Peoples' Rights on the Rights of Women in Africa (adopted 01 July 2003, entered into force 25 November 2005).

[3] United Nations, 'Sendai Framework for Disaster Risk Reduction 2015–2030' (United Nations 2015) A/RES/69/283. <http://www.un.org/ga/search/view_doc.asp?symbol=/RES/69> accessed 17 October 2021.

[4] Yeonsoo Lee et al., 'Women's Health in Times of Emergency: We Must Take Action' (2021) 30 Journal of Women's Health.

was disrupted leading to a loss of income.[5] Even though works of literature have identified these vast concerns of women during emergencies.[6] Still, there are gaps in the preparedness of West African nations to SRH issues in times of crisis. From a legal perspective, it is expedient that the formal system of governance suspends its toga to accommodate evolving concerns in times of emergencies as was seen during the COVID-19 lockdown. Hence, a look at a more informal adaptive regime with a more collaborative structure.

West Africa has gone through two major public health outbreaks with major impact on human existence in the last decade in particular the COVID-19 pandemic and Ebola outbreak in 2015. The response from sub-regional governments has permeated different socio, economic, and legal means or interactions of one to the other. It thus shows and reflects the boundaries of law to human survival and co-existence. For example, the Ebola outbreak led to collaborations from different stakeholders to wipe out the scourge; however, it seemed that those avenues did not outlive the pandemic,[7] hence, jeopardizing smooth and quick response in case of future public health occurrences. The COVID-19 pandemic has again confirmed that human beings and, rightly so, women need avenues to consult when in emergencies. For example, in most West Africa, women have low-income levels, and less job security and thus easily affected by emergencies that threaten the family. This is partly due to the patriarchal culture in most West African countries where women are expected to sacrifice their jobs for the family when emergencies arise and demand children stay at home.

[5] 'Policy Brief: The Impact of Covid-19 on Women' <https://www.un.org/sexualviolenceinconflict/wp-content/uploads/2020/06/report/policy-brief-the-impact-of-covid-19-on-women/policy-brief-the-impact-of-covid-19-on-women-en-1.pdf> accessed 10 November 2021.

[6] World Health Organization, 'Sexual Reproductive Health and Rights in Emergencies' <https://www.who.int/health-cluster/about/work/other-collaborations/sexual-reproductive-health-rights/en/> accessed 11 September 2021; Yeonsoo Lee et al. (n 4).

[7] Akin Abayomi et al., 'From Ebola to Covid-19: Emergency Preparedness and Response Plans and Actions in Lagos, Nigeria' (2021) 17 Globalization and Health 1, 2–6; Alexandre Delamou et al., 'Public Health Impact of the 2014–2015 Ebola Outbreak in West Africa: Seizing Opportunities for the Future' (2016) 2 BMJ Global Health <https://gh.bmj.com/content/2/2/e000202> accessed 8 October 2021.

At the outbreak of the COVID-19 pandemic in early 2020, national governments across the globe started making laws to stem the spread of the virus through government pronouncement of lockdown measures. These restrictions included closing border ports, worship centres, work environments, schools, and market squares for weeks and months. For instance, the response from the Nigerian government was an instant executive order leading to the lockdown of the three most populated states in the country.[8] An exercise implemented under the extant Nigerian Quarantine Act of 1926,[9] which gives the President of the Federal Republic competence to make such restrictive regulations if needed.[10] In a similar manner, regional states replicated such measures. In all of the COVID-19 safety measures at different levels of governance, there seemed to be minimal protection for a large spectrum of informal sectors. These vulnerable groups, as we know are prone to negative consequences of lockdown measures. These phases of closures, now starting to ease were the case worldwide in all its shades—partial, hard, soft, or total lockdown depending on the data on confirmed cases.[11] Restrictive measures to some meant significant breaches to fundamental human rights in some quarters; yet, nations allege exceptions under public health safety to achieve compliance and contain the spread of the virus.[12] This scenario is particularly true "...at the societal level including economic contraction and recession, disruption of supply systems, aggravation of social tensions and the potential for the lockdown to lead to the long-term erosion of human rights and civil liberties".[13] This introduction sets the scene for this paper. The next section discusses the concepts of reproductive rights framework in Africa. The following section analyses the sexual and reproductive health (SRH) during the lockdown, and next is SRH within selected West

[8] Fidelis Mbah, 'Nigeria Announces Lockdown of Major Cities to Curb Coronavirus' (30 March 2020) <https://www.aljazeera.com/economy/2020/3/30/nigeria-announces-lockdown-of-major-cities-to-curb-coronavirus> accessed 24 May 2022.

[9] Nigeria Quarantine Act 1926 (Cap Q2 LFN 2004).

[10] COVID-19 Regulations 2020 pursuant to the provision of The Quarantine Act of the Federal Republic of Nigeria COVID-19 REGULATIONS 2020 (nipc.gov).

[11] Najmul Haider et al., 'Lockdown Measures in Response to COVID-19 in Nine Sub-Saharan African Countries' 5 BMJ Global Health.

[12] Kelli Hall et al., 'Centring Sexual and Reproductive Health and Justice in the Global COVID-19 Response' (2020) 395 Lancet Global Health 1175, 1176.

[13] Najmul Haider et al. (n 11) 3.

African countries post-COVID-19 recovery plans. The subsequent section demonstrates emerging ideas through adaptive governance to SHR, and finally, the conclusion.

6.2 Legal Contexts of Reproductive Rights

Reproductive health has been defined as "a state of complete physical, mental and social wellbeing, not merely the absence of disease or infirmity, in all matters relating to the reproductive system and to its functions and processes.... therefore, implies that people are able to have a satisfying and safe sex life and that they have the capacity to reproduce and the freedom to decide if, when and how often to do so".[14] Women have enjoyed legal recognition at every level of governance. As earlier mentioned, the human rights provisions premised other key regulations to protect this vulnerable group. For example, the Convention on the Elimination of All Forms of Discrimination against Women (CEDAW)[15] demonstrates the importance of culture and value systems in the promotion of women's and girls' rights. Within the context of SRH, the CEDAW highlights the increasing gap in knowledge on family planning[16] and child spacing.[17] CEDAW maintains that there must be increasing energy to family planning education facilitated by state and non-state actors. Regardless of the harmful practices that may characterize a given culture, protecting women's health and safety in working conditions, including the safeguarding of reproduction's function, is germane.[18] All of these services to reproductive health, according to CEDAW, should be free, accessible, and meet emergency needs.[19]

[14] United Nations, 'Reproductive Rights Are Human Rights: A Handbook for National Human Rights Institution' 18 <https://www.ohchr.org/documents/publications/nhrihandbook.pdf> accessed 5 October 2021.

[15] UN General Assembly, Convention on the Elimination of All Forms of Discrimination Against Women (Adopted 18 December 1979, entered into force 3 September 1981) 1249 UNTS 13 (CEDAW).

[16] Article 10 (h) CEDAW.

[17] Article 16 (2).

[18] Article 11 (f).

[19] Ibid. Art 11, 12, and 14.

The Maputo Protocol,[20] among other things, makes provision for a detailed SRH norm for the African States to follow. It provides that

> ...sexual and reproductive health of women shall be "respected and promoted," including

> (a) the right to control their fertility;
> (b) the right to decide whether to have children, the number ... and spacing of children;
> (c) the right to choose any method of contraception;
> (d) the right to self-protection and to be protected against sexually transmitted infections, including HIV/AIDS;
> (e) the right to be informed on one's health status, particularly if affected with sexually transmitted infections, including HIV/AIDS, in accordance with internationally recognized standards and best practices;
> (f) the right to have family planning education.[21]

This all-encompassing provision totally agrees that women have the right, decision-making obligations, and absolute control of their imbued reproductive workings. Thus, they are in a better position to decide the timing for sex, contraception, and child spacing. The United Nations highlights the main component of reproductive health to include

> Ensuring contraceptive choice and safety and infertility services; improving maternal and new born health; reducing sexually transmitted infections, including HIV, and other reproductive morbidities; eliminating unsafe abortion and providing post-abortion care; and promoting healthy sexuality, including adolescent health, and reducing harmful practices.[22]

[20] Protocol to the African Charter on Human and Peoples' Rights on the Rights of Women in Africa (adopted 01 July 2003, entered into force 25 November 2005).

[21] Ibid., Article 14 (1).

[22] United Nations (n 14) 24.

In essence, an effective system of SRH must be accessible to the people it seeks to protect. Such access must be of a high standard, not discriminatory, affordable, and accessible in all ramifications that are physically, financially, and information-wise.

Reproductive rights could mean the "rest on the recognition of the basic rights of all couples and individuals to decide freely and responsibly the number, spacing, and timing of their children and to have the information and means to do so, and the right to attain the highest standard of sexual and reproductive health".[23] With this in mind, the next session will demonstrate how the recent global lockdown from the pandemic affects impacted the reproductive rights of women and girls.

6.3 Sexual and Reproductive Health During COVID-19 in West Africa

Over 200 million people need reproductive health in Africa.[24] This situation was further compounded by the COVID-19 pandemic which places tension on accessing this critical health compartment.[25] Vulnerable groups, including women, encountered difficulties during the pandemic. Most of the issues were more into the lockdown measures from different nations to curtail the spread of the virus. Impact experienced from all over the world ranges from shortages of contraception, reduced access to family planning methods, increased rate of abortions, miscarriages, trauma, and others.[26] SRH issues do not make it to the agenda in strategic emergency stakeholder or task force meetings for deliberation. Such social concern can be perceived as secondary and carry less weight than other "seemingly" political and economic within the polity.[27]

The word "lockdown" can be termed "as a set of measures aimed at reducing transmission of COVID-19 that are mandatory, applied indiscriminately to a general population, and involve some restrictions on the

[23] Ibid., 19.

[24] Leopold Ouedraogo et al., 'Continuity of Essential Sexual and Reproductive Health Services during Covid-19 Pandemic in the WHO African Region' <https://www.afro.who.int/sites/default/files/2021-04/CONTINUITY%20OF%20ESSENTIAL%20SRHR%20SERVICES%20LEOrevised2.pdf> accessed 23 September 2021.

[25] Ibid., 1.

[26] Kelli Hall et al. (n 12) 1175–6.

[27] Ibid., 1175.

established pattern of social and economic life".[28] Najmul Haider et al. further enumerate the types of lockdowns employed during the pandemic by different nations. One that was profound was the border lockdown to restrict movement from place to place to mitigate the spread of the virus. Most, if not all countries, closed all non-essential services. For about a month, initial measures from certain nations targeted a few states with the largest population before extending to other regional states.

The impact of these measures is mostly seen in contraceptive services.[29] It was the case that self-care saw tremendous support in family planning as most women were not ready for babies. However, the early period of the pandemic saw a decrease in the supply of contraceptives.[30] In African states, there was no change recorded in abortion care as some countries forbid such practice, Nigeria for instance.[31]

According to Leopold et al., the critical challenges to family planning and SRH during the pandemic were excruciating for women and their mental health. Enforcement of the lockdown measures means they could not go out, access a variety of SRH commodities, and lack infrastructure to access support from civil societies.[32] The study, however, demonstrates the urgent need for information dissemination, collaboration, support, capacity building, and advocacy geared towards mitigating huge impacts on SRH during emergencies, such as the COVID-19 pandemic. For all of the latter to happen, policy initiatives must involve the "engagement of various stakeholders in the provision of services as well as possible alternatives to the health service systems in place". Outside of telemedicine, an informal support group could actively engage in the timely provision of SRH needs to women, especially in rural communities, to boost communal resilience. Lockdown measures caused many disruptions, such as limited supplies, besides initial challenges experienced by this sector before the pandemic. Commentators found that women struggled in

[28] Najmul Haider et al. (n 11) 2.

[29] Shannon Wood et al., 'Need for and Use of Contraception by Women before and During COVID-19 in Four Sud-Saharan African Geographies: Results from Population-Based National or Regional Cohort Surveys' (2021) Lancet Global Health 793, 793–4.

[30] Leopold Ouedraogo et al. (n 24).

[31] Ibid., 6.

[32] Ibid., 7.

getting the required help during this time despite the increased telehealth platform; it failed to correspond with existing infrastructure.[33] From the United States', (USA) lockdown experience, Malia Maier et al. find that policy must rise to meet these challenges and cover the wide gaps noticed during the COVID-19 pandemic for the next generation. The stay-at-home measures saw limited access to healthcare facilities and those in emergencies or related to the rave of the moment "COVID-19". Therefore, other related issues like the SRH were pushed to the back as though not important for over a year. Like situations in developing nations, commentators bemoan the policy response in a developed country like the US, where challenges related to SRH, including abortion, contraceptive were disregarded like a pinch of salt. At such times in the future, policy initiatives must show preparedness and support to SRH as a priority sector that is occupied as well as "unambiguous".[34]

Additionally, as may be the case with other developed economies, the COVID-19 lockdown measures by state actors came with myriads of negative impact on the enjoyment of civil rights, especially in Africa. For instance, the suspension and modification of the human rights of the citizens, in particular, to SRH. It was a challenging period for women at different stages of growth, all in a bid to curtail the spread of the virus. These lockdown measures led to the partial or total shutdown of health clinics, and some that opened could not cater to the people's needs. This was particularly true of "maternity services, where some poor women chose to give birth at home without skilled birth attendants. Others lost their lives in hospitals due to negligence and lack of treatment by healthcare workers....".[35] Even where some health facilities opened for business, they were "dead" and scared of contracting the virus, leading to a shortfall of healthcare officers.[36]

Experience from Africa further confirms that lockdown measures, no matter how structured, impact women's health. To a certain extent, in

[33] Malia Maier et al., '"Scrambling to Figure out What to Do": A Mixed Method Analysis of Covid-19's Impact on Sexual and Reproductive Health and Rights in the United States' (2021) BMJ Sex Reproductive Health 1, 4.

[34] Ibid., 7.

[35] Nkemdilim Anazonwu et al., 'State Actors, Human Rights Violations and Informal Livelihoods during the COVID-19 Pandemic in Nigeria' (2021) Territory, Politics, Governance 1, 8–9.

[36] Nkemdilim Anazonwu et al. (n 35).

most African countries, applicable to the lockdown measures, are time curfew, which implies that you cannot be seen in the public space around certain times at night until dawn. For example, Ghana's partial lockdown in response to the pandemic began on 30 March 2020.[37] Owing to the nature of the restriction that affected the movement, it was pertinent that citizens, including women and girls, stay indoors to avoid public sanctions, such as fines and imprisonment. Given these circumstances, Nasreen Solomon and Harsha Gihwala allude to the astronomical rise in cases of informal abortion as women resort to unsafe clinics, and maternity centres to have an abortion.[38] This situation was compounded when abortion results in death. Thus, informed decisions on keeping unwanted pregnancies that might lead to an increased population in the short term.[39] Historically, sub-Saharan Africa has been beleaguered with many disasters, emergencies, pandemics, and other political issues.[40] As earlier stated that, notable among which was the Ebola outbreak in 2014–2015, which saw nations frightened before interventions were agreed upon and reached. This period affected the right of women, more particularly in the area of SRH. Although it was not as pronounced as the COVID-19 pandemic, it moved the critical strata of the economy, and affected international travel, movement, and public gatherings. This was a lesson for the century for Africa in which writers believed that Africa and, more closely, West Africa would have been prepared and ready to respond to future outbreaks. Some commentators highlight that "Only a strong focus on empowerment and capacity building at the community level, including targeted health education initiatives, will ensure community-level cooperation and result in sustained behavioural changes and community resilience".[41] The extent of applicability of the resilience framework is yet to be seen on

[37] The promulgation of Coronavirus Disease (COVID-19) Pandemic (No. 2) Instrument, 2020 (Executive Instrument 65 of 2020), Centre for Human Rights: University of Pretoria, 'Ghana' (*A Nature and Description of Emergency Covid-19 Measures*) <https://www.chr.up.ac.za/covid19-database/ghana> accessed 20 October 2021.

[38] Nasreen Solomons & Harsha Gihwala, 'The Right to Sexual and Reproductive Health: Challenges and Possibilities During Covid-19' <https://www.ohchr.org/Documents/Issues/Health/sexual-reproductive-health-covid/CSOs/ngo.ghjru.pdf> accessed 12 October 2021.

[39] Ibid., 8.

[40] Najmul Haider et al. (n 11).

[41] Leopold Ouedraogo et al. (n 24).

SRH concerns during emergencies. Countries in general and West Africa Nation States, in particular, are somewhat overwhelmed by the astronomical rate of casualties at such uncertain times, forgetting preparedness in times of comfort.[42]

From a political point of view, the pandemic swayed global attention primarily to COVID-19, away from the safety of people. There was a lack of political will for law-making, a low attention span for legal matters even in our courts, as well as clinic closure.[43] Endler et al. demonstrate that the pandemic saw healthcare professionals shaken by COVID-19, unlike other emergencies even when they seem most critical.[44] This distinction could then mean that healthcare workers fear contracting the disease from unnecessary exposure to the disease on the one hand and the fear of being sanctioned for breaking lockdown measures, including curfew on the other hand. The writers allude that the outright situational shift to COVID-19 reflects the lack of interest of different governments in Sexual and Reproductive Health Rights to the typical person and another gender agenda.[45] However, policy initiatives around telemedicine continue to be relevant to SRH and remarkably accurate at the hit of the pandemic, and recommend that States continue to direct policy and legislative debate for the future. However, for such initiative to be effective, there must be local community inclusion, and not limited to a top-to-bottom "justice and formal policy agenda" which resides at the heart of the COVID-19 response.[46] In the same way, attaining justice and human rights in emergencies means eliminating all forms of restrictive policies towards SHR concerns and other women-limiting devices, such as the "gagging clauses" that render women voiceless at such priceless times.[47]

[42] United Nations (n 3); Barbara Cosens et al., 'Designing Law to Enable Adaptive Governance of Modern Wicked Problems' (2020) 73 Vanderbilt Law Review 1687.

[43] Margit Endler et al., 'How the Coronavirus Disease 2019 Pandemic Is Impacting Sexual and Reproductive Health and Rights and Response: Results from a Global Survey of Providers, Researchers, and Policy-Makers' (2021) 100 Acta Obstet Gynecol Scand. 571.

[44] Ibid.

[45] Ibid.

[46] Kelli Hall et al. (n 12) 1177.

[47] Leopold Ouedraogo et al. (n 24) 1177.

6.4 Sexual and Reproductive Health in Post-COVID-19 Economic Recovery Plans

The outbreak of the COVID-19 pandemic saw a paradigm shift in political structure, awareness and outlook, and budgets, thus necessitating new knowledge in line with the new realities created by the pandemic. Hence, nations came up with policy documents with diverse nomenclature towards charting a new course of action for the country post-COVID-19. The pandemic hits hard on sub-Saharan women in every facet of womanhood and the SRH in particular.[48] For example, World Health Organization (WHO) case assessment shows that more than 30% of women in West Africa suffered a form of disruption or the other in relation to SRH in the second phase of the pandemic.[49] This section will now examine two case documents from West African states and their implications for SRH. SRH, according to available data experienced a downward turn following the outbreak of COVID-19 at least when read together with the noticeable asymmetry in the socio-economic condition of the people.[50] In addition, the choice of West Africa aligns with the convention of this Series as well as gives a significant sample representation considering the sub-region's population size, and cultural practices.[51] For this chapter, Nigeria and Ghana comes to mind judging

[48] Luisa Flor et al., 'Quantifying the Effects of the COVID-19 Pandemic on Gender Equality on Health, Social, and Economic Indicators: A Comprehensive Review of Data from March, 2020, to September, 2021' Lancet Global Health.

[49] World Health Organization, 'Second Round of the National Pulse Survey on Continuity of Essential Health Services During the COVID-19 Pandemic' (WHO 2021) WHO/2019-nCoV/EHS_continuity/survey/2021.1 <https://www.who.int/publications/i/item/WHO-2019-nCoV-EHS-continuity-survey-2021.1> accessed 15 November 2021; Fatouma Laouan, 'Rapid Gender Analysis—COVID-19 (West Africa—April 2020)' <https://www.care-international.org/files/files/CARE_West_Africa_Rapid_Gender_Analysis_COVID-19_May_2020_final_EN.pdf> accessed 22 November 2021.

[50] Venkatraman Chandra-Mouli et al., 'Adolescent Sexual and Reproductive Health for All in Sub-Saharan: A Spotlight on Inequalities' (2021) 18 Reproductive Health 1.

[51] Department of Sexual and Reproductive Health and Research, 'Ghana Contraceptive Within the Context of Adolescents' Sexual and Reproductive Lives: Country Profile' (World Health Organization 2020) WHO/SRH/20.17 <https://apps.who.int/iris/bitstream/handle/10665/339394/WHO-SRH-20.17-eng.pdf> accessed 1 February 2022; International Federation of Women Lawyers (FIDA) Nigeria, 'The Urgent Need to Address the Gendered Impact of COVID-19 on Violence Against Women and Girls in West African Commonwealth Countries' <https://fida.org.ng/wp-content/uploads/2021/08/FIDA-Nigeria-Policy-Brief.pdf> accessed 2 April 2022.

from the recorded cases of COVID-19 (as the most hit nations in West Africa after Algeria).[52] That said, these West African States give the best possible outlook to the context of SRH, COVID-19 lockdown and post pandemic based on accessible documents garnered through the authors desk research.

Ghana, a significant country in West Africa with appreciable number of women populations,[53] did also experience some setback to this group during the lockdown. The UN Policy Brief on COVID-19 highlights the spike in domestic violence and other health crises among women with most of these numbers exempted from medical insurance.[54] In addition, women had more work to do, "With an increased exposure to violence and household income shocks due to the pandemic, social and economic pressure may lead to a rising incidence of child marriage and adolescent pregnancy as a result of sexual exploitation and sexual violence".[55] The UNICEF report highlights varying concerns of women during the pandemic to include nutrition, work-life balance, and reproduction, among others. At the time, the policy options seemed not to be working or instead inundated with pressing issues of COVID-19, although expected but not well managed.[56] The report recommends the importance of emergency preparedness and meaningful collaborations with other sectors to ease these tensions in the future.

Given this background, the UN's Ghana post-COVID-19 recovery plans demonstrate support for women and other ancillary matters like reproductive health.[57] The document notes that women are essential to

[52] Statista, 'Coronavirus Cases in Africa as of March 02, 2022, by Country' (4 March 2022) <https://www.statista.com/statistics/1170463/coronavirus-cases-in-africa/> accessed 30 March 2022.

[53] World Bank, 'Population, Female- Sub-Saharan Africa' <https://data.worldbank.org/indicator/SP.POP.TOTL.FE.IN?locations=ZG> accessed 15 October 2021.

[54] 'Policy Brief: The Impact of Covid-19 on Women' (n 5).

[55] UNICEF, 'Primary and Secondary Impacts of the COVID-19 Pandemic on Children in Ghana' <https://www.unicef.org/ghana/media/3486/file/Effects%20of%20COVID-19%20on%20Women%20and%20Children%20in%20Ghana%20(II).pdf> accessed 1 November 2021.

[56] Ibid.

[57] 'United Nations Development System in Ghana: Building Back Better From COVID-19, Common Country Analysis (CCA) and Socio-Economic Response and Recovery Plan (SERRP)' <https://ghana.un.org/sites/default/files/2020-11/United%20Nations%20Ghana%20SERRP_%20Final.pdf> accessed 3 October 2021.

Ghana in her recovery plans; the policy outlines five fundamental pillars: priority in health, protection for people, economic plus macroeconomic response and recovery, multidimensional collaboration, social interaction and community resilience.[58] The idea behind this recovery plan heavily relies on people, especially the restoration of women. The 72-page document highlights the universality of healthcare restrictions, particularly for women folks who could not access those facilities during the pandemic. Regarding SRH, the period saw an increase in sexually transmitted diseases, abortion, and unwanted pregnancies, particularly among adolescent girls.[59] All of these show that the necessary and diligent forecast on available data to better prepare going forward. It acknowledges the use of telemedicine, technologies, research, "innovative resource-efficiency techniques and deflect pressure from the health system to benefit people". Some of these innovations include scaling up the supply chain for SRH products and mainstreaming preparedness schemes in emergencies for the future. Ghana's recovery plans post-COVID-19 has shown zest for gender and women issues, an example other nation can pursue with a broad focus. However, it may be too early to discuss the effectiveness of the use of the process.

In contrast is Nigeria's post-COVID-19 framework document that incidentally revolves around economic recovery. According to the World Bank, Nigeria is the largest economy in West Africa.[60] Like every other nation, Nigeria was dramatically impacted by the COVID-19 pandemic. The COVID-19 lockdown measures rolled out by the Nigerian Government just like the rest of the world, disrupted economic activities and better amplified SRH concerns for women and girls. In the heat of the pandemic, Nigeria came up with the post-COVID-19 recovery document to cater for the aftermath of the crisis, compounded with earlier recession and other social disruptions.[61] The paper highlighted fundamental areas that the Government must concentrate on and direct its finances in the short term. From the gender and reproductive context,

[58] Ibid.

[59] UNICEF (n 55).

[60] World Bank, 'Africa Overview' <https://www.worldbank.org/en/region/afr/overview> accessed 1 November 2021.

[61] Federal Government of Nigeria, 'Bouncing Back: Nigeria Economic Sustainability Plan' (2020) <https://media.premiumtimesng.com/wp-content/files/2020/06/ESC-Plan-compressed-1.pdf> accessed 1 January 2021.

the Government overlooks reproductive and mental health relevance for women. An essential reference on women states that the Government will support the "Provision of start-up capital and entrepreneurship skills for young Nigerian people and women".[62] Arguably, Nigeria emphasizes socio-economic issues as outlined in the document; however, support may not have been on the top for women issues during emergencies like the pandemic present. While it is commendable that the various African States currently divert attention to foreign direct investment, debt relief, COVID-19 vaccine rollout, it may be ideal to consider other global issues of women during emergencies. Promotion and policy integration of reproductive problems must be undoubtedly seen in action to realize sustainable growth post-pandemic.

Nigeria may have shown a lack of zest and attention to these issues via policy documents. Still, more is required from other non-state actors as a coping strategy and not displace these magnificent gender issues. This section highlights that the Nigerian governments post-COVID-19 document highly concentrates on an economic recovery outlook that focuses on "deepening reforms that create jobs, encourage investment, and enhance competitiveness".[63] It is bizarre that African countries have forgotten the ripple effect of women's emancipation that constitutes most of their governance matters. Remarkably, the Sendai framework encapsulates the workings of national governance structures to accommodate and invest in women's issues for far-reaching economic growth.[64] According to the Sendai framework, women can enjoy these ripple benefits in times of crises subject to the willingness of the national Government to domestic this adaptive legal norm

> *To strengthen the design and implementation of inclusive policies and social safety-net mechanisms, including through community involvement, integrated with livelihood enhancement programmes, and access to basic*

[62] Ibid., 45.

[63] Federal Government of Nigeria (n 61).

[64] United Nations (n 3). Article 29 "Public and private investment in disaster risk prevention and reduction through structural and non-structural measures are essential to enhance the economic, social, health and cultural resilience of persons, communities, countries and their assets, as well as the environment. These can be drivers of innovation, growth and job creation. Such measures are cost-effective and instrumental to save lives, prevent and reduce losses and ensure effective recovery and rehabilitation. National and local levels".

> *healthcare services, including maternal, new born and child health, sexual and reproductive health, food security and nutrition, housing and education, towards the eradication of poverty, to find durable solutions in the post-disaster phase and to empower and assist people disproportionately affected by disasters...*[65]

This salient provision envisions the integration of an adaptive and more inclusive approach to reproductive matters in times of emergency. The next section provides more insight into informal approaches to reproductive health concerns in West Africa.

6.5 Pathway to Informal Adaptive Governance Process to SRH in West Africa

Recent emergencies increasingly reflect the urgency for a more robust approach to governance structure to solve emerging challenges, particularly in democratic settings. These governance settings to which most nations subscribe are drastically changing ideologies that may require other efforts outside Government and its apparatus to include informal systems such as the adaptive governance model.[66] This accelerating change arguably demonstrates that governance issues may go beyond standard-setting boundaries that call for a plan to bring it back to base, through AG context of resilience in difficult seasons.[67] Some of these running issues are primarily social and informal problems that are unequivocally complex, including pandemics, disasters, and climate change.[68] In these situations, for there to be calm and order, the existing systems may have to be reworked pending the emergence of a new structure to complement the current order. In essence, the sudden appearance of concerns brought about by the unexpected may cause a paradigm shift. According to Barbara Cosens et al., "A deep understanding of a complex problem and its setting, the inclusion of local knowledge and perspective, and tailoring of governance to that context are required yet are impossible to achieve through government programs alone. In particular, when

[65] Ibid., Article 30.

[66] Barbara Cosens et al. (n 42) 1691.

[67] Ibid., 1696.

[68] Ibid., 1699.

humans are involved, issues of power and agency enter into the context, further adding to the complexity challenge for governance".[69] The emerging structure around this study—adaptive community programs (ACP)—recognizes law's significance, especially private law even in reproductive health matters. This context appreciates interaction with each field of law without any setbacks while also providing innovative approaches to issues arising through accelerated change. Exchange of such nature could create "small-scale innovation while creating stability at higher levels".[70] For example, periodic communal trainings in SRH with local midwives and mothers as facilitators, enhanced by the SRH supplies from health ministries and international health organisation such as the WHO.

These seemingly private governance structures could help fast-track communities laced with transparency, accountability, and participation. Unlike the existing public law system that is hell-bent on retaining positive law for all purposes "in the face of unprecedented rates of change could itself be destabilizing",[71] ACP in SRH combines these governance structures for a more robust preparedness and collaborative coping measures during emergencies.

As odd as it may sound, the West African governments must align themselves to different coping mechanisms to these "accelerating changes" to SRH governance. This sudden show of concern brought about by the unexpected should not jeopardize the integrity of women and girl children. To this end, the instrument of law can set in motion networking groups with constructive feedback to set up of non-linear, cross-scale interactions to address tipping points in SRH during and after pandemics.

To enhance the adaptive capacity of the womenfolk, SRH policies and legal frameworks must align with the dynamics of the population. To achieve this, advocacy groups, lawmakers, and civil societies can assist with information support, the inclusion of community representations, and the effective dissemination of decisions on SRH.[72] In this prism of public health and a large spectrum of pressing harm surges, policymakers can see the urgency for a continuous SRH adaptation program. This section

[69] Ibid., 1701.

[70] Ibid., 1703.

[71] Ibid., 1724.

[72] Leopold Ouedraogo et al. (n 24) 8–9.

maintains that SRH governance structures must adapt to these changing realities in the face of rapid emergency nuances.

Taking this discussion further is the insightful study of Elena Gartner that highlights the interaction of reproductive and environmental rights.[73] The author posits that these civil rights demonstrate in absolute terms that SRH during the pandemic resides within public health campaign that requires immediate action and justice discourse that is also true of environmental harm scholarship. Gartner maintains that with the pandemic creating "social inequality" amidst all levels of governance, it then means that reproductive health may widen up the space to justice scholarship. The author draws similarities between reproductive health, environmental protection, and sustainable development. The legal responses aim to "stop harmful pollution and stabilize the climate for the wellbeing of future generations, increase public participation, transparency, access to lawyers, and proper dissemination of data and medical research".[74] Similar to environmental issues, reproductive concerns in women revolve around other socio-economic problems, such as discrimination, and pollution that all need urgent international attention.[75] Admittedly, these public health concerns put together must look within the context of an adaptive framework for normalcy. It is the assumption that such a process should entrench a "bottom-up" approach for an inclusive outcome directed at reducing "persistent growing global inequalities"—aggravated by the pandemic. According to Gartner, "the COVID-19 pandemic brings into sharp focus how international environmental health issues intersect with existing inequalities to devastating effect, highlighting the need for stronger international coordination and safeguards".[76] In support of bottom-up arguments for SHR concerns are intense public awareness, advocacy plans, and international support through capacity building, education, and finance. These efforts, where intensely facilitated with a clear vision, could lead to a policy framework that breaks the chain of oppression, sexual abuse, and exclusion of women gender from reproductive matters.

[73] Elena Gartner, 'From Civil Rights to Human Rights: The Pandemic's Aftermath Requires Environmental and Repreductive Justice Mechanisms to Reinforce Global Public Health' (2020) 24 Human Rights Brief 42.

[74] Ibid., 44.

[75] Ibid., 45.

[76] Ibid., 47.

6.6 Conclusion

Drawing upon the provision of the Sendai Framework on Disaster Risk,

> Women and their participation are critical to effectively managing disaster risk and designing, resourcing and implementing gender-sensitive disaster risk reduction policies, plans and programmes; and adequate capacity building measures need to be taken to empower women for preparedness as well as to build their capacity to secure alternate means of livelihood in post-disaster situations.[77]

Such adaptation document considers women as significant stakeholders in times of disaster and emergencies as we had during COVID-19. For all intents and purposes, it is the recommendation of this chapter that every community must, in collaboration with intergovernmental agencies, set out plans for resilience programs to cater to SRH issues. Some areas beyond formal norms are training and retraining of the patrilineal community to understand sex, pregnancies, and abortion. While the Government may be overwhelmed during these periods, legislative processes would be underway, passed to law, and undertake a pilot study on compulsory empowerment of women. Implementing this requires an independent local task force, a toll-free line, and other whistle-blowing channels for reporting and documenting SRH risks. As a means of empowerment, local midwives must undergo intensive care training with facilities in place. In this way, we reduce the strain on health facilities and the effects of lockdown measures in times of disaster. Remarkably, this research identifies financing, international support, capacity building, and most importantly, continuous adaptation training as practical means of SRH in emergencies for West African communities.

In the same line of thought is regulated synergy of all measures of adaptive processes to human rights laws to create a path in open discussion and information gathering with all stakeholders within the prism of confidentiality (least petrified of reprisal or retaliation amongst the group). All of these be covered in supposed informal guidelines or regulations for emergencies, such as the lockdown regulations and the ensuing economic recovery plans.

[77] Para 36 (a) (i) Sendai Framework.

Bibliography

Akin Abayomi et al, 'From Ebola to Covid-19: Emergency Preparedness and Response Plans and Actions in Lagos, Nigeria' (2021) 17 Globalization and Health 1.

Alexandre Delamou et al, 'Public Health Impact of the 2014–2015 Ebola Outbreak in West Africa: Seizing Opportunities for the Future' (2016) 2 BMJ Global Health <https://gh.bmj.com/content/2/2/e000202> accessed 8 October 2021.

Barbara Cosens et al, 'Designing Law to Enable Adaptive Governance of Modern Wicked Problems' (2020) 73 Vanderbilt Law Review 1687.

Centre for Human Rights: University of Pretoria, 'Ghana' (*A Nature and Description of Emergency Covid-19 Measures*) <https://www.chr.up.ac.za/covid19-database/ghana> accessed 20 October 2021.

Cheluchi Onyemelukwe, 'The Law and Human Rights in Nigeria's Response to the COVID-19 Pandemic' <https://blog.petrieflom.law.harvard.edu/2020/06/04/the-law-and-human-rights-in-nigerias-response-to-the-covid-19-pandemic/> accessed 15 October 2021.

Christina Hill and Lucy Manne, 'Women's Vision for Reform: An Agenda for Corporate Accountability in Australia's Mining Sector' <https://actionaid.org.au/wp-content/uploads/2018/09/MINING-CORP-ACCT-REPORT-v4.pdf> accessed 30 September 2021.

Convention on the Elimination of All Forms of Discrimination Against Women 1979.

Dennis Asante et al, 'A Socio-Geographic Perspective of Health and Economic Impacts of COVID-19 on Poor Households in Ghana' (2021) GeoJournal.

Department of Sexual and Reproductive Health and Research, 'Ghana Contraceptive Within the Context of Adolescents' Sexual and Reproductive Lives: Country Profile' (World Health Organization 2020) WHO/SRH/20.17 <https://apps.who.int/iris/bitstream/handle/10665/339394/WHO-SRH-20.17-eng.pdf> accessed 1 February 2022.

Elena Gartner, 'From Civil Rights to Human Rights: The Pandemic's Aftermath Requires Environmental and Reproductive Justice Mechanisms to Reinforce Global Public Health' (2020) 24 Human Rights Brief 42.

Fatouma Laouan, 'Rapid Gender Analysis—COVID-19 (West Africa—April 2020)' <https://www.care-international.org/files/files/CARE_West_Africa_Rapid_Gender_Analysis_COVID-19_May_2020_final_EN.pdf> accessed 22 November 2021.

Fidelis Mbah, 'Nigeria Announces Lockdown of Major Cities to Curb Coronavirus' (30 March 2020) <https://www.aljazeera.com/economy/2020/3/30/nigeria-announces-lockdown-of-major-cities-to-curb-coronavirus> accessed 24 May 2022.

International Federation of Women Lawyers (FIDA) Nigeria, 'The Urgent Need to Address the Gendered Impact of COVID-19 on Violence Against Women and Girls in West African Commonwealth Countries' <https://fida.org.ng/wp-content/uploads/2021/08/FIDA-Nigeria-Policy-Brief.pdf> accessed 2 April 2022.

Jennifer Nash, 'Home Is Where the Birth Is: Race, Risk, and Labour During Covid-19' (2021) 32 Yale Journal of Law & Feminism 103.

Karen Hardee et al, 'Family Planning and Resilience: Associations Found in a Population, Health, and Environment (PHE) Project in Western Tanzania' (2018) 40 Population and Environment 204.

Kelli Hall et al, 'Centring Sexual and Reproductive Health and Justice in the Global COVID-19 Response' (2020) 395 Lancet Global Health 1175.

Leopold Ouedraogo et al, 'Continuity of Essential Sexual and Reproductive Health Services During Covid-19 Pandemic in the WHO African Region' <https://www.afro.who.int/sites/default/files/2021-04/CONTINUITY%20OF%20ESSENTIAL%20SRHR%20SERVICES%20LEOrevised2.pdf> accessed 23 September 2021.

Luisa Flor et al, 'Quantifying the Effects of the COVID-19 Pandemic on Gender Equality on Health, Social, and Economic Indicators: A Comprehensive Review of Data from March, 2020, to September, 2021' Lancet Global Health.

Malia Maier et al, '"Scrambling to Figure out What to Do": A Mixed Method Analysis of Covid-19's Impact on Sexual and Reproductive Health and Rights in the United States' (2021) BMJ Sex Reproductive Health 1.

Margit Endler et al, 'How the Coronavirus Disease 2019 Pandemic Is Impacting Sexual and Reproductive Health and Rights and Response: Results from a Global Survey of Providers, Researchers, and Policy-Makers' (2021) 100 Acta Obstet Gynecol Scand. 571.

Najmul Haider et al, 'Lockdown Measures in Response to COVID-19 in Nine Sub-Saharan African Countries' 5 BMJ Global Health.

Nasreen Solomons & Harsha Gihwala, 'The Right to Sexual and Reproductive Health: Challenges and Possibilities During Covid-19' <https://www.ohchr.org/Documents/Issues/Health/sexual-reproductive-health-covid/CSOs/ngo.ghjru.pdf> accessed 12 October 2021.

Nkemdilim Anazonwu et al, 'State Actors, Human Rights Violations and Informal Livelihoods During the COVID-19 Pandemic in Nigeria' (2021) Territory, Politics, Governance 1.

'Policy Brief: The Impact of Covid-19 on Women' <https://www.un.org/sexualviolenceinconflict/wp-content/uploads/2020/06/report/policy-brief-the-impact-of-covid-19-on-women/policy-brief-the-impact-of-covid-19-on-women-en-1.pdf> accessed 10 November 2021.

Shannon Wood et al, 'Need for and Use of Contraception by Women before and During COVID-19 in Four Sud-Saharan African Geographies: Results from Population-Based National or Regional Cohort Surveys' (2021) Lancet Global Health 793.

Statista, 'Coronavirus Cases in Africa as of March 02, 2022, by Country' (4 March 2022) <https://www.statista.com/statistics/1170463/coronavirus-cases-in-africa/> accessed 30 March 2022.

UNICEF, 'Primary and Secondary Impacts of the COVID-19 Pandemic on Children in Ghana' <https://www.unicef.org/ghana/media/3486/file/Effects%20of%20COVID-19%20on%20Women%20and%20Children%20in%20Ghana%20(II).pdf> accessed 1 November 2021.

United Nations, 'Reproductive Rights Are Human Rights: A Handbook for National Human Rights Institution' <https://www.ohchr.org/documents/publications/nhrihandbook.pdf> accessed 5 October 2021.

———, 'Sendai Framework for Disaster Risk Reduction 2015–2030' (United Nations 2015) A/RES/69/283 <https://doi.org/.un.org/ga/search/view_doc.asp?symbol=A/RES/69> accessed 17 October 2021.

'United Nations Development System in Ghana: Building Back Better From COVID-19, Common Country Analysis (CCA) and Socio-Economic Response and Recovery Plan (SERRP)' <https://ghana.un.org/sites/default/files/2020-11/United%20Nations%20Ghana%20SERRP_%20Final.pdf> accessed 3 October 2021.

Venkatraman Chandra-Mouli et al, 'Adolescent Sexual and Reproductive Health for All in Sub-Saharan: A Spotlight on Inequalities' (2021) 18 Reproductive Health 1.

World Bank, 'Africa Overview' <https://www.worldbank.org/en/region/afr/overview> accessed 1 November 2021.

———, 'Amid Recession, Sub-Saharan Africa Poised for Recovery' (2021) 2021/106/AFR <https://www.worldbank.org/en/news/press-release/2021/03/31/amid-recession-sub-saharan-africa-poised-for-recovery> accessed 2 November 2021.

———, 'Population, Female-Sub-Saharan Africa' <https://data.worldbank.org/indicator/SP.POP.TOTL.FE.IN?locations=ZG> accessed 15 October 2021.

World Health Organization, 'Integrating Sexual and Reproductive Health into Health Emergency and Disaster Risk Management' <https://www.who.int/hac/techguidance/preparedness/SRH_HERM_Policy_brief_A4.pdf> accessed 11 September 2021.

———, 'Second Round of the National Pulse Survey on Continuity of Essential Health Services During the COVID-19 Pandemic' (WHO 2021) WHO/2019-nCoV/EHS_continuity/survey/2021.1 <https://www.who.int/publications/i/item/WHO-2019-nCoV-EHS-continuity-survey-2021.1> accessed 15 November 2021.

———, 'Sexual Reproductive Health and Rights in Emergencies' <https://www.who.int/health-cluster/about/work/other-collaborations/sexual-reproductive-health-rights/en/> accessed 11 September 2021.

Yeonsoo Lee et al, 'Women's Health in Times of Emergency: We Must Take Action' (2021) 30 Journal of Women's Health.

CHAPTER 7

Reproductive Health Rights in Liberia: The Case of (Il)Legal and (Un)Safe Abortion

Veronica Fynn Bruey

7.1 Introduction: Brief Background History

With a population of 3.5 million people (in 2008), Liberia is Africa's oldest republic, comprising 15 political counties, with 17 distinct Indigenous language groups, 86 per cent Christian, 12 per cent Islam, and 1.8 per cent other religion.[1] Although archaeological evidence supporting prehistoric habitation of the Grain Coast is scarce, the Indigenous People of Liberia existed long before 1822, when formerly enslaved Black

[1] Liberia Institute of Statistics and Geo-Information Services, '2008 Population and Housing Census: Final Results' (Liberia Institute of Statistics and Geo-Information Services 2009) Government vii, 4, 18–19.

V. F. Bruey (✉)
Legal Studies, Athabasca University, Edmonton, AB, Canada
e-mail: vfynnbruey@athabascau.ca

O. S. Adelakun and E. Ndoni (eds.), *Reproductive Health and Assisted Reproductive Technologies In Sub-Saharan Africa*,
Sustainable Development Goals Series,
https://doi.org/10.1007/978-981-99-2411-0_7

Africans returned to the continent.[2] The arrival of former African slaves from the United States and the Caribbean as Black settler-colonists, assisted by the American Colonisation Society and its auxiliaries, sowed a seed of systemic violence, which culminated in a full-blown civil war after 167 years (1822–1989) of discrimination against Indigenous Liberians.[3]

As a complex by-product of the inhumane transatlantic slave trade, Liberia epitomises the United States' colonising project, bearing the torch of patriarchy, masculinity, and misogyny, all of which were exacerbated by the civil war. The Liberian civil war started on 29 December 1989 and lasted for 14 years, with eight different warring factions responsible for 250,000–270,000 deaths and the displacement of another 800,000–1,000,000 people.[4] Perceived as the 'spoils of war,' 80 per cent of girls and women endured all manner of sexual exploitation and abuse, including rape, forced marriage, forced prostitution, forced pregnancy, and forced conscription. Sexual violence was used as a 'weapon of war'

[2] Joseph Saye Guannu, *Liberian History Before 1857: A Reference for Elementary Pupils* (1st edn, Exposition Press 1977) 10; Abayomi Karnga, *History of Liberia* (D H Tyte 1926) 20; Ray Cavanaugh, 'Discovery of 1821 Document Sheds Light on Liberia Purchase—The Washington Post' *Washington Post* (Washington, DC, 20 November 2021) <https://www.washingtonpost.com/history/2021/11/20/liberia-purchase-agreement-1821-burrowes/> accessed 20 November 2021; Frederick D McEvoy, 'Some Proposals for Liberian Archaeology' (1970) 111 Liberian Studies Journal 129; Nnamdi Azikiwe, *Liberia in World Politics* (University of Michigan 1934) 22–23; D Elwood Dunn, *A History of the Episcopal Church in Liberia, 1821–1980* (American Theological Library Association and The Scarecrow Press 1992) 9; Amos Sawyer, *The Emergence of Autocracy in Liberia: Tragedy and Challenge* (Institute for Contemporary Studies 1992) 44–48; Amos Jones Beyan, 'Transatlantic Trade and the Coastal Area of Pre-Liberia' (1995) 57 The Historian 757; Andreas W Massing, 'An Inferential History of Pre-Liberia, 1460–1490: Mapping Liberia—A Conjectural History of Early Liberia' (German Technical Corporation (GTZ), Monrovia, Liberia, 23 March 2007) <http://www.onliberia.org/A%20conjectural%20history%20of%20early%20Liberia.ppt>.

[3] Veronica Fynn Bruey, 'Systematic Gender Violence and the Rule of Law: Aboriginal Communities in Australia and Post-War Liberia' (PhD Thesis, The Australian National University 2016) 352–353 <https://openresearch-repository.anu.edu.au/handle/1885/159520>.

[4] Veronica Nmoma, 'The Civil War and the Refugee Crisis in Liberia' (1997) XVII 1997; United Nations High Commission for Human Rights, 'Liberia: Strategies & Program' <http://www.unhcr.org/home/PROTECTION/43eb16254.pdf> accessed 15 December 2011.

to terrorise and violate girls' and women's reproductive rights.[5] An estimated 15,000–20,000 children, mostly primary school age, were forcibly enlisted, mutilated, raped, beaten, murdered, and enticed to commit egregious crimes against humanity.[6]

Violation of girls' and women's reproductive rights in Liberia is not only inextricably tied to their sexual health but also entrenched institutionally, structurally, and inter-personally. Systemic violence against girls and women in Liberia occurs at six intricate levels paired at the institutional/state, cultural/structural, and community/interpersonal. As alluded to above, the 14-year civil war accentuated the prevalence of violence against girls and women in Liberia, with sexual abuse and exploitation, particularly statutory rape, being strongly correlated with a number of indicators and risk factors of unsafe abortion.

Safeguarding girls' and women's reproductive rights in Liberia is an all-round lose-lose situation. Carrying a child full-term in Liberia is risky and, in some instances, deadly. Goal #3 (ensure healthy lives and promote well-being for all at all ages) of the 17 Sustainable Development Goals (SDGs) targets reduction in maternal mortality (Goal #: 3.1) and preventable deaths of newborns and children under 5 years of age (Goal #: 3.2) as well as ensuring universal access to sexual and reproductive heathcare services (obviously, abortion services included). Liberia ranks the ninth highest of 184 countries in the world, with a maternal mortality rate of 661–1071 per 100,000 live births by women ranging between the ages of 15 and 49 years.[7] Unfortunately, there is no indication that Liberia will be achieving the SDG's maternal, newborn, and child health targets for

[5] UNICEF-Liberia, 'Child, Maternal and Newborn Health' (*Maternal and Newborn Health*, 2018) 618 <https://www.unicef.org/liberia/child-maternal-and-newborn-health> accessed 18 October 2021.

[6] Philip Marcelo, 'Rebuilding Liberia: Child Soldiers and the Youth Problem in Liberia' (*providencejournal.com*, 1 August 2013) <http://www.providencejournal.com/article/20130801/SPECIAL-REPORTS/308019903> accessed 31 August 2016; Tony Tate, 'How to Fight, How to Kill: Child Soldiers in Liberia' (Human Rights Watch 2004) NGO Report Vol 16, No 2 (A) 1 <https://www.hrw.org/reports/2004/liberia0204/liberia0204.pdf>, update the dates when the sources were accessed. A source accessed 31 August 2016 does not show currency for this project.

[7] UNICEF-Liberia (n 5); Government of Liberia, 'Investment Case for Reproductive, Maternal, Newborn, Child and Adolescent Health, 2016–2020' (Ministry of Health and Social Welfare 2016) Government Report 11 <https://www.globalfinancingfacility.org/sites/gff_new/files/documents/Liberia%20RMNCAH%20Investment%20Case%202016%20-%202020.pdf>.

2021 and 2030.[8] In fact, a recent assessment carried out on Liberia's 701 health services, with emphasis on family planning, antenatal, and delivery care across the 15 counties, made no mention of access to abortion.[9]

Meanwhile, the major causes of maternal mortality in Liberia are post-partum haemorrhage (25 per cent), hypertensive disorders of pregnancy (16 per cent), sepsis (10 per cent), and unsafe abortion (10 per cent).[10] For mothers fortunate to have live births, 84.6 per 1000 (i.e., 13,365 in 2019) of their infants will not see their fifth birthday.[11] An estimated 60 per cent of neonatal deaths occur among adolescent girls, compared with 6 per cent for those over the age of 19.[12] Thirty-one per cent of adolescent girls also account for the high teenage pregnancy rate, with 30 per cent of those ending in an abortion.[13] The high occurrence of maternal mortality, neonatal deaths, sexual exploitation and abuse, and poor access to reproductive health services by adolescent girls and teenagers are intertwined with the (il)legal abortion practices.

There are many reasons why a prospective mother may not be able to carry a pregnancy for a full term. Sometimes the only option is to abort the pregnancy, whatever the reason. In Liberia, a woman's choice to abort a pregnancy is restrained by law. Many vulnerable adolescent and teenage girls become pregnant as a result of statutory rape, transactional sex, forced marriage, trafficking in person, and lack of information

[8] Ulrich Laaser et al., 'Delays in Achieving Maternal, Newborn, and Child Health Targets for 2021 and 2030 in Liberia' (2019) 7 Frontiers in Public Health 386, 3.

[9] Roland Y Kesselly et al., 'The Status of Health Services in the 15 Counties of Liberia' (2018) Volume X South Eastern European Journal of Public Health (SEEJPH) 2018, 4 <https://www.seejph.com/index.php/seejph/article/view/1873> accessed 20 November 2021; Sanni Yaya, Olalekan A. Uthman, Ghose Bishwajit, and Michael EKholuenetale, 'Maternal Health Care Service Utilization in Post-War Liberia: Analysis of Nationally Representative Cross-Sectional Household Surveys' (2019) 19 BMC Public Health 28, 2 <https://bmcpublichealth.biomedcentral.com/articles/10.1186/s12889-018-6365-x> accessed 16 November 2021.

[10] Elsie G. Karmbor-Ballah et al., 'Maternal Mortality and the Metempsychosis of User Fees in Liberia: A Mixed-Methods Analysis' (2019) 3 Scientific African e00050, 2; Yaya et al. (n 9) 2; Government of Liberia (n 7) 11.

[11] UNICEF, 'Liberia—Demographics, Health & Infant Mortality' (*Country Profile*, 2019) <https://data.unicef.org/country/lbr/#> accessed 21 November 2021.

[12] Sanni Yaya et al., 'Maternal Health Care Service Utilization in Post-War Liberia: Analysis of Nationally Representative Cross-Sectional Household Surveys' (2019) 19 BMC Public Health 28, 2; Government of Liberia (n 7) 26.

[13] Government of Liberia (n 7) 11.

on sexual health and access to reproductive services. The act of abortion (or 'spoiling the belly,'[14] in Liberian parlance) is generally shrouded in secrecy, mainly due to criminalisation of the practice and stigmatisation in a heavily religious country. Apart from a few anecdotes and case studies, there is very little research or case law to support evidence for the occurrence of abortion practices in Liberia. Thus, the importance of the *Investment Case for Reproductive, Maternal, New born, Child and Adolescent Health*, 2016–2020—an 86-page strategic roadmap embarking on a journey to transform Liberia's collapsed healthcare delivery system and to improve maternal health.[15]

The *Liberian Penal Law—Title 26 Revised*, 1976 criminalises abortion as an offense against the family. Precisely, it is a felony to terminate a pregnancy beyond the 24th week except when it is carried out by a licensed physician believing that there is a substantial risk to the physical and mental health of the mother or the child, or the pregnancy resulted from rape, incest, or other felonious intercourse (Section 16.3 (1) and (2). In a country with a negative annual GDP growth rate of–2.278 (2020); a patient–doctor ratio of 1:15,000 (i.e., 298 doctors for a projected population of 4.5 million (2020); the World Health Organisation recommends 1:1000); a relatively high incidence of rape, where more than 600 cases were reported between January and June of 2020; and a life expectancy of 64.1 years, there is no denying the challenge of securing girls' and women's reproductive rights.[16]

[14] Katherine Thomas, '"Spoiling the Belly": The Dangers of Backstreet Abortions in Liberia' *Women and Girls* (New York, NY, 2017) <https://deeply.thenewhumanitarian.org/womenandgirls/articles/2017/04/21/spoiling-the-belly-the-dangers-of-backstreet-abortions-in-liberia> accessed 17 November 2021.

[15] (n 7) 6.

[16] Rodney Sieh, 'Liberia: More Than 600 Cases of Rape, Sodomy, Abuses During COVID-19 State of Emergency' *FrontPage Africa* (Monrovia, Liberia, 13 July 2020) <https://frontpageafricaonline.com/front-slider/liberia-more-than-600-cases-of-rape-sodomy-abuses-during-covid-19-state-of-emergency/> accessed 18 October 2021; Adam Gaber, 'Liberia Adopts Yale Capstone Recommendations for Medical Education Reform' *YaleNews* (New Haven, CT, 30 April 2018) <https://news.yale.edu/2018/04/30/liberia-adopts-yale-capstone-recommendations-medical-education-reform> accessed 18 October 2021; World Bank, 'Life Expectancy at Birth, Total (Years)—Liberia' (*Data*, 2021) <https://data.worldbank.org/indicator/SP.DYN.LE00.IN?locations=LR> accessed 23 November 2021; Lucinda Rouse, 'Africa's COVID Threat Hits "New Level" as Delta Variant Spreads' *Al Jazeera* (Monrovia, Liberia, 1

Compounded by the post-war reconstruction, the recent Ebola Virus Disease crisis in 2014–2015,[17] and now challenged by a third wave of the Covid-19 pandemic, the need to protect the reproductive health rights of girls and women, especially adolescents and teenage girls living in rural communities, is ever pressing. Liberia is a youthful nation. According to the latest census (2008), those between the ages of 0 and 19 make up 53 per cent of Liberia's 3.5 million people, and those under 25 years are 63 per cent, while 77 per cent of the population is below the age of 35.[18] Informed by the rights-based approach and feminist (legal) theories/feminist jurisprudence, with emphasis on adolescent and teenage girls, the goal of the chapter is to use case law, case studies, and content analysis methodology to examine the efficacy of Liberian abortion law in protecting girls' and women's reproductive rights.

7.1.1 Structure and Flow

The chapter begins with an introduction outlining a brief historical background of Liberia in the context of civil war and the state of reproductive health rights. Following is a review of the literature where key terms are defined while expanding on the theoretical and legal approach adopted in the chapter. Description of terms further elaborates on the risk factors, health indicators, impact, and consequences of unsafe abortion on girls and women in Liberia. A summary of (inter)national laws and policy on women's reproductive right in Liberia assesses Liberia's obligation to

July 2021) <https://www.aljazeera.com/news/2021/7/1/africa-covid-threat-hits-new-level-delta-variant-spreads> accessed 27 November 2021.

[17] Adrienne E Strong and David A Schwartz, 'Effects of the West African Ebola Epidemic on Health Care of Pregnant Women: Stigmatization with and without Infection' in David A Schwartz, Julienne Ngoundoung Anoko and Sharon A Abramowitz (eds), *Pregnant in the Time of Ebola* (Springer International Publishing 2019) 11 <http://link.springer.com/10.1007/978-3-319-97637-2_2> accessed 17 November 2021; Veronica Fynn Bruey, 'Maternal and Reproductive Rights: Ebola and the Law in Liberia' in Sharon A Abramowitz, Julienne Ngoundoung Anoko and David A Schwartz (eds), *Pregnant in the Time of Ebola: Women and Their Children in the 2013–2015 West African Epidemic* (1st ed. 2019, Springer International Publishing: Imprint: Springer 2019) 219.

[18] Liberia Institute of Statistics and Geo-Information Services, 'National Population and Housing Census' (Liberia Institute of Statistics and Geo-Information Services 2009) Government Report A1-4.

protect girls' and women's reproductive rights and their access to abortion services in Liberia. Due to its practice in secrecy and lack of empirical research on the topic, a few studies and anecdotes are used to contextualise the everyday lives of girls' and women's experiences with (il)legal and (un)safe abortion practices in Liberia. The chapter's overall examination of the statistical analysis, health indicators, risk factors, conceptual framework, and legal instruments is critical to devising and recommending appropriate intervention programs to address the issue of illegal and unsafe abortion in Liberia. The chapter concludes with recommendations on how to prevent unsafe abortion and improve girls' and women's reproductive rights to abortion in Liberia.

7.2 Literature Review: Definitions, Theories, Legal Framework

7.2.1 Definition and Explanation of Key Terms Reflecting Health Risks, Indicators, Impact, and Outcomes of (Un)Safe Abortion Practices in Liberia

Abortion is the loss of pregnancy before foetal viability (i.e., before the foetus becomes capable of surviving on its own outside of the uterus).[19] Abortion can be induced, spontaneous or unsafe. When abortion is induced it is a deliberate action to terminate pregnancy by drug, surgery, or other means.[20] Spontaneous abortion or (or miscarriage) is a natural loss of pregnancy before 20 weeks of gestation.[21] An unsafe abortion is the termination of an unintended pregnancy by person(s) lacking adequate skills or in an environment that does not conform to minimal

[19] Onikepe Owolabi, 'Towards Improving the Measurement of Unsafe Abortion: Substantive Estimates and Methodological Insights from Zambia.' (PhD Thesis, London School of Hygiene and Tropical Medicine 2017) 17 <http://researchonline.lshtm.ac.uk/id/eprint/3548894> accessed 24 November 2021; Kate Greasley, *Arguments About Abortion: Personhood, Morality, and Law* (1st edn, Oxford University Press 2017) 2.

[20] International Federation of Gynecology and Obstetric, 'Induced Abortion—An Overview | ScienceDirect Topics', *International Encyclopaedia of Public Health* (ScienceDirect 2008) <https://www.sciencedirect.com/topics/medicine-and-dentistry/induced-abortion> accessed 24 November 2021.

[21] Clark Alves and Amanda Rapp, 'Spontaneous Abortion', *StatPearls* (StatPearls Publishing 2021) <http://www.ncbi.nlm.nih.gov/books/NBK560521/> accessed 24 November 2021.

medical standards, or both.[22] This definition of unsafe abortion, which is taken from the World Health Organisation's Technical Working Group Report published in 1993,[23] is critiqued for being unclear about who safe abortion providers ought to be or the appropriate medical skills they should have. The issue of safe abortion providers is of utmost importance in Liberia where the prevalence and incident rates of abortion strongly correlate with not having safe abortion providers.

To ensure a correct interpretation of unsafe abortion, it is recommended that the following explanation must accompany the above definition: '[t]he persons, skills and medical standards considered safe in the provision of abortion are different for medical and surgical abortion and depend on the duration of the pregnancy. What is considered "safe" should be interpreted in line with current WHO technical and policy guidance.'[24] Meanwhile, methods used to identify and measure estimates of unsafe abortion are subject to error due to the lack or restriction of data collection.[25] Estimates from 2010 to 2014 show approximately 45 per cent (25 million) of all abortions (55.7 million) were unsafe, with 97 per cent (24.3 million) of those occurring in developing countries, mainly due to religious, social, political, and legal obstacles.[26] Between 2015 and 2019, at least 121 million unintended pregnancies occurred worldwide, 61 per cent (73 million) of which ended in abortion per year worldwide.[27]

[22] World Health Organisation, 'The Prevention and Management of Unsafe Abortion: Report of the Technical Working Group, Geneva 12–15 April 1992' (World Health Organisation 1993) 3.

[23] Ibid.

[24] Bela Ganatra et al., 'From Concept to Measurement: Operationalizing WHO's Definition of Unsafe Abortion' (2014) 92 Bulletin of the World Health Organization 155, 155.

[25] Owolabi (n 19) 31.

[26] Lisa B Haddad and Nawal M Nour, 'Unsafe Abortion: Unnecessary Maternal Mortality' (2009) 2 Reviews in Obstetrics & Gynecology 122, 122; World Health Organisation, 'Preventing Unsafe Abortion' (*Key Facts*, 25 September 2020) <https://www.who.int/news-room/fact-sheets/detail/preventing-unsafe-abortion> accessed 25 November 2021; Bela Ganatra et al., 'Global, Regional, and Subregional Classification of Abortions by Safety, 2010–14: Estimates from a Bayesian Hierarchical Model' (2017) 390 The Lancet 2372, 2372.

[27] World Health Organisation (n 26).

Disregarding the existence of Indigenous Peoples who practice African traditional religion, Liberia, as a colony of the United States, claims to have been founded on Christian principles. Being a Christian in Liberia means honouring the principles of the Holy Bible, including one of the Ten Commandments which says '[t]hou shalt not kill' (Exodus 20:13, King James Version). In 1973, the term 'pro-life' was coined by anti-abortion crusaders to recriminalise abortion after the Supreme Court ruled in *Roe v Wade* that the Constitution of the United States protects abortion rights. As the 'stepchild'[28] of the United States, the Roman Catholic Church in Liberia holds an 'absolute and extreme position against abortion'.[29]

Buried deep within the psyche of this religion is a blissful idealism of the right to life and the dignity of a foetus, despite the indelible stench of poverty, subjugation, power, and outright control over the female's body and her ability to choose what's right for her. In a statement signed by Archbishop Lewis Zeigler, Metropolitan Archbishop of Monrovia and President of the Catholic Bishop Conference of Liberia; the Most Reverend Andrew Karnley, Bishop of Cape Palmas; and the Most Reverend Anthony Borwah, Bishop of Gbarnga, the Catholic Bishop Conference of Liberia (CABICOL).

> ...denounce any attempt by anyone or any institution to promote same sex marriage, abortion and contraceptives. Thus, we call upon all, especially our government to reject the acceptance of this incipient culture of death as a pre-requisite for developmental and financial aid...[w]e therefore calls on all Liberians to join us in our efforts to promote peace and the respect for the fundamental rights and dignity of every person.[30]

[28] Nancee Oku Bright, *Liberia: America's Stepchild* (Grain Coast Productions 2002) <http://www.pbs.org/wgbh/globalconnections/liberia/film/overview.html>.

[29] Frances Kissling, 'Religion and Abortion: Roman Catholicism Lost in the Pelvic Zone' (1993) 3 Women's Health Issues 132, 132.

[30] Staff Reporter, 'Liberia's Catholic Bishops Against Abortion, Same Sex Marriage' *FrontPage Africa* (Monrovia, Liberia, 12 April 2016) <https://frontpageafricaonline.com/politics/liberia-s-catholic-bishops-against-abortion-same-sex-marriage/> accessed 23 November 2021.

Considering that 61 per cent (58–73 million) of 121 million unintended pregnancies annually between 2015 and 2019 ended in abortion,[31] the CABICOL statement (above) raises the question of why adolescent and teenage girls, from the squalor of Liberia, with no formal education, end up dying because they become targets of rape, forced marriage, female genital cutting, trafficking, and a host of sexual exploitation and abuse spiralling down into systemic violence.[32]

Like gender, violence is a complex concept, which varies in severity that is categorically representative of injury, pain, suffering, and death. Violence can be subtle, nuanced, or overt and is almost always a conscious manifestation of conscious human behaviour. Shaped by social implications, violence occurs at the state or institutional, structural/cultural, and community/interpersonal level, collectively called systemic violence.[33] The power and meaning given to violence embody the various forms of sexual exploitation and abuse that affect adolescent and teenage girls' reproductive health in Liberia.

In Liberia—a severely economically deprived country—sexual exploitation and abuse often occur when (predominantly) men in positions of power and authority exploit or abuse girls and women for sexual purposes. Sexual exploitation refers to 'any actual or attempted abuse of a position of vulnerability, differential power, or trust, for sexual purposes, including, but not limited to, profiting monetarily, socially or politically from the sexual exploitation of another'.[34] Sexual abuse is the 'actual or threatened physical intrusion of a sexual nature, whether by force or under unequal

[31] Jonathan Bearak et al., 'Unintended Pregnancy and Abortion by Income, Region, and the Legal Status of Abortion: Estimates from a Comprehensive Model for 1990–2019' (2020) 8 The Lancet Global Health e1152, e1152.

[32] Tamba Saah Alpha et al., 'Review of Maternal Deaths in Lofa County, Liberia, 2015–2017' (2021) 4 Journal of Interventional Epidemiology and Public Health 6, 7; Faiza Mohamed, 'Justice for Ruth Berry Peal, Who Was Forcibly Mutilated in Liberia, but Still No Ban on FGM' *Independent* (Monrovia, Liberia, 8 April 2013) <https://www.independent.co.uk/voices/comment/justice-for-ruth-berry-peal-who-was-forcibly-mutilated-in-liberia-but-still-no-ban-on-fgm-8564214.html> accessed 26 November 2021.

[33] Fynn Bruey, 'Systematic Gender Violence and the Rule of Law: Aboriginal Communities in Australia and Post-War Liberia' (n 3) 15, 104–107.

[34] United Nations Secretariat, 'Special Measures for Protection from Sexual Exploitation and Sexual Abuse' (United Nations 2003) UN Document ST/SGB/2003/13 1 <https://content.unops.org/service-Line-Documents/IAIG/ST-SGB-2003-13_EN.pdf>.

or coercive conditions'.[35] Sexual exploitation and abuse (SEA) has always been a serious concern for adolescent and teenage girls who make up nearly half of Liberia's population and therefore are most at risk for unsafe abortion. Sadly, during the civil war and in post-war Liberia, the arrival of hundreds of thousands United Nations and Economic Committee of West African States (ECOWAS) peacekeepers and humanitarian/aid workers intensified the prevalence of SEA in Liberia.[36]

A Save the Children United Kingdom study documented the incidence of transactional sex between children and humanitarian/aid workers. As a means of survival, children, particularly young girls under the age of 18, were engaged in exchanging sex for food, money, hygiene products, perfume, mobile phones, and access to entertainment centres (e.g., video clubs, night clubs, bars, etc.).[37] One young adolescent girl emphasised how '[i]t's difficult to escape the trap of those (NGO) people; [because] they use the food as bait to get you to sex with them'.[38] Another commented on older men, including UN employees and aid workers, raping young girls: '[t]he youngest [girls] are loving to big, big men [sugar daddies] for money…[u]nderage children are forced "to reach life stage" (sexual maturity) and because of this, teenage pregnancy is on the increase'.[39] More than two decades after his mother was impregnated by

[35] United Nations Secretariat (n 34).

[36] Bernd Beber et al., 'Peacekeeping, Compliance with International Norms, and Transactional Sex in Monrovia, Liberia' (2017) 71 International Organization 1, 1.

[37] Rosa Freedman, Sarah Blakemore and Camilla Barker, 'Safeguarding Children from UN Peacekeeper Sexual Exploitation and Abuse in Liberia' (Keeping Children Safe 2017) 5 <https://research.reading.ac.uk/safeguarding-children/wp-content/uploads/sites/56/Unorganized/KCS_LiberiaReport_web_112018.pdf>; United Nations High Commissioner for Refugees and Save the Children UK, 'Sexual Violence and Exploitation: The Experience of Refugee Children in Guinea, Liberia and Sierra Leone—Based on Initial Findings and Recommendations from Assessment Mission 22 October–30 November 2001' (United Nations High Commission for Refugees 2002) UN Report <https://www.savethechildren.org.uk/sites/default/files/docs/sexual_violence_and_exploitation_1.pdf>.

[38] United Nations High Commissioner for Refugees and Save the Children UK (n 37) 4.

[39] Save the Children UK, 'From Camp to Community: Liberia Study on Exploitation of Children' (Save the Children—UK 2006) 10 <https://resourcecentre.savethechildren.net/pdf/save_uk_liberia.pdf/>.

a peacekeeper, 21-year-old Moses Z Kaine says, 'I was still in my mother's womb when my father ended his duties and left Liberia'[40] He made a plea, asking his father and all peacekeepers who left their children behind in Liberia to return and support them.

Expanding on the enormity of risk factors (e.g., prostitution, trafficking in persons, harmful traditional practice, such as female genital cutting, forced marriage, sex-for-grades, single parenting, high illiteracy rate, unemployment, caregiver/parental abuse, stigma, etc.) that make adolescent and teenage girls more vulnerable to engaging in unsafe abortion practices is beyond the scope of this chapter.[41] Notwithstanding, the chapter explicates four theoretical frameworks to help understand girls' and women's reproductive rights and their increased exposure to relatively high maternal deaths due to (il)legal and (un)safe abortion.

7.2.2 *Theorising Reproductive Health Rights of Adolescent and Teenage Girls*

There is plenty of research as well as many publications dedicated to theories of abortion, namely pro-life, pro-choice theory on the sacredness of life, free will, and the theory of person or conscious entity.[42] This chapter draws on three approaches to explain the reproductive health rights of adolescent and teen girls in Liberia. They are the human rights-based

[40] Jonathan Paye-Layeh and Carley Petesch, 'Peacekeepers Left More than 6000 Children in Liberia' *AP NEWS* (Monrovia, Liberia, 21 November 2018) <https://apnews.com/article/monrovia-ap-top-news-africa-international-news-west-africa-ccbbddfcab8f45d48d0d3b40a81dbf3d> accessed 26 November 2021.

[41] UNICEF—Liberia, 'Child Protection' (*Programme*, 2016) <https://www.unicef.org/liberia/child-protection> accessed 26 November 2021; Gabrielle Alexis, 'Child Prostitution: Inadequate Responses by the Church' (Master of Arts, Liberty University 2016) 39 <https://digitalcommons.liberty.edu/cgi/viewcontent.cgi?article=1417&context=masters>; Thomas Jaye, 'The Security Culture of the ECOWAS: Origins, Development and the Challenge of Child Trafficking' (2008) 26 Journal of Contemporary African Studies 151, 151; Monica Ruiz-Casares, 'Child Protection Knowledge, Attitudes, and Practices in Central and Western Liberia' (USAID and Save the Children 2011) 37–41 <https://bettercarenetwork.org/sites/default/files/2020-09/kap_finalreport_2011_8appendices_v2.1.pdf>; Mohamed (n 32); Emma Batha, 'Liberia Bans Female Genital Mutilation—But Only for a Year' *Reuters* (Monrovia, Liberia, 25 January 2018) <https://www.reuters.com/article/us-liberia-fgm-law/liberia-bans-female-genital-mutilation-but-only-for-a-year-idUSKBN1FE1N7> accessed 18 April 2018.

[42] Mohammad Rasekh, 'Battle of Life: A Brief Study of Theories on Abortion' (2003) 4 Journal of Reproduction and Infertility 220, 220.

approach, asking the girl/woman question, and speaking up/out. These theories discussed are drawn from interdisciplinary scholarship based on the author's expertise in law, public health, psychology, and gender/ women's studies.

The first theory, critical to safeguarding girls' and women's reproductive rights, is the Rights-Based Approach (hereafter RBA). Applying a human rights-based approach to an issue involves providing States with an intrinsic and instrumental rationale to take action to ensure human rights are protected. An intrinsic rationale 'acknowledg[es] that a human rights-based approach is the right thing to do, morally or legally', whereas an instrumental rationale, 'recognize[es] that a human rights-based approach leads to better and more sustainable human development outcomes'.[43] The RBA identifies poverty as a form of injustice, targeted at marginalising, discriminating, and exploiting vulnerable groups, which include girls and women at risk for unsafe abortion.[44] Therefore, applying the RBA places an intrinsic moral and legalistic duty on Liberia to protect girls' and women's reproductive rights.

One way Liberia could respect girls' and women's reproductive rights is by conducting research to establish and inform evidence-based practice. The efficacy of quality research and service delivery of the highest ethical standard is achievable with an adoption of the 'asking the [girl/] woman question'[45]—a major feminist legal theory. Feminist legal theory or feminist jurisprudence argues that since the law is masculine, mostly written, enforced, and adjudicated by men, girls' and women's critical perspectives are required to ensure equality and justice for all. Notably, the same law that liberates girls and women from social injustices is also responsible for discriminating, subjugating, and excluding them as equal participants in the legal arena.[46] Against this backdrop, feminist legal theory offers

[43] Suman Momin, 'A Human Rights Based Approach to Refugees: A Look at the Syrian Refugee Crisis and the Responses from Germany and the United States' (2017) 9 Duke Forum for Law & Social Change 55, 57.

[44] Jakob Kirkemann Boesen and Tomas Martin, *Applying a Rights-Based Approach: An Inspirational Guide for Civil Society* (Danish Institute for Human Rights 2007) 9.

[45] Katharine T Bartlett, 'Feminist Legal Methods' (1990) 103 Harvard Law Review 829, 829.

[46] Veronica Fynn Bruey, 'Indigenous Women and International Law', *Research Handbook on Feminist Engagement with International Law* (Edward Elgar 2019) 15.

mechanisms to expose biases in the judicial process, to critique legal precedents and, most importantly, to allow girls and women to reclaim/rewrite laws written by and for men. Drawing on feminist legal theory is also crucial for explaining a paradigmatic shift from using patriarchal dominance towards effecting realistic change by preventing the deaths and ill-health of girls and women at risk for unsafe abortion.

To be clear, women are traditionally viewed not only as different in the eyes of the law but also as subordinate, a status that is enforced by institutional, cultural, and interpersonal interactions and social practices of coercion and violence.[47] The girl/woman question is a rhetorical phraseology used in the feminist legal research method to explore gender implications of a social (e.g., health, law, and education) practice of rule (e.g., (il)legal or (un)safe abortion). Asking girl/woman questions assumes authorities in health and law are neutral and male-centred. The girl/woman question not only upholds the integrity, dignity, and agency of the female person, but it also exposes paternalistic and misogynistic features—how they operate and how they might be corrected.[48] This misogynistic philosophical foundation of the law demands that legal justice informed by evidence-based research must be reformed by women's experiences to achieve any semblance of equality and fairness.[49] If Liberian girls' and women's perspectives about the law and their health are not understood, their claims to legal discourse regarding their reproductive rights will not be perceived as legitimate.

In validating their claim to reproductive justice, Liberian girls and women are speaking up and speaking out in several ways. First and foremost, though silent in death (i.e., high maternal mortality rates), their anecdotal stories and unique case studies (see below) are the loudest alarm in their speaking up/out moment. A principal tactic for girls and women in fighting against violation of their reproductive rights is to break the silence and fear that prejudice, stigma, stereotype, traditional beliefs,

[47] Patricia Smith, 'Four Themes in Feminist Legal Theory: Difference, Dominance, Domesticity, and Denial' in Martin P Golding and William A Edmundson (eds), *The Blackwell Guide to the Philosophy of Law and Legal Theory* (Blackwell Pub 2005) 3.

[48] Fynn Bruey, 'Systematic Gender Violence and the Rule of Law: Aboriginal Communities in Australia and Post-War Liberia' (n 3) 227–228.

[49] Veronica Fynn Bruey, 'Human Trafficking and the Law in Canada' in Elisha Jasper Dung and Augustine Avwunudiogba (eds), *Human trafficking: Global History and Perspectives* (Lexington Books 2021) 110–111.

and religion imposed by speaking out/up.[50] 'Speak-outs' or 'speak-ups' are transgressive in that they challenge conventional arrangements and are presumed antithetical to the dominant discourse (e.g., abortion is a shameful act and should not be spoken of in public).[51] Speaking out/up notifies male oppressors of young women's refusal to be muzzled while alerting the wider society of the injustice, trauma, abuse, and violation they suffered as a result of illegal and unsafe abortion practices. To preclude marginalised girls and women who dare to speak out/up requires carefully examining where the impetus to speak originates and what power relations and domination exist between the one speaking out/up and the one to whom the disclosure is directed.[52] The need to speak out/up is about enabling Liberian girls and women to make the transition from being so-called passive victims of systemic violence to becoming active advocates of reproductive rights and gender justice.

7.2.3 *(Inter)national Instruments for Protecting Girls' and Women's Reproductive Rights in Liberia*

Enacting laws domestically, regionally, and internationally to protect the reproductive health rights of girls and women is critical to the survival of the strength of the enforceability of such laws. Liberia is yet to have the (il)legality of abortion adjudicated in the court of law.[53] Also, the Liberian Constitution does not include a provision that 'guarantees the right to the highest attainable standard of health, including reproductive health'. Notwithstanding, Liberia does have an obligation under inter(national) law and other local policy framework to protect girls' and women's reproductive rights to safe abortion. As one of the original 50 countries (one of two from Africa) to sign the *UN Charter* on 26 June 1945, the Republic of Liberia must uphold the *Universal Declaration of Human Rights*,

[50] Veronica Fynn Bruey (ed), *Patriarchy and Gender in Africa* (Lexington Books 2021) 198.

[51] Linda Alcoff and Laura Gray, 'Survivor Discourse: Transgression or Recuperation?' (1993) 18 Signs: Journal of Women in Culture and Society 260, 260, 267–268.

[52] Ibid 284.

[53] Malawi is one of very few African countries to adjudicate abortion publicly in the court of law. *See, The State (On the Application by HM (Guardian) on behalf of CM (Minor) v The Hospital Director of Queen Elizabeth Central Hospital & The Minister of Health*, 2021).

1948, although it is not legally binding under customary international law. Article 1 of the Universal Declaration states, '[a]ll human beings are born free and equal in dignity and rights. They are endowed with reason and conscience and should act towards one another in a spirit of [sisterhood].' Liberia ratified the *African Charter on Human and Peoples' Rights*, 1981 (hereafter the Banjul Charter) on 29 December 1987.

The Banjul Charter guarantees enjoyment of the rights and freedom without distinction to ethnic group, sex, religion, *inter alia*[54] equal protection of the law[55] right to life (*see* article 4); and prohibition of torture and cruel, inhuman, and degrading treatment.[56] Liberia is signatory to the *International Covenant on Civil and Political Rights,* 1966[57]; the *International Covenant on Economic, Social and Cultural Rights*, 1966[58]; the *Convention on the Elimination of All Forms of Discrimination against Women*, 1979[59]; the *Convention on the Rights of the Child*, 1990 and its *Optional Protocol*[60]; and *Convention against Torture and Other Cruel Inhuman or Degrading Treatment or Punishment*, 1984 (*see* article 1).[61] Regionally, Liberia has also signed the *African Charter on the Rights and Welfare of the Child*, 1990,[62] and the *Protocol to the African Charter on Human and Peoples' Rights on the Rights of Women in Africa*, 2003 (or the Maputo Protocol).[63]

At the national level, even though chapter three of the *Liberian Constitution*, 1986 enshrines citizens' fundamental rights to equal protection under the law, life, security of person, *inter alia*, Section 16.3 (1) and

[54] *See* article 2 of the Banjul Charter.

[55] *See* article 3 of the Banjul Charter.

[56] *See* article 5 of the Banjul Charter.

[57] Signed on 18 April 1967 and ratified on 22 September 2004. Also see, article 7 of the Banjul Charter.

[58] Signed on 18 April 1967 and ratified on 22 September 2004. Also *see* articles 3 and 12 of the Banjul Charter.

[59] Ratified on 17 July 1984. Also *see* articles 4 and 5 of the Banjul Charter.

[60] Signed on 26 April 1990 and ratified on 04 June 1993. Also *see* articles 3, 4, 6, 10, 19, 37, 39 *inter alia* of the Banjul Charter.

[61] Ratified on 22 September 2004.

[62] Signed on 14 May 1992 and ratified on 01 August 2007. Also *see* articles 3, 4, 11, 14, 15, 16, 21, 27, 29, *inter alia*.

[63] Signed 12 December 2003 and ratified on 14 December 2007. Also *see* articles 2, 3, 4, 5, 6, 8, 12, 13, 14, 18, *inter alia* of the Banjul Charter.

(2) of the *Liberian Penal Code*, 1976 criminalises abortion except when the termination of the pregnancy is performed by a licensed physician '...if he believes there is substantial risk that continuance of the pregnancy would gravely impair the physical or mental health of the mother or that the child would be born with grave physical or mental defect, or that the pregnancy resulted from rape, incest, or other felonious intercourse Article 16 (3) of the *Liberian Penal Code* deems '[n]o abortion shall be performed in Liberia unless two physicians, one of whom may be the person performing the abortion, shall have certified in writing the circumstances which they believe to justify the abortion'. Not only is this law unenforceable it is also unrealistic. In Liberia, where the patient–doctor ratio is 1:15,000, it is impossible for most girls or women, especially those in rural Liberia, to have any access to a medical facility, let alone to have two certifying medical personnel justifying with one certified physician performing a legal abortion.

Other national laws pertinent to girls' and women's reproductive rights include but are not limited to the *Public Health Law*, 1976 which protects Liberians' health through preventive health measures). The *Ministry of Health and Social Welfare Act*, 1972 prevents and abates conditions hazardous to public health). The *Ministry of Health Act*, 2015 moves away from primary care, emphasising secondary and tertiary care for all Liberians. The *Ministry of Gender and Development Act*, 2001 seeks to enhance and protect women's rights). The *Ministry of Gender, Children and Social Protection Act*, 2013 mainstreams government-wide efforts to ensure gender equality and empowerment of women and development of children.[64] Additionally, the *Children's Law*, 2011 facilitates the respect, protection, promotion, and provision of the realisation of child rights in order to make maximum contribution to the survival, development, participation, and protection of every child in Liberia. The *Mental Health Act*, 2017 provides for and protects the civil, social, and health rights of all persons with mental disorders and promotes and regulates equitable and effective access to mental health care, treatment, habituation, and rehabilitation for all persons in Liberia.[65]

64 Veronica Fynn Bruey, 'The Liberian Public Health System', *Liberia in the Twenty-First Century: Issues and Perspectives* (Nova Science Publishers 2019) 217–221.

65 Ibid 224–226.

Policy-wise, the *Basic Package of Health Services*, 2008[66] was created on the fundamental principles of primary health care (i.e., prevention of disease and ill-health) and decentralisation of health services management to target maternal, child, adolescent, reproductive, mental health, communicable disease control, and emergency care. The *National Health Policy Plan*, 2011[67] is the first-ever *National Health and Social Welfare Financing Policy and Plan,* established in 2007 to supervise and standardise the finances to implement the National Health and Social Welfare Policy and Plan, 2011–2021.[68] Of significance is the *Investment Case for Reproductive, Maternal, Newborn, Child, and Adolescent Health mentioned above*, 2016–2020.[69] The 86-page strategic roadmap embarks on a journey to transform Liberia's collapsed healthcare delivery system to improve maternal health in the face of the Ebola Virus Disease crisis and the COVID-19 pandemic. Liberia affirms its responsibility as signatory to United Nations' Sustainable Development Goals 2030 (SDGs); Every Woman, Every Child Initiative; Family Planning 2020; African Health Strategy; Paris Declaration; Maputo Call to Action; and the UN Secretary General's Global Strategy for Reproductive, Maternal, Newborn, Child, and Adolescent Accountability and Results by commitment of at least 10 per cent of the health sector to reproductive, maternal, newborn, child, and adolescent health. Noteworthy, Liberia has no specific law on reproductive health, medical health/health care, or abortion.

As Liberia is an economically deprived society, with an overburdened healthcare system still struggling to provide universal access to basic health needs in the post-war reconstruction period, pursuing legal recourse through the court systems is not a primary option for many girls and women seeking justice for violation of their reproductive rights. In the absence of expensive court proceedings, with no guarantee to a remedy, the government of Liberia, precisely, the Ministry of Health

[66] Government of Liberia, 'Basic Package of Health and Social Welfare Services for Liberia' (Ministry of Health and Social Welfare 2008) Government Policy <http://www.basics.org/documents/Basic-Package-of-Health-and-Social-Welfare-Services_Liberia.pdf>.

[67] Ministry of Health and Social Welfare, 'National Health Policy on Contracting 2008–2011' <http://liberiamohsw.org/Policies%20&%20Plans/Contracting%20policy%20doc_MOHSW_%20Oct.%2014%20-%2008.doc> accessed 7 February 2017.

[68] Fynn Bruey, 'Liberia in the Twenty-First Century' (n 64) 226–228.

[69] Government of Liberia (n 7).

and Social Welfare, the Ministry of Gender, Children, and Social Protection; Ministry of Education, and Ministry of Internal Affairs could fulfil their collective goals by scaling up equitable access to (sexual and reproductive health) education, family planning, and safe abortion services. Drawing on both international and national legal instruments, emphasis must be placed on adolescent and teenage girls and women in rural communities outside of Monrovia since they are at a higher risk of female genital cutting, trafficking in persons, illiteracy, child abuse/labour, child marriages, statutory rape, incest, unsafe abortion, and maternal mortality.

7.3 Anecdotes and Reported Studies: Some Points for Discussion

In 2017, a study conducted in Liberia used satellite imagery and Global Positioning System (GPS) locators to randomly select 1381 households and randomly sampled 475 women between the ages of 18–30.[70] Preserving their anonymity, women responded to questions about their sexual histories. The research results showed that more than half of the respondents engaged in transactional sex, more than 75 per cent with UN personnel.[71] This research finding raises serious concern about Liberia's ability to achieve the UN SDG's goal #5 when the establishing institution continues to sabotage its own agenda by being the perpetrator of violence against girls and women. Unsafe abortion and the consequential high prevalence of maternal mortality rate is explicit violence against girls and women in Liberia.

As noted elsewhere, empirical studies about (unsafe) abortion in Liberia are at best scanty. The recent study conducted in 2021 was carried out on the 358,612 inhabitants of Lofa county in Liberia, of whom 23 per cent (82,480) are women of reproductive age, and is the only research that infer presentation events likely tied to fatal abortion outcomes.[72] The cumulative number of women who attended antenatal care between the years 2015 to 2017 was 7539, where 57 out of 59 health facilities in the county provide reproductive and maternal health services.[73] In Lofa

[70] Beber et al. (n 36) 1.

[71] Ibid.

[72] Alpha et al. (n 32).

[73] Ibid.

county, only one referral hospital (i.e., a hospital with a lot more resources to take on emergency and non-emergency care) has an obstetric specialist, with two obstetric technicians; the rest of the hospitals have two medical doctors a piece, both of whom are general practitioners.[74] There are no other gynaecological/obstetric specialists or technicians apart from those assigned to the referral hospital. Findings from the study analysis show the overall maternal mortality rate in Lofa county for the three-year period was 142 per 100,000 live births, with the highest being 615 per 100,000 live births, recorded in May 2016.[75] Although, reproductive and maternal health care is provided in 98 per cent of health facilities, there is incongruence between the care and the relatively high maternal mortality rate, which without doubt includes death caused by unsafe abortion.

The major cause of maternal death includes post-partum haemorrhage (37 per cent), sepsis (22 per cent), ruptured uterus (13 per cent), eclampsia (hypertension) (8 per cent), and abortion (8 per cent). Women with no formal education accounted for 74 per cent (i.e., 34/46) of maternal deaths.[76] Generally, 'three delays' are documented as major contributing factors to maternal mortality: (1) delay in deciding to seek appropriate medical help, (2) delay in reaching an appropriate medical facility, and (3) delay in receiving adequate care when a facility is reached.[77] Lofa County, located northwest in rural Liberia, is 357.3 km from Monrovia, the capital city is neglected and underserved, and thus neatly fits the description of the three delays.

The story of Mamie Tarr, taken off the Deeply Humanitarian news blog, epitomises the gut-wrenching situation of most girls and women seeking abortion services in Liberia.

> ...during Liberia's Ebola outbreak, Mamie Tarr began hemorrhaging. When she arrived at the clinic, clutching her abdomen and complaining of intense pain, health workers at first suspected Ebola. In fact, without telling her family, the 30-year-old had visited a backstreet abortionist who used a combination of herbs, chalk and a rusty syringe to terminate her five-month pregnancy. At the time, Mamie's husband, Edwin, was sick. "My wife saw me being carried to the Ebola treatment center as a suspected

[74] Ibid.

[75] Ibid.

[76] Ibid.

[77] Ibid.

> Ebola case, and she thought I was going to die," he said. "She got scared about raising the child without me, so she spoiled her belly. Then she just closed her mouth, she said nothing, until she started bleeding." Edwin was released from the Ebola treatment center without ever testing positive for the virus, but Mamie died from complications of the botched abortion.[78]

The final study to highlight the traumatising and deadly lived experiences of many girls and women in Liberia is a study done by the Planned Parenthood Association of Liberia, with support from the Foundation for Women's Health, Research and Development in the United Kingdom. *In Their Own Words: Girls from Liberia on Sexuality, Pregnancy and Services* reflects the lives of girls and women living in the squalor of Monrovia and their daily challenges as pregnant teenagers and mothers. The following quotations from the report are extracted from training and research conducted by the Planned Parenthood Association of Liberia[79]:

> A girl began having sex at the age of 14 and she got pregnant because she had no information from her parents and others, so she ended up going to her friend to get an abortion and it caused a rupture of her womb. (p. 35)

> Most girls will try an abortion as the first stop anyway and some are successful at getting rid of the baby. They will pay someone to help them with this or they will just take some remedy for it at home—sometimes it ruins their stomach and womb, sometimes they even die from this. (p. 35)

> They use country herbs, special portions, all types of things. They also use the special chalk, they put it inside themselves, sometimes they put it in by themselves, sometimes the boyfriend will put it on his penis to insert it, other times it will be the traditional healer that will put it on his penis for you. Other people use a mixture of ground cassava leaves, ground up glass bottles, and mix with blue (bleach for clothes) and they drink it. It damages you so much it even kills you. But they will have to do it anyway. (p. 35)

[78] Thomas (n 14).

[79] Foundation for Women's Health, Research and Development and International Planned Parenthood Federation, 'In Their Own Words: Girls from Liberia on Sexuality, Pregnancy and Services' (International Planned Parenthood Federation 2012) <https://www.forwarduk.org.uk/wp-content/uploads/2019/06/Girls-from-Liberia-on-Sexuality-Pregnancy-and-Services.pdf>.

> The bad thing is that whenever you are affected with or by something and go for services the people there will talk to you very bad or even curse you before tending to you. (p. 37)

> If you are young and pregnant, nurses can make you feel so bad, they can even beat you. There are some kind nurses but very few. Most are mean, they are old and they talk at you and beat you. (p. 37)

> There was a 12-year-old girl in my community who got pregnant but when she went to deliver her and the baby died in the process. All of the midwives said that the girl was too small to make it through. (p. 38)

> ...When her parents finally found out about it (pregnancy) they decided to let her keep the pregnancy but she died in childbirth anyway, so that was her end. (p. 38)

> ...She was struggling through the pregnancy because there wasn't enough money to support her. She gave birth to the baby and because there were not enough funds to support her and the baby, the child was not taken care of properly. The baby was very sickly and, in the end, died. (p. 38)

7.4 Conclusion: Recommendation for Protection and Prevention

The illegality of abortion in Liberia makes it unsafe. In addition, the lack of health services and providers targeting the reproductive health needs of girls and women put them at greater risk for maternal and child mortality. While it is argued that the problem of abortion is more philosophical than jurisprudential,[80] this chapter discusses the life-and-death situation Liberian girls and women, particularly adolescent and teenage girls in rural communities, face each day when it comes to their reproductive health rights. This chapter calls for a more humane and compassionate approach to treating girls and women as equal agents of change, capable of making decisions and exercising control over their bodies. Disrupting patriarchal forces that arm boys and men with the power to exploit and abuse girls and women, compelling them to risk

[80] Mohammad Rasekh, 'The Problem of Abortion: Jurisprudential or Philosophical?' (2005) 16 Islam and Christian—Muslim Relations 251, 251.

their survival, leaving them with only the option of becoming a single parent, is critical for protecting girls' and women's reproductive rights and ensuring sustainable development.

Without access to hard evidence on the ground, it is challenging to assess Liberia's progress with respect to achieving its reproductive, maternal, newborn, child, and adolescent health targets in line with SDGs goal #3. However, with the Ebola Virus Disease crisis in 2014–2015 and now the Covid-19 pandemic, it is safe to assume that there are significant barriers to implementing the strategic plans of the *Investment Case for Reproductive, Maternal, Newborn, Child and Adolescent Health*, 2016–2020.

Finally, seeking justice for the violation of girls' and women's reproductive rights in Liberia is a progressive realisation; the government of Liberia must continue to prioritise primary care health measures by providing equitable access to (sexual and reproductive health) education, family planning, and safe abortion services for girls and women in rural Liberia. Honouring their responsibility under international, regional, and national laws, the government of Liberia must address the issue of sexual abuse and exploitation by UN humanitarian/aid workers, female genital cutting, trafficking of girls, parental neglect/abuse, child abuse/labour, child marriages, statutory rape, and incest, which are major contributing factors, resulting in the high prevalence of unsafe abortion practices, and hence, maternal mortality.

Bibliography

Primary Resources

International Law

Convention against Torture and Other Cruel Inhuman or Degrading Treatment or Punishment, 1984.

Convention on the Elimination of All Forms of Discrimination against Women, 1979.

Convention on the Rights of the Child, 1990.

International Covenant on Civil and Political Rights, 1966.

International Covenant on Economic, Social and Cultural Rights, 1966.

Protocol to the African Charter on Human and Peoples' Rights on the Rights of Women in Africa, 2003.

UN Charter, 1945.

Universal Declaration of Human Rights, 1948.

Regional Instruments

African Charter on Human and Peoples' Rights, 1981.
African Charter on the Rights and Welfare of the Child, 1990.

Domestic Statutes

Children's Law, 2011.
Liberian Constitution, 1986.
Liberian Penal Code, 1976.
Mental Health Act, 2017.
Ministry of Gender, Children and Social Protection Act, 2013.
Ministry of Gender and Development Act, 2001.
Ministry of Health Act, 2015.
Ministry of Health and Social Welfare Act, 1972.
Public Health Law, 1976.

Case Law

Roe v Wade, 1973.
The State (On the Application by HM (Guardian) on behalf of CM (Minor) vs The Hospital Director of Queen Elizabeth Central Hospital & The Minister of Health: Judicial Review Cause Number 03 of 2021 (unreported) (High Court of Malawi, Zomba District Registry) Decision of 15 June 2021.

Secondary Resources

Alcoff L and Gray L, 'Survivor Discourse: Transgression or Recuperation?' (1993) 18 Signs: Journal of Women in Culture and Society 260.
Alexis G, 'Child Prostitution: Inadequate Responses by the Church' (Master of Arts, Liberty University 2016) <https://digitalcommons.liberty.edu/cgi/viewcontent.cgi?article=1417&context=masters>.
Alpha TS et al., 'Review of Maternal Deaths in Lofa County, Liberia, 2015–2017' (2021) 4 Journal of Interventional Epidemiology and Public Health 6.
Alves C and Rapp A, 'Spontaneous Abortion', *StatPearls* (StatPearls Publishing 2021) <http://www.ncbi.nlm.nih.gov/books/NBK560521/> accessed 24 November 2021.
Azikiwe N, *Liberia in World Politics* (University of Michigan 1934).
Bartlett KT, 'Feminist Legal Methods' (1990) 103 Harvard Law Review 829.

Batha E, 'Liberia Bans Female Genital Mutilation—But Only for a Year' *Reuters* (Monrovia, Liberia, 25 January 2018) <https://www.reuters.com/article/us-liberia-fgm-law/liberia-bans-female-genital-mutilation-but-only-for-a-year-idUSKBN1FE1N7> accessed 18 April 2018.

Bearak J et al., 'Unintended Pregnancy and Abortion by Income, Region, and the Legal Status of Abortion: Estimates from a Comprehensive Model for 1990–2019' (2020) 8 The Lancet Global Health e1152.

Beber B et al., 'Peacekeeping, Compliance with International Norms, and Transactional Sex in Monrovia, Liberia' (2017) 71 International Organization 1.

Beyan AJ, 'Transatlantic Trade and the Coastal Area of Pre-Liberia' (1995) 57 The Historian 757.

Boesen JK and Martin T, *Applying a Rights-Based Approach: An Inspirational Guide for Civil Society* (Danish Institute for Human Rights 2007).

Bright NO, *Liberia: America's Stepchild* (Grain Coast Productions 2002) <http://www.pbs.org/wgbh/globalconnections/liberia/film/overview.html>.

Cavanaugh R, 'Discovery of 1821 Document Sheds Light on Liberia Purchase—The Washington Post' *Washington Post* (Washington, DC, 20 November 2021) <https://www.washingtonpost.com/history/2021/11/20/liberia-purchase-agreement-1821-burrowes/> accessed 20 November 2021.

Dunn DE, *A History of the Episcopal Church in Liberia, 1821–1980* (American Theological Library Association and The Scarecrow Press 1992).

Foundation for Women's Health, Research and Development and International Planned Parenthood Federation, 'In Their Own Words: Girls from Liberia on Sexuality, Pregnancy and Services' (International Planned Parenthood Federation 2012) <https://www.forwarduk.org.uk/wp-content/uploads/2019/06/Girls-from-Liberia-on-Sexuality-Pregnancy-and-Services.pdf>.

Freedman R, Blakemore S and Barker C, 'Safeguarding Children from UN Peacekeeper Sexual Exploitation and Abuse in Liberia' (Keeping Children Safe 2017) <https://research.reading.ac.uk/safeguarding-children/wp-content/uploads/sites/56/Unorganized/KCS_LiberiaReport_web_112018.pdf>.

Fynn Bruey V, 'Systematic Gender Violence and the Rule of Law: Aboriginal Communities in Australia and Post-War Liberia' (PhD Thesis, The Australian National University 2016) <https://openresearch-repository.anu.edu.au/handle/1885/159520>.

Fynn Bruey V, 'Indigenous Women and International Law', *Research Handbook on Feminist Engagement with International Law* (Edward Elgar 2019).

Fynn Bruey V, 'Maternal and Reproductive Rights: Ebola and the Law in Liberia' in Sharon A Abramowitz, Julienne Ngoundoung Anoko and David A Schwartz (eds), *Pregnant in the Time of Ebola: Women and Their Children in*

the 2013–2015 West African Epidemic (1st ed. 2019, Springer International Publishing: Imprint: Springer 2019).
Fynn Bruey V, 'The Liberian Public Health System', *Liberia in the twenty-first century: issues and perspectives* (Nova Science Publishers 2019).
Fynn Bruey V, 'Human Trafficking and the Law in Canada' in Elisha Jasper Dung and Augustine Avwunudiogba (eds), *Human trafficking: Global History and Perspectives* (Lexington Books 2021).
Fynn Bruey V, (ed), *Patriarchy and Gender in Africa* (Lexington Books 2021).
Gaber A, 'Liberia Adopts Yale Capstone Recommendations for Medical Education Reform' *YaleNews* (New Haven, CT, 30 April 2018) <https://news.yale.edu/2018/04/30/liberia-adopts-yale-capstone-recommendations-medical-education-reform> accessed 18 October 2021.
Ganatra B et al., 'From Concept to Measurement: Operationalizing WHO's Definition of Unsafe Abortion' (2014) 92 Bulletin of the World Health Organization 155.
Ganatra B et al., 'Global, Regional, and Subregional Classification of Abortions by Safety, 2010–14: Estimates from a Bayesian Hierarchical Model' (2017) 390 The Lancet 2372.
Government of Liberia, 'Basic Package of Health and Social Welfare Services for Liberia' (Ministry of Health and Social Welfare 2008) Government Policy <http://www.basics.org/documents/Basic-Package-of-Health-and-Social-Welfare-Services_Liberia.pdf>.
Government of Liberia, 'Investment Case for Reproductive, Maternal, Newborn, Child and Adolescent Health, 2016–2020' (Ministry of Health and Social Welfare 2016) Government Report <https://www.globalfinancingfacility.org/sites/gff_new/files/documents/Liberia%20RMNCAH%20Investment%20Case%202016%20-%202020.pdf>.
Greasley K, *Arguments About Abortion: Personhood, Morality, and Law* (1st edn, Oxford University Press 2017).
Guannu JS, *Liberian History Before 1857: A Reference for Elementary Pupils* (1st edn, Exposition Press 1977).
Haddad LB and Nour NM, 'Unsafe Abortion: Unnecessary Maternal Mortality' (2009) 2 Reviews in Obstetrics & Gynecology 122.
International Federation of Gynecology and Obstetric, 'Induced Abortion—An Overview | ScienceDirect Topics', *International Encyclopaedia of Public Health* (ScienceDirect 2008) <https://www.sciencedirect.com/topics/medicine-and-dentistry/induced-abortion> accessed 24 November 2021.
Jaye T, 'The Security Culture of the ECOWAS: Origins, Development and the Challenge of Child Trafficking' (2008) 26 Journal of Contemporary African Studies 151.

Karmbor-Ballah EG et al., 'Maternal Mortality and the Metempsychosis of User Fees in Liberia: A Mixed-Methods Analysis' (2019) 3 Scientific African e00050.

Karnga A, *History of Liberia* (D H Tyte 1926).

Kesselly RY et al., 'The Status of Health Services in the 15 Counties of Liberia' (2018) Volume X South Eastern European Journal of Public Health (SEEJPH) 2018.

Kissling F, 'Religion and Abortion: Roman Catholicism Lost in the Pelvic Zone' (1993) 3 Women's Health Issues 132.

Laaser U et al., 'Delays in Achieving Maternal, Newborn, and Child Health Targets for 2021 and 2030 in Liberia' (2019) 7 Frontiers in Public Health 386.

Liberia Institute of Statistics and Geo-Information Services, 'National Population and Housing Census' (Liberia Institute of Statistics and Geo-Information Services 2009) Government Report.

Liberia Institute of Statistics and Geo-Information Services, '2008 Population and Housing Census: Final Results' (Liberia Institute of Statistics and Geo-Information Services 2009) Government.

Marcelo P, 'Rebuilding Liberia: Child Soldiers and the Youth Problem in Liberia' (*providencejournal.com*, 1 August 2013) <http://www.providencejournal.com/article/20130801/SPECIAL-REPORTS/308019903> accessed 31 August 2016.

Massing AW, 'An Inferential History of Pre-Liberia, 1460–1490: Mapping Liberia—A Conjectural History of Early Liberia' (German Technical Corporation (GTZ), Monrovia, Liberia, 23 March 2007) <http://www.onliberia.org/A%20conjectural%20history%20of%20early%20Liberia.ppt>.

McEvoy FD, 'Some Proposals for Liberian Archaeology' (1970) 111 Liberian Studies Journal 129.

Ministry of Health and Social Welfare, 'National Health Policy on Contracting 2008–2011' <http://liberiamohsw.org/Policies%20&%20Plans/Contracting%20policy%20doc_MOHSW_%20Oct.%2014%20-%2008.doc> accessed 7 February 2017.

Mohamed F, 'Justice for Ruth Berry Peal, Who Was Forcibly Mutilated in Liberia, but Still No Ban on FGM' *Independent* (Monrovia, Liberia, 8 April 2013) <https://www.independent.co.uk/voices/comment/justice-for-ruth-berry-peal-who-was-forcibly-mutilated-in-liberia-but-still-no-ban-on-fgm-8564214.html> accessed 26 November 2021.

Momin S, 'A Human Rights Based Approach to Refugees: A Look at the Syrian Refugee Crisis and the Responses from Germany and the United States' (2017) 9 Duke Forum for Law & Social Change 55.

Nmoma V, 'The Civil War and the Refugee Crisis in Liberia' (1997) XVII 1997.

Owolabi O, 'Towards Improving the Measurement of Unsafe Abortion: Substantive Estimates and Methodological Insights from Zambia.' (PhD Thesis, London School of Hygiene and Tropical Medicine 2017) <http://researchonline.lshtm.ac.uk/id/eprint/3548894> accessed 24 November 2021.

Paye-Layeh J and Petesch C, 'Peacekeepers Left More than 6,000 Children in Liberia' *AP NEWS* (Monrovia, Liberia, 21 November 2018) <https://apnews.com/article/monrovia-ap-top-news-africa-international-news-west-africa-ccbbddfcab8f45d48d0d3b40a81dbf3d> accessed 26 November 2021.

Rasekh M, 'Battle of Life: A Brief Study of Theories on Abortion' (2003) 4 Journal of Reproduction and Infertility 220.

Rasekh M, 'The Problem of Abortion: Jurisprudential or Philosophical?' (2005) 16 Islam and Christian—Muslim Relations 251.

Rouse L, 'Africa's COVID Threat Hits "New Level" as Delta Variant Spreads' *Al Jazeera* (Monrovia, Liberia, 1 July 2021) <https://www.aljazeera.com/news/2021/7/1/africa-covid-threat-hits-new-level-delta-variant-spreads> accessed 27 November 2021.

Ruiz-Casares M, 'Child Protection Knowledge, Attitudes, and Practices in Central and Western Liberia' (USAID and Save the Children 2011) <https://bettercarenetwork.org/sites/default/files/2020-09/kap_finalreport_2011_8appendices_v2.1.pdf>.

Save the Children UK, 'From Camp to Community: Liberia Study on Exploitation of Children' (Save the Children—UK 2006) <https://resourcecentre.savethechildren.net/pdf/save_uk_liberia.pdf/>.

Sawyer A, *The Emergence of Autocracy in Liberia: Tragedy and Challenge* (Institute for Contemporary Studies 1992).

Sieh R, 'Liberia: More Than 600 Cases of Rape, Sodomy, Abuses During COVID-19 State of Emergency' *FrontPage Africa* (Monrovia, Liberia, 13 July 2020) <https://frontpageafricaonline.com/front-slider/liberia-more-than-600-cases-of-rape-sodomy-abuses-during-covid-19-state-of-emergency/> accessed 18 October 2021.

Smith P, 'Four Themes in Feminist Legal Theory: Difference, Dominance, Domesticity, and Denial' in Martin P Golding and William A Edmundson (eds), *The Blackwell Guide to the Philosophy of Law and Legal Theory* (Blackwell Pub 2005).

Staff Reporter, 'Liberia's Catholic Bishops Against Abortion, Same Sex Marriage' *FrontPage Africa* (Monrovia, Liberia, 12 April 2016) <https://frontpageafricaonline.com/politics/liberia-s-catholic-bishops-against-abortion-same-sex-marriage/> accessed 23 November 2021.

Strong AE and Schwartz DA, 'Effects of the West African Ebola Epidemic on Health Care of Pregnant Women: Stigmatization with and without Infection' in David A Schwartz, Julienne Ngoundoung Anoko and Sharon A Abramowitz (eds), *Pregnant in the Time of Ebola* (Springer International

Publishing 2019) <http://link.springer.com/10.1007/978-3-319-97637-2_2> accessed 17 November 2021.

Tate T, 'How to Fight, How to Kill: Child Soldiers in Liberia' (Human Rights Watch 2004) NGO Report Vol 16, No 2 (A) <https://www.hrw.org/reports/2004/liberia0204/liberia0204.pdf>.

Thomas K, '"Spoiling the Belly": The Dangers of Backstreet Abortions in Liberia' *Women and Girls* (New York, NY, 2017) <https://deeply.thenewhumanitarian.org/womenandgirls/articles/2017/04/21/spoiling-the-belly-the-dangers-of-backstreet-abortions-in-liberia> accessed 17 November 2021.

UNICEF, 'Liberia—Demographics, Health & Infant Mortality' (*Country Profile*, 2019) <https://data.unicef.org/country/lbr/#> accessed 21 November 2021.

UNICEF-Liberia, 'Child Protection' (*Programme*, 2016) <https://www.unicef.org/liberia/child-protection> accessed 26 November 2021.

UNICEF-Liberia, 'Child, Maternal and Newborn Health' (*Maternal and Newborn Health*, 2018) <https://www.unicef.org/liberia/child-maternal-and-newborn-health> accessed 18 October 2021.

United Nations High Commission for Human Rights, 'Liberia: Strategies & Program' <http://www.unhcr.org/home/PROTECTION/43eb16254.pdf> accessed 15 December 2011.

United Nations High Commissioner for Refugees and Save the Children UK, 'Sexual Violence and Exploitation: The Experience of Refugee Children in Guinea, Liberia and Sierra Leone—Based on Initial Findings and Recommendations from Assessment Mission 22 October–30 November 2001' (United Nations High Commission for Refugees 2002) UN Report <https://www.savethechildren.org.uk/sites/default/files/docs/sexual_violence_and_exploitation_1.pdf>.

United Nations Secretariat, 'Special Measures for Protection from Sexual Exploitation and Sexual Abuse' (United Nations 2003) UN Document ST/SGB/2003/13 <https://content.unops.org/service-Line-Documents/IAIG/ST-SGB-2003-13_EN.pdf>.

World Bank, 'Life Expectancy at Birth, Total (Years)—Liberia' (*Data*, 2021) <https://data.worldbank.org/indicator/SP.DYN.LE00.IN?locations=LR> accessed 23 November 2021.

World Health Organisation, 'The Prevention and Management of Unsafe Abortion: Report of the Technical Working Group, Geneva 12–15 April 1992' (World Health Organisation 1993).

World Health Organisation, 'Preventing Unsafe Abortion' (*Key Facts*, 25 September 2020) <https://www.who.int/news-room/fact-sheets/detail/preventing-unsafe-abortion> accessed 25 November 2021.

Yaya S et al., 'Maternal Health Care Service Utilization in Post-War Liberia: Analysis of Nationally Representative Cross-Sectional Household Surveys' (2019) 19 BMC Public Health 28 <https://bmcpublichealth.biomedcentral.com/articles/10.1186/s12889-018-6365-x> accessed 16 November 2021.

PART III

Assisted Reproductive Technologies

CHAPTER 8

Reproductive Health Rights and the Regulation of Assisted Reproductive Technologies (Art) Services in Nigeria

Grace Titilayo Kolawole-Amao

8.1 Introduction

Reproduction is a natural phenomenon of every living thing, humanity inclusive. As humans, there are rights that accrue because we are humans. In other words, by being human everyone has human rights that cuts across every area of human existence. Thus, Thus, RHRs are rights that are very prime to human existence. With the drastic increase in the rate of infertility globally, and inventions of alternative methods in reproductive medicine, RHRs have become very imperative. Advancements which have made it possible for couples with infertility to experience biological reproduction is actually preferred to adoption, particularly in African setup because of the belief that bearing children is one of the important

G. T. Kolawole-Amao (✉)
Bowen University, Iwo, Osun State, Nigeria
e-mail: titilayoakinola@ymail.com

O. S. Adelakun and E. Ndoni (eds.), *Reproductive Health and Assisted Reproductive Technologies In Sub-Saharan Africa*,
Sustainable Development Goals Series,
https://doi.org/10.1007/978-981-99-2411-0_8

purposes of marriage. The development in reproductive medicine which paved way for Assisted Reproductive Technologies (ART) has given rise to RHRs issues both in its practice and in its service provision. Thus, in as much as ART has brought great relief in reproductive medicine, RHRs and how ART is regulated is an important aspect of ART practice that should be addressed to prevent abuses and violations of rights. This chapter examines RHRs and the regulation of ART practice in Nigeria.

8.2 Reproductive Health Rights in the Context of Human Rights

Human rights are rights that we have because we are humans. Human rights are pennants that recognise that the dignity of all human beings should be protected.[1] They are universal and **innate** to all persons, notwithstanding the nationality, sex, ethnic origin, colour, religion, language or any other status that may be in question.[2] There basic principles of human rights, first of which is its universality because everyone is equally entitled to his/her human rights. The principle of **universality** of human rights is the foundation of international human rights law and this was clearly accentuated in the Universal Declaration of Human Rights (UDHR) and many international human rights documents after it.[3] Secondly, human rights are inalienable. Generally, no one should be deprived of their human rights except in express cases stated by the law.[4] Lastly, human rights are regarded as indivisible and interdependent, i.e. human rights can only be enjoyed fully when they are inseparable. All rights are dependent on each other to be fully enjoyed.[5]

[1] 'What Are Human Rights?' (UNICEF) <https://www.unicef.org/child-rights-convention/what-are-human-rights> accessed 25 August 2021.

[2] 'What Are Human Rights?' (United Nations (UN) Human Rights) <https://www.ohchr.org/en/issues/pages/whatarehumanrights.aspx> accessed 25 August 2021.

[3] International Covenant on Civil and Political Rights (ICCPR); International Covenant on Economic, Social and Cultural Rights (ICESCR); Convention on the Rights of the Child (CRC); Convention on the Rights of Persons with Disabilities; Convention on the Elimination of All Forms of Discrimination against Women (CEDAW); Vienna Declaration and Programme of Action; Declaration on the Elimination of Violence against Women (DEVAW) etc.

[4] E.g., Section 45 of the 1999 Constitution of the Federal Republic of Nigeria states instances where fundamental rights can be derogatory.

[5] 'What Are Human Rights?' (United Nations (UN) Human Rights) (n. 2).

8.3 Reproductive Health Rights

Understating what RHRs are required an in-depth understating of the concept of reproductive health. According to the “International Conference on Population and Development (ICPD) Programme of Action”[6]:

> Reproductive health is a state of complete physical, mental and social well-being in all matters relating to the reproductive system and to its functions and processes.

In the opinion of “World Health Organization (WHO)”[7]:

> Reproductive health is a state of complete physical, mental and social well-being and not merely the absence of disease or infirmity, in all matters relating to the reproductive system and to its functions and processes.

Simply put, reproductive health implies that people are able to practice safe sex life as well as the capacity to reproduce and deciding when or how often to do so.[8] This requires informed choice and access to safe, effective, affordable and acceptable health-care services.[9] Reproductive health is concerned with all stages of human reproduction. Reproductive health implies that a person is free from the danger of sexually transmitted diseases, has the right to take decisions on his/her fertility with full access to the necessary information, and controlling his/her sexuality as he deems fit without discrimination on whatever grounds.[10] Thus, reproductive health is a whole wellness in terms of reproduction and the reproductive system of a person.

[6] ‘Programme of Action’ Adopted at the ICPD Cairo, 5–13 September 1994, p. 59. <https://www.unfpa.org/sites/default/files/pub-pdf/programme_of_action_Web%20ENGLISH.pdf> accessed 15 September 2021.

[7] ‘Reproductive Health in Western Pacific’ <https://www.who.int/westernpacific/health-topics/reproductive-health> accessed 15 September 2021.

[8] ‘Programme of Action of ICPD’, (n. 7).

[9] ‘Sexual and Reproductive Health and Rights: A Position Paper’ (Department for International development; 2004) p. 4. <https://www2.ohchr.org/english/issues/development/docs/rights_reproductive_health.pdf> accessed 15 September 2021.

[10] J.K. Meena, A. Verma, J. Kishore and G.K. Ingle, ‘Sexual and Reproductive Health: Knowledge, Attitude, and Perceptions among Young Unmarried Male Residents of Delhi’ (2015) *International Journal of Reproductive Medicine* 1 <https://doi.org/10.1155/2015/431460> accessed 15 September 2021.

RHRs can therefore be defined as the rights of a person to take decisions on different aspects of his/her reproductive health. RHRs are dependent on the recognition of rights of all persons to decide without discrimination on their reproductive ability such as deciding to have children, deciding the number of children and the time to have them, as well as adequate access to information on sexual and reproductive health as it is clearly stated in human rights documents[11] RHRs are founded on existing human rights recognised in international human rights law i.e. in treaties, conventions, declarations and other instruments. RHRs in other words, can be garnered from existing human rights that are provided for in national laws, international and regional documents on human rights and other human rights supporting documents. Thus, the discourse on reproductive health rights is incomplete if it occurs outside the ambit of human rights.

8.4 Reproductive Health Rights in International Human Rights Law

RHRs have come to be recognised as human rights at the international level. As earlier stated, RHRs are garnered from existing human rights provisions. In international human rights law (IHRL), RHRs consist of human rights recognised in existing conventions, treaties, declarations and other instruments. There is no specific human rights instrument on RHRs. Rather, the existing international and regional human rights instruments make provisions for the protection of the different aspects of reproductive rights.[12] In other words, "*it is clear that reproductive rights are not a new set of rights but a constellation of freedoms and entitlements that are already recognized in national laws, international human rights instruments and other consensus documents.*"[13] Thus, there are specific human rights relevant to reproductive health and are therefore referred to as RHRs. The following human rights can be said to collectively constitute RHRs:

[11] 'Programme of Action of ICPD' (n. 7) at p. 60.

[12] 'Reproductive Rights Are Human Rights: A Handbook for National Human Rights Institutions' (United Nations, 2014) p. 21. <https://www.ohchr.org/documents/publications/nhrihandbook.pdf> accessed 24 September 2021.

[13] Ibid.

8.4.1 Right to Life

The right to life is a fundamental right protected by numerous international documents.[14] Relating the right to life to reproductive health, it includes the right to prevent avoidable death, both of the mother and the child, during and after pregnancy and at childbirth. Thus, the right not to die from preventable pregnancy-related causes is a RHRs rooted in the right to life. In the report of the "Human Rights Council on its Eleventh Session", the report stated that WHO opined that maternal mortality is the leading cause of death among women and girls of reproductive age globally, while also recognising that preventable maternal mortality is a health and human rights challenge that requires the effective protection of the human rights of women and girls, in particular their rights to life.[15]

8.4.2 Right to Health

The right to health is also a key right recognised by numerous international documents.[16] Standard of living that will support good health and the well-being of every person is what the right to health entails e.g. food, clothing, shelter, medical care and information, necessary social services and security. The "*Right to the highest attainable standard of health*" is recognised as a crucial aspect of RHRs in IHRL. Health was defined in the "preamble of the 1946 Constitution of the WHO" "*as a state of complete physical, mental and social well-being and not merely the absence of disease or infirmity*".[17] The "Convention on the Elimination of All

[14] Article 3 of the Universal Declaration of Human Rights (UDHR); Article 6 of the International Covenant on Civil and Political Rights (ICCPR); Article 6 of the Convention on the Rights of the Child (CRC).

[15] United Nations (UN) General Assembly, 'Report of the Human Rights Council on its eleventh session (A/HRC/11/L.16/Rev.1. 16 October 2009)' p. 45. <https://undocs.org/pdf?symbol=en/A/HRC/11/37> accessed 24 September 2021.

[16] Article 25 of the UDHR; Article 12 of International Covenant on Economic, Social and Cultural Rights (ICESCR); Article 5 of International Convention on the Elimination of All Forms of Racial Discrimination (ICERD); Article 12 of Convention on the Elimination of All Forms of Discrimination Against Women (CEDAW); Article 24 of CRC; Article 25 of Convention on the Rights of Persons with Disabilities (CRPD).

[17] 'The Right to Health Fact Sheet No. 31 Office of the UN High Commissioner for Human Rights and World Health Organisation 1.

Forms of Discrimination against Women (CEDAW)" and the "International Covenant on Economic, Social and Cultural Rights (CESCR)" have both clearly opined that reproductive health falls within the ambit of the right to health.

8.4.3 Right to Liberty and Security

The Right to Liberty and Security of Person focuses on protecting every person's personal freedom and personal safety. RHRs have been affirmed to include the right to liberty and security of person which includes the freedom to control one's reproductive life. The right to liberty and security of person is provided for in IHRL by numerous international conventions, treaties and documents.[18] Principle 1 of ICPD Programme of Action recognises that everyone has the right to life, liberty and security of persons.[19] The ICPD Programme of Action further states that the right to make decisions concerning one's reproduction without discrimination is a human right.[20] The "Beijing Platform for Action" also clearly states that every woman has the right to control and decide on matters relating to her reproductive and sexual life as a component of her human rights.[21] Thus, existing human rights can be applied to and used to advocate for and against the reproductive health of persons e.g. focal abortion, forced sterilisation, laws of practices requiring special/parental consent for contraceptive or abortion, female genital mutilation, protection from unwanted medical intervention, etc.[22]

[18] Article 3 of UDHR; Article 9 of ICCPR; Article 14 of CRPD.

[19] 'Programme of Action of ICPD' (n. 7).

[20] Ibid.; paragraph 7.3 of the Programme of Action of ICPD (n. 7).

[21] Paragraph 96 of Beijing Platform for Action: "*The human rights of women include their right to have control over and decide freely and responsibly on matters related to their sexuality, including sexual and reproductive health, free of coercion, discrimination and violence.*" <https://www.unwomen.org/~/media/headquarters/attachments/sections/csw/pfa_e_final_web.pdf> accessed 5 October 2021.

[22] 'IPPF Charter Guidelines on Sexual and Reproductive Rights (International Planned Parenthood Federation 1997)' p. 7. <https://www.sm.ee/sites/default/files/content-editors/eesmargiEncd_ja_tegevused/Tervis/Tervislik_eluviis/ippf_charter_srh_rights_2003.pdf> accessed 5 October 2021.

8.4.4 Reproductive Right

Right to decide the number of spacing of children is a human right key to RHRs. It includes the right to make reproductive decisions and to make family planning choices.[23] There are international treaties and conventions that provide for this right.[24] The "Beijing Platform for Action" also affirms that reproductive rights encompass the right of a person to decide the number of children, timing and spacing.[25]

8.4.5 Right to Marry

Right to consensual to marriage and equality in marriage is also key to RHRs. Marriage is key to the reproduction of a person. The right of all persons to choose freely whether or not to marry and who to marry is a right that is crucial to RHRs. The right can be used to campaign against child marriage, forced pregnancy, forced sterilisation and can be used to argue for fair and unbiased reproductive health services.[26] International conventions, treaties and documents provide for this right.[27] The "Beijing Platform for Action" states that it is obligatory for governments to put law in place to ensure free and consensual marriage as well as minimum marriageable age to prevent the occurrence of child marriage.[28]

[23] Julia Gebhard and Diana Trimino, 'Reproductive Rights, International Regulation' (Max Planck Encyclopedia of Public Law, 2012). p. 2. <https://www.corteidh.or.cr/tablas/r16912.pdf> accessed 20 September 2021.

[24] Article 16(1) of CEDAW; Article 23(1) of CRPD; Principles 7.3, 7.12 and 8 Programme of Action of ICPD.

[25] Paragraph 223 of Beijing Platform for Action: "*...the Fourth World Conference on Women reaffirms that reproductive rights rest on the recognition of the basic right of all couples and individuals to decide freely and responsibly the number, spacing and timing of their children and to have the information and means to do so...*".

[26] 'IPPF Charter Guidelines on Sexual and Reproductive Rights' (n. 23) p. 12.

[27] Article 16 of UDHR; Article 23 of ICCPR; Article 10 of ICESCR; Article 16 of CEDAW; Article 23 of CRPD; Principle 9 of Programme of Action of ICPD.

[28] Paragraph 274 (e) of Beijing Platform for Action: Actions to be taken by Governments: "*Enact and strictly enforce laws to ensure that marriage is only entered into with the free and full consent of the intending spouses; in addition, enact and strictly enforce laws concerning the minimum legal age of consent and the minimum age for marriage and raise the minimum age for marriage where necessary*".

8.4.6 Right to Privacy

Right to Privacy includes the right to decide freely without arbitrary interference with one's reproductive functions. Right to privacy is linked to RHRs. The right to make decisions about one's reproductive life and to have the privacy to do so is also important in reproductive health. Thus, the right to medical confidentiality in a doctor-patient relationship stems from the right to privacy. The right to privacy can be an advocacy tool for reproductive health information and services with respect to the right to privacy and confidentiality as well as a tool against forced pregnancy, laws or practices requiring spousal/parental consent for contraception or abortion.[29] The "Beijing Platform of Action" also supports health services that support privacy and confidentiality of patients in any health-care procedure and that access to information on reproductive health should take into account privacy and confidentiality.[30]

8.4.7 Right to Equality

The Right to Equality and Non-Discrimination simply means that no person should be discriminated against in any area of life including reproductive health. The right to equality and non-discrimination entails that all persons are born equal and no one should be discriminated against on any grounds or status.[31] The "Vienna Declaration and Programme of Action" emphasise the importance of eradicating all forms of discrimination against women and the girl-child.[32] The "Beijing Platform for

[29] 'IPPF Charter Guidelines on Sexual and Reproductive Rights' (n. 23) p. 9.

[30] Paragraph 106 (f) of Beijing Platform of Action: Government should "*Redesign health information, services and training for health workers so that they are gender-sensitive and reflect the user's perspectives with regard to interpersonal and communications skills and the user's right to privacy and confidentiality...*"; Paragraph 107 (e) of Beijing Platform of Action: "*Prepare and disseminate accessible information, through public health campaigns, the media, reliable counselling and the education system, designed to ensure that women and men, particularly young people, can acquire knowledge about their health, especially information on sexuality and reproduction, taking into account the rights of the child to access to information, privacy, confidentiality, respect and informed consent...*".

[31] Article 2 of UDHR; Article 2 of ICCPR; Article 2 of ICESCR; Article 1 of CEDAW; Article 2 of CRC; Article 6 of CRPD; Principle 1 of ICPD Programme of Action; Paragraphs 4.4. and 7.45 of Programme of Action of ICPD.

[32] Paragraph 18 of the Vienna Declaration and Programme of Action (1993): "*The human rights of women and of the girl-child are an inalienable, integral and indivisible*

Action" also urges governments to put measures in place for the enjoyment of all human rights and freedoms for women and girls without barriers and discrimination and to ensure the promotion and protection of the full and equal enjoyment of all human rights by women and men.[33] Equality and non-discrimination is a core principle guiding the human rights system and the right is an anchor to the enjoyment and fulfilment of all other human rights.[34] Thus, the right to control one's fertility without discrimination can be said to be fundamental to the enjoyment of all other human rights.[35]

8.4.8 Freedom from Harmful Practices

The right to be free from practices that harm women and girls. Practices that harm women and girls' reproduction can be subsumed under this right and can be regarded as part of RHRs. Practices that are prejudicial to the women/girls' reproductive health should be prevented and it is a reproductive health right. International treaties, conventions and documents also recognise this right.[36]

8.4.9 Right Not to Be Subjected to Torture

The right not to be subjected to torture or cruel inhuman and degrading treatment is a crucial human right all persons are entitled to. This right is also linked to reproductive health and ensures that ethical professional standards and medical/scientific treatment conform to human rights and

part of universal human rights. The full and equal participation of women in political, civil, economic, social and cultural life, at the national, regional and international levels, and the eradication of all forms of discrimination on grounds of sex are priority objectives of the international community" <https://www.ohchr.org/en/professionalinterest/pages/vienna.aspx> accessed 21 October 2021.

[33] Paragraphs 32 and 232 (a) of Beijing Platform for Action.

[34] United Nations, 'Reproductive Rights Are Human Rights: A Handbook for National Human Rights Institutions' (United Nations, 2014). p. 90. <https://www.ohchr.org/documents/publications/nhrihandbook.pdf> accessed 24 September 2021.

[35] Cook Rebecca; 'International Protection of Women's Reproductive Rights' (1991–1992) 24 New York University, *Journal of International Law and Politics*, 645.

[36] Articles 2 and 5 CEDAW; Article 24.3 of CRC; Paragraphs 38 and 49 of Vienna Declaration and Programme of Action; Paragraph 5.5 of Programme of Action of ICPD; Paragraph of 224 of Beijing Platform for Action.

are applied to health service delivery. The right is provided for in IHRL in conventions, treaties and other documents.[37] The right implies that all persons have the right to control their own bodies, including their sexual and reproductive life, and be free from any intervention, medical or otherwise, except with their full, free and informed consent. In the report of UN Human Rights Council, the "UN Special Rapporteur on Torture and other Cruel, Inhuman or degrading treatment or punishment" emphasised that forced abortions and sterilisation of women with disabilities against their will may constitute torture or ill-treatment.[38] Degrading treatment such as forced abortion, female genital mutilation, early marriage, medical trials or experimentation related to sexuality at fertility conducted without free and informed consent of persons involved, prohibition of abortion on the grounds of rape; violence against a person in relation to their sexuality and reproduction during armed conflicts will prevent the actualisation of reproductive rights.

8.4.10 *Right to Be Free from Violence*

The right to be free from sexual and gender-based violence is also crucial to reproductive health. Violence against women and girls is an affront to the health and autonomy of victims. Victims can likewise suffer reproductive health consequences ranging from forced pregnancy, unsafe abortions, STDs, traumatic fistula and even death. In other words, the right is key to RHRs. IHRL conventions, treaties and other documents also recognise the right to be free from violence in all ways, whether sexual or gender-based.[39]

[37] Article 5 of UDHR; Article 7 of ICCPR; Article 1 of Convention against Torture and Other Cruel, Inhuman or Degrading Treatment or Punishment; Article 37 of CRC; Article 15 of CRPD; Paragraph 56 of Vienna Declaration and Programme of Action; Paragraph 4.10 of Programme of Action of ICPD.

[38] Manfred Nowak, 'Promotion and Protection of All Human Rights, Civil, Political, Economic, Social and Cultural Rights, including the Right to Development' (Report of the Special Rapporteur on torture and other cruel, inhuman or degrading treatment or punishment, 15 January 2008) Paragraph 38. <https://www.refworld.org/docid/47c2c5452.html> accessed 21 October 2021.

[39] Article 5 of CEDAW; Article 19(1) of CRC; Article 16 of CRPD; Article 7(1) of Rome Statute of International Criminal Court; Paragraph 18 of Vienna Declaration and Programme of Action; Principle 4 of Programme of Action of ICPD.

8.4.11 Right to Reproductive Health Information

The right to have access to sexual and reproductive health education encompasses the right to access information on reproductive health and to be adequately informed about risks and effective methods relating to one's reproductive health. The right to information and education is key to RHRs because information and education makes one aware of one's health status and the right one is entitled to. Thus, barriers preventing access to information and education must be removed. Certain international conventions, treaties and other documents recognise this right.[40] The information relating to sexual and reproductive health should be gender-sensitive and age appropriate, free from stereotypes and presented in an objective, critical and pluralistic manner and the information should enable all persons to make decision related to their sexual and reproductive life with free and informed consent.[41]

8.4.12 Right to Enjoy Scientific Progress

The right to enjoy scientific progress is a right that includes scientific progress/inventions in all areas including reproductive health. This right is key to RHRs because it includes access to benefits from reproductive health technology on contraception and infertility treatment and the right that such reproductive technology should be accessible to all. International conventions/treaties and other documents recognise the right of all persons to enjoy the benefits of scientific innovations.[42]

[40] Article 10 of CEDAW; Article 23(1) of CRPD; Article 17 of CRC; Article 19 of ICCPR; Paragraphs 7.45 and 7.46 of the Programme of Action of ICPD; Paragraphs 74 and 106 (e) of Beijing Platform for Action.

[41] United Nations, 'Reproductive Rights Are Human Rights: A Handbook for National Human Rights Institutions' (n. 35), pp. 107–108.

[42] Article 15 of ICESCR; Article 27(1) of UDHR, Article 7 of ICCPR; Paragraph 11 of Vienna Declaration and Programme of Action.

8.5 African Human Rights System and Reproductive Health Rights

The African Human Rights System also recognises and affirms human rights that are key to RHRs. The "African Charter on Human and Peoples Rights (ACHPR)"[43] recognises the rights key to reproductive health, being the right to life,[44] the right to liberty and security of person,[45] the right to health,[46] the right to equality and non-discrimination,[47] the right not to be subjected to torture and other cruel, inhumane or degrading treatment/punishment,[48] the right to access reproductive health education and information.[49] Furthermore, the protocol to the ACHPR on the rights of women in Africa (the Maputo Protocol) also affirms women's RHRs as human rights such as the right to life,[50] the right to health, including reproductive health,[51] the right to decide the number of spacing of children,[52] the right to consent to marriage and equality in marriage,[53] the right to be free from practices that harm women and girls,[54] the right to be free from sexual and gender-based violence,[55] and the right to access sexual/reproductive health education and information.[56] Apart from the existing human rights that are key to reproductive health, the Maputo Protocol recognises expressly the RHRs of women ranging from the right to control their fertility, the right to

[43] 1981, Banjul Charter.

[44] Article 4 of the ACHPR.

[45] Article 6 of ACHPR.

[46] Article 16 of ACHPR.

[47] Articles 18 and 28 of ACHPR.

[48] Article 5 of ACHPR.

[49] Article 9 of ACHPR.

[50] Article 4 of the Maputo Protocol.

[51] Article 14 of Maputo Protocol.

[52] Ibid.

[53] Article 6 of Maputo Protocol.

[54] Articles 2 and 5 of Maputo Protocol.

[55] Articles 3 and 4 of Maputo Protocol.

[56] Article 14 of Maputo Protocol.

choose any method of contraception, the right to family planning education and right to decide whether to have children, the number of children, spacing and timing.[57]

The Maputo Protocol has contributed greatly to the development and recognition of RHRs of women in Africa. In the South African case of *Treatment Action Campaign v. Ministry of Health Case* (TAC)[58] the court held the South African government accountable for failing to ensure access to anti-retroviral drugs that can prevent mother-to-child transmission of HIV. The continued respect, promotion and protection of reproductive health rights of all is imperative at the international, regional and national levels. The "General Comment No. 2 on Article 14 of the Maputo Protocol" provide interpretative guidance to Article 14 of the Maputo Protocol. In summary, it clarifies the obligations of states with respect to reproductive health rights that are guaranteed under the protocol.[59]

8.6 Reproductive Health Rights in Nigeria

Nigeria is a state party to numerous international and regional conventions/treaties with some ratified and domesticated. Therefore, the discussion on human rights is not novel to Nigeria. The "Constitution of the Federal Republic of Nigeria (FRN)" makes provision for fundamental rights which are key to RHRs[60] such as the right to life,[61] the right to dignity of human person,[62] the right to personal liberty,[63] the

[57] Article 14(1) of Maputo Protocol.

[58] [2002] 5 SA 721 (CC).

[59] 'General Comment No. 2 on Article 14.1 (a), (b), (c) and (f) and Article 14. 2 (a) and (c) of the Protocol to the African Charter on Human and Peoples' Rights on the Rights of Women in Africa.' <https://www.achpr.org/legalinstruments/detail?id=13#:~:text=Under%20Article%2014%20(2)%20(,physical%20health%20of%20the%20mother> accessed 10 August 2021.

[60] Chapter IV of the 1999 Constitution of the FRN.

[61] Section 33 of the 1999 Constitution of the FRN.

[62] Section 34 of the 1999 Constitution of the FRN.

[63] Section 35 of the 1999 Constitution of the FRN.

right to privacy and family life,[64] the right to be free from discrimination.[65] The right to health is not listed among the fundamental rights in Nigeria. Thus, the Nigerian Constitution provides for the right to health in Chapter II, but together with other social and economic rights, they are non-justiciable.[66] Simply put, there is a legal recognition of the right to health under the Constitution, but unlike the fundamental rights in Chapter IV of the Constitution, it is part of the fundamental objectives of the government which is merely a directory and not obligatory. In *Archbishop Olubunmi Okogie & ors, v. A.G of Lagos State*[67] the court held according to Section 6(6)(c) of the Constitution, the fundamental objectives of state policy are non-justiciable and therefore the courts lack jurisdiction to deal with them. These has made the enforcement of the right to health generally difficult. Be that as it may, the ACHPR has been domesticated in Nigeria as the African Charter (Ratification and Enforcement) Act 2004. It has been used and applied by the courts in Nigeria to enforce the right to health in some cases. The court has, in practice, made reference to the ACHPR in enforcing the right to health even though the right to health is non-justiciable under the constitution. In *Ahanefule v. Imperial Medical & anor.*[68] the court held that the defendant's action in denying the plaintiff medical care on grounds of her HIV positive status constituted a flagrant violation of the right to health guaranteed under Article 16 of the ACHPR.

Also, in *Odafe & ors. v. A.G.*[69] the plaintiffs were prison inmates diagnosed with HIV, and they alleged that they were denied access to medical treatment based on their HIV positive status and was therefore discriminatory, violating their rights under the Constitution and the African Charter. The court held that the defendants were liable for the violation of the right to health as guaranteed under the African Charter. In *Gbemre v. Shell petroleum Development Company Nigeria*

[64] Section 37 of the 1999 Constitution of the FRN.

[65] Section 42 of the 1999 Constitution of the FRN.

[66] Section 17 of the 1999 Constitution of Nigeria.

[67] [1981] NCLR 625; *Adeyinka Badejo v. Federal Minister of Education & ors.* [1996] 8 NWLR (Pt. 464) 15.

[68] [2012] <https://www.escr-net.org/caselaw/2012/georgina-ahamefule-v-imperial-medical-centre-dr-alex-molokwu-suit-no-id16272000> accessed 26 October 2021.

[69] [2004] AHRLR 205.

Ltd. & Ors,[70] the applicant, who instituted the action as a human rights matter and in a representative capacity for himself and on behalf of the Iwherekan community in Delta State of Nigeria, contended that the constitutionally guaranteed fundamental rights to life and dignity of human person provided under the Constitution of Federal Republic of Nigeria, 1999 and reinforced by the African Charter on Human and Peoples' Rights (Ratification and Enforcement) Act inevitably includes the right to clean poison-free, pollution-free and healthy environment and that consequently the continued flaring of gas in the area constituted a grave violation of the applicant's constitutional rights. Applicant's submission in this regard was upheld by the court and the respondents restrained from further flaring of gas in the said community. The court in this case acknowledged that gas flaring is harmful as well as a threat to human life. The court regardless assumed a wider role of interpreting and applying the right to health by inference from the right to life in *Gbemre's* case.

Apart from the right to health, the ACHPR also provides for certain human rights key to reproductive health that are not expressly stated in the Constitution of the FRN. It is important that the right to health be moved to the realm of fundamental rights in Nigeria because all other human rights will not be enjoyable if the right to health is not protected and justiciable.

8.7 The Concept of Assisted Reproductive Technologies (ART)

ART can be referred to as methods of fertility treatments in reproductive medicine. ART is the assistance provided to aid human reproduction when reproduction seems naturally impossible. According to the "Centres for Disease Control and Prevention" ART includes all fertility treatments in which either eggs or embryos are handled. In general, ART procedures involve surgically removing eggs from a woman's ovaries, combining them with sperm in the laboratory, and returning them to the woman's body or donating them to another woman. ART therefore incorporates a wide range of procedures that are used to overcome natural barriers in fertilisation by directly collecting and in-vitro handling of

[70] [2005] AHRLR 151.

human gametes and replacement of embryo into the uterus.[71] There are various procedures used in fertility treatments under ART. They include the following:

8.7.1 In Vitro Fertilisation (IVF)

IVF is a method of assisted reproduction in which sperm and eggs are combined outside of the body in a laboratory dish. After fertilisation, the fertilised eggs (embryos) will be transferred into the woman's uterus, where they may implant in the uterine lining and develop.[72] IVF has been declared to be one of the most successful ART procedures with a success rate of about 15–25% per cycle, in addition it often produces multiple embryos thereby increasing the likelihood of multiple babies.[73] Excess embryos may be cryopreserved (frozen) for future use. Initially, IVF was used to treat women with blocked, damaged, or absent fallopian tubes. Today, IVF is used to treat many causes of infertility, whether from the man or woman.[74]

8.7.2 Ovarian Stimulation/Induction

This method may be used by women who are not ovulating regularly. During ovarian stimulation/ovulation induction, hormone medications (it could be tablet or injection) are used to stimulate multiple eggs to grow in the ovaries rather than the single egg that normally develops each month.[75] The intention is that if such a couple have intercourse around this time, there is an increased chance of conception or rather the stimulated eggs could be retrieved for IVF procedure.

[71] S. Amjad and R. Rehman, 'Assisted Reproductive Techniques' in Rehana Rehman and Aisha Sheikh (eds), *Subfertility* (Elsevier Inc. 2021) p. 185.

[72] 'Assisted Reproductive Technology: A Guide for Patients' (American Society for Reproductive Medicine 2018) p. 4. <https://www.reproductivefacts.org/globalassets/rf/news-and-publications/bookletsfact-sheets/english-fact-sheets-and-info-booklets/art-booklet2.pdf> accessed 11 October 2021.

[73] 'What Are the Different Types of Assisted Reproductive Technology (ART)' (Centre of Reproductive Medicine) <https://infertilitytexas.com/blog/what-are-the-different-types-of-assisted-reproductive-technology-art/> accessed 11 October 2021.

[74] 'Assisted Reproductive Technology: A Guide for Patients' (American Society for Reproductive Medicine 2018) (n. 74).

[75] Ibid.

8.7.3 Artificial Insemination (AI)

AI is technologically the simplest means of reproduction and has been used for the longest period of time. AI is a fertility procedure used to introduce sperm directly to the cervix or uterus via the vagina at the time or just before ovulation with the hopes that it will result in pregnancy. There are two approaches to AI, there is the intrauterine insemination (IUI) and intra-cervical insemination (ICI). The ICI involves the insertion of sperm into the cervix (passageway outside the uterus) of the woman while IUI involves the insertion/deposit of sperm directly into the woman's uterus.[76] AI can be used to treat women and men who have normal and healthy reproductive system but for unknown reasons cannot conceive which may be due to certain difficulties with intercourse. Also, if the man is unable to achieve an erection or has structural problems of the penis after trauma or surgery or when semen has been frozen due to male partner's or husband's absence or prior to certain medical treatment that may eventually affect sperm quality/production e.g. cancer.

8.7.4 Intra Cytoplasmic Sperm Injection (ICSI)

There are times where sperm may be unable to fertilise egg, for example, maybe because the outer layer of the egg is thick or hard or the sperm itself is not viable, in such cases the ICSI procedure may be employed. ICSI is a process where one or more eggs are taken from the woman's body and are injected with a single healthy sperm and after fertilisation are placed into the woman's uterus for growth.[77] ICSI is different from IVF in that, for IVF the eggs and sperm are fertilised in a cell-culture dish unaided before placing in the uterus but in an ICSI procedure the fertilisation is aided by injecting the eggs with a single sperm to fertilise before putting in the uterus. ICSI can be used when there are serious sperm issues such as low sperm motility or very few quality sperm. ICSI allows a

[76] 'Everything You Need to Know about Artificial Insemination' (22 December 2017) <https://www.healthline.com/health/artificial-insemination#process> accessed 11 October 2021.

[77] 'What Is Intracytoplasmic Sperm Injection (ICSI)?' (American Society for Reproductive Medicine 2014) <https://www.reproductivefacts.org/news-and-publications/patient-fact-sheets-and-booklets/documents/fact-sheets-and-info-booklets/what-is-intracytoplasmic-sperm-injection-icsi/> accessed 11 October 2021.

doctor to select the healthiest sperm and implant it in the egg. A woman can also take fertility drugs to boost egg production and normalise her cycle before an ICSI implantation.[78]

8.7.5 Gamete Intra Fallopian Transfer (GIFT)

This procedure is a modified version of the IVF procedure. The procedure, like IVF, also involves retrieving eggs from the woman but instead of fertilisation occurring in a cell-culture dish or test tube in a laboratory, the eggs retrieved are placed with the sperm into a thin flexible tube and injected into the woman's fallopian tubes for fertilisation to occur naturally. Based on religious/ethical beliefs, fertilisation should occur inside the woman's body, thus, this procedure is preferable to people that belong to that school of thought.[79] Thus, unlike IVF, the sperm and eggs are deposited in the fallopian tubes for fertilisation.

8.7.6 Zygote Intra Fallopian Transfer (ZIFT)

This procedure is also a modified version of the IVF procedure. This procedure, like the IVF, also involves retrieving eggs from the woman and combining them with sperm in a cell-culture dish in the lab, but unlike in IVF where the embryos, after fertilisation, are observed for 3–5 days before placing in the woman's uterus, for ZIFT, the embryo (zygotes) is inserted into the fallopian tubes within 24 hours after fertilisation.[80] The goal is for the zygote to implant in the uterus and develop into a foetus.

8.7.7 Preimplantation Genetic Diagnosis (PGD)

PGD is testing the embryo for any abnormality/disease that intending parents may have to determine if it is present in the embryo before

[78] 'What Are the Different Types of Assisted Reproductive Technology (ART)' (Centre of Reproductive Medicine) (n. 75).

[79] Ibid.

[80] N. Todd, 'GIFT AND ZIFT' (*WebMD*, 19 June 2020) <https://www.webmd.com/infertility-and-reproduction/gift-and-zift> accessed 11 October 2021.

implantation.[81] It is a prenatal diagnosis used to detect early form of genetic disease in an embryo for the purpose of prevention.[82] The aim of PGD is to prevent any transmission of known genetic diseases/ abnormality from intending parents to the foetus and used where intending parents are aware of any family history of genetic abnormality that their offspring might be exposed to. Thus, PGD gives intending parents opportunity to reduce drastically the risk of passing any known genetic disease to their children before fertilisation.[83] In PGD, embryos are generated through the process of IVF or ICSI and then screened for any genetic disorder after which a selected healthy embryo will be placed in the woman's uterus.

8.7.8 Surrogacy

This is another method that assist couples to reproduce. Surrogacy is an alternative method for couples who are unable to reproduce. Surrogacy refers to a contract in which a woman carries a pregnancy for another woman/couple. After the birth of the child, the surrogate mother hands over the child to the intending parents. Intending Parents may seek surrogacy arrangement when pregnancy is medically impossible, pregnancy risks present an unacceptable danger to the mother's health, or a number of other reasons. This is usually achieved through ART e.g. IVF, artificial insemination or any other ART method.

8.8 Reproductive Health Rights and ART

The key human rights to ART are the right to access sexual and reproductive health education and information and the right to enjoy scientific progress in the area of reproductive health. Reproductive medicine has made progress over the years and the right to access information on such advancement is a reproductive right in order to inform reproductive health choices. Also, the right to enjoy such reproductive advancement is

[81] M.B. Dayal, 'Preimplantation Genetic Diagnosis' *Medscape* (29 August 2018) <https://emedicine.medscape.com/article/273415-overview> accessed 11 October 2021.

[82] S.J. Fasouliotis and J.G. Schenker, 'Preimplantation Genetic Diagnosis Principles and Ethics' (1998) 13 (8) *Human Reproduction* 2238–2245, 2238.

[83] Ibid.

important which should include the accessibility and affordability of such scientific progress in reproductive medicine. It is an obligation States must see as very important. The burden that comes with infertility and the succour brought to couples with fertility issues by ART cannot be underestimated and these ART should be celebrated and accessible to all. In *AB and another v Minister of Social Development*,[84] the South African Constitutional Court gave a description of the gap ART fills when it comes to bearing the burden of infertility as follows:

> We are not in any way short of words when it comes to describing the effects of experiencing infertility: grief; sadness; despair; panic; helplessness; and isolation are but a few of the feelings that often ensue. For a large number of people, infertility has been "the most upsetting experience of their lives". For others, infertility is rated as comparably stressful to the loss of a partner or a child. The likelihood of depression has been shown to double for women who are infertile. Disturbingly, infertility levels are on the rise globally, with one in every ten people facing infertility problems. We are fortunate, however, to live in an era where the effects of infertility can be ameliorated to a large extent through assistive reproductive technologies. The technological advances seen over the last half century have greatly expanded the reproductive avenues available to the infertile. These reproductive avenues should be celebrated as they allow our society to flourish in ways previously impossible.

Thus, with reproductive avenues made available by ART, couples with infertility should not be denied the chance of reproducing where reproductive rights of access to reproductive education/information and access to reproductive advancements are not protected and adequately enjoyed.

8.9 ART in Nigeria

Infertility is prevalent globally, though more prevalent in the developing countries of Africa, Nigeria not being an exemption. High value is placed on fertility and human reproduction in Nigeria, and has been perceived over time as the most important purpose of a marriage union. ART, in reproductive medicine, is no doubt a welcomed feat in the Nigerian health-care system. In Nigeria, Oladapo Ashiru pioneered ART in reproductive medicine in 1984 and the first baby was birthed through

[84] [2016] ZACC 4 paras 2–3.

the IVF method in 1989.[85] Also in Anambra State at the Life Specialist Hospital Nnewi, a team led by Joseph Ikechebelu delivered the first IVF baby in August 2011.[86] Since then, ART has thrived and series of births have emerged through both public and private facilities in Nigeria with IVF procedure largely subscribed to by couples. There are a number of government-owned fertility centres situated at public hospitals in Nigeria, and they include the University of Benin Hospital, Edo State, Garki Hospital, FCT Abuja, National Hospital, FCT, Abuja, University of Ilorin Teaching Hospital, Kwara State, University College Hospital, Ibadan, Oyo State and Lagos University Teaching Hospital.[87] Furthermore, there are also some known private-owned facilities that offer ART services across Nigeria such as George's Memorial Centre, Lagos State, Nordica Fertility Centre, Lagos State, The Olive Branch Clinic, Lagos State, The Bridge Clinic, Lagos State, St. Ives Specialist Hospital, Lagos State, Truecare Fertility Clinic, Medical ART Centre, Lagos State, Hope Valley Clinic, Lagos State, Vine Branch, Ibadan, Oyo State, Gynascope Specialist Hospital, Port Harcourt, Rivers State, Diff Hospital, FCT, Abuja, Lily Fertility Centre, Warri, Delta State, Nisa Premier Hospital, FCT, Abuja to mention a few.[88] In summary, ART services in Nigeria are majorly rendered by private-owned facilities compared to the few owned by government facilities.

8.10 Regulatory Framework on ART in Nigeria

ART is an important aspect of human interaction that needs to be regulated by law, thus, an effective regulatory instrument is germane to ensure efficacy in the application of ART. There are salient legal issues

[85] L.O. Omokanye et al., 'Assisted Reproduction Technology in Nigeria: Challenges and the Way Forward' (2018) 3 (1) *African Journal for Infertility and Assisted Conception* 2-5, 2.

[86] I.S. Okwelogu, E.C. Azuike, J.I. Ikechebelu and C.K.C. Nnebue, 'In-Vitro Fertilization Practice: Awareness and Perceptions Among Women Attending Fertility Clinics in Okija, Anambra State, Nigeria' (2012) 3 (2) *Afrimedic Journal* 5–10, 5.

[87] 'Top Government Owned IVF Centres in Nigeria' (Fertility Hub, Nigeria) <https://www.fertilityhubnigeria.com/top-government-owned-ivf-centres-nigeria/> accessed 12 October 2021.

[88] 'A Comprehensive Ranking of Fertility Clinics in Nigeria' (Fertility Hub, Nigeria) <https://www.fertilityhubnigeria.com/comprehensive-ranking-fertility-clinics-nigeria/> accessed 12 October 2021.

surrounding ART practice and the question of what parameters should be acceptable needs to be addressed. It is important to answer the question: are there laws governing ART practice in Nigeria? In as much as there is no specific and concise legal response to ART practice in Nigeria, there are laws and regulations that impliedly have an impact on ART practice to some extent in Nigeria.

The National Health Act (NHA) 2014 is a regulatory framework on the national health-care system in Nigeria. There are few provisions in the NHA that can be applied to ART practice in Nigeria. Section 26 of the NHA recognise the right to confidentiality of a patient except in certain situations.[89] This means that couple's information and treatment during ART procedures remain confidential and can only be disclosed with their consent. Also, section 44 paragraph 6 of the "*Rules of Professional Conduct for Medical and Dental Practitioners (Code on Medical Ethics)*"[90] in Nigeria provides for confidentiality in a doctor-patient relationship. The Code of Medical Ethics further explains that the duty of confidentiality on the part of a medical practitioner includes:

> The protection of medical records, maintenance of confidentiality in the process of further consultation, cryptic utilisation of anonymised clinical material for teaching or publication in professional journals, judicious balance between maintenance of confidentiality for an under-aged patient and simultaneously making available necessary information to the parent or guardian, presentation of a patient at a scientific meeting only following informed consent of the patient and acceptance by the audience to maintain confidentiality etc.[91]

[89] Section 26 (1) of the NHA states that: "*All information concerning a user, including information relating to his or her health status, treatment or stay in a health establishment is confidential.*"

[90] Section 44 paragraph 6 of the Code of Medical Ethics: "*It is the duty of a doctor to preserve his patient's confidences. This duty out-lasts the doctor's employment, and it extends as well to his employees; and none of them should accept employment which involves, or may involve the disclosure or use of these confidences, either for the private advantage of the doctor or his employees, or to the disadvantage of the patient without the patient's knowledge and consent, and even if there are other available sources of such information. This duty to maintain a patient's secrets subsists even after the patient has died and a doctor should not continue in a particular employment when he discovers that this obligation prevents the performance of his full duty to his former or to his new patient.*"

[91] Section 44 paragraph 5 of the Code of Medical Ethics.

In Part VI of the NHA, there are provisions that can be applied to ART practice in Nigeria. Particularly, Section 50 of the NHA prohibits the unethical dealing in gametes. It prohibits the manipulation of gametes including embryo splitting, engaging in any exercise that involves the transfer or embryo splitting for the purpose of the cloning of human being and the importation or exportation of human zygotes or embryos.[92] These provisions are not adequate to address issues on ART practice in Nigeria. There is a need for a more robust and ART-specific regulatory framework.

Over the years, there have been some legislative attempts at providing a legal framework for ART practice in Nigeria. There has been a number of proposed Bills specifically on ART in Nigeria but were not passed into law. The first attempt was made in May 2012 following a presentation of "*A Bill to provide National a framework for the regulation and supervision of reproductive technology and matters connected therewith*" at the House of Representatives. The Bill was read for the second time but was not passed into law. Moreover, the Nigerian Medical Association (NMA) and the Society for Obstetrics and Gynaecology of Nigeria (SOGON) denied having anything to do with the Bill nor did they contribute to its contents.[93]

An attempt was also made to amend NHA in 2016 with the presentation of "*A Bill for an Act to amend the National Health Act to provide for regulation of assisted birth technology, for safe and ethical practice of assisted reproductive technology services and for related matters.*" The Bill was presented to the National Assembly but was not passed into law. The proposed Bill will empower the Federal Ministry of Health to make new regulations along that provided by the NHA on ART procedures among other things.[94] The Bill also recommends that a registry of ART clinics and banks at the national level should be established in Nigeria

[92] Section 50 of the NHA: "*(1) A person shall not: - (a) manipulate any genetic material, including genetic material of human gametes, zygotes or embryos; or (b) engage in any activity including nuclear transfer or embryo splitting for the purpose of the cloning of human being. (c) import or export human zygotes or embryos.*"

[93] E.M. Akpambang and M. Amujo-Akomolafe, "Legal Position on Surrogacy Arrangements in Nigeria and Some Selected Jurisdictions" [2020] 7(3) *International Journal of Research in Humanities and Social Studies* 18–39 at.30. <http://www.ijrhss.org/papers/v7-i3/3.pdf> accessed 29 October 2021.

[94] Section 59 of the Bill to provide National a framework for the regulation and supervision of reproductive technology and matters connected therewith 2012.

that will serve as the central database for ART clinics and banks and to include information on the nature/types of services they provide and other relevant information.[95] The Bill also makes it mandatory for every ART clinic/bank to be registered with the Ministry of Health and all existing ART clinic/bank before the commencement of the Act must take reasonable steps within 90 days of the commencement of the Act to be registered.[96] The power of inspection of any ART clinic/bank also lies with the Ministry, with or without prior notice.[97] The Bill saddles ART clinics/banks with the duty to ensure eligibility of patients, donors of gametes and surrogates for ART procedures as specified by the provisions and regulations of the Act such as medical fitness i.e. medical examination for diseases that may endanger the health of the parties involved and the child.[98] The Bill further protects the rights to medical confidentiality of all parties involved, be it the donor or couples, and requires informed consent.[99] Records of all gametes donor, embryos used, the method used and details of the commission couple or surrogate they were used for must be adequately documented, it prohibits improper dealing dealings with gamete and embryos and sex selection except to treat a sex-linked disorder/disease.[100] The Bill provides for the rights of all parties involved including parental right over the child conceived.[101]

[95] Section 60 of the Bill to provide National a framework for the regulation and supervision of reproductive technology and matters connected therewith 2012.

[96] Section 62 of the Bill to provide National a framework for the regulation and supervision of reproductive technology and matters connected therewith 2012.

[97] Section 61 of the Bill to provide National a framework for the regulation and supervision of reproductive technology and matters connected therewith 2012.

[98] Section 68 of the Bill to provide National a framework for the regulation and supervision of reproductive technology and matters connected therewith 2012.

[99] Sections 68(3–9), 69 and 74(3–4) of the Bill to provide National a framework for the regulation and supervision of reproductive technology and matters connected therewith 2012.

[100] Sections 70, 71, 72 and 77 of the Bill to provide National a framework for the regulation and supervision of reproductive technology and matters connected therewith 2012.

[101] Section 76 of the Bill to provide National a framework for the regulation and supervision of reproductive technology and matters connected therewith 2012.

On the 24th of October 2017,[102] two Bills: "*A Bill for an Act for the regulations of in-vitro fertilization to prohibit certain practices in connection with in-vitro fertilization, to establish an in-vitro fertilization authority to make provision in respect of children born of in-vitro fertilization process and for connected purposes, 2017*" and "*A Bill for an Act to provide for regulation and supervision of Assisted Reproductive Technology and for matters Connected therewith, 2017*" were presented to the Senate for second reading.[103] The Bill for an Act to provide for regulation and supervision of Assisted Reproductive Technology proposed rules on the regulation of ART in Nigeria. The Bill requires the registration of ART clinic before the registration authority before a clinic can practice ART[104] and provides for different ART procedures that can be carried out such as infertility treatment, IUI, Artificial Insemination, IVF, surrogacy.[105] The Bill also protects the rights to medical confidentiality of all parties involved be it the donor or couples and informed consent.[106] Records of all donor gametes, embryos, the procedure used and information on the commission couple or surrogate they were used for must be adequately documented as well as the deoxyribonucleic acid (DNA) fingerprint of the individual/couple and the child born as a result of ART treatment or procedure.[107] The Bill provides for professional ethics in the practice of ART such as the required number of embryos that may be placed in a woman in one cycle, the kind of gametes/embryos that can be placed in a woman, non-mixing of semen from two individuals, multiple pregnancy and the mandatory requirement of informing the patient immediately of the medical implications, medical analysis of semen before use in any ART

[102] 'Nigerian Senate proceeding of 24th October, 2017' *Vanguard Newspaper* (24 October 2017). <https://www.vanguardngr.com/2017/10/read-nigerian-senates-proceeding-tuesday-october-24th-2017/> accessed 29 October 2021.

[103] D.Z. Adeniran, 'Reproductive Technology Bills Scale Second Reading in Senate' (*Order Paper*, 25 October 2017) <https://orderpaper.ng/reproductive-technology-bills-scale-second-reading-senate/> accessed 29 October 2021.

[104] Section 11 of the Bill for an Act to provide for regulation and supervision of Assisted Reproductive Technology.

[105] Sections 13 and 20(10) of the Bill for an Act to provide for regulation and supervision of Assisted Reproductive Technology.

[106] Sections 20 (1–9) and 21 of the Bill for an Act to provide for regulation and supervision of Assisted Reproductive Technology.

[107] Sections 22 and 28 of the Bill for an Act to provide for regulation and supervision of Assisted Reproductive Technology.

procedure, conditions in which pre-implantation genetic diagnosis can be done, prohibition of pre-determined sex of a child or sex selection procedure in ART, prohibition of exportation/transfer of gametes, zygotes and embryos except for personal use with permission of the authority, sale of gametes except for use by ART clinic for treating infertility.[108] The Bill further provides rules to regulate gametes and embryos collection, storage, screening and handling by ART banks operating independent of any ART clinic to avoid abuse.[109] The Bill provides for the rights and duties of patients, donors, surrogates and the children born from the ART procedure.[110]

The Bill on regulations of in-vitro fertilisation (IVF) focused on IVF as an ART procedure proposed the establishment of the IVF Human Fertilisation Authority with functions of developing standards, regulations and guidelines on IVF human fertilisation and also disseminate information on IVF among other functions.[111] The Bill prohibits the dealing with embryos by an unauthorised person not specified under the Act and the Bill makes informed consent mandatory.[112] The Bill provides for the eligibility criteria for IVF treatment such as for the purpose of procreation only for persons certified by a medical doctor as incapable of naturally conceiving, restriction to the use of only human embryo for IVF etc.[113] The Bill also protects the rights to medical confidentiality of all parties involved, be it the donor or couples as well as right to informed consent.[114] The Bill provides for the rights of parents, donors, and the children born[115] and also provides rules to guide IVF procedure using surrogate mother and the parental rights over such child.[116] The

[108] Sections 23, 24, 25 and 29 of the Bill for an Act to provide for regulation and supervision of Assisted Reproductive Technology.

[109] Sections 26 and 27 of the Bill for an Act to provide for regulation and supervision of Assisted Reproductive Technology.

[110] Sections 32–36 of the Bill for an Act to provide for regulation and supervision of Assisted Reproductive Technology.

[111] Sections 4 and 5 of the Bill on regulations of in-vitro fertilization (IVF).

[112] Sections 18–20 of the Bill on regulations of in-vitro fertilization (IVF).

[113] Sections 21–24 of the Bill on regulations of in-vitro fertilization (IVF).

[114] Sections 36–38 and 27 of the Bill on regulations of in-vitro fertilization (IVF).

[115] Section 28 of the Bill on regulations of in-vitro fertilization (IVF).

[116] Section 32 of the Bill on regulations of in-vitro fertilization (IVF).

authority is required to keep records of IVF treatment services rendered to persons, gametes of persons used, donors of embryos and gametes and children conceived of IVF treatment.[117] The Bill prohibits the carrying out of IVF procedure without obtaining licence from the authority, the conditions for obtaining licence as well as conditions that may warrant the revocation of licence and temporary suspension of a licence.[118] The two Bills were consolidated and scheduled to be reviewed by the Committee on health of the Senate and presented for third reading and then to be passed into law thereafter. The consolidated Bill lapsed with the 8th Assembly, thus the hope of a law on ART arising from the consolidated Bill is dead. In the current 9th Assembly, a new Bill on In-Vitro Fertilisation was introduced by Senator Barau Jibril, one of the sponsors of the two Bills consolidated which lapsed with the 8th Assembly. The Bill was presented to the Senate and passed the first reading stage on 9th November 2021.[119] Hopefully, a law will emanate from this new Bill before the end of the 9th Assembly.

As at today, the only regulatory provisions on ART practice in Nigeria is the NHA and the Code of Medical Ethics earlier mentioned which are inadequate to address salient legal and ethical issues on ART practice in Nigeria. All the proposed Bills should be consolidated to a single Bill after careful consideration of the peculiarities of a country like Nigeria and then passed into law to serve as the regulatory framework on ART in Nigeria noting that the time for a regulatory framework for ART in Nigeria is overdue.

8.11 Challenges to the Enjoyment of Reproductive Health Rights to ART in Nigeria

A major challenge to the enjoyment of RHRs to ART in Nigeria is the lack of a regulatory framework on ART practice in Nigeria. For every societal development, a legal response to such development is important for social control. For ART, there are legal and ethical issues that impact on the RHRs of parties and resulting children that needs to be adequately

[117] Section 34 of the Bill on regulations of in-vitro fertilization (IVF).

[118] Sections 39–47 and 50 of the Bill on regulations of in-vitro fertilization (IVF).

[119] 'In-Vitro Fertilisation Bill, 2021' <https://placbillstrack.org/view.php?getid=8675> accessed 27 March 2022.

addressed and regulated to avoid abuse, such as rules guiding ART procedures, dealing with surplus embryos, storage of embryos and length of storage etc. The lack of a legal response to ART services in Nigeria leaves a gap in reproductive medicine that needs to be earnestly filled to avoid abuse and to protect RHRs in Nigeria. A likely legal issue that may arise in Nigeria is a case that happened in California. A California couple sued an IVF clinic for alleged IVF swap after the woman was implanted with the wrong embryo by the fertility clinic. The couple alleged medical malpractice, negligence and fraudulent concealment on the part of the fertility clinic. DNA evidence showed that the child born was not theirs, but that of another couple whose embryo was swapped with theirs and they had to swap the babies after giving birth to them.[120] It shows that so many things can go wrong during ART procedures, a legal framework to regulate its practice will go a long way to ensure ethical professionalism and to prevent violation of reproductive rights of parties involved. One of the obligations of state parties to international/regional human rights treaties and conventions is that laws should be enacted to protect human rights and provide platforms for their enjoyment.

Accessibility to ART in Nigeria is another stumbling block to the enjoyment of reproductive rights as it relates to ART. One of the key components of reproductive rights is the right to enjoy scientific progress. Where people cannot access advancements/progress in reproductive medicine such as ART services, the right to enjoy scientific progress is violated. In Nigeria as earlier discussed, the practice of ART is done by a few fertility clinics concentrated basically in urban areas of the country, particularly in large cities. Persons willing to access ART treatments who are not domiciled in these areas need to commute to a nearby city where the service is available. The right to have access to reproductive health education which includes the right to access information on reproductive health and to be adequately informed about the risks and effective methods relating to one's reproductive health should be improved in Nigeria. Social media will also help a great deal in making reproductive education accessible including information on ART. Efforts should be made to set up more fertility clinics in locations where it will be accessible to all regardless of their places of domicile.

[120] 'California Couple Sue Clinic for Alleged IVF Swap Horror' *Arise News* (9 November 2021) <https://www.arise.tv/california-couple-sue-clinic-for-alleged-ivf-swap-horror/> accessed 11 November 2021.

Affordability of ART procedures is another major challenge to the enjoyment of reproductive rights in Nigeria. Currently, ART procedures are quite expensive in Nigeria, with a little cost difference in government-owned fertility clinics. It can be presumed that only the financially capable persons can enjoy ART services in Nigeria. The right to enjoy scientific advancement includes affordability of such scientific progress but this cannot be said to be the case in Nigeria as just few people can afford it. Efforts should be made by the government to enable a subsidised plan for every class of person to be able to access ART services because ART fills a huge gap in reproductive medicine by giving hope to infertile persons who would otherwise not have their own biological children.

8.12 Conclusion

ART has provided human society hope and solace to people who would have not been able to conceive naturally so that they can now conceive. ART is a welcomed global development in reproductive medicine and has a great impact on RHRs. The need to create a balanced ART practice and protection of the RHRs of those concerned is germane in order to prevent abuse. Nigeria still has a long way to go in ART practice and the enjoyment of reproductive health rights, hence, the need to regulate ART services as well as protect reproductive health rights in Nigeria has become imperative. The chapter recommends that:

- Nigeria should earnestly put in place a legal framework to regulate ART practice and to protect RHRs. It is an obligation that must be addressed with utmost importance.
- Mechanisms should be put in place for the availability and affordability of scientific advancement in reproductive medicine (ART) because it is important and key to the enjoyment of RHRs.
- Access to information on ART is a reproductive right and should be improved by using all possible mediums available to reach all classes of persons. The right to health is key to the actualisation of reproductive health rights and should be recognised as fundamental rights in the Constitution of FRN rather than seen as merely directive. Right to health is a fundamental right to RHRs. In Nigeria the right to health is a socio-economic right and are non-justiciable like other fundamental rights provided in the Constitution, therefore the

courts lack jurisdiction to deal with them. This has made the enforcement of the right to health in Nigeria difficult. The right to health should be moved to the realm of fundamental rights in Nigeria to further reinforce the enjoyment of reproductive rights in Nigeria.

Bibliography

Books

Amjad S, and Rehman R, 'Assisted Reproductive Techniques' in Rehana Rehman and Aisha Sheikh (eds), *Subfertility* (Elsevier Inc. 2021).

Gebhard J, and Trimino D, 'Reproductive Rights, International Regulation' (Max Planck Encyclopedia of Public Law, 2012) <https://www.corteidh.or.cr/tablas/r16912.pdf>.

United Nations, 'Reproductive Rights Are Human Rights: A Handbook for National Human Rights Institutions' (United Nations, 2014) <https://www.ohchr.org/documents/publications/nhrihandbook.pdf>.

Journals

Akpambang E M, and Amujo-Akomolafe M, 'Legal Position on Surrogacy Arrangements in Nigeria and Some Selected Jurisdictions' [2020] 7(3) *International Journal of Research in Humanities and Social Studies* 18–39 <http://www.ijrhss.org/papers/v7-i3/3.pdf>.

Cook R, 'International Protection of Women's Reproductive Rights' (1991–1992) 24 New York University, *Journal of International Law and Politics*, 645.

Fasouliotis S J, and Schenker J G, 'Preimplantation Genetic Diagnosis Principles and Ethics' (1998) *Human Reproduction* 13 (8) 2238–2245, 2238.

Meena J.K, Verma A, Kishore J, and Ingle G K, 'Sexual and Reproductive Health: Knowledge, Attitude, and Perceptions among Young Unmarried Male Residents of Delhi' (2015) *International Journal of Reproductive Medicine* <https://doi.org/10.1155/2015/431460>.

Okwelogu I S, Azuike E C, Ikechebelu J I, and Nnebue C K C, 'In-Vitro Fertilization Practice: Awareness and Perceptions Among Women Attending Fertility Clinics in Okija, Anambra State, Nigeria' (2012) 3 (2) *Afrimedic Journal* 5–10.

Omokanye L O et al, 'Assisted Reproduction Technology in Nigeria: Challenges and the Way Forward' (2018) 3 (1) *African Journal for Infertility and Assisted Conception* 2–5.

Statutes and Bills

A Bill for an Act to amend the National Health Act to provide for regulation of assisted birth technology, for safe and ethical practice of assisted reproductive technology services and for related matters 2016.

A Bill for an Act to provide for regulation and supervision of Assisted Reproductive Technology and for matters connected therewith 2017.

A Bill on regulations of *in-vitro* fertilization (IVF) 2017.

A Bill to provide National a framework for the regulation and supervision of reproductive technology and matters connected therewith 2012.

Constitution of the Federal Republic of Nigeria 1999.

National Health Act 2004.

Rules of Professional Conduct for Medical and Dental Practitioners (Code of Medical Ethics) 2004.

International Documents

African Charter on Human and Peoples Rights (ACHPR) (Banjul Charter) 1981.

Beijing Platform for Action 1995.

Convention on the Rights of the Child (CRC) 1990.

Convention on the Rights of Persons with Disabilities (CRPD) 2008.

Convention on the Elimination of All Forms of Discrimination against Women (CEDAW) 1981.

Convention against Torture and Other Cruel, Inhuman or Degrading Treatment or Punishment 1987.

Declaration on the Elimination of Violence against Women (DEVAW) 1993.

International Covenant on Civil and Political Rights (ICCPR) 1976.

International Covenant on Economic, Social and Cultural Rights (ICESCR) 1976.

International Convention on the Elimination of All Forms of Racial Discrimination (ICERD) 1969.

Nowak M, 'Promotion and Protection of All Human Rights, Civil, Political, Economic, Social and Cultural Rights, including the Right to Development' (Report of the Special Rapporteur on torture and other cruel, inhuman or degrading treatment or punishment, 15 January 2008) <https://www.refworld.org/docid/47c2c5452.html>.

Protocol to the ACHPR on the Rights of Women in Africa (Maputo Protocol) 2005.

Rome Statute of International Criminal Court 2002.

The Right to Health Fact Sheet No. 31 Office of the UN High Commissioner for Human Rights and World Health Organisation.

Universal Declaration of Human Rights (UDHR) 1948.

Vienna Declaration and Programme of Action 1993.

Internet

A Comprehensive Ranking of Fertility Clinics in Nigeria (Fertility Hub, Nigeria) <https://www.fertilityhubnigeria.com/comprehensive-ranking-fertility-clinics-nigeria/>.

Adeniran D Z, 'Reproductive Technology Bills Scale Second Reading in Senate' *Order Paper* (25 October 2017) <https://orderpaper.ng/reproductive-technology-bills-scale-second-reading-senate/>.

Assisted Reproductive Technology: A Guide for Patients (American Society for Reproductive Medicine 2018) p. 4. <https://www.reproductivefacts.org/globalassets/rf/news-and-publications/bookletsfact-sheets/english-fact-sheets-and-info-booklets/art-booklet2.pdf>.

California Couple Sue Clinic for Alleged IVF Swap Horror, *Arise News* (9 November 2021) <https://www.arise.tv/california-couple-sue-clinic-for-alleged-ivf-swap-horror/>.

Dayal M B, 'Preimplantation Genetic Diagnosis' *Medscape* (29 August 2018) <https://emedicine.medscape.com/article/273415-overview>.

Everything You Need to Know about Artificial Insemination (22 December 2017) <https://www.healthline.com/health/artificial-insemination#process>.

General Comment No. 2 on Article 14.1 (a), (b), (c) and (f) and Article 14. 2 (a) and (c) of the Protocol to the African Charter on Human and Peoples' Rights on the Rights of Women in Africa. https://www.achpr.org/legalinstruments/detail?id=13#:~:text=Under%20Article%2014%20(2)%20(,physical%20health%20of%20the%20mother.

In-Vitro Fertilisation Bill, 2021 <https://placbillstrack.org/view.php?getid=8675>.

IPPF Charter Guidelines on Sexual and Reproductive Rights (International Planned Parenthood Federation 1997)' <https://www.sm.ee/sites/default/files/contenteditors/eesmargiEncd_ja_tegevused/Tervis/Tervislik_eluviis/ippf_charter_srh_rights_2003.pdf>.

Nigerian Senate proceeding of 24th October, 2017 *Vanguard Newspaper* (24 October 2017). <https://www.vanguardngr.com/2017/10/read-nigerian-senates-proceeding-tuesday-october-24th-2017/>.

Programme of Action Adopted at the ICPD Cairo. <https://www.unfpa.org/sites/default/files/pubpdf/programme_of_action_Web%20ENGLISH.pdf>.

Reproductive Health in Western Pacific <https://www.who.int/westernpacific/health-topics/reproductive-health>.

Reproductive Rights are Human Rights: A Handbook for National Human Rights Institutions' (United Nations, 2014) <https://www.ohchr.org/documents/publications/nhrihandbook.pdf>.

Sexual and Reproductive Health and Rights: A Position Paper (Department for International development; 2004) <https://www2.ohchr.org/english/issues/development/docs/rights_reproductive_health.pdf>.

Todd N, 'GIFT AND ZIFT' (*WebMD*, 19 June 2020) <https://www.webmd.com/infertility-and-reproduction/gift-and-zift>.

Top Government Owned IVF Centres in Nigeria (Fertility Hub, Nigeria) <https://www.fertilityhubnigeria.com/top-government-owned-ivf-centres-nigeria/>.

United Nations (UN) General Assembly, 'Report of the Human Rights Council on its eleventh session (A/HRC/11/L.16/Rev.1. 16 October 2009)' <https://undocs.org/pdf?symbol=en/A/HRC/11/37>.

What Are the Different Types of Assisted Reproductive Technology (ART) (Centre of Reproductive Medicine) <https://infertilitytexas.com/blog/what-are-the-different-types-of-assisted-reproductive-technology-art/>.

What Are Human Rights? (UNICEF) <https://www.unicef.org/child-rights-convention/what-are-human-rights>.

What Are Human Rights? (United Nations (UN) Human Rights) <https://www.ohchr.org/en/issues/pages/whatarehumanrights.aspx>.

What Is Intracytoplasmic Sperm Injection (ICSI)?' (American Society for Reproductive Medicine 2014) <https://www.reproductivefacts.org/news-and-publications/patient-fact-sheets-and-booklets/documents/fact-sheets-and-info-booklets/what-is-intracytoplasmic-sperm-injection-icsi/>.

Cases

AB and Another v. Minister of Social Development [2016] ZACC 4.

Adeyinka Badejo v. Federal Minister of Education & Ors. [1996] 8 NWLR (Pt. 464) 15.

Ahanefule v. Imperial Medical & anor [2012] <https://www.escr-net.org/caselaw/2012/georgina-ahamefule-v-imperial-medical-centre-dr-alex-molokwu-suit-no-id16272000>.

Archbishop Olubunmi Okogie & ors, v. A.G of Lagos State [1981] NCLR 625.

Gbemre v. Shell petroleum Development Company Nigeria Ltd. & Ors [2005] AHRLR 151.

Odafe & ors. v. A.G [2004] AHRLR 205.

Treatment Action Campaign v. Ministry of Health Case (TAC) [2002] 5 SA 721 (CC).

CHAPTER 9

New Frontiers for Reproductive Health Rights: Contemporary Developments in the Regulation of Assisted Reproductive Technologies in South Africa

Bonginkosi Shozi, Aliki Edgcumbe, and Donrich Thaldar

South Africa has seen a boom of legislation and case law explicitly on medically assisted reproduction in the past decade. This area of law—also known as reproductive law—is a developing area in South African law, and one in need of in-depth analysis. To this end, this chapter provides an overview of the emergent law relating to the use of assisted reproductive technologies (ARTs), covering core concepts, relevant legislation and case law. Reflecting on how reproductive health rights are enshrined in the Constitution of South Africa, reproductive law in South Africa is founded on the state's commitment to reproductive health rights—which

B. Shozi · A. Edgcumbe · D. Thaldar (✉)
University of KwaZulu-Natal, Durban, South Africa
e-mail: ThaldarD@ukzn.ac.za

O. S. Adelakun and E. Ndoni (eds.), *Reproductive Health and Assisted Reproductive Technologies In Sub-Saharan Africa*,
Sustainable Development Goals Series,
https://doi.org/10.1007/978-981-99-2411-0_9

includes the use of ARTs. This is illustrated through analyses of three subject areas that have been (and continue to be) areas of legal developments and thus represent the frontier of reproductive health rights in South Africa: gamete donation, surrogacy and genetic testing. South Africa's reproductive law takes a generally permissive stance on the use of ARTs, which represents a recognition and manifestation of reproductive health rights by the state. However, there are certain areas of South Africa's reproductive law that are highly regulated and where the state has attempted to significantly restrict the use of ARTs. These areas represent cases where the court has endeavoured to strike a balance between reproductive health rights and countervailing state interests but has failed to strike that balance well.

9.1 Introduction

a. From gametes to birth: Reproductive law as a developing discipline in South African law

While laws specifically addressing assisted reproductive technologies (ARTs) have existed in South Africa since the 1983 Human Tissue Act,[1] early legislation in this area did little more than give legal recognition to the current practice. With a dearth of legal development to give substance to the regulation of medically assisted human reproduction, this area of law—also known as reproductive law—has long been regarded as a small and insubstantial sub-discipline under the umbrella of family law in South Africa. But reproductive law does not always fit well under this umbrella. Family law, which concerns familial relations, is primarily focused on the relationships between people who already exist. In other words, much of family law is about what happens after a person is born. Reproductive law, on the other hand, is predominantly focused on what happens before that. It is about the journey from gamete to birth, and the kinds of decisions people can make that define what this journey looks like—for both the child who may be born because of these decisions (the prospective child) and for the person whose decisions may cause the existence of a child that they intend to parent (the prospective parent).

[1] Human Tissue Act 65 of 1983.

Fuelled, in part, by rapid technological advances that have made ARTs more accessible to South Africans,[2] South African law has seen a boom of legislation and case law explicitly on medically assisted reproduction in the past decade. It is, at this point, beyond doubt that reproductive law has become an area of law in its own right. This burgeoning area of law is one deserving of in-depth legal analysis. Such an in-depth analysis is what this chapter provides.

b. Roadmap

The evolution of reproductive law in South Africa has been enabled by the recognition of reproductive health rights in the South African Constitution.[3] As such, this chapter begins by outlining these rights, and considers their implications for how ARTs must be regulated. Thereafter, we briefly outline the core relevant legislation that gives substance to the reproductive health rights of South Africans. The remainder of the chapter provides a succinct overview of the state of reproductive law in South Africa, which begins with an introduction to core concepts. This is followed by analyses of three subject areas that have been (and continue to be) areas of legal developments and thus represent the frontier of reproductive health rights in South Africa: gamete donation, surrogacy and genetic testing.

9.2 Reproductive Health Rights in the South African Constitution

Reproductive health rights received official recognition as fundamental human rights that protect the freedom of the individuals to choose the number, spacing and timing of their children, as well as their right to the information and means necessary to make reproductive decisions at the International Conference on Population and Development (ICPD) in 1994.[4] The events leading up to this coincided with the drafting

[2] Silke Dyer and others, 'Assisted Reproductive Technology in Africa: A 5-Year Trend Analysis from the African Network and Registry for ART' (2020) 41 Reproductive BioMedicine Online 604, 607.

[3] Constitution of the Republic of South Africa, 1996 (Constitution of South Africa).

[4] UN Population Fund, 'Report of the International Conference on Population and Development' (1994) 1995 UN Doc A/CONF.171/13/Rev.1 117.

of the Constitution of the Republic of South Africa—with the Interim Constitution being assented to in the same year, and the 'final Constitution' coming into effect just 4 years later. The ICPD, like many major international human rights laws at the time,[5] had a direct influence on the Constitution.[6] This is evident in how reproductive rights are provided for both as part of the right to bodily and psychological integrity (section 12(2)) and the right to access health care (section 27), as well as in how the terminology used in these provisions draw directly from the Programme of Action adopted at the ICPD, as illustrated in Table 9.1.

Reproductive health rights are capable of being exercised through *negative* reproductive decisions—those related to abstaining from reproduction—or through *positive* reproductive decisions—those related to choosing to have children. In both cases, individuals are entitled to the 'information and means' necessary to act on their reproductive plans through family planning services and access to medical services and technology.[7]

Historically, negative reproductive decisions have been the focus of reproductive rights in international human rights law.[8] Similarly, negative reproductive decisions have traditionally been the focus of reproductive rights in South African law. The earliest cases where reference was made to reproductive health rights in South African law were cases where these rights were used to shore up the validity of South Africa's permissive legislation on the termination of pregnancy.[9] However, positive reproductive decisions are becoming increasingly relevant in South African law as the use of ARTs becomes more prevalent—most notably in the

[5] See, John Dugard, 'The Influence of International Human Rights Law on the South African Constitution' (1996) 49 Current Legal Problems 305.

[6] Bonginkosi Shozi, 'Something Old, Something New: Applying Reproductive Rights to New Reproductive Technologies in South Africa' (2020) 36 South African Journal on Human Rights 1, 5–6.

[7] See, African Union, 'Protocol to the African Charter on Human and People's Rights on the Rights of Women in Africa' (2003).

[8] Shozi, 'Something Old, Something New: Applying Reproductive Rights to New Reproductive Technologies in South Africa' (n 6), 3–4.

[9] *Christian Lawyers Association of South Africa v Minister of Health* 1998 (4) SA 111 3 (T) (*Christian Lawyers* I); *Christian Lawyers Association of South Africa v Minister of Health* 2005 (1) SA 509 (T) (*Christian Lawyers* II). See below heading '9.3(a) A paradigm shift for reproductive healthcare policy: The Choice on Termination of Pregnancy Act'.

Table 9.1 Terminology in ICPD programme of action compared to the constitution

ICPD Programme of Action (1994)[10]	*Constitution of the Republic of South Africa (1996)*
Article 7.3: 'Reproductive rights embrace certain human rights that are already recognised in national laws, international human rights documents and other consensus documents. These rights rest on the recognition of the basic right of all couples and individuals to decide freely and responsibly the number, spacing and timing of their children and have the information and means to do so, and the right to attain the highest standard of sexual and reproductive health. It also includes their right to make **decisions concerning reproduction** free of discrimination, coercion and violence, as expressed in human rights documents'	Section 12: '(2) Everyone has the right to bodily and psychological integrity, which includes (a) the right to make **decisions concerning reproduction**'
Article 7.2: **Reproductive health** is a state of complete physical, mental and social wellbeing and not merely the absence of disease or infirmity, in all matters relating to the reproductive system and to its functions and processes	Section 27: '(1) Everyone has the right to have access to – (a) health care services, including **reproductive health** care'

landmark Constitutional Court judgement in *AB v Minister of Social Development*.[11]

While this case is significant in recognising reproductive health rights as applicable to the use of ARTs, the way in which the scope of these rights was defined by the Constitutional Court has been a subject of extensive criticism.[12] Given the controversy in this area, and the importance of this

[10] UN Population Fund, 'Programme of Action' adopted at the International Conference on Population and Development (1994).

[11] *AB v Minister of Social Development* 2017 (3) SA 570 (CC) (*AB* Constitutional Court judgment).

[12] See, Donrich Thaldar, 'Post-Truth Jurisprudence: The Case of *AB v Minister of Social Development*' (2018) 34 South African Journal on Human Rights 231; Denise Meyerson, 'Surrogacy, Geneticism and Equality: The Case of *AB v Minister of Social Development*' (2019) 9 Constitutional Court Review 317; Catherine Albertyn, 'Abortion,

decision, the scope of reproductive health rights in South Africa in light of the *AB* judgement is discussed below.

a. Defining the scope of reproductive health rights: Section 12(2)(a)

Section 12 of the Constitution is divided into two distinct rights: (1) the right to freedom and security of the person in section 12(1), and (2) the right to bodily and psychological integrity in section 12(2). Section 12(2)(a) stands as an affirmative recognition of reproductive health rights by protecting the freedom of all persons to make 'decisions concerning reproduction', but the wording of section 12(2) has led to debates regarding the scope of this right in the context of using ARTs. The debate centres around whether the use of the words 'bodily and psychological integrity' should be interpreted to mean that section 12(2)(a) is only infringed by the state when *both* the bodily integrity and psychological integrity of a person are impacted by a particular state act, or whether state action needs only impact bodily integrity *or* psychological integrity. Crucial to the resolution of this debate is an understanding of the relationship between section 12(1) and section 12(2).

This debate regarding the scope of section 12(2) of the Constitution, and by extension the reproductive health rights as enshrined in section 12(2)(a), emanates from *AB v Minister of Social Development*.[13] The case centred around an infertile woman, AB, who wanted to have a child through surrogacy using donor gametes. Although she had a willing surrogate mother, section 294 of the Children's Act[14] requires that single surrogacy commissioning parents, such as AB, use their own gametes for the conception of the child. Given the medical fact that AB's own eggs were not of sufficient quality to be used, section 294 had the effect of excluding her from using surrogacy. She challenged the constitutionality of section 294 on a variety of grounds, among others the infringement of her section 12(2) right to bodily and psychological

Reproductive Rights and the Possibilities of Reproductive Justice in South African Courts' (2019) University of Oxford Human Rights Hub Journal 87.

[13] *AB v Minister of Social Development* 2016 (2) SA 27 (GP) (*AB* High Court judgement); *AB* Constitutional Court judgement (n 11).

[14] Children's Act 38 of 2005, s 294 (Children's Act).

integrity, and in particular 12(2)(a), namely the right to make decisions concerning reproduction.

This was the first Constitutional Court judgement to consider reproductive health rights in the context of the use of ARTs, and which critically engaged with the content of the provisions of the Constitution that undergirded these rights. In this case, a majority of the Constitutional Court interpreted section 12(2)(a) as being infringed only where a particular state action had an impact upon both the bodily integrity *and* the psychological integrity of the individual bringing the claim.[15] In other words, a majority of the Constitutional Court in *AB* viewed section 12(2) as inextricably bound to 12(1) and, therefore, to the concept of bodily integrity such that persons must show that their bodily integrity has been impacted upon in order to claim that their right 'to make decisions concerning reproduction' was infringed. This has the effect that section 12(2)(a) (and by extension, reproductive health rights generally) are limited only to uses of ARTs involving *the use of one's own body*, because it is only in such cases that an act which prevents the use of said ARTs can be said to impact on their bodily integrity.

Part of the majority's justification for its finding was that section 12(2) derived from section 11 of the Interim Constitution (titled 'Freedom and security of the person'[16]) and, since the scope of which was determined to be the protection of bodily integrity in *Ferreira v Levin NO*,[17] the same went for section 12(2). The minority judgement, on the other hand, challenged this justification, taking the view that *Ferreira* was irrelevant to the interpretation of section 12(2) on the grounds that the right to bodily and psychological integrity is a significant departure from section 11 of the Interim Constitution.[18] As stated in the judgement, the minority took the view that, 'the focus in *Ferreira* was on freedom and security of the person—a right now protected explicitly by section 12(1). *Ferreira* should

[15] *AB* Constitutional Court judgement (n 11) [315].

[16] The text of section 11 of the Interim Constitution of the Republic of South Africa, 1993 is as follows: '(1) Every person shall have the right to freedom and security of the person, which shall include the right not to be detained without trial. (2) No person shall be subject to torture of any kind, whether physical, mental or emotional, nor shall any person be subject to cruel, inhuman or degrading treatment or punishment'.

[17] Ferreira v Levin; Vryenhoek v Powell 1996 (1) SA 984 (CC) [54].

[18] This is evident from the text of section 11 of the Constitution, which does not feature the words 'bodily', 'psychological' or 'integrity'.

therefore not be used as an ill-fitting interpretative crow-bar to pry open other freedom rights.[19] From this exchange, we see that the difference of viewpoints by the majority and minority of the Constitutional Court centres on the question of whether the right of freedom and security of the person as per section 12(1) (and its concomitant confinement to the domain of bodily integrity as per the case of *Ferreira*) is something that applies to all of section 12—including 12(2)(a)—or just 12(1). Put differently, is section 12(2) essentially an extension of section 12(1) in being an expression of the right to 'freedom and security of the person' (as it once existed in section 11 of the interim Constitution)? Or is section 12(2) a new right, standing apart from section 12(1) such that its scope should not be limited to infringements of bodily integrity in the same section 12(1) is?

In other cases where the courts have engaged with the relationship between section 12(1) and section 12(2), while some overlap between the two has been recognised, courts have typically applied either one or the other—a decision based on which of the two was deemed more appropriate to apply in the circumstances of that case.[20] For instance, in *Christian Lawyers' Association v National Minister of Health and Others*,[21] the court remarks that the right of a woman to determine the fate of her own pregnancy could be based on section 12(1), but finds that such a conclusion is unnecessary because section 12(2) was more specifically related to issues relating to women's reproductive choices.[22] Ergo, while the scope of section 12(1) and section 12(2) may sometimes overlap such that both provisions may be applicable, it seems each of these provisions has long been interpreted as being separate and independent—calling into question the finding of the majority of *AB* that seemingly conflated the two as aspects of one and the same right.

[19] *AB* Constitutional Court judgement (n 11) [77].

[20] The potential distinction between s 12(1) and s 12(2) is one which the Constitutional Court acknowledged but declined to deal with in *Law Society of South Africa v Minister for Transport* 2011 (1) SA 400 (CC) [57]. The Constitutional Court accepted the decision by the court *a quo* not to apply s 12(2) and instead based its decision on 12(1)(c). The court *a quo*'s finding that 12(2), 'does not apply, nor was it intended to apply, to victims of motor vehicle accidents in the context of the State being obliged to afford "an appropriate remedy" to such victims'.

[21] *Christian Lawyers* II (n 10).

[22] Ibid. [46].

Another important distinction between section 12(1) and section 12(2) is the element of psychological integrity, which finds mention only in the latter of the two provisions. Despite the fact psychological integrity is not one of the rights included under 'security of the person' in our law as it is in the Canadian Charter of Human Rights and Freedoms,[23] the majority of the Constitutional Court in *AB* refers to this provision in justifying its view that the scope of section 12(2)—like section 12(1)—is inextricably bound to bodily integrity such that reproductive health rights cannot be applied to uses of ARTs that do not involve the use of one's own body. In making reference to Canadian jurisprudence, the majority states: 'Jurisprudence in comparable jurisdictions also shows that security of the person encompasses personal autonomy involving control over a person's bodily integrity'.[24] Regrettably, the majority misrepresents the state of Canadian law by stating that the right to 'security of the person' encompasses bodily integrity as if it does not also encompass psychological integrity.

In Canadian law, bodily integrity and psychological integrity are both protected, independently, under the right to security of the person.[25] This is illustrated in *R. v. Morgentaler* (to which the majority refers), where the Canadian Supreme Court interpreted bodily integrity and psychological integrity as two separate rights, and concluded that state limitation on access to abortion was an infringement of each one of these rights.[26] In other words, in Canadian law, persons may claim that their rights are infringed by state policy that limits their use of reproductive technologies, even if said policy impacts upon *just their psychological integrity*. These claims must show that a particular occurrence had (1) a profound impact on them psychologically and (2) resulted from state action.[27] This

[23] Peter Hogg, *Constitutional Law of Canada* (3 edn, Carswell, 1992) [44.8].

[24] *AB* Constitutional Court judgement (n 11) [314].

[25] *R v Morgentaler* [1988] 1 SCR 30.

[26] Ibid. [54]. Given that the Canadian Supreme Court explicitly rejects arguments made by the Crown that the scope of security of the person is limited to bodily integrity it hard to see how this case could be used as evidence to support the assertion that section 12(2) is primarily concerned with bodily integrity.

[27] See, *Blencoe v British Columbia (Human Rights Commission)* [2000] 2 SCR 307 [60]–[61]; *New Brunswick (Minister of Health and Community Services) v G(J)* [1999] 3 SCR 46; *B(R) v Children's Aid Society of Metropolitan Toronto* [1995] 1 SCR 315; *Winnipeg Child and Family Services v KLW* [2000] 2 SCR 519 [59].

jurisprudence, it seems, supports the contrary position to the one taken by the majority, i.e., that section 12(2) must be interpreted as its own right which is capable of being infringed by acts that impact upon a person's bodily integrity *or just their psychological integrity*—rather than as constrained to acts that impact on bodily integrity as section 12(1) is.

The imperative for recognising a self-standing right that is infringed by acts that only impact upon psychological integrity is especially apparent in instances where a particular state action clearly has a serious effect on the mental and emotional wellbeing of a person, without interfering with their body. In *New Brunswick (Minister of Health and Community Services) v. G (J)*,[28] the Canadian Supreme Court held that the state arbitrarily depriving parents of custody over their children was a violation of the parents' right to security of the person, because this amounts to a serious interference with the psychological integrity of the parents.[29] The approach taken in *AB* would preclude such claims from being brought under section 12(2) even though the wording of the provision explicitly refers to psychological integrity. Given that psychological harms can have a severely deleterious impact on the dignity of the individual, his or her personal autonomy and ability to feel safe and secure, it does not appear that the position taken in *AB* is in line with the values of the Constitution.

All these factors, considered together, cast serious doubt on the justification of the Constitutional Court in reaching its conclusion in *AB*. It is, thus, unsurprising that subsequent judgments dealing with the interpretation of section 12(2)(a) in relation to the use of ARTs have not followed the trend set by *AB*. In the recent case of *Surrogacy Advisory Group v Minister of Health*,[30] the applicant challenged the constitutionality of certain provisions in the regulations governing the use ARTs in South Africa. One of the provisions challenged by the applicant was the prohibition on non-medical preimplantation sex selection, which it argued violated, inter alia, prospective parents' rights in terms of section 12(2)(a) and (b).[31] The court was confronted with the question of whether section 12(2)(a) applied, as the respondent—the Minister of Health—argued that a prohibition on non-medical preimplantation

[28] *New Brunswick* (n 27).

[29] Ibid. [58]–[61].

[30] *Surrogacy Advisory Group v Minister of Health* 2023 (1) SA 241 (GP).

[31] Ibid. [113].

sex selection cannot infringe section 12(2)(a) because the act of non-medical preimplantation sex selection is performed outside the woman's body (i.e., on an in vitro embryo), and thus her body, and rights in terms of section 12(2)(a), are not affected. Rejecting this line of argument, the court in *Surrogacy Advisory Group* concludes that: '[section] 12(2)(a) does not reduce reproductive choices to only when an embryo is inside a woman's body'.[32] On this basis, the court found that the provision prohibiting non-medical preimplantation sex selection was an infringement of the right to bodily and psychological integrity.[33]

Importantly, the court in *Surrogacy Advisory Group* does not seem to regard its interpretation of section 12(2)(a) as being at odds with the interpretation of the majority in *AB*:

> In *AB v Minister of Social Development* [2016] ZACC 43 par 314 the court clarified that in the case of surrogacy, s 12(2)(a) is only applicable to a woman's own body and not the body of another woman (i.e., the person carrying the child). This is not the case here, as the woman who seeks protection is the person carrying the child.[34]

This seemingly innocuous comment, made in a footnote, has potentially far-reaching consequences as it suggests the interpretation given to section 12(2)(a) in *AB* only applies to surrogacy. Ergo, persons claiming a violation to their right to make decisions concerning reproduction in all other cases need not demonstrate that both bodily and psychology integrity had been affected. What is clear in the wake of *Surrogacy Advisory Group* is that the scope of section 12(2)(a) is not constrained to one's own body, but is rather (as the court puts it) relevant to all one's 'reproductive choices'.[35] In conclusion, the scope of reproductive health rights includes the use of ARTs, and laws that constrain reproductive choice that involves the use of ARTs may be struck down as unconstitutional.

[32] Ibid. [157].

[33] Ibid. [168] (a).

[34] Ibid. [158], footnote 135.

[35] Ibid. [168] (a).

b. Defining the scope of reproductive health rights: Section 27(1)(a)

For clarity of interpretation and application, section 12(2)(a) must be read together with section 27(1)(a)—the right to reproductive healthcare. Section 27 of the Constitution contains socio-economic rights, which were included in the Constitution not as self-standing rights, but with the view that they would perform a 'norm setting' function for the state in the new constitutional dispensation—placing a duty on the state to ensure the substantive realisation of certain aspirations.[36]

Section 27(1)(a) specifically enjoins the state to 'take reasonable legislative and other measures' to ensure the realisation of the right to reproductive healthcare. The exact nature of what these measures must entail is unclear. It has been argued that section 27(1)(a), at the least, requires the state to make law that facilitates health care including access to ARTs,[37] and this is a view that finds support in preceding jurisprudence on socio-economic rights.[38]

When the *AB* case first came before the courts, the High Court of South Africa found that the right to access reproductive healthcare included the use ARTs, including in the context of double-donor surrogacy, and that this right had been infringed.[39] The majority of the Constitutional Court reasoned that (as a socio-economic right) section 27(1)(a) is not a self-standing right that is independently enforceable.[40] But the majority did not oppose the view that section 27(1)(a) could apply to ARTs. And in *Surrogacy Advisory Group*, the view that section 27(1)(a) can apply to ARTs was explicitly endorsed. The applicant argued that section 27(1)(a) gives rise to a negative duty on the state to refrain from limiting access to healthcare, therefore a provision requiring certain persons to undergo psychological evaluation in order to use ARTs

[36] Christof Heyns and Danie Brand, 'Introduction to Socio-Economic Rights in the South African Constitution' (1998) 2 Law, Democracy & Development 153, 155.

[37] Annelize Nienaber, 'The Grave's a Fine and Private Place: A Preliminary Exploration of the Law Relating to Posthumous Sperm Retrieval for Procreation' (2010) 25 Southern African Public Law 1, 8.

[38] *Government of the Republic of South Africa v Grootboom* 2001 (1) SA 46 (CC).

[39] *AB* High Court judgement (n 13) [137].

[40] *AB* Constitutional Court judgement (n 11) [322].

was unconstitutional.[41] The court agreed, finding that this psychological evaluation requirement unjustifiably infringed on section 27(1)(a).[42] This is a clear affirmation that the act of promulgating law regulating assisted human reproduction is one that the state is duty-bound to do with regard to their duty to provide access to reproductive healthcare. Ergo, the legislative framework relating to the use of ARTs that we discuss below is a manifestation of the state's duty in terms of section 27(1)(a).

9.3 Relevant Legislation

South Africa has three core statutory instruments relating to the use of ARTs for the purpose of medically assisted reproduction (MAR) in humans. These are: (i) the National Health Act 61 of 2003; (ii) the Children's Act 38 of 2005; and (iii) Regulations Relating to the Artificial Fertilisation of Persons. Each of these three core statutes will be briefly described below.

Before beginning our discussion of the core statutes, it is necessary to discuss another statute which is less directly related to MAR—the Choice on Termination of Pregnancy Act.[43] This is necessary because of how the rise to prominence of reproductive health rights shaped the development of this statute, and how the statute was the forebearer of a paradigm shift in the regulatory approach of the South African government towards reproductive healthcare. It is important to reflect on the history and development of this legislation, to properly understand and contextualise the current regulatory framework.

a. A paradigm shift for reproductive healthcare policy: The Choice on Termination of Pregnancy Act

Prior to the new constitutional dispensation, termination of pregnancy in South Africa was regulated by the Abortion and Sterilization Act.[44] This statute prescribed that termination of pregnancy was generally prohibited unless (i) the continued pregnancy endangered the woman's life; (ii)

[41] *Surrogacy Advisory Group* (n 30) [68].

[42] Ibid. [88].

[43] Choice on Termination of Pregnancy Act 92 of 1996 (Choice Act).

[44] Abortion and Sterilization Act 2 of 1975.

the continued pregnancy was a serious threat to the woman's physical or mental health and will cause permanent damage; (iii) there was a serious risk that the child to be born will suffer a physical or mental defect of such a nature that it will be irreparably seriously handicapped; (iv) or the foetus has allegedly been conceived as a result of rape or incest, or the foetus was conceived in illegitimate carnal intercourse with a woman who was—due to a permanent mental handicap or other medical defect—unable to comprehend the consequential implications of or bear the parental responsibility for the prospective child.[45] As is apparent from the criteria listed here, underlying the government's position on the termination of pregnancy was the notion that the state had an interest in limiting abortions on the grounds that the destruction of a human foetus is somehow morally objectionable. Similar policies, driven by the same normative underpinnings, existed all around the world.[46] It is because of these normative underpinnings that the law permitted termination of pregnancy only where doing so was perceived a lesser evil than the continued pregnancy.

In the course of South Africa's transition into a multi-racial constitutional democracy founded on values such as autonomy, such a restrictive stance on abortion became untenable. Accordingly, in 1996, the Abortion Act was repealed by the Choice on Termination of Pregnancy Act (the Choice Act). This new legislation was an about-turn by our state on termination of pregnancy, influenced by the recognition of reproductive health rights in both international human rights law, and in the South African Constitution. This is acknowledged in the Preamble of the Choice Act, which expressly provides that it: 'repeals the restrictive and inaccessible provisions of the Abortion and Sterilization Act, 1975 (Act No. 2 of 1975), and promotes reproductive rights'. This legislation thus marks the first manifestation of the state's commitment to realising reproductive health rights.

In recognition of women's reproductive health rights, the Choice Act does not place a blanket prohibition on abortion subject to certain morally driven justification criteria as its predecessor did. However, it also does not grant carte blanche on termination of pregnancy with no

[45] Ibid. s 3.

[46] Marge Berer, 'Abortion Law and Policy Around the World' (2017) 19 Health and Human Rights 13, 14.

regard for the perceived normative significance of the human foetus that was at the heart of the position in the Abortion and Sterilization Act. Rather, the Choice Act is a compromise between these two positions, in limiting access to termination of pregnancy only after the first trimester,[47] and these limitations become more restrictive as the pregnancy (and accordingly the foetus) advances as described below.

A pregnant woman has the freedom to terminate within the first 12 weeks of the pregnancy, for any reason, without needing to provide any justification for doing so.[48] At week 13 of the pregnancy, the Act restricts the pregnant woman's freedom to terminate marginally by allowing termination of pregnancy only where it can be shown that the pregnancy: (i) risks physical or mental injury to the mother; (ii) causes substantial risk of physical or mental abnormality to the foetus; (iii) is due to incest or rape; (iv) will affect the socio-economic circumstances of the pregnant woman.[49] After 20 weeks, the pregnancy may be terminated if the continued pregnancy will endanger the woman's life or the foetus will be severely deformed or there is risk of injury to the foetus.[50]

Predictably, this paradigm shift in the state's approach to the termination of pregnancy led to controversy, particularly among religious organisations. This led to the first Constitutional Court judgement that engaged with the content of reproductive health rights in South Africa: *Christian Lawyers Association of South Africa v Minister of Health*.[51] In this case, the Christian Lawyers Association challenged the constitutionality of the Choice Act, arguing, inter alia, that the Choice Act was unconstitutional on the basis that it permits the termination of a human foetus, an act they argued violated the foetus' right to life (section 11 of the Constitution). The court dismissed the argument that a foetus has a right to life, on the grounds that personhood in South Africa does not begin at conception but at birth.[52] What is more, the court affirmed the constitutionality of the Choice Act as being founded upon, and underscored by, a woman's reproductive health rights as enshrined in

[47] Choice Act (n 44), s 2(1)(a).

[48] Ibid.

[49] Ibid. s 2(1)(b).

[50] Ibid. s 2(1)(c).

[51] *Christian Lawyers* I (n 10).

[52] Ibid. [1122B-F].

the Constitution.[53] This finding finds support in subsequent judgments relating to the constitutionality of the Choice Act.[54]

In light of the foregoing, it is beyond doubt that the constitutionalisation of reproductive health rights set the tone for subsequent legislation relating to human reproduction. Since the promulgation of the Choice Act, the default position in the state's approach to reproductive health issues has been permissive in a way that is mindful of these reproductive health rights, although limitations have been imposed with the view of balancing reproductive health rights with countervailing state interests. Whether this balance is always well struck is, however, an open question.

b. Core statutes

i. National Health Act

The National Health Act 61 of 2003 (the National Health Act) is the principal legislation governing South Africa's national healthcare system. Chapter 8 of the National Health is of specific relevance to MAR, as this part of the NHA regulates human biological material. This includes gametes and embryos.[55] The NHA takes a broadly permissive position of MAR, as it, in several instances, recognises that gametes and embryos may be used for reproductive purposes provided that the relevant requirements are complied with. For instance, the NHA prescribes that informed consent must be given in writing prior to gametes being removed from a living person.[56] As the primary legislation in healthcare (including reproductive healthcare), all other laws, regulations, policies and guidelines that regulate some aspect of MAR must conform to the prescripts of the NHA.

ii. Children's Act

The Children's Act 38 of 2005 (the Children's Act) is the primary legislation for all matters relating to children. Though the Children's Act primarily focuses on children that already exist, it also attends to matters that relate to children that are yet to exist—such as those to be born

[53] Ibid. [1441J]–[1442A].

[54] *Christian Lawyers* II (n 10) [528D].

[55] National Health Act 61 of 2003, s 1 (National Health Act).

[56] Ibid. s 55(a).

via MAR (i.e., prospective children). The Children's Act regulates three specific areas where MAR intersects with the interests and wellbeing of the prospective child: (i) the acquisition of parental responsibilities and rights relating to children conceived via MAR[57]; (ii) the rights of children conceived via MAR[58]; and (iii) surrogacy.[59]

iii. Regulations Relating to the Artificial Fertilisation of Persons

In addition to containing general provisions relating to the use of human biological material, including gametes as embryos, the National Health Act in section 68 empowers the Minister of Health to promulgate regulations pertaining to any matters that fall within the remit of Chapter 8.[60] One of the matters listed in section 68 is 'the artificial fertilisation of persons' (i.e., MAR). As such, in 2012, the Minister published the Regulations Relating to the Artificial Fertilisation of Persons (the 2012 Regulations).[61] The 2012 Regulations provide for various aspects relating to 'the withdrawal of gametes from and for use in living persons'[62] including removal or withdrawal of gametes and their storage,[63] practices related to gamete donation,[64] and general requirements for the provision of MAR services.[65]

Since 2012, revised draft regulations have been published in 2016 (2016 Regulations),[66] but these never became law. In March 2021, another set of revised draft regulations (2021 Regulations)[67] were

[57] Children's Act (n 14), s 19(3), s 26(2)(b), s 40(3).

[58] Ibid. s 40, s 41.

[59] Ibid. s 296.

[60] National Heath Act (n 55), s 68.

[61] Regulations Relating to the Artificial Fertilisation of Persons GN R175, GG 35099 (2 March 2012) (2012 Regulations).

[62] Ibid. reg 2.

[63] Ibid. reg 3.

[64] Ibid. reg 6, reg 7, reg 8.

[65] Ibid. reg 9, reg 10, reg 11, reg 12.

[66] [Draft] Regulations Relating to the Artificial Fertilisation of Persons GN 1165, GG 40312, 30 September 2016.

[67] [Draft] Regulations Relating to Assisted Conception of Persons GN 251, GG 44321, 25 March 2021.

published for public comment. However, given the extensive criticism levied against the contents of these regulations,[68] it seems unlikely that they will be promulgated any time soon, and without extensive revision.

9.4 Core Concepts in South African Reproductive Law

a. A woman's right to access MAR healthcare services

The regulation of MAR in South Africa centres, to a large extent, on the 'recipient', i.e., the woman who intends to carry the MAR-induced pregnancy. Any woman can access MAR healthcare services; accordingly, any woman who intends to become pregnant through MAR qualifies as a recipient. Importantly, the woman does not need to have any medical reason to access MAR herself. She can do so for any reason that she herself finds sufficient. For example, a woman in a lesbian marriage or a single woman can access MAR in South Africa. Note, however, that medical reasons are required if a woman intends to become a surrogacy commissioning parent—surrogate motherhood is discussed in more detail below.

b. The recipient's right to use donor gametes

When using MAR, a recipient has the right to use donor gametes (male, female, or both).[69] Again, no medical reason is required. Furthermore, the recipient has the right to select her gamete donor based on characteristics including eye colour, hair colour, race, complexion, religion, occupation, educational qualifications and fields of interest.[70] The treating health care professional at a fertility clinic has a legal duty to ensure that the recipient's wishes regarding gamete donor characteristics

[68] Donrich Thaldar and Bonginkosi Shozi, 'South Africa's Latest Medically Assisted Reproduction Draft Regulations: Close, but No Cigar' [2022] Tydskrif vir die Suid-Afrikaanse Reg 1.

[69] 2012 Regulation (n 61), reg 10(2)(a).

[70] Ibid. reg 14(1)(a)(iii).

are adhered to.[71] The use of donor gametes is accepted medical practice in South Africa.[72]

c. Ownership of reproductive material

The 2012 Regulations provide for the ownership of reproductive material.[73] As a rule, a person who provides his or her gametes for purposes of MAR is deemed the owner of his or her gametes. The exception is where a man provides his sperm for use by a woman who is not his wife—whether she is identified or not. This would typically include anonymous sperm donors, but may also include other categories of men who make use of MAR, such as gay couples. In such a case, namely where a man provides his sperm for use by a woman who is not his wife, the sperm is owned by the fertility clinic or sperm bank where the man donated his sperm. Once an in vitro embryo is created, the embryo is owned by the recipient—irrespective of whether her own egg was used or not.[74]

Importantly, although the Regulations provide who initially acquires ownership in reproductive material when it is produced or created, the Regulations do not limit the contractual freedom of persons to transfer ownership. Accordingly, persons involved with MAR are free to arrange the ownership of reproductive material as they deem fit.

d. Parental rights and responsibilities

Except in the case of surrogacy,[75] the woman who gives birth to a child is the legal mother of the child—irrespective of whether she has a genetic link with the child.[76] The woman's husband at the time of either (a)

[71] Ibid. reg 11(c)(ii).

[72] Dr. Rodrigues, Expert opinion (filed in *AB* High Court judgement (n 13) and *AB* Constitutional Court judgement (n 11)).

[73] 2012 Regulation (n 61), reg 18.

[74] For a critique of the way in which the Regulations provide for ownership of reproductive material, see Donrich Thaldar, 'The In Vitro Embryo and the Law: The Ownership Issue and a Response to Robinson' [2020] Potchefstroom Electronic Law Journal 1.

[75] See below heading '9.6 Surrogate motherhood'.

[76] Children's Act (n 14), s 40(2).

the creation of the in vitro embryo that resulted in the child, or (b) the transfer of the in vitro embryo that resulted in the child,[77] is deemed to be the legal father of the child—irrespective of whether he has a genetic link with the child.[78]

In this context, the Pretoria High Court recently held that the use of the word 'husband' excludes lesbian couples and constitutes an unjustified limitation of their right to equality.[79] As a remedy, the court replaced the word 'husband' with 'spouse'. Note that this judgement will only enter into effect once—and if—confirmed by the Constitutional Court.

Gamete donors have no parental rights and responsibilities in respect of the donor-conceived child.[80] Note that a person can only be a gamete donor in the context of MAR, not in the context of reproduction through sexual intercourse.[81] Accordingly, a man who conceives a child through sexual intercourse with a woman can never be deemed the child's 'sperm donor'.[82] The fact that gamete donors have no parental rights or responsibilities in respect of the donor-conceived child does not mean that they are legally barred from acquiring such rights and responsibilities.[83] Similar to any other person who has a 'tangible and clearly demonstrable interest and connection' with a child, a gamete donor can, in principle, apply to the court to be granted parental rights and responsibilities in respect of a child.[84] Note that any number of persons can have parental rights and responsibilities in respect of a child—it is not limited by law.[85] If a gamete donor applies to court for parental rights and responsibilities in respect of the child, the fact that there is a genetic link between the applicant and the child will be irrelevant to the court's decision.[86] A person who applies to the court to be granted parental rights and responsibilities in respect of

[77] Ibid. s 1: Definition of 'artificial fertilisation'.

[78] Ibid. s 40(3).

[79] *VJV v Minister of Social Development* unreported case 27706/2021 ZAGPPHC (24 February 2022).

[80] Children's Act (n 14), s 26(2)(b).

[81] Ibid. s 26(2)(b).

[82] *BR v LS* 2018 (5) SA 308 (KZD).

[83] *QG v CS* 2021 (7) ECL 54 (GP).

[84] Ibid.

[85] Children's Act (n 14), s 41.

[86] *QG v CS* (n 83).

a child must prove that granting such parental rights and responsibilities would be in the best interest of the child.[87] Given that the stability of the child's existing family unit is in the best interest of the child,[88] an applicant would probably only be successful if he or she has already fulfilled an actual and valuable parent-like role in the child's life.[89]

e. The hush rule

South African sperm banks and egg donation agencies only offer anonymous gamete donors, as it is generally assumed that donor anonymity is a legal requirement in South Africa.[90] The 2012 Regulations indeed provide that it is unlawful to disclose the identity of (a) a person who has donated gametes for use in MAR, (b) a person who underwent MAR or (c) a person who was born as a result of MAR.[91] The clear purpose of this provision is to protect the privacy of persons in (a) to (c).[92] However, the provision in the 2012 Regulations is formulated so overbroad that it renders it unlawful for persons in (a) to (c) to themselves disclose their involvement in MAR. This is clearly problematic and has resulted in litigation against the state.[93] The Pretoria High Court held that the relevant regulation must be 'read down' to allow persons in (a) to (c) to disclose their own identities.[94]

[87] Children's Act (n 14), s 41.

[88] Ibid. 7(1)(k).

[89] See: Bonginkosi Shozi, Roasia Hazarilall and Donrich Thaldar, 'Blood Is Thicker Than Water, but Is It Thicker Than Ink? An Analysis of Parenthood and Sperm Donor Agreements in the Wake of *QG v CS*' (2022) 33 Stellenbosch Law Review 529. See also Professor Donrich Thaldar's ***amicus curiae*** heads of argument (*QG v CS* 2021 (7) ECL 54 (GP)) https://thaldtian.files.wordpress.com/2021/07/heads-of-argument6-anon.pdf. Accessed 19 June 2022.

[90] Donrich Thaldar and Bonginkosi Shozi, 'Is Open-Identity Gamete Donation Lawful in South Africa?' (2022) 112 South African Medical Journal 1.

[91] 2012 Regulation (n 61), reg 19.

[92] Thaldar and Shozi 'Is Open-Identity Gamete Donation Lawful in South Africa?' (n 90).

[93] *Surrogacy Advisory Group* (n 30).

[94] Ibid. [199].

Importantly, another set of regulations[95] made in terms of the National Health Act—the General Control Regulations—provides that the gamete donor's identity can indeed be disclosed—subject only to his or her consent.[96]

9.5 Gamete Donation

a. General provisions

Gamete donation entails the removal of sperm or eggs from a living person for use in MAR, which may only be performed by a 'competent person' in terms of the 2012 Regulations.[97] One qualifies as a competent person if he or she is: a gynaecologist with training in reproductive medicine; or a medical scientist, medical technologist or clinical technologist with training in reproductive biology and related laboratory practices.[98] It is also a requirement that the donated gametes only be used for MAR at an 'authorised institution'—which refers to an institution duly authorised to provide MAR services such as gamete bank or fertility clinic.[99] The competent person must ensure that not more than six children are conceived using gametes from a single donor.[100]

b. Who is a gamete donor?

In order to be a gamete donor, a person must provide written consent,[101] be at least 18 years old,[102] and be subjected to testing and analysis to ensure their suitability as a donor.[103] Typically, the term 'gamete donor' refers to a person who is providing his or her gametes to another person

[95] Regulations regarding the General Control of Human Bodies, Tissue, Blood, Blood Products and Gametes GN R180, GG 35099 (2 March 2012).

[96] Ibid. reg 24(1)(c).

[97] 2012 Regulation (n 61), reg 3(1).

[98] Ibid. reg 1.

[99] Ibid. reg 9(1).

[100] Ibid. reg 6.

[101] Ibid. reg 7(e).

[102] Ibid. reg 10(1)(c).

[103] Ibid. reg 10(1)(b).

(or other persons) for said person(s) to use in MAR, with the expectation that the person(s) using the gametes will play the role of the parent(s) of the donor-conceived child, and not the donor. The 2012 Regulations take a broader approach, defining a gamete donor as: '[a] living person from whose body a gamete or gametes are removed or withdrawn, for the purpose of artificial fertilisation'.[104] In other words, the 2012 Regulations define gamete donor in a way that includes all persons who provide their gametes for MAR, regardless of whether they are in fact ***donating*** their gametes (i.e., transferring ownership of them to another person).[105] This means that persons are gamete donors:

(i) in the typical case, where they are providing gametes, on an anonymous basis, to a person not known to them, but also;
(ii) where they are providing the gametes for their *own* MAR, such as where a woman has an egg removed for the purposes of IVF with donor sperm, and the resultant embryo is then implanted in her uterus. This woman is, confusingly, her own donor in terms of the 2012 regulations; and
(iii) where they are providing gametes for the MAR of someone known to them, such as a husband providing sperm for the artificial insemination of his wife.

This overbroad definition has a number of anomalous consequences, much of which relate to the fact that criteria ostensibly intended for gamete donors in the typical case of (i)—such as the requirement that identifying information about the donor not be disclosed[106]—on a plain reading of the text of the 2012 Regulations, also apply to gamete donors in cases (ii) and (iii).[107]

[104] Ibid. reg 1.

[105] See above heading '9.4(c) Ownership of reproductive material'.

[106] See below heading '9.5(c) Known donors vs unknown donors'.

[107] Thaldar and Shozi, 'South Africa's Latest Medically Assisted Reproduction Draft Regulations: Close, but No Cigar' (n 68), 4.

c. Known donors versus unknown donors

Within the broad umbrella of 'gamete donor' as defined in the 2012 Regulations, a distinction is made between two specific kinds of donors: donors who are *not* known to the person(s) who will be using their gametes for MAR at the time the donation occurs (unknown donors), and donors who *are* known to person(s) who will be using their gametes for MAR (known donors).

Typically, unknown donors will be individuals recruited by a gamete donor bank or fertility clinic, whose gametes have been removed and stored by the gamete donor bank or fertility clinic. In such cases, a person seeking to have children using donor gametes shall have the opportunity to select from the donor gametes the gamete bank or fertility clinic has available. In such cases the person seeking to make use of the donor gametes, the gamete bank or fertility clinic offering the donor gametes is not permitted to reveal identifying information about the gamete donor to prospective parents.[108] However, they may have non-identifying information—including the gamete donor's race, religion, hair colour, eye colour and level of educational qualification—which prospective parents may use in making their choice of donor.[109] Even after the birth of a child, gamete banks and fertility clinics are enjoined not to reveal any information to the donor-conceived child or their legal guardian that would reveal the identity of an unknown donor.[110]

With known donors, on the other hand, the onus on gamete banks and fertility clinics to keep identifying information secret falls away because the prospective parent and the gamete donor are known to each other. Most commonly, this will be because the gamete donor is either 'donating' gametes for their own MAR—such as where the 'gamete donor' is a man who is the husband or life partner of a woman who intends to be the recipient of his sperm via artificial insemination.[111] But South African law also provides for circumstances where a person other than a

[108] 2012 Regulations (n 61), reg 19.

[109] Ibid. reg 14(1)(a)(iii), reg 11(c)(ii).

[110] Children's Act (n 14), s 41(2).

[111] See above heading '9.4(a) A woman's right to access MAR healthcare services'.

spouse or life partner becomes a gamete donor to a person who is known to them.[112] This could be a close family member or friend, although it is becoming increasingly common for prospective parents and potential gamete donors to find each other on the internet via social media platforms like Facebook.[113]

Known donors must provide written confirmation that they are known to each other, and both the donor and the recipient must undergo psychological evaluations before gamete removal can occur.[114] It is also advisable for known gamete donors who are not a spouse or life partner to provide informed consent, in writing, to being a known donor, as well as arranging for if, when and what identifying information about them will be shared with the donor-conceived child.[115]

d. Compensation

Notwithstanding the fact that gametes can be owned,[116] the sale or trade of gametes and embryos is strictly prohibited.[117] As such, gamete donors cannot be paid by a gamete bank or fertility clinic for making their donations. They may, however, be reimbursed for reasonable expenses incurred in the process of making the donation.

e. Extraordinary cases

In recent years, cases have come before the courts that have confronted legal 'grey areas' concerning (i) the removal of gametes from a person who is rendered medically incapable of providing consent (i.e., comatose), and (ii) the use of donor gametes. These cases and their implications are discussed briefly below.

[112] Regulations Regarding the General Control of Human Bodies, Tissue, Blood, Blood Products and Gametes (n 95), reg 24(1)(c). For a comprehensive discussion of this issue, see, Thaldar and Shozi, 'Is open-identity gamete donation lawful in South Africa?' (n 90).

[113] This is what happened in the case of *QG v CS* (n 83).

[114] 2012 Regulations (n 61), reg 7(j)(i) (ii).

[115] Thaldar and Shozi, 'Is Open-Identity Gamete Donation Lawful in South Africa?' (n 90), 4.

[116] See 2012 Regulations (n 61), reg 3(c).

[117] National Health Act (n 55), s 60(4)(a).

i. Comatose gamete removal

In the case of *Ex Parte SN*, the court granted an order allowing a woman to have her comatose (and dying) husband's sperm removed from him and stored, with the intention of using it for MAR after her husband died.[118] Notably, this order permitted comatose gamete removal not only without the man's written consent, but without any other evidence proving his consent to, or desire for, comatose gamete removal and posthumous reproduction. The wife, as the husband's *curatix ad personam*, was legally empowered to consent to the gamete removal on the husband's behalf in terms of section 7(1) of the National Health Act, which described the circumstances within which one can give consent to health services on behalf of another.[119]

This case established that in cases where an individual is incapable of giving consent, an individual empowered to provide consent to health services on behalf of that person may give consent to gamete removal. The subsequent use of said gametes, however, is a separate issue. The court in *Ex Parte SN* refused to adjudicate whether the use of the gametes of the husband after his death would be lawful.

ii. Posthumous reproduction

In the 2018 judgement of *NC v Aevitas*, the court granted an order allowing a woman to use her deceased husband's sperm for MAR.[120] The couple had chosen to have the husband's sperm cryopreserved after he had been diagnosed with cancer and learning he would have to undergo chemotherapy, in order to preserve their dream of having children that were genetically related to both of them.[121] At the fertility clinic, the consent form contained a section where he was asked what ought to happen to his sperm in the event of his death. The husband made the

[118] *Ex Parte SN* unreported case 2020/10242 ZAGHC (7 May 2020).

[119] Bonginkosi Shozi, 'Legal Issues in Posthumous Conception Using Gametes Removed from a Comatose Male: The Case of *Ex Parte SN*' (2021) 14 South African Journal of Bioethics and Law 28, 29.

[120] *NC v Drs Aevitas Inc t/a Aevitas Fertility Clinic* unreported case 23236/2017 ZAWCHC (23 January 2018).

[121] Bonginkosi Shozi, 'A Human Rights Analysis of Posthumous Reproduction' (Master's Dissertation, University of KwaZulu-Natal 2018) 44.

election that his sperm should be assigned to the care of his wife on his death, indicating his approval of her use of said sperm.

The *Aevitas* judgement confirmed that posthumous conception is legal—at least in cases where the deceased spouses consent to having their gametes used by their surviving spouses after their death is clear and uncontested.[122]

9.6 Surrogate Motherhood

a. General provisions

Surrogacy is specifically regulated in South Africa by Chapter 19 of the Children's Act. The 'commissioning parent' is defined in the Children's Act as the person who 'enters into a surrogate motherhood agreement with a surrogate mother'.[123] It may be more helpful to define the commissioning parent as the parent who intends to raise the child.[124] The Act defines a 'surrogate mother' as the 'adult woman who enters into a surrogate motherhood agreement with the commissioning parent'.[125] The surrogate mother must understand and accept the legal consequences of the surrogacy arrangement[126] and have a living child of her own.[127] The surrogate mother agrees to be the 'gestational mother', willing to carry the child but without intending to raise the child; rather the child is handed over to the commissioning parent to raise.[128] Altruistic surrogacy

[122] See, Donrich Thaldar, 'Posthumous Conception: Recent Legal Developments in South Africa' (2018) 108 South African Medical Journal 471.

[123] Children's Act (n 14), s 1(1).

[124] Samantha Vanessa Lewis, 'The Constitutional and Contractual Implications of the Application of Chapter 19 of the Children's Act 38 of 2005' (LLM dissertation, University of Western Cape 2011), 13. In fact, commissioning parents are often referred to as the 'intended parents', which is precisely what they are—those intending to parent the child born to the surrogate.

[125] Ibid. Surrogate means 'substitute' or 'stand-in'—an apt description as the surrogate is the woman who 'stands in' for another person who is unable to successfully carry a child.

[126] Children's Act (n 14), s 295(c)(iii).

[127] Ibid. s 295(c)(viii).

[128] Ibid. s 1(1): 'an agreement between a surrogate mother and a commissioning parent in which it is agreed that the surrogate mother will be artificially fertilised for the purpose

is available to a single person and to opposite-sex or same-sex couples who are permanently and irreversibly unable to give birth to a child.[129]

b. Compensation in respect of a surrogate motherhood agreement

Commercial surrogacy is not permitted in South Africa.[130] No person in connection with a surrogate motherhood agreement may receive reward or compensation, except to cover specific expenses: the artificial fertilisation of the surrogate mother, any loss of earnings suffered by the surrogate mother as a result of the surrogate motherhood agreement, as well as insurance to cover the surrogate in the event of her death or disability brought on by the pregnancy.[131] In addition, the commissioning parents can reimburse the surrogate mother on a monthly basis for her pregnancy-related expenses. Table 9.2 provides the monthly budget for reimbursable expenses that was approved by the Johannesburg High Court in 2018.[132] These amounts should be adapted for inflation on an annual basis. Legal and medical professional persons offering their professional services related to surrogacy are entitled to reasonable compensation.[133]

c. The surrogate motherhood agreement

To enter into a valid surrogacy arrangement, the commissioning parents and the surrogate mother, as well as the surrogate mother's husband or permanent partner,[134] sign a surrogate motherhood agreement that must

of bearing a child for the commissioning parent and in which the surrogate mother undertakes to hand over such a child to the commissioning parent upon its birth, or within a reasonable time thereafter, with the intention that the child concerned becomes the legitimate child of the commissioning parent'.

129 Ibid. s 295(a). Regarding the meaning of 'permanently and irreversibly unable to give birth to a child', see: Donrich W. Jordaan, 'Legal Access to Surrogate Motherhood in Illness That Does Not Cause Infertility' (2016) 106 South African Medical Journal 684.

130 Children's Act (n 14), s 295(c)(iv), s 301.

131 Ibid. s 301(1), s 301(2).

132 *Ex Parte KAF* [2018] ZAGPJHC 529.

133 Children's Act (n 14), s 301(3).

134 Children's Act (n 14), s 293.

Table 9.2 Budget for reimbursable expenses (2018)[135]

Expense by surrogate mother	*Amount*	*Period*
Cellular phone calls	R500 per month	From the confirmation of the surrogacy agreement until the birth of the child
Vitamins, nutritional supplements and scar creams	R1500 per month	For the duration of the pregnancy
Domestic worker	R3500 per month	From the onset of pregnancy, until three months thereafter
Maternity clothing	R6750	This amount is not per month, but for the duration of the pregnancy

first be confirmed by the High Court[136] before the artificial fertilisation of the surrogate mother takes place.[137] At least one of the commissioning parents at the time of entering into the agreement must be domiciled within South Africa.[138] The surrogate is also required to be domiciled within South Africa, although the court may do away with this requirement where good cause is shown.[139]

d. The effect of the surrogate motherhood agreement

In South Africa, two types of surrogacy are recognised—full and partial surrogacy. Full surrogacy is where the surrogate mother is merely the gestational mother and is not the genetic mother; her eggs are not used in the artificial fertilisation.[140] Partial surrogacy, on the other hand, is achieved by means of the artificial insemination of the surrogate mother with the sperm of the commissioning parent. In this case, the surrogate

[135] Donrich Thaldar, 'Criteria for assessing the suitability of intended surrogate mothers in South Africa: Reflections on *Ex Parte KAF* II' (2019) 12 South African Journal of Bioethics and Law 61.

[136] Ibid. s 292.

[137] Ibid. s 292(1)(a), s 292(1)(b).

[138] Ibid. s 292(1)(c).

[139] Ibid. s 292(1)(a).

[140] Parliamentary Ad Hoc Committee, Report by the Parliamentary Ad Hoc Committee on the South African Law Commission Report on Surrogate Motherhood (Cape Town: PAHC, 1999), 8.

mother is both the genetic and gestational mother since her egg has been utilised in the process of creating the embryo.[141] The effect of the surrogacy agreement is that any child born of the surrogate mother will be deemed the child of the commissioning parents from the moment of the birth of the child.[142] The surrogate mother is obliged to hand over the child as soon as possible after birth, and she enjoys no rights over the child.[143] However, in the case of partial surrogacy, the surrogate mother is given the option to terminate the surrogate motherhood agreement within sixty days of the birth of the child and acquire parental rights in respect of the child. Should this occur, the commissioning parents lose their parental rights over the child.[144] The commissioning father may retain his parental rights in situations where the surrogate mother is a single woman.[145] Given that full surrogacy provides legal certainty, it is preferred in practice. There has never been a reported case of partial surrogacy.

e. The genetic origins of the child

Commissioning parents must use their own gametes for the conception of the surrogacy child.[146] If this is not possible due to medical, biological or other valid reasons, at least one commissioning parent's gametes must be used.[147] In the case of a single commissioning parent, that parent's gametes must be used.[148] This 'genetic origins' requirement has been controversial and led to litigation against the state. However, in 2016, a 7–4 majority of the Constitutional Court held that this requirement

[141] Ibid.

[142] Children's Act (n 14), s 297(1)(a).

[143] Ibid. s 299 (b), s 299(c).

[144] Ibid. s 299(a).

[145] Ibid. s 299(a).

[146] Ibid. s 294.

[147] Ibid.

[148] Ibid.

was indeed constitutional.[149] The majority's judgement has been universally criticised in the academic literature.[150] Based on different facts, the genetic origins requirement is again heading to the Constitutional Court.[151]

f. The best interests of the child

The best interest of the child to be born is given careful consideration by the courts[152] and is a constitutional imperative in all matters affecting children. The court in *Ex Parte WH* saw its role in surrogacy matters as two-fold: 'On the one hand the court's role is that of facilitator of surrogate agreements and, on the other, it plays the role of gatekeeper and protector of the rights of the parties and the children born as a result of the agreement'.[153] It is important to note that the concept of the 'child to be born' is a mental construct and does not refer to the physical embryos.[154] Section 28(2) of the Constitution of South Africa provides that '[a] child's best interests are of paramount importance in every matter concerning the child'.[155] In considering the wording of this constitutional provision, the court in *S v M*[156] held that the language is both 'comprehensive and emphatic', and indicates that law enforcement must always be 'child-sensitive' and that 'statutes must be interpreted and the common law developed in a manner which favours protecting

[149] *AB* Constitutional Court judgement (n 11).

[150] Shozi 'Something Old, Something New: Applying Reproductive Rights to New Reproductive Technologies in South Africa' (n 6); Donrich Thaldar, 'The Constitution as an Instrument of Prejudice: A Critique of *AB v Minister of Social Development*' (2019) 9 Constitutional Court Review 343; Donrich Thaldar, 'Post-Truth Jurisprudence: The Case of *AB v Minister of Social Development*' (n 12); Carmel Van Niekerk, 'Section 294 of the Children's Act: Do Roots Really Matter?' (2015) 18 Potchefstroom Electronic Law Journal/Potchefstroomse Elektroniese Regsblad 397; Meyerson (n 12), 294.

[151] *KB v Minister of Social Development* [2023] ZAMPMBHC 12.

[152] Children's Act (n 14), s 295(e).

[153] *Ex Parte WH* 2011 6 SA 514 (GNP) [63].

[154] *Ex Parte KAF* (n 132) [14]. The court held that 'not one of these embryos can be legally equated with the child that is to be born,' and that 'the embryos are merely the human biological material that may give rise to the child that is to be born'.

[155] Constitution of South Africa (n 3).

[156] *S v M* 2007 (2) SACR 539 (CC).

and advancing the interests of children'.[157] The best interest principle has not, however, been given an exhaustive content, but rather the standard is flexible, allowing courts to take an individualised approach based on the specifics of the situation.[158] This is a fundamental feature in the conservation of children's rights,[159] clearly asserted in *S v M*:

> A truly principled child-centred approach requires a close and individualised examination of the precise real-life situation of the particular child involved. To apply a pre-determined formula for the sake of certainty, irrespective of the circumstances, would in fact be contrary to the best interests of the child concerned.[160]

Furthermore, the court clarified that the 'best interests of the child' is by no means an 'overbearing and unrealistic' trump over all rights, and may be limited appropriately[161]; however, it remains a right which is granted a degree of privilege in the balancing of rights.[162] In *Ex Parte JCR*, the Pretoria High Court, per Neukircher J, extended the best interest assessment to include the existing children of commissioning parents and those of the surrogate mother.[163] To this end, the court required that the existing children of the commissioning parents and those of the surrogate mother consult a clinical psychologist to (a) prepare the children for the surrogate pregnancy and/or the new child, (b) make any recommendation that is in the interests of the children including whether they may need further therapy, and (c) report on the effect that any previous surrogacy has had on the children.[164] While the court intended to safeguard the interests of any children impacted by the surrogacy arrangement,[165] it

157 Ibid. [15].

158 *Ex Parte WH* (n 153) [61].

159 J Sloth-Nielsen, 'Children's Rights Jurisprudence in South Africa' (2019) 52 De Jure 501,516.

160 *S v M* (n 156) [24].

161 Ibid. [26].

162 Sloth-Nielsen, 'Children's Rights Jurisprudence in South Africa' (n 159), 517.

163 *Ex Parte JCR* [2022] ZAGPPHC 209 [36.1]–[36.2].

164 Ibid. [36.1]–[36.2].

165 Ibid. [35].

has been argued that these new requirements go too far and are unconstitutional.[166] Requiring the existing children to first be assessed by a clinical psychologist has been criticised since it infringes on the right of infertile individuals and couples to reproductive autonomy, by essentially making their reproductive decisions subject to their children's wishes.[167] The judgement in *Ex Parte JCR* was overturned by a full bench of the Pretoria High Court in *Ex parte Three Surrogacy Applications*.[168] The full bench held that the subjection of the existing children of the commissioning parents and those of the surrogate mother to psychological evaluation should not be a standard requirement, and should only ordered by the court if the circumstances of a particular case so require.

g. Suitability of the commissioning parents

When deciding on the suitability of a parent, the court suggested that an objective test should be applied which would include 'an enquiry into the ability of the parents to care for the child both emotionally and financially and to provide an environment for the harmonious growth and development of the child' while always having due regard for constitutional principles.[169]

h. Suitability of the surrogate mother

The following eight criteria to assess the suitability of a prospective surrogate mother have crystalised in case law: The surrogate mother should: (1) understand the nature of surrogate motherhood; (2) agree with the commissioning parents regarding selective reduction; (3) be motivated by altruism; (4) enjoy good mental health; (5) be emotionally well-resourced; (6) be emotionally available for her own child or children; (7) be free of unhealthy substances; and (8) be financially stable.[170]

166 Holness and others, 'A Parenting License, Granted by One's Existing Children? Reflections on *Ex Parte JCR*' (forthcoming in the Potchefstroom Electronic Law Journal).

167 Ibid.

168 *Ex parte Three Surrogacy Applications* 2023 (1) SA 627 (GP).

169 *Ex parte WH* (n 153) [63].

170 Donrich Thaldar, 'Criteria for Assessing The Suitability of Intended Surrogate Mothers in South Africa: Reflections on *Ex Parte KAF* II' (n 132). See also: Donrich

9.7 Genetic Testing

a. Preimplantation genetic testing for aneuploidy (PGT-A)

A recipient can have her in vitro embryos tested for chromosomal abnormalities (aneuploidy) before any of them are transferred to her uterus. This is done by taking a biopsy of a few cells from the trophectoderm of a blastocyst (the embryo at 5 days after fertilisation), which cells are then used to conduct a genetic test, called preimplantation genetic testing for aneuploidy (PGT-A). In this way, she can ensure that only embryos that are chromosomally normal (euploid) are selected to be transferred to her uterus. This increases her chances of a successful pregnancy and avoids having a child with a disability such as Down's syndrome.[171]

Given that PGT-A tests all the chromosomes, it also provides information on the sex chromosomes, and reveals the embryo's sex.[172] While PGT-A in general is unregulated, using PGT-A for sex selection—i.e., using PGT-A to select an embryo for transfer to the recipient's uterus based on the embryo's sex—was made unlawful in 2012, except if such sex selection is done to avoid a sex-linked genetic disorder.[173] In other words, 'social' sex selection was unlawful, while 'therapeutic' sex selection was lawful. However, the Pretoria High Court declared the ban on 'social' sex selection unconstitutional in July 2022.[174] If the Minister of Health fails to amend the ban to allow for 'social' sex selection, the ban will automatically become invalid in July 2023. In other words, from July 2023 it will be legal for intended parents to use PGT-A to select—based purely on their personal preferences—an embryo of their desired sex for transfer to the recipient's uterus.

Thaldar, 'The Need to Develop Objective Criteria for Suitability as a Surrogate Mother: Reflections on *Ex Parte KAF*' (2018) 11 South African Journal of Bioethics and Law 35.

[171] Dr. Rodrigues, Expert opinion (n 72) [14]–[16].

[172] Ibid. [17].

[173] 2012 Regulation (n 61), reg 13. For a critical analysis of the ban on social sex selection, see: Donrich Thaldar, 'Is It Time to Reconsider the Ban on Non-therapeutic Pre-implantation Sex Selection?' (2019) 136 South African Law Journal 223.

[174] *Surrogacy Advisory Group* (n 30).

b. Non-invasive prenatal testing (NIPT)

A pregnant woman can, at ten weeks of pregnancy, have the embryo tested for chromosomal abnormalities (aneuploidy). This is done by taking a blood sample from the woman and isolating the free-floating DNA of the embryo that is present in the woman's blood. This is called non-invasive prenatal testing (NIPT).[175] Since the woman should have the results within two weeks, she can then terminate her pregnancy if any aneuploidy is reported. In South Africa, a pregnant woman can have her pregnancy terminated within the first trimester without having to provide any reasons.

Similar to PGT-A, NIPT also reveals the sex of the embryo.[176] Accordingly, the possibility exists that the pregnant woman can use NIPT for social sex selection by terminating the pregnancy if the embryo is not of the desired sex, and then falling pregnant until she is pregnant with an embryo of the desired sex. Again, similar to PGT-A, the use of NIPT for social sex selection was banned.[177] However, as discussed above, the Pretoria High Court declared the ban on 'social' sex selection unconstitutional in July 2022.[178] From July 2023 it will be legal for a pregnant woman to use NIPT for social sex selection.

c. From genetic testing to heritable genome editing?

In South African law, the recipient's reproductive autonomy entails wide-ranging rights related to determining the genetic traits of her prospective child. For example, she can choose to use MAR, select certain gamete donors based on their characteristics (most of which have a genetic component, such as race, complexion and eye colour), and use PGT-A to make a further selection based on genetic traits—the sensitive issue of social sex selection being the only exception. In future, heritable genome editing may offer the possibility of determining the genetic

[175] Dr. Rodrigues, Expert opinion (n 72) [20].

[176] Ibid. [21].

[177] 2012 Regulation (n 61), reg 13.

[178] *Surrogacy Advisory Group* (n 30).

traits of a prospective child with even more precision.[179] This will probably start with health-related interventions, such as correcting genetic defects and making the prospective child immune against certain diseases. In time, heritable genome editing may even offer non-health-related interventions—commonly referred to as 'enhancements' in the academic literature—such as higher intelligence, a preferred skin complexion and a preferred eye colour.[180] If heritable genome editing is proven to be safe and effective, the right to reproductive autonomy in South African law appears likely to embrace this new technology.[181] Limits on its use would only be justified in cases where it presents harm to the prospective child, for example where it is misused to cause a child to be born with a disability.[182]

[179] Heritable genome editing means making changes to—editing—the genetic material of eggs, sperm or early embryos, and establishing a pregnancy. These genetic changes will then be present in all the cells of the eventual individual, and will, like any other genetic trait, be inherited by the individual's offspring.

[180] Bonginkosi Shozi, 'A Critical Review of the Ethical and Legal Issues in Human Germline Gene Editing: Considering Human Rights and a Call for an African Perspective' (2020) 13 South African Journal of Bioethics and Law 62, 63. See also: Andrew McGee, 'Using the Therapy and Enhancement Distinction in Law and Policy' (2020) 34 Bioethics 70; Rasmus Bjerregaard Mikkelsen and others, 'Genetic Protection Modifications: Moving Beyond the Binary Distinction Between Therapy and Enhancement for Human Genome Editing' (2019) 2 CRISPR Journal 362.

[181] Donrich Thaldar and others, 'Human Germline Editing: Legal-Ethical Guidelines for South Africa' (2020) 116 South African Journal of Science 1. See also: Donrich Thaldar, Bonginkosi Shozi and Tamanda Kamwendo, 'Culture and Context: Why the Global Discourse on Heritable Genome Editing Should Be Broadened from the South African Perspective' (2021) 4 BioLaw Journal 409; Bonginkosi Shozi and others, 'The Future of Global Regulation of Human Genome Editing: A South African Perspective on the WHO Draft Governance Framework on Human Genome Editing' (2022) 48 Journal of Medical Ethics 165; Donrich Thaldar and Bonginkosi Shozi, 'An Imbalanced Approach to Governance? An Analysis of the WHO's Position on Human Genome Editing' (2023) Bioethics 1; Bonginkosi Shozi and Donrich Thaldar, 'Promoting Equality in the Governance of Heritable Human Genome Editing Through Ubuntu: Reflecting on a South African Public Engagement Study' (2023) 23 The American Journal of Bioethics 43.

[182] Donrich Thaldar and Bonginkosi Shozi, 'Procreative Non-maleficence: A South African Human Rights Perspective on Heritable Human Genome Editing' (2020) 3 CRISPR Journal 32.

9.8 Conclusion

In this chapter, we have shown that South African reproductive law is founded upon the state's commitment to give life to reproductive health rights. It is as a result of this that South African policy on MAR is relatively permissive, allowing all kinds of people to make use of ARTs, and not placing limits on them such as mandating they have a medical indication.[183] A similarly permissive approach has been taken by our courts, in empowering individuals to make use of ARTs even where the current legislation does not strictly provide for it—such as by allowing surviving spouses to have children with gametes of their deceased husband or wife.[184]

In certain areas, however, there have been attempts made by the state to limit the use of ARTs, with the view of balancing the reproductive health rights underlying the use of said ARTs with countervailing state interests. These attempts have not always been well executed. For instance, the current policy requiring commissioning parents to have a 'genetic link' with their child, thereby barring double-donor surrogacy, is founded on little more than an arbitrary preference for genetic relatedness.[185] It is in cases such as these that judicial intervention becomes increasingly important, as this is the only true counterweight to unbalanced approaches to policy development on MAR by vindicating the reproductive health rights of those affected by these policies.

Accordingly, as new frontiers such as NIPT[186] and heritable human genome editing[187] emerge and transform the landscape of what is possible in the domain of MAR, so too should our understanding of reproductive health rights transform in light of these developments. As famously put by former Constitutional Court Justice Albie Sachs:

> Indeed, rights by their nature will atrophy if they are frozen. As the conditions of humanity alter and as ideas of justice and equity evolve, so do

[183] See above heading '9.4(a) The 'recipient'; a woman's right to access MAR healthcare services'.

[184] See above heading '9.5(e) Extraordinary cases'.

[185] See above heading '9.6(e) The genetic origins of the child'.

[186] See above heading '9.7(b) Non-invasive prenatal testing (NIPT)'.

[187] See above heading '9.7(c) From genetic testing to heritable genome editing?'.

concepts of rights take on new texture and meaning. The horizon of rights is as limitless as the hopes and expectations of humanity.[188]

Table of Cases

South African Cases

AB v Minister of Social Development 2016 (2) SA 27 (GP).
AB v Minister of Social Development 2017 (3) SA 570 (CC).
BR v LS 2018 (5) SA 308 (KZD).
Christian Lawyers Association of South Africa v Minister of Health 1998 (4) SA 111 3 (T).
Christian Lawyers Association of South Africa v Minister of Health 2005 (1) SA 509 (T).
Ex Parte JCR [2022] ZAGPPHC 209.
Ex Parte KAF [2018] ZAGPJHC 529.
Ex Parte SN unreported case 2020/10242 ZAGHC (7 May 2020).
Ex parte Three Surrogacy Applications 2023 (1) SA 627 (GP).
Ferreira v Levin 1996 (1) SA 984 (CC).
Government of the Republic of South Africa v Grootboom 2001 (1) SA 46 (CC).
KB v Minister of Social Development [2023] ZAMPMBHC 12.
Law Society of South Africa v Minister for Transport 2011 (1) SA 400 (CC).
Minister of Home Affairs v Fourie 2006 (1) SA 524 (CC).
NC v Drs Aevitas Inc t/a Aevitas Fertility Clinic unreported case 23236/2017 ZAWCHC (23 January 2018).
QG v CS 2021 (7) ECL 54 (GP).
S v M 2007 (2) SACR 539 (CC).
Surrogacy Advisory Group v Minister of Health 2023 (1) SA 241 (GP).
VJV v Minister of Social Development unreported case 27706/2021 ZAGPPHC (24 February 2022).

Canadian Cases

B(R) v Children's Aid Society of Metropolitan Toronto [1995] 1 SCR 315.
Blencoe v British Columbia (Human Rights Commission) [2000] 2 SCR 307.
New Brunswick (Minister of Health and Community Services) v G(J) [1999] 3 SCR 46.

[188] *Minister of Home Affairs v Fourie* 2006 (1) SA 524 (CC) [102].

R v Morgentaler [1988] 1 SCR 30.
Winnipeg Child and Family Services v KLW [2000] 2 SCR 519.

Table of Legislation

South African Statutes

Abortion and Sterilization Act 2 of 1975.
Children's Act 38 of 2005.
Choice on Termination of Pregnancy Act 92 of 1996.
Constitution of the Republic of South Africa, 1996.
Human Tissue Act 65 of 1983.
Interim Constitution of the Republic of South Africa, 1993.
National Health Act 61 of 2003.

South African Statutory Instruments

[Draft] Regulations Relating to Assisted Conception of Persons GN 251, GG 44321, 25 March 2021.
[Draft] Regulations Relating to the Artificial Fertilisation of Persons GN 1165, GG 40312, 30 September 2016.
Regulations Regarding the General Control of Human Bodies, Tissue, Blood, Blood Products and Gametes GN R175, GG 35099 (2 March 2012).
Regulations Relating to the Artificial Fertilisation of Persons GN R175, GG 35099 (2 March 2012).

Bibliography

African Union, 'Protocol to the African Charter on Human and People's Rights on the Rights of Women in Africa' (2003).
Albertyn C, 'Abortion, Reproductive Rights, and the Possibilities of Reproductive Justice in South African Courts' (2019) University of Oxford Human Rights Hub Journal 87.
Berer M, 'Abortion Law and Policy Around the World' (2017) 19 Health and Human Rights 13.
Dugard J, 'The Influence of International Human Rights Law on the South African Constitution' (1996) 49 Current Legal Problems 305.
Dyer S and others, 'Assisted Reproductive Technology in Africa: A 5-Year Trend Analysis from the African Network and Registry for ART' (2020) 41 Reproductive BioMedicine Online 604.
Heyns C and D Brand, 'Introduction to Socio-Economic Rights in the South African Constitution' (1998) 2 Law, Democracy & Development 153.
Hogg P, Constitutional Law of Canada (3 edn, Carswell, 1992).

Holness and others, 'A Parenting License, Granted by One's Existing Children? Reflections on Ex Parte JCR' (forthcoming in the Potchefstroom Electronic Law Journal).
Jordaan DW, 'Legal Access to Surrogate Motherhood in Illness That Does Not Cause Infertility' (2016) 106 South African Medical Journal 684.
Lewis SV, 'The Constitutional and Contractual Implications of the Application of Chapter 19 of the Children's Act 38 of 2005' (LLM dissertation, University of Western Cape 2011).
McGee A, 'Using the Therapy and Enhancement Distinction in Law and Policy' (2020) 34 Bioethics 70.
Meyerson D, 'Surrogacy, Geneticism and Equality: The Case of AB v Minister of Social Development' (2019) 9 Constitutional Court Review 317.
Mikkelsen RB and others, 'Genetic Protection Modifications: Moving Beyond the Binary Distinction Between Therapy and Enhancement for Human Genome Editing' (2019) 2 CRISPR Journal 362.
Nienaber A, 'The Grave's a Fine and Private Place: A Preliminary Exploration of the Law Relating to Posthumous Sperm Retrieval for Procreation' (2010) 25 Southern African Public Law 1.
Parliamentary Ad Hoc Committee, Report by the Parliamentary Ad Hoc Committee on the South African Law Commission Report on Surrogate Motherhood (Cape Town: PAHC, 1999).
Rodrigues Expert Opinion (AB v Minister of Social Development 2016 (2) SA 27 (GP) and AB v Minister of Social Development 2017 (3) SA 570 (CC)).
Shozi B, 'A Human Rights Analysis of Posthumous Reproduction' (Master's Dissertation, University of KwaZulu-Natal, 2018).
——— 'Something Old, Something New: Applying Reproductive Rights to New Reproductive Technologies in South Africa' (2020) 36 South African Journal on Human Rights 1.
——— 'Legal Issues in Posthumous Conception Using Gametes Removed from a Comatose Male: The Case of *Ex Parte SN*' (2021) 14 South African Journal of Bioethics and Law 28.
——— and others, 'The Future of Global Regulation of Human Genome Editing: A South African perspective on the WHO Draft Governance Framework on Human Genome Editing' (2022) 48 Journal of Medical Ethics 165.
——— Hazarilall R and D Thaldar, 'Blood Is Thicker Than Water, but Is It Thicker Than Ink? An Analysis of Parenthood and Sperm Donor Agreements in the Wake of QG v CS' (2022) 33 Stellenbosch Law Review 529.
——— and D Thaldar, 'Promoting Equality in the Governance of Heritable Human Genome Editing Through Ubuntu: Reflecting on a South African Public Engagement Study' (2023) 23 The American Journal of Bioethics 43.

Sloth-Nielsen J, 'Children's Rights Jurisprudence in South Africa' (2019) 52 De Jure 501.

Thaldar D, 'Posthumous Conception: Recent Legal Developments in South Africa' (2018) 108 South African Medical Journal 471.

——— 'Post-Truth Jurisprudence: The Case of *AB v Minister of Social Development*' (2018) 34 South African Journal on Human Rights 231.

——— 'The Need to Develop Objective Criteria for Suitability as a Surrogate Mother: Reflections on *Ex Parte KAF*' (2018) 11 South African Journal of Bioethics and Law 35.

——— 'Criteria for Assessing the Suitability of Intended Surrogate Mothers in South Africa: Reflections on *Ex Parte KAF* II' (2019) 12 South African Journal of Bioethics and Law 61.

——— 'Is It Time to Reconsider the Ban on Non-therapeutic Pre-implantation Sex Selection?' (2019) 136 South African Law Journal 223.

——— 'The Constitution as an Instrument of Prejudice: A Critique of *AB v Minister of Social Development*' (2019) 9 Constitutional Court Review 343.

——— and Shozi B, 'Procreative Non-maleficence: A South African Human Rights Perspective on Heritable Human Genome Editing' (2020) 3 CRISPR Journal 32.

——— and others, 'Human Germline Editing: Legal-Ethical Guidelines for South Africa' (2020) 116 South African Journal of Science 1.

——— 'The In Vitro Embryo and the Law: The Ownership Issue and a Response to Robinson' (2020) Potchefstroom Electronic Law Journal 1.

——— *Amicus curiae* heads of argument (QG v CS 2021 (7) ECL 54 (GP)) https://thaldtian.files.wordpress.com/2021/07/heads-of-argument6-anon.pdf. Accessed 19 June 2022.

——— Shozi B and T Kamwendo, 'Culture and Context: Why the Global Discourse on Heritable Genome Editing Should Be Broadened from the South African Perspective' (2021) 4 BioLaw Journal 409.

——— and Shozi B, 'Is Open-Identity Gamete Donation Lawful in South Africa?' (2022) 112 South African Medical Journal 1.

——— and Shozi B, 'South Africa's Latest Medically Assisted Reproduction Draft Regulations: Close, but No Cigar' (2022) Tydskrif vir die Suid-Afrikaanse Reg 1.

——— and Shozi B, 'An Imbalanced Approach to Governance? An Analysis of the WHO's Position on Human Genome Editing' (2023) Bioethics 1.

UN Population Fund, 'Programme of Action' Adopted at the International Conference on Population and Development (1994).

——— 'Report of the International Conference on Population and Development' (1994) 1995 UN Doc A/CONF.171/13/Rev.1 117.

Van Niekerk C, 'Section 294 of the Children's Act: Do Roots Really Matter?' (2015) 18 Potchefstroom Electronic Law Journal/Potchefstroomse Elektroniese Regsblad 39.

CHAPTER 10

Informed Consent and Ethical Considerations in Assisted Reproductive Technology in Nigeria: Options and Challenges

Folakemi O. Ajagunna

10.1 Introduction

Assisted Reproductive Technology (ART) refers to a collection of treatments that deal with both sperm and eggs.[1] It includes procedures involving the in vitro handling of human oocytes and sperm or embryos in order to achieve a pregnancy. Such procedures include in vitro fertilisation, transcervical embryo transfer, intrafallopian gamete transfer, intrafallopian zygote transfer, tubal embryo transfer, gamete and embryo

[1] J. Medina, 'In-vitro Fertilisation: The Right to Give Life or Taking the Fundamental Right to Take Life' Law School Student Scholarship Paper [2015] 795.

F. O. Ajagunna (✉)
University of Ibadan, Ibadan, Nigeria
e-mail: fo.ajagunna@mail.ui.edu.ng

O. S. Adelakun and E. Ndoni (eds.), *Reproductive Health and Assisted Reproductive Technologies In Sub-Saharan Africa*,
Sustainable Development Goals Series,
https://doi.org/10.1007/978-981-99-2411-0_10

cryopreservation, oocyte and embryo donation and gestational surrogacy.[2] ART has been practised in Nigeria over the past three decades, yet the practice is not regulated under any statutory framework. In the absence of a regulatory framework, clinics offering ART services in Nigeria develop internal rules which serve as guidelines for this reproductive process to curtail inherent unethical practices associated with that development.[3] One such concerned unethical practice relates to the practice of obtaining informed consent in assisted conception treatments.[4]

Informed consent refers to the legal and ethical requirement in medical treatments involving the process of giving individual adequate information about all aspects of the treatment he or she is involved in. This principle is enshrined in the right to autonomy which is guaranteed in a number of international human rights documents and some legislation. In particular, the Nigerian National Health Act of 2014 and the Nigerian Code of Medical Ethics provide for informed consent. The essence of the informed consent process is to enable the patient to make a decision concerning his or her treatment and to voluntarily participate in the treatment process.[5] The implication of the principles of informed consent is that the medical personnel must obtain consent from the patient before carrying out the medical procedure. The process of obtaining informed consent begins with giving the patient full and adequate information about the procedure to be undertaken and information on the risks, benefits and outcome of the proposed treatment.[6] There exists a widely

[2] SO Koyonda, 'Assisted Reproductive Technology in Nigeria: Placing the Law above the Medical' Journal of Indian Law Institute [2009] 25.

[3] L.O. Omokanye, O.A. Olatinwo, G.A. Salahudeen, K.A. Durowade, A.A. Panti, and R.O. Balogun 'Assisted Reproduction Technology in Nigeria: Challenges and the Way Forward' (2018) (3) African Journal for Infertility and Assisted Conception <http://www.afrijac.org> accessed 27 October 2021.

[4] Chinelo A. Ekechi-Agwu and Anthony O. Nwafor 'Regulating Assisted Reproductive Technologies in Nigeria: Lessons from Australia and the United Kingdom' (2020) (24) African Journal of Reproductive Health <http://ajol.info> accessed 22 October 2021.

[5] Nijhawan P. Lokesh, Manthan Krishman, Muddu Krishna, Prashant B. Musmade 'Informed Consent: Issues and Challenges' Journal of Advanced Pharmaceutical Technology and Research [2013] 134.

[6] Yinka Olomojobi, *Medical and Health Law: The Right to Health* (1st ed., Princeton Publishing, 2019), 127.

held belief[7] that informed consent has to do with documents obtained by the health practitioner from the patient before a medical procedure is to be embarked upon, however, this is not necessarily so because the process of informed consent ought to relate to every communication which an individual has with the health facility. It has been described by Coleman et al.[8] as the primary mechanism with which prospective patients can indicate their preferences, fears, values and expectations into decisions about their treatment. Previous researches have documented issues relating to informed consent in various aspects of medical treatment in Nigeria, however, not much has been done on informed consent in ART which is a relatively new and growing industry in Nigeria . For instance, in a study conducted by Adotey and Jebbin[9] on informed consent practices in surgical procedures in clinical settings, it was reported that about 74.6% of the patients got information about their diagnosis, while 36.7% were informed of the possible complications of their surgery. Only 35% of the patients in the study signed the requisite consent forms. Ezeuko[10] in another study similarly reported that although guidelines exist in Nigeria on informed consent, however, most medical practitioners fail to abide by all the guidelines prescribed in the Code of Medical Ethics. This chapter therefore examines issues relating to informed consent emanating from the practice of ART in fertility clinics in Nigeria. It adopts a socio-legal approach through the use of in-depth and key-informant interviews to document opinions of relevant stakeholder on practices relating to informed consent in ART clinics in Nigeria. The book chapter posits that although regulations exist in the form of ethical guidelines and laws on informed consent in Nigeria, however what these guidelines and laws recommend is not a reflection of what obtains in practice. The chapter

[7] Irehobinde O. Iyioha and Oluchi Aniaka 'Informed Consent' <www.lawexplorer.com/informedconsent> accessed 21 February 2023.

[8] Carl H. Coleman, Jerry A. Menkoff, Jesse A. Goldner, Nancy N. Dubler, *The Ethics and Regulation of Research with Human Subjects* (Lexis Nexis 2005) 297.

[9] JN Jebbin and JM Adotey, 'Informed Consent: How Informed are Patients?' (2004) (13) Nigerian Journal of Medicine <http://ajol/info> accessed 19 October 2021.

[10] Mabel Ijeoma Ezeuko 'Nigerian Laws on Informed Consent Before a Surgical Procedure' (2019) (87) Medico-Legal Journal <www.journals.sagepub.com> accessed 26 October 2021.

argues that the process of obtaining consent should rather be a continuous process throughout the ART treatment regimen and not a singular event done in the course of treatment.

10.2 Regulatory Framework for Informed Consent in Nigeria

There are two ambits to the principle of informed consent. The first is the principle of informed consent as applicable to medical care and the second is informed consent in research settings. The application of informed consent in medical care serves as a foundation for understanding informed consent in research settings. This is mainly because the ethics of informed consent arose from the Hippocratic Oath which enjoins the physician to direct their commitment to the health and wellbeing of their patients. Principles of informed consent also emanate from the ethical principles guiding research as enshrined in the Belmont Report of 1979, the Helsinki Declaration and the Nuremberg Code of 1947. For instance, the Nuremberg Code provides thus

> The voluntary consent of the human subject is absolutely essential. This means that the person involved should have legal capacity to give consent; should be so situated as to be able to exercise free power of choice, without the intervention of any element of force, fraud, deceit, duress, overreaching, or other ulterior form of constraint or coercion; and should have sufficient knowledge and comprehension of the elements of the subject matter involved as to enable him to make an understanding and enlightened decision.[11]

Historically, the focus of informed consent had been paternalism which had the physician more in focus and recognised that the physician had the right to determine what was in the best interest of the patient. A dramatic shift later occurred in the late 1950s and the 1960s wherein judges[12] began to propose opinions which focused on patient's autonomy

[11] British Medical Journal 'The Nuremberg Code and Nuremberg Doctor's Trial' (1996) 7070(313) 1448 <https://www.bmj> accessed 21 October 2021.

[12] The case of *Salga v Leland Stanfors Jr University Board of Trustees* (1957) 154 Cal App 2d, 560, 317 is instructive to note here. In this case, the judgement identified the need to focus attention on fulfilling the requirements of providing patients with information on any medical procedure to be carried out.

and the right of the patient to determine what was in their own best interest, arising from sufficient information given to the patient.[13] The basic ethical principles that serve as a foundation for informed consent are respect for persons, beneficence and justice. These principles are general judgments that serve as a basic explanation for the varying moral assessments of human actions. The principle of respect for persons advances two ethical convictions. The first being that all persons should be treated as autonomous agents, and secondly, that persons with diminished autonomy are entitled to protection. This principle thus necessitates protection for these categories of persons. Where a person is autonomous, he is said to be capable of making decisions about his personal actions after deliberating on such course of action.

The principal framework for informed consent in research in Nigeria is the National Code of Research Ethics (NHREC). The provisions of the NHREC are not examined in this chapter as the scope of this research is limited to informed consent in medical treatment, and not informed consent in research.

The National Health Act 2014 is the law that regulates the development and administration of the health system in Nigeria. In its functions, the Act provides the minimum standard for operating health services in the country. The Act was passed in October 2014, and it has been said that not much has been done to operationalise the provisions of the Act.[14] The Act contains seven parts, each dealing with varying components of the health system. Part III of the Act provides for rights and obligations of users and healthcare personnel. Section 23 of the Act states that every health care provider shall give a user relevant information pertaining to his state of health and necessary treatment relating thereto including information relating to his health status, range of diagnostic procedures and treatments options available, the benefits, risks, costs and consequences associated with each option and the implications and risks associated with the treatments. Although the provisions of this section deal with aspects of information on proposed medical procedures and treatments, it appears that emphasis is made rather on full information or disclosure to patients

[13] Ted J. Ruback 'Informed Consent' in Richard W. Dehn and David P. Asprey (eds) *Essential Clinical Procedures* (Elsevier 2002).

[14] O Enabulele, 'Nigeria's National Health Act 2014; A Review of Some of Its Implications and Challenges' (2017) (16) 2 Annals of Biomedical Sciences <https://ajol.info> accessed 24 October 2021.

and not on the right to give consent based on the information received by the patient. In addition, the provisions of this section do not stipulate the level of information to be given for consent to be an informed one. Generally, the right to informed consent is embedded in the fiduciary relationship wherein one party has differential power, and thus that party has the inherent duty to share required information with the other.[15]

The Nigerian Code of Medical Ethics provides ethical guidelines for medical and dental practice in Nigeria. Rule 19 provides for informed consent by stating that practitioners involved in procedures requiring the consent of the patient, his relation or appropriate public authority must ensure that the appropriate consent is obtained before such procedures, either for surgery or diagnostic purposes, are done, be they invasive or non-invasive. It also provides that consent forms should be in printed or written form either as a part of case notes or in separate sheets with the institution's name boldly indicated. The importance of informed consent was recognised in the case of *Medical & Dental Practitioner's Disciplinary Tribunal v Okonkwo*[16] where the Supreme Court held that the consent of a patient is paramount. At the onset of the case, the Medical and Dental Practitioners' Tribunal had considered the determination of the appropriate course of action to take by a medical practitioner where the patient had denied informed consent in order to carry out a life-saving measure on him or her. Upon appeal, the appellate court held that since the patient's relationship with the practitioner is based on consensus, it follows that the choice of an adult patient with a sound mind to refuse informed consent to medical treatment, barring state intervention through judicial process, leaves the practitioner helpless to impose treatment on the patient.

10.3 Essential Components of Informed Consent

Legal and ethical angles have been attributed to informed consent. The ethical angle relates to patients' autonomy to which every individual approaching medical care is entitled. In addition to this, every patient has his or her basic human rights which are fundamentally guaranteed in the Constitution. The foremost fundamental human right that enshrines

[15] Ted J. Ruback (n. 13) 4.

[16] [2001] 7 NWLR, 71, 79.

the principle of informed consent is contained in section 34(1) of the 1999 Constitution (as amended). This section provides that every individual is entitled to the dignity of his person. When applied to informed consent, this implies that each person has a right to determine what happens to his or her body.[17] Failure to respect these rights can result into battery or physical assault which are punishable under the laws of the land. In instances where the medical practitioner does not obtain informed consent, and the patient gets injured, the patient may have grounds to sue the doctor for medical malpractice. For informed consent to be an effective one, three essential conditions must be met. The first is that the patient must have the capacity to give consent or the competence to make an informed decision. The second is that the patient must be given sufficient information about the procedure or treatment and the alternatives available, to allow him or her to make an informed choice and lastly that the patient must give consent to treatment voluntarily, without coercion, manipulation, or duress.[18] These essential conditions will be examined in turn.

10.3.1 Capacity to Give Consent

There are different tests of a patient's capacity to consent to treatment, however, in general, an adult is presumed to be legally competent unless he or she has been formally and legally declared incompetent.[19] Competence is established by an assessment of the patient's capacity to comprehend the nature of his or her state and the choices of options existing and to determine whether or not he or she is able to make a rational decision. In the English case of *S v McC*,[20] Lord Reid affirmed that English law does go to a great length in the protection of a person of full age and capacity from undue interference with his personal liberty in order to make an informed choice. Patients must be able to appreciate the nature of available treatments and the possible outcome in each case.

[17] Patricia Imode Gbobo and Mercy Oke-Chinda 'An Analysis of the Doctrine of Informed Consent in Nigeria's Healthcare Services' (2018) (69) Journal of Law Policy and Globalization <https://www.liste.org> accessed 15 October 2021.

[18] Yinka Olomojobi (n. 6) 177.

[19] Ted J. Ruback (n. 13) 3.

[20] [1972] AC. 24. 83. This case substantially predates the case of *Montgomery*, which brought 'informed consent' into UK law.

They must be able to deliberate and consider their options and weigh them against one another to choose the best alternative. They must also be able to communicate their assessment and judgement in some way.[21]

10.3.2 Adequate Information

Another important aspect of informed consent is that the patient must be given adequate information about the nature of the process to be carried out. Adequate information warrants that patients are able to use the information disclosed to them in their decision-making and such information should be disclosed clearly, in a conversant language and at an appropriate level of complexity.[22] A distinction should be made between full and adequate information. In the opinion of the author of this book chapter, full information depicts that every iota of information about the medical procedure has been given to the patient while adequate information depicts that what is given to the patient is the required amount of information needed by the patient in order to arrive at a decision whether to continue with the treatment or not.

Various requirements have been proposed as both legal and moral standards for what constitutes adequate information. The 'reasonable physician' standard bases disclosure of information on the prevailing practice within the profession. It is guided by providing an answer to the question 'What would a typical health care provider in the same specialty and "community" disclose to his patient about this procedure?' Going by this standard, the health practitioner is allowed to decide what information is relevant to be disclosed and what is not needed to be disclosed. This standard aligns with the paternalism which has been discussed previously in this book chapter. Millium[23] equates this standard of disclosure to the standard of understanding i.e. the requirement of disclosure must be synonymous with the requirement of understanding. This legal standard also influenced the courts in adjudging the actions of

[21] Festus Emiri, *Medical Law and Ethics in Nigeria* (Malthouse Books, 2012).

[22] Millium Joseph and Bromwich Danielle 'Informed Consent: What Must Be Disclosed and What Must Be Understood' (2021) (21) 973 The American Journal of Bioethics <https://www.tandfonline.com> accessed 25 October 2021.

[23] Ibid.

medical practitioners. This standard has more often than not been criticised for not representing a true reflection of patients' autonomy which the principle of informed consent stands upon.[24]

Another standard of disclosure is the reasonable man's standard which featured more prominently after the early '70s. This standard warrants the medical practitioner to disclose to the patient any ***material information*** *(emphasis mine)* that any reasonable man in the same circumstances would consider necessary to arrive at a decision about the proposed treatment. The implication of this is to place relevance on the patient's preferences as opposed to the health practitioner's choices. This test has been described as beneficial as it emphasises the patient's choices, thus the quantum of information disclosed must be at the patient's level of understanding. However, this standard merely bases this information requirement on what any reasonable man would need and not what each particular patient needs. The inherent disadvantage posed by the adoption of this test leads to the subjective test. The subjective test identifies the need to address each patient's particular information need in order to arrive at an informed decision. It allows greater differentiation based on patient preference, relying on the unique nature and abilities of the individual patient to determine the degree of disclosure needed to satisfy the requirements of informed consent.

The 2014 National Health Act uses the word 'relevant information' in order to describe the amount of information required before informed consent can be taken. It also provides thereafter, that the healthcare provider shall where possible inform the user in a language that the user understands and in a manner which takes into account the user's level of literacy. This provision impliedly suggests that the Nigerian Health Act imposes a reasonable man's standard on the medical practitioner in Nigeria. On a closer look as well, it appears it also adopts the subjective test when it takes into account the literacy level of the user before arriving at the understanding of the user on the components of informed consent. This book chapter posits that taking into consideration the user's level of literacy and language in determining the level of information for consent to be an informed one has taken into effect what each patient requires for comprehension as opposed to a blanket requirement.

[24] J. Pugh 'Informed Consent, Autonomy and Beliefs' in ***Autonomy, Rationality and Contemporary Beliefs*** (Oxford University Press 2020) <www.ncbi.nih.gov/books> accessed 21 February 2023.

According to Nnebue,[25] effective communication is the key to enabling potential patients to make informed decisions about their involvement in the course of treatment. It is also essential that adequate information be given about each step of the medical treatment apart from the initial information given at the onset of treatment. As argued by Rao, the nature of modern-day treatment makes patients approach the medical practitioner with different demands and varying expectations which necessitates providing patients with adequate information before any procedure is commenced.[26]

(a) Voluntary consent

The legal doctrine of informed consent specifies that the health professional should disclose to a patient all information relevant to making a decision whether to undergo or forgo a proposed treatment or diagnostic procedure. All aspects of informed consent obtained at this point must be voluntary and without any form of coercion, duress or manipulation. A number of exceptions to the requirement for informed consent have been identified. These include instances where the patient is incapacitated and thus lacks the ability to give an informed consent. Another instance arises where there is a life-threatening emergency that leaves little or no time at all to obtain consent. Informed consent can also be waived voluntarily. Generally, where patient's ability to make decisions is not certain, a psychiatrist may be commissioned to conduct an evaluation to ascertain the competency of the patient.[27]

[25] C. Nnebue, 'Informed Consent in Research' (2010) (1) Afrimedic Journal <https://www.ajol.info> accessed 20 October 2021.

[26] KH Rao 'Informed Consent: An Ethical Obligation or Legal Compulsion' [2008] Journal of Cutaneous & Aesthetic Surgery 33.

[27] Parth Shah, Imani Thorton, Danielle Turrin, and John E. Hipskind *Informed Consent* (Stat Pearls Publishing, 2021) <www.ncbi.nih.gov/books> accessed 25 October 2021.

10.4 Models of Informed Consent

Two models of informed consent have been identified by Lidz and Appelbaum.[28] These are the 'event model' and the 'process model'. The event model considers informed consent as a procedure to be performed once in each treatment course and which, as a matter of necessity, covers all elements of informed consent at once. Thus, informed consent under the event model is a once and for all occurrence. Consent, as an event model depicts a discrete act of decision-making that takes place at a particular time usually before the commencement of treatment. It does not acknowledge any information given prior to the time the consent is obtained. The shortcoming of this model is that it fails to determine whether the consent given is obtained after a full and adequate understanding of the information given to the patient. The process begins when health personnel produce the consent form and set out the requisite information on the benefits and risks of the procedures. The event model is not without its benefits. One of such is that it presents a clear picture of the roles and responsibilities of the parties before the treatment or procedure begins. It has likewise been considered by some others as being ineffective and inappropriate for medical treatments because it is meant to cover all the legal elements in that precise moment when the patient is about to sign the consent forms.[29]

The 'process model' on the other hand, regards informed consent as an integral and continuing aspect of the physician–patient relationship. The model envisages active patient participation in all stages of the relationship. It commences with taking decisions on diagnosis to setting goals for treatments and selecting best approaches for treatment and evaluating the treatment.[30] Thus, informed consent under the process model is a continuum which requires that the patient and doctor enter into an ongoing dialogue which is described as 'mutual monitoring'.

[28] Charles S. Lidz and Paul S. Appelbaum 'Two Models of Informed Consent' (1998) (148) Archives of Internal Medicine <http://pubmed.ncbi.nim.nih.gov> accessed 26 October 2021. This is a dated reference; scholarship may have moved on.

[29] Virginnia Recchia, Anthonio Dodaro and Larissa Braga 'Event-Based Versus Process Based Informed Consent to Address Scientific Evidence and Uncertainties in Ionising Medical Imaging' (2013)(4)5 Insights Imaging <http://www.ncbi.nim.nih.gov> accessed 26 October 2021.

[30] Charles S. Lidz and Paul S. Appelbaum (n. 28).

10.5 Materials and Methods

This research employed a socio-legal approach to elicit information from a section of participants. The socio-legal approach involved the use of in-depth and key-informant interviews. There is a paucity of data on the percentage of persons who use ART services in Nigeria as activities in this sector have been mainly uncoordinated,[31] and unregulated. According to the World Report on Assisted Reproductive Technology, as stated by Adamson et al.,[32] data from Africa represents only 1 per cent of global ART activity, this world report further states that there are about 12 self-registered IVF units in Nigeria. Provision of ART services in Nigeria is mainly done by private health facilities. A few tertiary health care facilities provide ART services while provision of ART services is rarely carried out in secondary and primary health care facilities[33] Presently in Nigeria, it is reported that there are about seventy IVF centres spread across Nigeria.[34] Out of this, large concentration of these centres is in Lagos, Abuja and Port-Harcourt.[35]

10.5.1 Sampling Technique and Sample Size

A sample size of 26 participants was used for this study. This sample size is broken down as follows

a. Fifteen adult female respondents
b. Nine medical doctors who are IVF specialists
c. Two embryologists

The convenience sampling technique was used to arrive at this number of participants as the previous researches conducted in different parts of

[31] Omokanye LO (n. 3).

[32] G.D. Adamson, J. DeMouzon, and S. Dyer 'ICMART World Report 2013' (2017) (32) Human Reproduction 64–65.

[33] World Health Organization. *The Nigerian Health System-Nigerian Plan Chapter.* <www.who.int/punch/countries/nigeria-plan> accessed October 9, 2020.

[34] The Cable News '*10 Percent of Nigerian Infertile Group Canvasses Use of Reproductive Technology*' <http://www.thecable.ng> accessed April 11, 2022.

[35] J.O. Fadare and A.A. Adeniyi 'Ethical Issues in Newer Assisted Reproductive Technologies: A View from Nigeria' Nigerian Journal of Clinical Practice [2015] 57–61.

Nigeria were carried out on infertile persons and their attitude, perception and willingness on ART services and not so much on participants who directly use IVF services.[36] The convenience sampling was adopted in this research due to the nature of the female respondents who had to be recruited into the study irrespective of their location in Nigeria. It is also believed that the size was adequate to sufficiently describe the various perspectives relating to issues relating to the informed consent in assisted reproduction in Nigeria. The interviews on the female IVF participants were carried out until saturation point when no new information was being added.

The medical doctors were purposively selected from Local Government Area (LGA) where fertility clinics are located, thus a prerequisite condition before any LGA was selected for the study was the presence of at least two fertility clinics within the LGA. The snowball sampling technique was used to identify the adult females interviewed in the study. Issues relating to childbearing, infertility and patronage at IVF clinics are considered as very personal and private in Nigeria. Thus, the snowball technique used in this study helped to identify the women who had undergone IVF treatment and their experiences in the fertility clinics visited were documented.

10.5.2 Study Population

The research participants in this research included women who patronised IVF clinics in Nigeria, embryologists and fertility doctors. The first study population comprised medical doctors who were experts in IVF. Nine respondents were interviewed in this category.

The second study group comprised fifteen adult females. The respondents were selected based on their willingness to participate in the study and their ability to give responses to questions asked. Due to the nature of the subject matter, the respondents were identified through snowballing technique irrespective of their location within the study areas. The third study group comprised embryologists who work in the laboratories in

[36] For instance, Akande et al. carried out a study on attitude and willingness of infertile persons towards the uptake of ART in Ibadan in 2019, similarly, Adesiyun conducted a study on awareness and perception of ART practice among women with infertility in Northern Nigeria.

fertility clinics. Two embryologists were interviewed in this research. One of them was located in Ibadan and the other was located in Abuja.

10.5.3 Study Area

This study was carried out in parts of Oyo State, Lagos State and the Federal Capital Territory, Abuja. These study areas were purposively selected for the research because they form a part of the states in Nigeria where there are main concentrations of fertility clinics.

10.5.4 Ethical Considerations

All ethical considerations were observed in this research and this included seeking the full informed consent of the respondents after the study was explained to them in clear terms. The respondents were also assured of their confidentiality and anonymity. No name was required; the tape recorder was used after the respondents gave consent for the researcher to use it. The respondents were informed that they could decide to end their participation whenever they no longer wished to continue. Interviews with the adult female respondents were held in privacy. The respondents identified a convenient time and place to be interviewed by the researcher. Ethical approval was obtained from the University of Ibadan Social Sciences and Humanities Ethical Review Committee (Approval No. UI/SSHEC/2021/00015).

10.6 Research Findings and Discussions

10.6.1 Socio-demographic Characteristics of Respondents

The female respondents were between the ages thirty-five and forty-five. They were mainly in their reproductive years (15–49) according to the Nigerian Demographic Health Survey 2018. Five of the respondents had tried IVF at least once in the past five years. Only two of the women had their babies from the IVF procedure. This reflects a thirteen per cent success rate in the interviewed respondents. The respondents were mainly residents in Ibadan, Abuja and Lagos. One of the respondents lived in Abeokuta and another of the respondents flew in from the United Kingdom to have her IVF sessions at a fertility clinic located in Abuja. Thirteen out of the fifteen female respondents were Yoruba women. Two of them were Ibos from the Eastern part of Nigeria, although they had their residence in Lagos State. The participants were all educated with the least form of education being the National Certificate of Education. Majority of the respondents were in the formal work sector (n-12), three of them had privately established businesses. All the female respondents were of the Christian faith.

The IVF doctors were all males with their ages between the range of 35–55 years. Two of the doctors were of the Igbo tribe, one was from the Middle Belt region (Benue State) while the rest were Yoruba tribe. The embryologists, a male and female, were located in Ibadan and Abuja. Respondents were asked questions on their knowledge of what constitutes informed consent and their experiences in the various fertility clinics visited. IVF doctors were interviewed on their knowledge of the various components of informed consent and practices in their fertility clinics. Themes and sub-themes were identified from the in-depth and key-informant interviews conducted in the study and they are presented in the paragraphs below.

10.6.2 Knowledge of What Constitutes Informed Consent

When participants were asked questions relating to what constitutes informed consent, various responses were received. These responses ranged from the affirmation by adult females that informed consent is the approval given to the medical doctors by the patient authorising the doctor to carry out ART procedures on them to a description of informed consent as a mere agreement that a patient has with the doctor treating her. Few ($n = 5$) of the women mentioned full information as part of their knowledge of what constitutes informed consent. This depicts that the women attributed informed consent to the aspect of the approval only. All the IVF doctors noted that informed consent was based on the provision of full and adequate information. They had varying responses on the meaning of 'adequate' as used within the context of ART. Two of the doctors were of the opinion that too much information should not be given to the patients in order not to scare them away. They felt that the patients just needed a summary of the steps to be taken by the medical doctors in the ART procedures. The implication of the response given by these doctors is to steer the meaning of adequate information away from the user's need to what the medical personnel feels and believes is enough for the patient. This runs contrary to the argument canvassed in this book chapter. Where the medical personnel is the umpire in determining the fate of his patient, such patient is eroded of his or right to autonomy and the ability to uphold it.

10.6.3 Nature of Information Given at Fertility Clinics

The female participants were asked questions relating to the nature of information given to them at the various IVF clinics visited and whether the information given emphasised the patient's role in decision-making. Participants stated the contents of the information given. For instance, P2 stated:

> I was told what to expect, the process involved, the medication I was to be administered with and the side effects of the medication as well as the duration of the treatment regime. (P2/Ibadan/45 years/Female)

Another participant stated that her decision to continue with the IVF treatment was based on the information she was given at the IVF clinic. She stated that the information was adequate and helped her in the decision she made.

P4, a Lagos-based respondent did not have a positive response on the nature of information given. In her words:

> ...the fertility clinic I patronised was more concerned about running promos to infertile couples. I personally felt they were insensitive. I was told I could get an IVF session done free if I paid for one. I had to leave the clinic for another one because they were more interested in what I could pay for rather than how I could get a baby of my own. (P4/Lagos/36 years/Female)

10.6.4 Procedure for Obtaining Informed Consent

According to Shah et al.,[37] implicit within the informed consent process is an assessment of the patient's understanding, rendering an actual recommendation and documentation of the process. Questions on the procedure of obtaining informed consent were responded to by the IVF doctors. They all agreed that there was a procedure adopted in their

[37] Parth Shah, Imani Thorton, Danielle Turrin and John E. Hipskind (n. 24).

respective clinics, but the patterns adopted varied. According to PD2, an Ibadan-based IVF doctor,

> What we are looking for when it comes to this issue of informed consent is a documentation that explains what we want to carry out on the patient and can also be used by the facility to absolve us of any liability if things don't go as planned. You know the nature of what we do is not 100 percent assured. We can say it is a 60-40 chance of success... so in essence, if it fails, our documentation will be brought out to say you were told as a patient and you cannot deny it because you signed the document. (PD2/ Ibadan/Male/37 years)

Another participant IVF Doctor in Lagos said:

> A lot of things are not as they should be in this industry and this is because the industry is not so regulated. Many patients are not informed about surplus embryos or leftover embryos while doctors are just more concerned with obtaining the three viable embryos needed for the treatment. People are doing what they feel is right in their own eyes. Our process of consent should be revisited every step all along the way. After counselling the patient and there is surplus embryo, we must obtain consent. (PD6/ Abuja/52 years/Male)

The response of the participant above reveals that it is expected that informed consent should be obtained at every stage of the IVF procedure and not only at the commencement of IVF treatment.

The IVF doctors were asked to respond to questions relating to the signing of documents before commencement of ART treatment. They all answered in the affirmative. when asked whether they sign documents before the commencement of ART procedures. In the words of PE1, an embryologist located in Abuja

> ...we do not do anything at all relating to assisted conception treatments until the patient has read and signed the requisite forms, this is a prerequisite that must be followed in our facility.

When this particular respondent was queried further on the necessity of signing the forms, he said that this was part of standard IVF protocols which must be followed. Another salient point he raised was that signing a form of this nature can absolve the IVF doctor and the fertility centre of any liability if things do not go as planned.

Female participants were asked questions on whether they signed any document after the nature of proposed treatment had been explained to them. All of the female participants affirmed that they all signed some documents before treatment. However, only 5 of these women could state what was contained in the forms.

In the United Kingdom, the Human Fertilisation and Embryology Act of 1990 as amended by the Human Fertility and Embryology Act 2008 is the main regulation of ART in the jurisdiction. By virtue of Section 13 of the 2008 Act, counselling of all parties involved in the medical procedure is required before any fertility service is offered to anyone. Consent of the donor and the person receiving treatment in relation to the gamete or embryo after effective counselling is emphasised by the Act. In line with this, in 2016 the UK government published guidelines for giving consent. The guidelines contain a step-by-step guide on issues relating to giving and obtaining informed consent in ART procedures. It is doubtful whether guidelines of this nature exist in Nigeria.[38] According to an IVF doctor based in Ibadan, in the absence of any specific regulation on ART in Nigeria, each clinic is guided by the ethos of the medical profession as contained in the Nigerian Code of Medical Ethics or by the standard IVF protocols in each facility. It should then be asked whether the existing provisions in this code of medical ethics can be sufficiently relied on or can adequately guide issues relating to consent in assisted conception procedures in Nigeria. The writer is of the opinion that the existing legal framework is grossly inadequate to guide this area of practice in Nigeria. This is because the practice of IVF and other assisted conception methods are of a very sensitive and confidential in nature. This necessitates that every component of informed consent must be followed in the procedures. It is not only sufficient for the patient to have general information about the procedure he or she is about to commence so as to sign the consent forms, in addition, consent must be involved in all other aspects of the treatment including consent to storage and disposal of formed leftover embryos.

[38] Oludoyinmola O. Ojifinni and Lateefat Ibisomi 'Preconception Care Practices in Nigeria: A Descriptive Qualitative Study' Reproductive Health [2020] 17, 172.

10.6.5 *Information on the Risks and Benefits of ART Procedure*

Information disclosure in ART procedures should include information about uncertainties of the process. This was largely absent in the information given to the participants in this research. A woman said:

> I was not given any full information, although I was given drugs and injections before the laboratory tests were carried out on me, I wasn't treated properly because I was not told that the procedure might not work even though I had paid the initial sum. It was a very painful and bitter experience for me. (P5/Ibadan/55 years/Female)

In a study carried out on the quality of informed consent for invasive procedures, Brezis et al.[39] found that about fifty per cent of patients did not receive explanations about risks and discussions about alternative options, while physicians also resisted attempts to improve informed consent. Brezis et al. therefore recommended that since patients differed in their modes of decision-making, then informed consent should be patient-specific. Similarly, in a study carried out by Okonta et al.,[40] several unethical practices were found and documented on ART provision in Nigeria; these included the inadequate provision of information and counselling on exploitation of egg donations and creation of embryos, thus necessitating the need for the regulation on informed consent aspects of ART in Nigeria.

10.7 Conclusion

This chapter examined informed consent in ART in Nigeria. The sociolegal approach adopted has enabled a factual assessment of field practices in relation to ART. It can be deduced from the findings in this study that the event model of consent is widely practised in the fertility clinics

[39] Mayer Brezis, Sarah Israel, Avital Weinstein, Prima Posoda, Ayelet Sharon and Renans Tauber 'Quality of informed Consent for Invasive Procedures' International Journal for Quality in Healthcare [2008] 352.

[40] Patrick I. Okonta, Kehinde Bamgbopa, Chizara C. Okeke, Kingsley Onwuzurigbo, Rose Ogbede and Richard Ajayi 'Ethical issues in the practice of Assisted Reproductive Technologies in Nigeria: Empirical Data from Fertility Practitioners' African Journal of Reproductive Health [2018] 51.

visited and from the interviews conducted with women who have patronised ART clinics. The process model of informed consent is rarely used and can be described as a more painstaking model. While knowledge of what constitutes informed consent is evident in the participants, especially the medical doctors, this has not necessarily translated to an objective practice of same in the participants. In fertility clinics where the event model is adopted and practised, there were reports that consent obtained did not emanate from full and adequate information as prescribed by law. The lack of regulation in the ART sector has invariably contributed to the chequered growth of the industry and the lack of uniformity in the guidelines adopted.

This research, based on the foregoing, recommends that the process model should be adopted in informed consent in Nigeria. This recommendation is premised on the need to give as much information as possible to patients patronising fertility clinics. It is of no doubt that all patients who have a need for one ART service or the other invariably part with huge sums of money to defray the costs of consultation, laboratory tests, medications and treatments in their efforts to conceive and bear children. In view of the foregoing, information on the risks and benefits of ART procedures should be conveyed with the utmost sense of urgency to the patients. The adoption of the process model of consent, if achieved, will go a long way to reduce incidences of medical mismanagement and other abuses in the sector.

Bibliography

Adamson, G. D., DeMouzon, J., and Dyer, S. 'ICMART World Report 2013' (2017) (32) 64–65 Human Reproduction.

Brezis, M., Israel, S., Weinstein, A., Prima Posoda, P., Sharon, A., and Tauber, R. 'Quality of Informed Consent for Invasive Procedures'. International Journal for Quality in Healthcare [2008] 352.

Coleman, C. H., Menkoff, J. A., Goldner, J. A., Dubler, N. N. *The Ethics and Regulation of Research with Human Subjects* (Lexis Nexis, 2005).

Ekechi-Agwu, C. A., and Nwafor, A. O. 'Regulating Assisted Reproductive Technologies in Nigeria: Lessons from Australia and the United Kingdom' (2020) (24) African Journal of Reproductive Health <http://ajol.info> accessed 22 October 2021.

Emiri, F. *Medical Law and Ethics in Nigeria* (Malthouse Books, 2012).

Enabulele, O. 'Nigeria's National Health Act 2014: A Review of Some of Its Implications and Challenges' (2017) (16) 2 Annals of Biomedical Sciences <https://ajol.info> accessed 24 October 2021.

Ezeuko, M. I. 'Nigerian Laws on Informed Consent Before a Surgical Procedure' (2019) (87) Medico-Legal Journal <www.journals.sagepub.com> accessed 26 October 2021.

Fadare, J. O., and Adeniyi, A. A. 'Ethical Issues in Newer Assisted Reproductive Technologies: A View from Nigeria' [2015] 57–61 Nigerian Journal of Clinical Practice.

Gbobo, P. I., and Oke-Chinda, M. 'An Analysis of the Doctrine of Informed Consent in Nigeria's Healthcare Services' (2018) (69) Journal of Law Policy and Globalization <https://www.liste.org> accessed 15 October 2021.

Iyioha, I. O., and Aniaka, O. 'Informed Consent' <www.lawexplorer.com/informedconsent> accessed 21 February 2023.

Jebbin, J. N., and Adotey, J. M. 'Informed Consent: How Informed Are Patients' (2004) (13) Nigerian Journal of Medicine <http://ajol/info> accessed 19 October 2021.

Joseph, M., and Danielle, B. 'Informed Consent: What Must Be Disclosed and What Must Be Understood' (2021) (21) 973 The American Journal of Bioethics <https://www.tandfonline.com> accessed 25 October 2021.

Koyonda, S. O. 'Assisted Reproductive Technology in Nigeria: Placing the Law above the Medical' [2009] Journal of Indian Law Institute.

Lidz, C. S., and Appelbaum, P. S. 'Two Models of Informed Consent' (1998) (148) Archives of Internal Medicine <http://pubmed.ncbi.nim.nih.gov> accessed 26 October 2021.

Lokesh, N. P., Krishman, M., Krishna, M., and Musmade, P. B. 'Informed Consent: Issues and Challenges' Journal of Advanced Pharmaceutical Technology and Research [2013].

Medina, J., 'In-vitro Fertilisation: The Right to Give Life or Taking the Fundamental Right to Take Life' [2015] Law School Student Scholarship Paper.

Nnebue, C. 'Informed Consent in Research' (2010) (1) Afrimedic Journal <https://www.ajol.info> accessed 20 October 2021.

Ojifinni, O. O., and Ibisomi, L. 'Preconception Care Practices in Nigeria: A Descriptive Qualitative Study' [2020] 17, 172 Reproductive Health.

Okonta, P. I., Bamgbopa, K., Okeke, C. C., Onwuzurigbo, O. P. R., and Ajayi, R. 'Ethical Issues in the Practice of Assisted Reproductive Technologies in Nigeria: Empirical Data from Fertility Practitioners' [2018] African Journal of Reproductive Health.

Olomojobi, Y. *Medical and Health Law: The Right to Health* (1st ed., Princeton Publishing 2019).

Omokanye, L. O., Olatinwo, O. A., Salahudeen, G. A., Durowade, K. A., Panti, A. A., and Balogun, R. O. 'Assisted Reproduction Technology in Nigeria: Challenges and the Way Forward' (2018) (3) African Journal for Infertility and Assisted Conception <http://www.afrijac.org> accessed 27 October 2021.

Parth Shah, P., Imani Thorton, I., Danielle Turrin, D., and Hipskind, J. E. *Informed Consent* (StatPearls Publishing, 2021) <www.ncbi.nih.gov/books> accessed 25 October, 2021.

Pugh, J. 'Informed Consent, Autonomy and Beliefs' in *Autonomy, Rationality and Contemporary Beliefs* (Oxford University Press 2020) <www.ncbi.nih.gov/books> accessed 21 February 2023

Rao, K. H. 'Informed Consent: An Ethical Obligation or Legal Compulsion' [2008] Journal of Cutaneous & Aesthetic Surgery.

Recchia, V., Dodaro, A., and Braga, L. 'Event-Based Versus Process Based Informed Consent to Address Scientific Evidence and Uncertainties in Ionising Medical Imaging' (2013) (4) 5 Insights Imaging <http://www.ncbi.nim.nih.gov> accessed 26 October 2021.

Ruback, T. J. 'Informed Consent' in Richard W. Dehn and David P. Asprey (eds) *Essential Clinical Procedures* (Elsevier 2002).

CHAPTER 11

Contract for Gestational Services: Examining the Legal Status and Enforceability of Surrogacy Arrangements in Nigeria

Amarachi Chizaram Okonkoh and Dorcas Odunaike

11.1 Introduction

Assisted Reproductive Technology (ART) refers to all treatments or procedures that include the in vitro handling of both human oocytes and sperm, or embryos, for the purpose of establishing a pregnancy. ART has been defined as:

> All interventions that include the in vitro handling of both human oocytes and sperm or embryos for the purpose of reproduction. This includes, but is not limited to, IVF and embryo transfer (ET), intracytoplasmic sperm

A. C. Okonkoh (✉) · D. Odunaike
Babcock University, Ilishan-Remo, Ogun State, Nigeria
e-mail: okonkoha@babcock.edu.ng

D. Odunaike
e-mail: odunaiked@babcock.edu.ng

O. S. Adelakun and E. Ndoni (eds.), *Reproductive Health and Assisted Reproductive Technologies In Sub-Saharan Africa*,
Sustainable Development Goals Series,
https://doi.org/10.1007/978-981-99-2411-0_11

injection (ICSI), embryo biopsy, preimplantation genetic testing (PGT), assisted hatching, gamete intrafallopian transfer (GIFT), zygote intrafallopian transfer, gamete and embryo cryopreservation, semen, oocyte and embryo donation, and gestational carrier cycles.[1]

Gestational surrogacy is a form of surrogacy arrangement where the surrogate contributes no genetic material to the creation of the child, she only offers gestational services, by making her womb available for the gestation of the child. Gestational surrogacy is the only form of surrogacy recognised and appropriately classified as a form of reproductive technology by the International Committee for Monitoring Assisted Reproductive Technology (ICMART).[2] Traditional surrogacy, a form of surrogacy where the surrogate contributes her own eggs to the creation of an embryo, and is both the biological and gestational mother of the child is not classified as ART. In Nigeria, traditional surrogacy is classified as a form of reproductive technology. Article 23 of The Nigerian Code of Medical Ethics issued by the Medical and Dental Council of Nigeria pursuant to the Medical and Dental Practitioners Act lists full surrogacy (traditional surrogacy) as a form of reproductive technology.[3] Thus, a surrogacy arrangement where the surrogate contributes both the genetic material—the egg, to the conception of the child and the gestation of the child is recognised as a form of ART in Nigeria.

A surrogacy contract is a contract that seeks to confer parental rights on intending parents, who commissioned the birth of a child through a surrogate. It does this by asserting the parental rights of the intending parents and clarifying that the surrogate shall have no parental rights over the resulting child and that she shall not assert any such right. By asserting the intending parent's parental rights in a surrogacy agreement, a surrogacy contract makes two key assumptions: the first is that parental rights are ordinarily vested in the surrogate. Secondly, the exercise of parental rights can be modified by contractual agreement. The first presumption is hinged on the maxim—*mater semper certa est* (the mother is always certain). This principle means that motherhood is acquired by giving birth to a child; that is, the woman who gives birth to a child is deemed to be

[1] Fernando Zegers-Hochschild and others, 'The International Glossary on Infertility and Fertility Care, 2017' (2017) 32(9) Human Reproduction 1786, 1790.

[2] Fernando Zegers-Hochschild and others (n 1).

[3] Cap M 20 Laws of the Federation of Nigeria (LFN) 2010, section 1(2) (c).

the mother of the child. The Nigerian courts have stated that 'the law has always acknowledged the right of a woman to say who the father of her child is, and of course, where a child is born within wedlock, the presumption is conclusive, that the child is the seed or product of the marriage'.[4] This rule is based on 'common sense', because as Hisano notes, the status of motherhood used to be evident by the pregnancy and birth of a child.[5]

One of the changes that ART has introduced to parentage is that it has fragmented and decentralised the process of making babies.[6] The decentralisation of the birth process by ART has resulted in distinct components of parentage being deposited in different persons, thus making it difficult to ascertain the legal parent. A gestational surrogate who shares no genetic connection with the child has a claim to parentage by virtue of her role in gestating and giving birth to the child. The gamete donor also has a recognisable claim to parentage by virtue of her genetic contribution to the conception of the child. The role of the intending parents who may or may not have contributed any genetic material to the conception of the child is also recognised, as their intention put into action is the 'first cause, or the prime movers, of the procreative relationship'.[7] It is within the context of the various fragments of parenthood that reside in different parties to the reproductive process and the surrogacy contract, that clarity on whom may exercise parental rights in a surrogacy arrangement is important. The essence of a surrogacy contract is therefore to clarify the rights and status of the parties to a surrogacy arrangement, especially the parental rights of intending parents, vis-a-vis the surrogate. It extinguishes the parental right of the surrogate- which resides in her by the presumption of law (since she gave birth to the child) and transfers or confers the same on the intending parents. This chapter examines the

[4] *Tony Anozie v Mrs Chizoba Uwakwe & Anor* (2016) LPELR-40554(CA).

[5] Erin Y Hisano, 'Gestational Surrogacy Maternity Disputes: Refocusing on the Child' (2011) 15 (2) Lewis & Clark Law Review 517, 520; Jane Stoll, Surrogacy Arrangements and Legal Parenthood: Swedish Law in a Comparative Context' (PhD Thesis, Uppsala Universitet 2013) 80.

[6] Pierce-Gealy, Michelle, '"Are You My Mother?": Ohio's Crazy-Making Baby-Making Produces a New Definition of "Mother"' (1995) 28(3) Akron Law Review 535, 542.

See also *Johnson v Calvert* 851 P.2d 776, 781–83 (Cal. 1993), where the court acknowledged that in a gestational surrogacy arrangement, both the surrogate and the intending mother (who is also the genetic mother) have each presented acceptable proof of maternity.

[7] *Johnson v Calvert* (supra).

legal status of a surrogacy contract under the Nigerian Legal System, in the absence of ART-specific laws and identifies the bases upon which a court may enforce or give effect to the terms of a gestational surrogacy contract in Nigeria.

11.2 Status of a Surrogacy Contract

Surrogacy 'is the process by which a woman makes a choice to become pregnant and then carry to full term and deliver a baby who, she intends, will be raised by someone else'.[8] The surrogate is the woman who carries the child, whereas the intended or commissioning parent refers to the person 'who manifests the intent to be legally bound as the parent of a child resulting from assisted or collaborative reproduction'.[9] There are generally two forms of surrogacy arrangements: gestational surrogacy and traditional surrogacy. A surrogacy arrangement may be altruistic or commercial/compensated. There are no available statistics on the number of surrogacy arrangements made in Nigeria annually. However, there is incontrovertible evidence that surrogacy is beginning to gain firm ground in Nigeria.[10] More and more families that have the means are resorting to surrogacy to establish their families.[11]

Despite the fact that the Nigerian Code of Medical Ethics recognises traditional surrogacy as a form of reproductive technology, the prevailing socio-legal realities indicate that the judicial treatment of traditional surrogacy contracts will differ from gestational surrogacy contracts. For example, in the case of *JF v DB*, the Ohio Supreme Court stated

[8] *P.M. and C.M., Appellees, v. T.B. and D.B.*, Appellants (2018) Supreme Court of Iowa, No 17–0376.

[9] *P.M. and C.M., Appellees, v. T.B. and D.B* (Supra).

[10] Joseph Ifeanyichukwu Ikechebelu and others, 'A Successful Gestational Surrogacy in Southeast Nigeria' (2017) 2(1) African Journal for Infertility and Assisted Conception 19 (note).

[11] The Media recently carried the news of a prominent Nigerian who used a surrogate to have her two children.

See 'Tinubu's Daughter, Folasade Welcomes Second Surrogate Baby Girl' (*PM News* 25 October 2019) <https://www.pmnewsnigeria.com/2019/10/25/tinubus-daughter-folasade-welcomes-second-surrogate-baby-girl/> accessed 27 October 2019: 'Nigerian Couples Cautiously Turn to Surrogacy to Ease Fertility Woes' (*New Vision* 27 December 2018) <https://www.newvision.co.ug/new_vision/news/1491806/nigerian-couples-cautiously-surrogacy-ease-fertility-woes> accessed 27 October 2019.

that '*we would be remiss to leave unstated the obvious fact that a gestational surrogate, whose pregnancy does not involve her own egg, may have a different legal position from a traditional surrogate, whose pregnancy does involve her own egg*'.[12]

The fundamental question which a surrogacy agreement raises is whether parental rights can be transferred, acquired, extinguished or modified by way of contract. This is what a surrogacy agreement purports to do; it seeks to confer on another, parental rights which, for the agreement would lie in the person transferring such rights. It also provides clarity on the person who may exercise parental rights in respect of a child born through a surrogacy arrangement. To be able to determine if parental rights can be the subject of a contractual agreement; that is, whether such rights can be extinguished and transferred to another through a surrogacy contract, it is apposite to first determine the legal status of a surrogacy contract under the Nigerian Law.

A surrogacy contract is either legal or illegal. If it is legal, it is valid if all the ingredients of a contract are present in it and therefore enforceable. If it is illegal, it is unenforceable, even if all the elements of a valid contract are present in it. Legality is governed by law. In *Bello v Attorney General Oyo State*, the word 'illegal' was defined to mean an act which the law directly forbids and which is declared to be unlawful.[13] In *Onyiuke III v Okeke*, the Nigerian Supreme Court stated what constitutes an illegal contract thus:

> It is the law that a contract is illegal if the consideration or the promise involves doing something illegal or contrary to public policy or if the intention of the parties in making the contract is thereby to promote something which is illegal or contrary to public policy; and an illegal contract is void and cannot be the foundation of any legal right.[14]

An illegal contract is therefore one which requires the doing of an act expressly prohibited by law or an act contrary to public policy. An illegal contract is unenforceable.[15] It is easy to determine acts that are expressly prohibited by law, however, what is challenging, is the determination of

[12] *JF v DB*, 116 Ohio St. 3d 363, 2007-Ohio-6750.

[13] (1986) LPELR-764(SC).

[14] (1976) LPELR-8039(SC).

[15] *Misa v Ahmad* (2018) LPELR-44247(CA).

acts that are contrary to public policy. Public policy is an amorphous concept almost incapable of a precise meaning and highly susceptible to subjective interpretations and definitions.[16]

11.3 Illegality, Public Policy and Surrogacy Contracts

11.3.1 Illegality and Surrogacy Contracts

Since ART began being utilised in Nigeria, no laws have been enacted to regulate its use and practice in the country and there are also no laws prohibiting its use. The absence of relevant laws regulating ART in Nigeria has created a regulatory gap and has perpetuated uncertainty in the law, rights and status of parties and even acts which constitute ART. This uncertainty notwithstanding, the only thing certain in the Nigerian legal landscape is the fact that there is no law in operation in Nigeria which prohibits surrogacy.

The only statute which has provisions relevant to surrogacy is the National Health Act (NHA) 2014. Section 50 of the NHA provides that:

> **50**.- {.1) A person shall not-
>
> (a) manipulate any genetic material, including genetic material of human gametes, zygotes or embryos; or
> (b) engage in any activity including nuclear transfer or embryo splitting **for the purpose of the cloning of human being;**
> (c) **import or export human zygotes or embryos.**[17]

ART generally and surrogacy specifically, involve the in vitro handling of sperm, eggs and embryos for the purpose of achieving pregnancy. The import of the provisions of section 50 of the NHA is that the manipulation of any genetic material, including human gametes and embryos is permitted under the law provided that such manipulation is **not** for the purpose of cloning a human being or importing or exporting a human

[16] Kojo Yelpaala, 'Restraining the Unruly Horse: The Use of Public Policy in Arbitration, Interstate and International' (1989) 2 Transnational Law 379, 381.

[17] Emphasis ours.

zygote or embryo. Surrogacy involves the in vitro handling of human gametes and embryos; however, the purpose is solely for the conception and birth of a child and nothing more and it does not fall within the exceptions provided for in section 50 of the National Health Act. Surrogacy is therefore not a violation of the provisions of the NHA. This position is fortified by a plethora of legal authorities. The Court in *Enyi V Benue State Judicial Service Commission* held that:

> The position of the Law is trite that the express mention of one or more things of a particular class may be regarded as silently excluding all other members of the class i.e., *expressum facit lessare taciturn*. This means that the express mention of one thing in a statutory provision or Constitution automatically excludes any other which otherwise would have been included by implication. It is also good Law that as a general rule of construction of statute or Constitution that a Court is not entitled to read into a Statute/Constitution word[s] which are excluded expressly, or impliedly from it as it is a well-established and cardinal principle of interpretation that where the ordinary meaning of the words used in a provision are clear and unambiguous, effect must be given to the words without resorting to any extrinsic aid.[18]

This was also the position in *Omatseye v FRN*, where the Court held that:

> It is trite that the express mention of one thing in a statutory provision automatically excludes any other which otherwise would have applied by implication with regard to the same issue. See the case of EHUWA V. O.S.I.E.C. (2006) 10 NWLR (PT.1012) 544 where the apex Court held: "It is now firmly established that in the construction of a Statutory provision, where a statute mentions specific things or persons, the intention is that those not mentioned are not intended to be included. The latin maxim is 'Expressio unius est exclusio alterius' - i.e., the expression of one thing is the exclusion of another".[19]

Thus, the non-mention of surrogacy and the in vitro handling of gametes and embryos for the purpose of achieving pregnancy and child birth is not an act prohibited under the law.

[18] (2021) LPELR-54437(CA).

[19] (2017) LPELR-42719(CA).

The increasing use and reliance on ART are expressly recognised under Nigerian law, however, there is no law that expressly prohibits, endorses or comprehensively regulates it. Presently, two key regulations provide some guidance on the clinical practice of ART in Nigeria; the Code of Medical Ethics and the ART Practice in Lagos State Regulations and Guidelines 2019 (the ART Regulation).[20] The Code is a subsidiary legislation that regulates the medical profession in Nigeria. 'A subsidiary legislation or enactment is one that was subsequently made or enacted under and pursuant to the powers conferred by the principal legislation or enactment. It derives its force and efficacy from the principal legislation to which it is therefore secondary and complementary'.[21] The Code is a national legal instrument, applicable only to medical practitioners across the entire federation. The Code acknowledges that there exists a lacuna in the absence of ART-specific statutes in Nigeria, to bridge the gap occasioned by the non-existence of relevant laws, it implores the medical practitioner involved in ART to resolve ethical matters that arise from embryo donation, gestational surrogacy and full surrogacy.[22]

The Lagos State ART Regulation on the other hand is only applicable to Lagos State. The Lagos State ART Regulation is described as a policy document. It is primarily intended to regulate the activities of fertility clinics, by spelling out the conditions which fertility centres must satisfy and the qualifications ART professionals are required to possess. However, the Lagos State ART Regulation extends to matters over which, by its enabling Act it has no authority to legislate on, like specifying an age limit for recipients of donor gametes, and requiring that gamete donation must be anonymous.[23] The Lagos State ART Regulation accurately notes that there are no laws currently regulating surrogacy in Nigeria. However, in an attempt to describe the legal landscape of surrogacy in Nigeria, it inaccurately states that because of the absence of such laws, surrogacy contracts are unenforceable. The absence of surrogacy laws does

[20] ART Practice in Lagos State Regulations and Guidelines 2019 (the ART Regulation) made pursuant to the Lagos State Health Reform Law of 2006.

[21] *Njoku & Ors V Iheanatu & Ors*, CA/PH/EPT/454/2007 (CON).

[22] Code of Medical Ethics, rule 23.

[23] The Lagos State ART Regulations is not properly numbered and divided into sections, thereby making proper referencing difficult.

not automatically make surrogacy contracts unenforceable in Nigeria, as such contracts may be enforced by invoking a number of legal principles enshrined under the law.

11.3.2 Public Policy and Surrogacy Contracts

Public policy has been described as an elusive concept,[24] it has also been most notably described as an unruly horse, argued only when all other points fail,[25] and which should be cautiously ridden.[26] Jurists like Lord Denning have forcefully asserted the relevance of public policy in achieving justice by attempting to discredit the ill notions associated with it. In *Enderby Town Football Club Ltd. v The Football Association Ltd.*, Lord Denning stated that:

> I know that over 300 years ago Hobart C.J. said that 'Public policy is an unruly horse'. It has often been repeated since. So unruly is the horse, it is said ... that no judge should ever try to mount it lest it run away with him. I disagree. With a good man in the saddle, the unruly horse can be kept in control. It can jump over obstacles. It can leap the fences put up by fictions and come down on the side of justice.[27]

Winfield has rightly observed, that it is 'a principle of judicial legislation or interpretation founded on the current needs of the community',[28] usually relied upon in the absence of relevant legislation. It can be the basis for the introduction of new rules,[29] and remains a veritable tool in the absence of statute or established legal rules that may be relied on in novel cases. It is acknowledged that the development of public policy cannot be divorced from 'when law had to be made in some way or other,

[24] Farshad Ghodoosi, 'The Concept of Public Policy in Law: Revisiting the Role of the Public Policy Doctrine in the Enforcement of Private Legal Arrangements' (2015) 94 Nebraska Law Review 685, 688.

[25] *Richardson v Mellish* (1824) 2 Bing 229, 252, per Burrough J.

[26] *Gray v Bar* [1971] 2 QB 554 (CA).

[27] [1971] Ch 591.

[28] Percy H Winfield, 'Public Policy in the English Common' (1928) 42(1) Harvard Law Review 76, 92.

[29] Stavros Brekoulakis, 'The Evolution of Public Policy and Judicial Function in English Law' [2019] Journal of International Dispute Settlement 1, 10.

and when there was not much statute law and practically no case law at all to summon to the judges' assistance'.[30] It was often cited as the basis for judicial decisions in cases where the law offered very little assistance. A judge faced with a legal situation for which neither statute nor case law provides any guide may rely on public policy to decide the question before him one way or the other, invoking public policy as the basis of the decision. Its most defining characteristic is its variability; which is both its strength and weakness.[31] Its inconsistency and flexibility permit the judicial resolution of disputes in accordance with the perceived prevailing public policy at every point in time.

The challenge with determining the legality or otherwise of an act by public policy is seen in the English Case of *Egerton v Earl of Brownlow* where sixteen judges gave varying opinions as to whether a clause under a Will was void as against public policy.[32] Parke B in that case summed up the challenges of relying on public policy in adjudication when he stated that:

> Public policy is a vague and unsatisfactory term, and calculated to lead to uncertainty and error, when applied to the decision of legal rights; it is capable of being understood in different senses; it may, and does, in its ordinary sense, mean 'political expedience' or that which is best for the common good of the community; and in that sense there may be every variety of opinion, according to education habits, talents and dispositions of each person, who is to decide whether an act is against public policy or not. To allow this to be a ground of judicial decision, would lead to the greatest uncertainty and confusion. It is the province of the statesman and not the lawyer, to discuss, and of the Legislature to determine what is best for the public good and to provide for it by proper enactments. It is the province of the judge to expound the law only; the written from the statutes; the unwritten or common law from the decisions of our predecessors and of our existing courts, from text writers of acknowledged authority, and upon the principles to be clearly deduced from them by sound reason and just inference; not to speculate upon what is the best, in his opinion, for the advantage of the community.[33]

[30] Winfield (n 28) 77.

[31] Though Winfield opines that the 'variability of public policy is a stone in the edifice of the doctrine, and not a missile to be flung at it'. See Winfield (n 28) 95.

[32] *Egerton V Brownlow* (1853) 4 HLC 1.

[33] *Egerton V Brownlow*.

In many jurisdictions of the world, the transfer of parental rights in exchange for money and the sale of children is prohibited. Surrogacy is not a baby-selling venture, however, offering financial compensation in exchange for reproductive services such as the sale of gametes and the gestation of a child could sometimes blur the lines between ethical and unethical conduct. Consequently, some jurists may consider surrogacy to be contrary to public policy, whereas, others may find that it is not. The determination of what constitutes or offends public policy may therefore in some cases be subjective. In *JF v DB*, the Ohio Supreme Court had to determine if a gestational surrogacy contract was contrary to the public policy of the state.[34] The Court in its lead judgement held that a gestational surrogacy contract does not violate public policy, even where the terms of the contract require the gestational surrogate not to assert parental rights over the children resulting from the arrangement that are not genetically related to her. In a rather interesting dissenting judgement, the minority held that the contract violates public policies which safeguard children. The dissenting judgement held that:

> Although the majority concludes that these statutes do not prohibit the contract at issue in this case, I respectfully disagree. The essence of this purported contract is an agreement among unrelated persons for the creation of a child for the payment of money. The contract document requires the surrogate mother and the egg donor to terminate any parental rights they may have to the resulting child, and should they fail to do so, they must return the money paid to them by J.F. to produce the child. Although the contract refers to the payment of money by J.F. to the egg donor and to the surrogate mother for their 'services', and not for their consent to adoption of the child or for the termination of any parental rights to the child, it is impossible to so precisely separate the conduct of the parties and the object of the payment of the money. The result of the contractual arrangement violates clearly stated public policy.[35]

It is unclear if the dissenting judges would have reached a different decision if the gestational surrogacy contract was an altruistic arrangement. The lead and dissenting judgement given in *JF v DB* validate the concerns expressed by Burrough J. when he exclaimed that:

[34] *JF v DB*.

[35] Ibid.

> I, for one, protest, as my Lord has done, against arguing too strongly upon public policy; it is a very unruly horse, and when you get astride it you never know where it will carry you. It may lead you from the sound law.[36]

The different decisions reached on the same issue, by the same court citing public policy emphasises the need for a law which expressly states the status of surrogacy arrangements and clear rules for its enforcement.

There is a dearth of Nigerian authorities on surrogacy. Currently, there is only one known case, where a Nigerian High Court held a surrogacy arrangement to be valid and enforced the same.[37] There are no known Court of Appeal or Supreme Court decisions on the legality and validity of surrogacy arrangements. The closest instance of a surrogacy arrangement that the Supreme Court has been privileged to consider was in *Meribe v Egwu*.[38] However, the question raised in *Meribe*'s case was an incidental question on the validity of a customary surrogacy method, which permitted a childless woman to procure another woman for her husband in order to procreate through her. According to the Igbo custom,[39] as pleaded in that case, a woman who was unable to have children, could marry a wife for the purpose of procreating through her. The children borne by the second wife are deemed under the custom and tradition of the people to belong to the first wife for all intents and purposes. The custom was explained as follows: 'It is the custom in our place that if a woman has no issue, she can marry another woman for her husband; any issue from the said married woman would be regarded as an issue from the woman who married her for the purpose of representation in respect of estate and inheritance'. The Supreme Court sanctioned the practice and held that:

[36] *Richardson v Mellish* (1824) 2 Bing 229, 252.

[37] *Re Olatunde* DHC/50/CS/2021 (Unreported) filed on 28 September 2021 in the Rivers State High Court, judgement was delivered on 29 November 2021.

[38] (1976) LPELR-1861 (SC).

[39] The customary law pleaded in this case is that of the Igbos of Ogbodi-Ukwu, Umuahia, of the present-day Abia state, Nigeria. However, this was a pervasive custom among the Igbos of Eastern Nigeria, but it is currently fading out due to modernisation, and more expedient means of having children such as adoption and ART.

> The facts disclosed in evidence did not show that Nwanyiakoli married Nwanyiocha for herself ... but that she 'married' her for her husband. The word "married" in that context is merely colloquial, the proper thing to say being that she procured Nwanyiocha for chief Cheghekwu to marry her. There was no suggestion in evidence that there was anything immoral in the transaction.

The implication of the Supreme Court's decision in *Meribe v Egwu* is that the court will respect methods adopted by persons who are unable to have children. However, such methods, must not be repugnant, immoral or contrary to public policy. The question then is what methods will be considered repugnant and immoral? The case of *Edet v Essien* gives insight into what the Nigerian Courts consider to be repugnant.[40] In *Edet v Essien*, the plaintiff had married a young lady, and when the marriage broke down, she remarried the defendant. According to the customary law of the Efik people of Cross-river State, Nigeria, a marriage is effectively terminated when the bride-price is returned to the groom's family. In this case, the bride-price was not returned and the plaintiff sought a declaration that the two children born to the defendant were his children (since they were born during the subsistence of the first marriage, which was not validly terminated). The native court awarded parentage to the plaintiff. Aggrieved, the defendant appealed, and the provincial court, upturning the decision of the lower court declared him to be the father of the children. The customary law of the Efik people that permitted the biological children of another, to be given to one with whom they had no biological connection was declared repugnant to natural justice, equity and good conscience. This decision was given many years before medical technology made it possible for more than two people of the opposite sex to be able to procreate. While the facts of *Edet v Essien* are different and not exactly applicable to surrogacy, it can be inferred from that decision that when parentage is split among different parties, the court may give preference to genetics. This shows that the courts will give weighty consideration to genetics in the consideration of surrogacy arrangements.

[40] (1932) 11 NLR 47.

11.4 Bases of Enforceability of Gestational Surrogacy Contracts

In jurisdictions where the courts have had the opportunity of pronouncing on the validity and enforceability of surrogacy contracts, it can be seen that the judicial treatment of traditional surrogacy contracts and gestational surrogacy contracts differ.[41] This section focuses primarily on the legal principles that may be invoked in the enforcement of gestational surrogacy contracts.

The validity and enforceability of surrogacy contracts in the absence of regulation is uncertain. Validity and enforceability are distinct questions of law which are governed by similar as well as different principles of law.[42] Though, where a contract is valid, it is often enforceable. A surrogacy arrangement is usually referred to as a contract because it has some resemblance with a contract properly so called and because it relies on settled contractual principles. First, it relies on the principles of offer and acceptance to come into existence. Second, it is often an agreement between two parties; the intending parents and the surrogates. In cases of commercial surrogacy, there is usually a consideration which is most often a monetary reward, paid to the surrogate in exchange for her to carry and bear a child for the commissioning parents. In furtherance of her commitment under the contract, the surrogate transfers all parental rights to the intending parents and hands over the baby to them at birth. Even in an altruistic surrogacy arrangement, where the surrogate is paid no fee for her services, promises are still exchanged. To ensure that the purpose of the contract is achieved, certain other terms and conditions are usually agreed upon by the parties. This undeniably brings a surrogacy agreement within the province of contract law. Yet, a surrogacy agreement does not fit absolutely within contract law alone. It extends to the province of family law and raises some human rights concern. The intersection of surrogacy contracts with contract law, human rights law and

[41] See *re Baby M*, 537 A.2d 1227 (NJ 1988).

[42] For example, altruistic surrogacy contracts are valid in the United Kingdom, but are unenforceable, while commercial surrogacy arrangements are illegal.

Surrogacy Arrangements Act 1985, section 1A; C Purshouse and K Bracegirdle, 'The Problem of Unenforceable Surrogacy Contracts: Can Unjust Enrichment Provide a Solution?' (2018) 26(4) Medical Law Review 5; Emily Jackson, 'UK Law and International Commercial Surrogacy: "The Very Antithesis of Sensible"' (2016) 4(3) Journal of Medical Law and Ethics 197.

family law leads to an important enquiry. Does the law permit parties to extinguish and acquire parental rights by virtue of an agreement? Is such a contract enforceable under the Nigerian law?

Another fundamental question that comes up in surrogacy matters, is the law that should govern a surrogacy arrangement: Human Rights Law? Family Law? Contract Law? Or a hybrid of all these laws? It has been argued that 'family law provides a rich source of norms, experience, and institutional guidance upon which the law can draw in attempting to predict behaviour and regulate contracts dealing with surrogacy.'[43] Yet, Family Law is sceptical of surrogacy contracts, because of the peculiar nature of the subject matter of the contract—human relationships, which are difficult to comprehend, predict or control.[44] Others have argued that surrogacy arrangements are contracts and should be governed by the law of contract. Courts have relied on the law of contract to enforce surrogacy arrangements. In *Re Baby M's* case, the trial court, in affirming the obligations created under the surrogacy contract and seeking to enforce same (though repulsed by the subject matter of the contract) stated that:

> The contract is not illusory... Mrs. Whitehead was anxious to contract. This court finds that she had changed her mind, reneged on her promise, and now seeks to avoid her obligations. A visitor from Mars would be surprised to discover that Mary Beth Whitehead was a mother and the article in dispute her child.[45]

In *JF v* JB, the Ohio Supreme Court emphasised the contractual nature of surrogacy arrangements and its enforceability. The court stated lucidly that a 'written contract defining the rights and obligations of the parties

[43] Peter H Schuck, 'Some Reflections on the Baby M Case', (1988) 76 Georgetown Law Journal 1793, 1809.

[44] Carl E Schneider, 'Surrogate Motherhood from the Perspective of Family Law' (1990) 13 Harvard Journal of Law and Public Policy 125, 127.

[45] *Re Baby M*.

The reaction of the public to the use of contract law to enforce a surrogacy contract at the time was hostile with one newspaper saying 'Here is a judge who would have used contract law to uphold Shylock's demand for a pound of flesh'. Richard Cohen, Philadelphia Inquirer, April 2, 1987 as cited in Audrey Wolfson Latourette, 'The Surrogate Mother Contract: In the Best Interests of Society?' (1990) 25(1) University of Richmond Law Review Volume 53, 58.

The decision of the trial Court was reversed on appeal to the New Jersey Supreme Court.

seems an appropriate way to enter into surrogacy agreement. If the parties understand their contract rights, requiring them to honour the contract they entered into is manifestly right and just'.[46] The court's position may be justified and supported on the basis of contractual autonomy.

Though the Law of Contract has been useful in regulating surrogacy arrangements, it is inadequate to address the complicated yet sensitive nature of a surrogacy contract. Its inadequacies lie in its remedies. Remedies like specific performance and damages may result in unintended consequences and harm the interests of the party in breach, while offering no real remedy to the party alleging the breach. In *Baby M's* case, the trial court's use of specific performance to compel the birth mother to hand over her child to another, was evidently distressing to her and raised some concerns about the morality of such a course.[47] Human Rights Law has also been invoked in the regulation and enforcement of surrogacy rights. Constitutional liberties, such as: the right of privacy and family life may be invoked to either enforce a surrogacy contract or to renege from its overreaching obligations.[48] A surrogacy contract is a contract with multiple legal flavours, because a surrogacy arrangement by its nature is pervasive and raises substantial questions of law bordering on family law, human rights, nationality, succession and conflict of laws or private international law. Thus, it is impracticable for it to be governed by a specific law. A surrogacy contract can therefore be governed by an amalgam of laws, including international law and child's right laws. The question of enforcement of a surrogacy contract is usually centred on the

[46] 879 NE 2d 740, 740 (Ohio 2007), 741.

[47] The Supreme Court of New Jersey on appeal noted that:

> We do not find it so clear that her efforts to keep her infant, when measured against the Sterns' efforts to take her away, make one, rather than the other, the wrongdoer. The Sterns suffered but so did she. And if we go beyond suffering to an evaluation of the human stakes involved in the struggle, how much weight should be given to her nine months of pregnancy, the labor of childbirth, and the risk to her life, compared to the payment of money, the anticipation of a child, and the donation of sperm.'

[48] The right to privacy is a constitutionally guaranteed right under section 37 of the Constitution of the Federal Republic of Nigeria, 1999 and the Nigerian Supreme Court has held that this right extends to the right to protect one's body from unwarranted invasion. See M.D.P.D.T v Okonkwo (2001) LPELR-1856 (SC).

determination of parental rights, and as the Indian Court has observed, babies conceived through surrogacy encounter a lot of complications on parentage issues.[49]

In the absence of statutory rules which govern the enforcement of surrogacy contracts, the court may rely on a number of legal principles to enforce a surrogacy contract. This is illustrated by the only known Nigerian gestational surrogacy case.[50] In *Re Olatunde*, the intending parents entered into a gestational surrogacy arrangement with a surrogate, the arrangement was brokered by a surrogacy agency, so the intending parents and the surrogate never met each other. After the child was born and handed over to the intending parents, a suit was filed by the intending parents, wherein they sought a declaration that they are the legal parents to the surrogate-born child, since surrogacy is not prohibited by any Nigerian law. In the course of trial, the court ordered parties to go for a DNA test, stating that the test 'does not impugn or disparage the efficacy and lawfulness of the act of surrogacy' which gave rise to the child, rather, it strengthened the right claimed by the applicants.[51] The test was done and the result transmitted directly to the court. The court, in its judgement held that surrogacy is a legal means of having children and does not offend against the law and it declared the intending parents to be the legal parents of the child.[52]

In Nigeria, gestational surrogacy contracts may be enforced on the following bases:

a. Genetics as a basis of enforcement;
b. Best Interest of the Child as a basis of enforcement;
c. Estoppel/Intent/Conduct as a basis of enforcement;

[49] *Jan Balaz (s) v Anand Municipality* (2009).

[50] *Re Olatunde* DHC/50/CS/2021 (Unreported) filed on 28 September 2021 in the Rivers State High Court, judgement was delivered on 29 November 2021.

[51] *Re Olatunde* DHC/50/CS/2021 (Unreported).

[52] This case was litigated by the first author. At the time of writing this chapter, the certified copy of the judgement was yet to be obtained, thus, making it impossible for the fuller reasons upon which the judgement was given to be discussed herein. However, the arguments adduced in this chapter as the basis upon which a court will enforce a gestational surrogacy arrangement were the arguments laid before the court.

11.4.1 Genetics as a Basis of Enforcement

In a gestational surrogacy, the child may be related to both or either of the intending parents, or the child may be genetically unrelated to both intending parents. There are therefore two types of gestational surrogacy arrangements: one in which the intending parents, or one of them contributes gametes to the reproductive process and one in which both of them contribute nothing. In a gestational surrogacy arrangement, the child is genetically unrelated to the surrogate, because the surrogate contributes no biological or genetic material, except the gestation service. Where the intending mother contributes her eggs to the procreation process, she undertakes a more active role in the reproductive process and is subjected to invasive surgical procedures in order to stimulate the production and retrieval of her eggs.[53] This emphasises her role in the reproductive process and diminishes concerns about baby selling which may often arise in traditional surrogacy cases.[54] Genetics as a basis of enforcement may work in two ways, however, its effect is usually to have the surrogacy contract enforced in favour of the intending parents or to have their legal parentage affirmed. The presence of a genetic connection could strengthen an intending parent's claim to legal parentage by its mere existence.[55] In other cases, the absence of a genetic connection between a child and the surrogate could weaken her claim to legal parentage, even where the intending parents are genetically unrelated to the child.[56] The consideration given to genetics in surrogacy arrangements is considerable, this explains why courts are unwilling to enforce traditional surrogacy contracts against a surrogate who is also the genetic/biological and birth mother of a child. It is in view of this same consideration that the courts will be more willing to enforce a gestational surrogacy contract in favour of the intending parents who are also the genetic parents of the child. This was acknowledged by the court in *In re Marriage of Moschetta* when it stated that infertile couples who use 'in vitro fertilization and embryo implantation in another woman's

[53] Pamela Laufer-Ukeles, 'Mothering for Money: Regulating Commercial Intimacy' 2013 (88) Indiana Law Journal 1223, 1260.

[54] Ibid.

[55] *Johnson v Calvert* 851 P.2d 776, 781–83 (Cal. 1993).

[56] *In Re Marriage of Buzzanca* (1998) [Nos. G022147, G022157. Fourth Dist., Div. Three. Mar 10, 1998.].

womb', that is couples who merely use a surrogate's womb, as opposed to using her eggs 'can be reasonably assured of being adjudged the legal parents of the child'.[57] Whereas, couples who resort to traditional surrogacy have no assurances that the court will honour their intentions, because 'biology is destiny'.[58]

In *Belsito v Clark*, the Ohio Court relied on genetics in awarding legal parentage to the intending parents.[59] The court stated its preference for genetics over the 'intent to procreate rule' laid down in *Johnson v Calvert* because the court in Johnson's case discarded both genetics and giving birth as means of identifying a natural mother and replaced both with intent. This, in the opinion of the court in *Belsito v Clark* affords a gestational surrogate the possibility of being recognised as a parent. However, it must be clarified that the court in *Johnson v Calvert* did not disregard genetics and giving birth as means of determining a natural mother. Indeed, it acknowledged that both genetic contribution and gestation could entitle a person to recognition as a natural mother, however, because both parties have each presented a valid fragment of motherhood, the tie breaker for legal parentage should be 'intent to procreate'. The merit of this rule lies in its relevance in gestational surrogacy arrangements where the intending parents are not the genetic parents. In any event, a gestational surrogate stands in a weaker position in relation to the intending parents and may be unable to successfully set up a claim to parentage in order to resile from a contract which she voluntarily entered into. This position was affirmed in *Johnson v Calvert*, where the Californian Supreme Court held that:

> We conclude that although the Act recognizes both genetic consanguinity and giving birth as means of establishing a mother and child relationship, when the two means do not coincide in one woman, she who intended to procreate the child—that is, she who intended to bring about the birth of a child that she intended to raise as her own—is the natural mother under California law.

[57] (1994) [Nos. G013880, G014430. Fourth Dist., Div. Three.

[58] *In re Marriage of Moschetta*.

[59] 67 Ohio Misc. 2d 54 (Ohio Com. Pleas 1994) • 644 N.E.2d 760 Decided Nov 14, 1994.

In the absence of statutory rules which prescribe genetics as a basis of enforcement of surrogacy contracts, genetics may not be the sole basis of enforcement. This is because in some cases, genetics and gestation may reside in distinct persons and no component of motherhood- genetic or biological may reside in the intending mother. In such cases, the court may invoke other principles and considerations in enforcing a surrogacy arrangement for the benefit of the intending parents, where sole reliance on genetics would result in absurdity. In *Re Marriage of Buzzanca*, the child born under a gestational surrogacy arrangement was unrelated to both the intending parents and the surrogate, the use of genetics alone in determining legal parentage would have resulted in the child being parentless, so the court adopted the 'intent to parent' and 'consent to procreate' considerations as the basis of affirming legal parentage.

The Nigerian Courts have, in recent times, recognised the use of blood and Deoxyribonucleic Acid (DNA) tests as a way to establish parentage. Section 63(1)(a) of the Child's Right Act states that:

> In any civil proceeding in which the paternity or maternity of a person falls to be determined by the Court hearing the proceedings, the Court may, on an application by a party to the proceedings, give a direction for – (a) the use of scientific tests, including blood tests and Deoxyribonucleic Acid tests, to ascertain whether the tests show that a party to the proceedings is or is not the father or mother of that person.

Also, in *Anozia v Nnani* the Nigerian Court of Appeal acknowledged the use of DNA in establishing paternity and held that:

> DNA test has to do with the use of genetic analysis, scientifically, to determine the paternity of a child, i.e., whose male spermatozoa fertilized the egg of a female, and, I think, this is usually applicable and relevant where there is dispute as to the paternity of a child, or where there is disputing claims or uncertainty as to the paternity of an individual, See the case of Olayinka Vs Adeparusi & Anor (2011) LPELR 8691 CA, where this Court, per Denton West JCA held: "... If a party is claiming paternity, it is trite that a Court of law should be allowed to determine same on proof of evidence relating to paternity, which could only be done by referral for a DNA test of the parties involved. After such test the Court has a duty to declare, the actual father of the child in dispute in consonance with the evidence at its disposal. DNA, that is, 'Deoxyribonucleic acid' is a molecule that contains the genetic code of any organism. It is hereditary and has

> become a euphemism for scientific analysis of genetic constitution, to determine one's roots... Of course, where one is a minor (not mature adult) and his paternity is in issue, the Court can order the conduct of DNA test, in the overall interest of the child, to ascertain where he belongs."[60]

The recognition of genetics and the use of DNA tests to determine parentage in Nigeria is a clear indication that the courts will be willing to receive evidence that rebuts the presumption that the birth mother/ surrogate is not the natural mother/genetic mother of a surrogate-born child and should not be declared the child's legal parent. In cases where the child is shown to be genetically unrelated to the surrogate as well as the intending parents, the court may rely on the 'intent' test laid down in *John v Calvert* or the best interest of the child rule in conferring legal parentage on the intending parents. It is inconceivable that a court will force a child on an unwilling parent/unwilling surrogate, who is genetically unrelated to the child and who at the point of entering into the surrogacy agreement had indicated no intention to assert parental rights over the child. Even if the surrogate is willing to assume parental rights over the child, it would be contrary to natural justice to confer parental rights on a surrogate who shares no genetic connection with the child. It is also unlikely that a court will permit intending parents to resile from an agreement which led to the birth of a child, that would not have been born but for their acted-on intention, even if they are genetically unrelated to the child. Genetics as a basis of enforcing obligations under a surrogacy agreement, in many cases guarantees the best interest of a child, nevertheless, this rule alone is insufficient for enforcing surrogacy contracts.

11.4.2 Best Interest of the Child as a Basis of Enforceability

The 'best interest of the child' is a principle firmly entrenched by statute, which requires that the best interest of a child should be given primary consideration in every action concerning a child.[61] This rule is a fundamental and overriding consideration in every action which concerns a child, undertaken by both public authorities and private persons. It is a pervasive rule, applicable in every determination involving a child.

[60] (2015) LPELR-24277(CA).

[61] Child's Right Act, section 1.

The rule has been described as 'a threefold concept', which embraces 'a substantive right; a fundamental, interpretative legal principle and a rule of procedure'.[62] The United Nations High Commissioner for Refugees (UNHCR) has explained that the best interest rule as a substantive right requires a child's best interest to be assessed and given primary consideration.[63] As a legal principle, it requires that where a legal provision has more than one provision, the interpretation which serves the child's best interest should be chosen.[64] While as a rule of procedure, it requires that whenever a decision will affect a child, the decision-making process should include an evaluation of both the negative and positive impact of that decision on the child concerned.[65] However, it has been conceded that while the best interest of the child should always be prioritised, the context in which questions surrounding the interest of a child arise determine the standard with which the child's interest is to be evaluated.[66]

Usually, in surrogacy cases, the court relies on other rules or principles in enforcing or refraining from enforcing a surrogacy arrangement and then justifies its decision with the best interest of the child rule. For example, in *Johnson v Calvert*, the court relied on the intent rule in enforcing a gestational surrogacy contract and justified its decision by stating that the rule will best promote certainty and stability for a child. In gestational surrogacy contracts, the courts are often of the opinion that a child's best interest will be better served if the legal parentage of the genetic parents are recognised and affirmed. In *Johnson v Calvert*, the court stated that:

> the interests of children, particularly at the outset of their lives, are '[un]likely to run contrary to those of adults who choose to bring them into being.' ... Thus, '[h]onoring the plans and expectations of adults who

[62] The UN High Commissioner for Refugees (UNHCR), '2021 UNHCR, 'Best Interests Procedure Guidelines: Assessing and Determining the Best Interests of The Child' (2021), 31.

[63] UNHCR (n 62) 32.

[64] Ibid.

[65] Ibid.

[66] *In Re: Roberts D.B* [Court of Appeals of Maryland. No. 110, Sept. Term, 2002, Decided: May 16, 2007].

will be responsible for a child's welfare is likely to correlate significantly with positive outcomes for parents and children alike.'

The positive intention of the intending parents put into action, by engaging a surrogate, supplying the gametes for the conception and bearing all costs associated with the reproductive process is a clear indication of how much they desire the child. This may be contrasted with the surrogate whose sole intention for undergoing childbirth is the contractual agreement between her and the intending parents. In cases of commercial/compensated gestational surrogacy arrangements, the financial compensation is usually a prime inducement for the surrogate to agree to act as a surrogate in the first instance.[67] It may therefore run contrary to the best interest of the child, for parental rights to be conferred on a surrogate, instead of the intending parents who engaged the surrogate. In *Belsito v Clark*, the court stated its preference for genetics as the basis of declaring the intending parents as both the natural and legal parents and anchored its decision on the best interest of the child. It held that:

> As has been stated, there is abundant precedent for using the genetics test for identifying a natural parent. For the best interest of the child and society, there are strong arguments to recognize the genetic parent as the natural parent. The genetic parent can guide the child from experience through the strengths and weaknesses of a common ancestry of genetic traits. Because that test has served so well, it should remain the primary test for determining the natural parent, or parents, in nongenetic-providing surrogacy cases.[68]

[67] For example, Statistics show that women who were willing to act as surrogates in India are women who come from the lower income bracket and who are poor. This is also the case in Nigeria, a country with high levels of poverty. A Nigerian surrogate sharing her reasons for choosing to act as a surrogate stated that:

I needed to support my family as we were in a finance crisis... I was out of work and needed something fulfilling and rewarding to do. It was a tough time for me and my family and I needed to do something quickly, else my family would be on the street. My friend told me that somebody needed a surrogate mother. That was how my journey into the world of surrogacy started. Healthwise, 'Why we carry pregnancies for fellow women—Nigerian surrogate mothers' *The Punch* (26 December 2020) <https://healthwise.punchng.com/why-we-carry-pregnancies-for-fellow-women-nigerian-surrogate-mothers/> accessed 28 November 2021.

See also Ranjana Kumari, 'Surrogate Motherhood-Ethical or Commercial' Center for Social Research, 40.

[68] *Belsito v Clark*.

Section 14(1) of the Nigerian Child's Right Act provides that 'every child has a right to parental care and protection, and accordingly, no child shall be separated from his parents against the wish of the child…'. In surrogacy cases, the child, being of tender years and lacking the capacity to speak or make decisions, is not in a position to express his preference for any of the parties as a parent. Thus, the state makes a decision on behalf of the child. The court therefore ought to concern itself with questions such as: Who is better suited to provide this child with parental care and protection? Who would this child consider to be a parent when he attains the age to make rational decisions for himself? The most logical answer seems to be that the intending parents are in a better position to provide parental care and protection. A lesson may be drawn from the experience of donor-conceived children in this regard. The experiences of some donor-conceived persons show that genes and genetics matter to them, as many of them desire to know their donors and get clarity as to their biological and ethnic origins.[69] Thus, it will be injudicious for a Nigerian court to refuse to enforce a gestational surrogacy contract on the grounds that it is a contract unknown to the Nigerian law or an agreement in violation of public policy. Where it is established that the child is genetically related to one or both of the genetic parents and unrelated to the surrogate, the court should enforce the agreement in favour of the intending parents. The intending parties are placed in a better legal position where the child is genetically related to at least one of them, as this may dispel concerns about baby selling, which is currently rife in Nigeria.[70] In Justice Kennard's dissenting judgement in *Johnson v Calvert*, she noted that the fact that the intending parents are paying a lot of money in order to have a child does not mean that they would be suitable parents. While this is

[69] See generally DR Beeson, PK Jennings and W Kramer, 'Offspring Searching for their Sperm Donors: How Family Type Shapes the Process' (2011) 26(9) Human Reproduction 2415; Sarah Zhang, 'The Children of Sperm Donors Want to Change the Rules of Conception: Does everyone have a right to know their biological parents? *The Atlantic* (15 October 2015) <https://www.theatlantic.com/science/archive/2021/10/do-we-have-right-know-our-biological-parents/620405/> accessed 28 November 2021.

[70] Ann Godwin, 'Upsurge in Baby Factories, Sale of Infants Raises Concerns' *The Guardian* (Port Harcourt, 5 September 2020) <https://guardian.ng/news/upsurge-in-baby-factories-sale-of-infants-raises-concerns/> accessed 28 November 2021; Isabelle Hamilton, 'The Dirty Business of Baby Factories in Nigeria' *The Organisation for World Peace* (15 December 2020) <https://theowp.org/reports/the-dirty-business-of-baby-factories-in-nigeria/> accessed 28 November 2021.

true, in gestational surrogacy arrangements, this is hardly a satisfactory reason to refuse to recognise the status of the intending parents as legal parents. Indeed, the law provides mechanisms for parents to be deprived of physical custody and parental rights over their children when they are shown to be unfit.[71] Thus, in determining who should be conferred with legal parentage of surrogate-born children, the determination of the question should not take the form of a comparison between the surrogate and the intending parents (genetic parents) parenting skills, rather, the court should inquire into who has a stronger claim to legal parentage in view of available facts, evidence and established legal principles. A child's best interest may therefore be better served when parental rights are awarded to persons who commissioned its birth and who may also be genetically related to it.

11.4.3 Estoppel/Intent/Conduct as a Basis of Enforcement

A surrogacy contract may be enforced by invoking principles like estoppel, intention and conduct within the realm of contract law. The enforcement of a surrogacy contract and the conferment of legal parentage on intending parents, using the contract model has been subjected to both praise and sharp criticisms. Those averse to the contract model as a basis of enforcement, cite the commodification of the reproductive process, life and the objectification of children as the reasons for their aversion.[72] Whereas, others rely on the protection of reasonable expectation as the basis for adopting the contract model.[73] The protection of reasonable

[71] Child's Right Act, section 50.

[72] *In re Baby M*; Deborah Zalesne, 'The Intersection of Contract Law, Reproductive Technology, and the Market: Families in the Age of ART' (2017) 51(2) University of Richmond Law Review 419, 431–433; Elizabeth S Scott, 'Surrogacy and The Politics of Commodification' (2009) 72 Journal of Law and Contemporary Problems 109, 110; Judith T Younger, 'What the Baby M Case Is Really All About' (1988) 6(2) Minnesota Journal of Law and Inequality 75.

[73] For instance, in *Re Marriage of Moschetta*, despite declining to enforce a traditional surrogacy contract in favour of the intending parents, the court observed how promises exchanged sets the surrogacy conception process in motion, and how the failure of the surrogate to keep her promises adversely affects the intending parents. The court stated that:

> Much has been written in the surrogacy area of the pain visited on the birth mother who contemplates giving up her child. Not so much appears to have been written

expectations has long been acknowledged as a fundamental principle of the law, even though it is often difficult to characterise what constitutes 'reasonable expectations'.[74] In the context of surrogacy, parties expect that promises made and backed by consideration should be enforceable in other to give effect to the reasonable expectations of the parties. Incidentally, it is not only the intending parents that have expectations that they expect to be fulfilled, the surrogate also has such expectations.[75] Generally, no surrogate will like to be stuck with a child she would not have had, but for a surrogacy arrangement, neither will intending parents prefer to be deprived of a child they went to great lengths to have. Yet, it is not every expectation that the law will consider to be reasonable and therefore consider eligible for legal protection,[76] it is for this reason that the courts sometimes decline to enforce a surrogacy contract.

Irrespective of the differing views held by scholars on the propriety or otherwise of adopting a contract model approach, the prevailing judicial practice indicts that contract principles continue to play a crucial role in the consideration and enforcement of surrogacy contracts.[77] It is impracticable to consider a surrogacy arrangement without reference to contract principles, the decision of the Court in *In Re Marriage of Buzzanca* illustrates this. In *Re Buzzanca*, the court in trying not to delimit the

about the disruption to the intended parents, who have-to put the matter in classic estoppel language-relied to their detriment in deciding to bring a child into the world. Let us be blunt here: Marissa would never have been born if Robert and Cynthia Moschetta had known Elvira Jordan would change her mind.

[74] Bailey H Kuklin, 'The Justification for Protecting Reasonable Expectations' (2001) 29(3) Hofstra Law Review 863, 864.

[75] See *In Re: Roberts D.B* [Court of Appeals of Maryland. No. 110, Sept. Term, 2002, Decided: May 16, 2007] where the surrogate disclosed that 'she had a reasonable expectation that her role in the lives of these children would terminate upon delivery of the children, and that the faithful performance of her duties under the agreement would not permanently impact her life...'.

[76] See *Re Marriage of Moschetta*, where the court affirmed this by stating that intending parents in a traditional surrogacy arrangement have no guarantees that their expectations will be honoured by the courts.

[77] Deborah Zalesne, 'The Intersection of Contract Law, Reproductive Technology, and the Market: Families in the Age of ART' (2017) 51(2) University of Richmond Law Review 419, 425.

question before it to the realm of contract, still placed reliance on contract principles in arriving at its decision. The Court stated that:

> In the case before us, we are not concerned ... with a question of the enforceability of the oral and written surrogacy contracts into which he entered... This case is not about 'transferring' parenthood pursuant to those agreements. We are, rather, concerned with the consequences of those agreements as acts which caused the birth of a child.

A surrogacy arrangement is first a contractual arrangement before anything else- this is therefore a justification for the use of contract principles in enforcing a surrogacy arrangement. Yet, the use of contract law for the enforcement of surrogacy arrangements does not translate to injustice. This is because contract law provides defences such as misrepresentation, duress and undue influence which can be relied on in repudiating a contract whose terms are unconscionable and unjust.[78] The enforcement of a surrogacy contract is also subject to other overriding legal principles, such as the best interest of the child and public policy.[79] These overriding consideration temper the hardship and injustice that may be associated with a strict enforcement of surrogacy contracts. Thus, despite the *Buzzanca* court's insistence that the matter before it was not concerned with the transfer of parentage pursuant to a surrogacy agreement, it could not ignore the implications of the contractual agreement on the rights and obligations of the parties before it.

As has been earlier stated, a surrogacy contract is a contract of multiple legal flavours, thus, it is not regulated by only contract law, but an amalgam of laws. It is for this reason that the breach of a surrogacy contract may not be treated as a breach of contract *simplicter*, falling strictly under contract law. To illustrate the influence that other areas of law have on surrogacy contracts, Lewis stated that when a breach occurs in a surrogacy contract, the 'judge steps away from contract law and looks to family law for an answer'.[80] The breach may therefore be categorised

[78] Ibid., 441; Yehezkel Margalit, 'In Defense of Surrogacy Agreements' (2014) 20 William & Mary Journal of Women and The Law 423, 449.

[79] *In re Baby M.*

[80] Browne C Lewis, 'Due Date: Enforcing Surrogacy Promises in the Best Interest of the Child' (2013) 87(4) St John's Law Review 899, 909.

as a custody dispute and resolved as one, guided in all cases by the best interest of the child as a paramount consideration.

Estoppel, intent and conduct are all interrelated as they look to a person's actions, representations and conduct in conferring or resolving a dispute involving parental rights. The decision in *Johnson v Calvert* is one of the celebrated surrogacy cases where the court relied on the intent rule in determining legal parentage. The court in *Johnson*'s case stated that because each of the parties had presented acceptable proof of maternity, it was essential to look into their intent, as expressed in the surrogacy agreement. The court noted that but for their acted-on intention, the child would never have been born. The court stated that 'The parties' aim was to bring Mark's and Crispina's child into the world, not for Mark and Crispina to donate a zygote to Anna'. This is accurate, because if the surrogate, Anna had indicated at the contract negotiation stage that she intended to keep the child for herself, Mark and Crispina would never have entered into an agreement with her, since their intention was to have a child of their own and not to help another create a child. It is illogical and contrary to common sense that a childless couple would have their embryos implanted in a woman who would otherwise be able to get pregnant without medical intervention, and then pay her to have a child and to keep the child for herself. The intent rule also binds the surrogate to her promise. For example, in *Johnson v Calvert*, the court emphasised that a woman who chooses to act as a gestational surrogate is not exercising her right to make procreative choices, rather she is agreeing to render a reproductive service, without any expectation that she will raise the child as hers. There is therefore no reason not to hold her bound to her promises, when she chooses to resile from it. Despite the critical gestational role played by the surrogate, the child would never have been born, but for the acted-on intentions of the intending parents.

The use of intent as a basis of enforcing surrogacy contracts also helps to adequately safeguard the best interest of a child, especially where both the gestating and genetic/intending parents refuse to assert parental rights in respect of a surrogate-born child. This will result in the entrenchment of clear and certain rules for the determination of legal parentage in surrogacy arrangements, which will in turn better safeguard the best interest of the child. Recent cases of child abandonment in gestational surrogacy arrangements,[81] show that the intent rule is best suited for determining parentage, independent of genetics. Relying on the intent to procreate and parent, courts have declared intending parents to be legal parents, even where the party who sought to refute parental obligations had contributed no genetic material to the creation of the child.[82] This rule ensures that surrogate-born children are not made legal orphans and that parentage is not unjustly foisted on a surrogate who had no intentions whatsoever to procreate, but for the surrogacy agreement.

Estoppel is a legal principle invoked to prevent a person from disavowing an earlier position, or conduct which he had expressed, that has caused others who relied on it to alter their positions. The Doctrine of Estoppel has been explained by the Nigerian Supreme Court in *Abalogu v SPDC Nigeria Limited* as follows:

> It is now well settled that where one party has, by his words or conduct, made to the other a promise or assurance which was intended to affect the

[81] Children are often rejected and abandoned by the intending parents for a plethora of reasons, some of which include the gender of the child, where the child is born with some disabilities or health conditions, divorce/separation of the intending parents before the child is born (especially where the child is unrelated to one or both of the intending parents).

See *In re Marriage of Buzzanca*; Andrea Whittaker, 'From 'Mung Ming' to 'Baby Gammy': A Local history of Assisted Reproduction in Thailand' (2016) 2 Reproductive Biomedicine & Society Online 71; Bridie Jabour, 'Baby Gammy: Conflicting Reports about Baby Boy 'Abandoned' in Thailand' *The Guardian* (Thailand, 4 August 2014) <https://www.theguardian.com/world/2014/aug/04/baby-gammy-conflicting-reports-about-baby-boy-abandoned-in-thailand> accessed 28 November 2021; Lindsay Murdoch and Saffron Howden, 'Abandoned Baby Gammy Rushed to Hospital in Thailand' *The Sydney Morning Herald* (2 August 2014) <https://www.smh.com.au/national/abandoned-baby-gammy-rushed-to-hospital-in-thailand-20140801-zzj76.html>; Jonathan Pearlman, 'Baby Gammy' was not Abandoned in Thailand, Court Rules' *The Telegraph* (Sydney, 14 April 2014) <https://www.telegraph.co.uk/news/2016/04/14/baby-gammy-was-not-abandoned-in-thailand-court-rules/#:~:text=A%20court%20in%20Australia%20has,keep%20his%20twin%20sister%20Pipah> accessed 28 November 2021; Doree Lewak, 'Sherri Shepherd Begged for a Family — Then She Abandoned us' *Pagesix* (13 March 2016) <https://pagesix.com/2016/03/13/sherri-shepherd-begged-for-a-child-and-then-abandoned-us/> accessed 28 November 2021.

[82] In re Marriage of Buzzanca; Joanna L Grossman, 'Baby Mama: Appellate Court Declares Sherri Shepherd is the Legal Mother of a Child Born to Her via Surrogate' [2015] 1; Jessica Grose, 'The Sherri Shepherd Surrogacy Case is a Mess. Prepare for More Like It' *Slate* (28 April 2015) <https://slate.com/human-interest/2015/04/sherri-shepherd-surrogacy-case-there-s-little-consensus-on-the-ethical-dimensions-of-surrogacy.html> accessed 28 November 2021.

> legal relations between them and to be acted on accordingly, then, once the other party had taken him at his word and acted on it, the one who gave the promise or assurance cannot afterwards be allowed to revert to the previous legal relations as if no such promise or assurance had been made by him. He must accept their legal relations as modified by himself, even though it is not supported in point of law by any consideration, but only by his word.[83]

Parties to a surrogacy contract exchange promises and assurances. The intending parents promise to accept custody and exercise parental rights over the child born, and the surrogate promises to hand over the child at birth and to make no claims whatsoever in respect of the child. On the strength of the promises exchanged, parties enter into a contract. It would be unjust to permit a party to deny the commitments made after parties have altered their positions. In the United States, estoppel has often been invoked in conferring parental rights and in stopping a person from refuting parental obligations, particularly in cases of artificial insemination and Assisted Reproductive Technology. In the United States case of *People v Sorensen* the principle was explained as follows:

> One who consents to the production of a child cannot create a temporary relation to be assumed and disclaimed at will, but the arrangement must be of such character as to impose an obligation of supporting those for whose existence he is directly responsible … it is safe to assume that without defendant's active participation and consent the child would not have been procreated.[84]

This principle was also applied in *In Re Marriage of Buzzanca* where the court stated that 'there are times when fatherhood can be established by conduct apart from giving birth or being genetically related to a child'. Therefore, when a person's actions result in the birth of a child, that would ordinarily not have been born, he acquires parental rights and responsibilities under the law and he will be estopped from denying his actions and the resultant implications of his action. Thus, in gestational

[83] (2003) LPELR-18(SC).

[84] (1968 Cal 2d 280).

surrogacy cases, the courts should affirm the agreement of the parties as reflected in their surrogacy contract, and no party should be allowed to resile therefrom.

11.5 Conclusion

A surrogacy arrangement by its very nature is fraught with a lot of ethical and legal questions, which may sometimes be difficult to resolve. These ethical and legal questions become more complicated in traditional surrogacy arrangements, hence, a gestational surrogacy arrangement is a safer option, especially in Nigeria, where there are no ART laws. The absence of ART laws creates uncertainty in the rights and obligations of parties to a surrogacy arrangement, and poses the risk of conflicting decisions and opinions on the legal status of surrogacy contracts. This uncertainty in the law is neither helpful nor safe as many Nigerians continue to turn to surrogacy to establish and complete their families. The interests of surrogate-born children are also left unprotected, as there are no measures in place to ensure that children are protected from limping/uncertain legal parentage, trafficking and exploitation in surrogacy arrangements. A Nigerian law on this subject is therefore urgently required. However, pending the enactment of an ART/surrogacy law, it is important for parties considering surrogacy to seek legal advice on how best to go about it, to ensure that their expectations are protected, especially in the event of a dispute. It is also prudent to enter into a surrogacy arrangement with the terms clearly spelt out in a surrogacy contract, giving due consideration to key contractual principles in order to aid its enforceability by a court of law.

Bibliography

Articles

Beeson DR, Jennings PK and Kramer W, 'Offspring Searching for Their Sperm Donors: How Family Type Shapes the Process' (2011) 26(9) Human Reproduction 2415.

Brekoulakis S, 'The Evolution of Public Policy and Judicial Function in English Law' [2019] Journal of International Dispute Settlement 1.

Ghodoosi F, 'The Concept of Public Policy in Law: Revisiting the Role of the Public Policy Doctrine in the Enforcement of Private Legal Arrangements' (2015) 94 Nebraska Law Review 685.
Grossman JL, 'Baby Mama: Appellate Court Declares Sherri Shepherd is the Legal Mother of a Child Born to Her via Surrogate' [2015] 1.
Hisano EY, 'Gestational Surrogacy Maternity Disputes: Refocusing on the Child' (2011) 15(2) Lewis & Clark Law Review 517.
Ikechebelu JI and others, 'A Successful Gestational Surrogacy in Southeast Nigeria' (2017) 2(1) African Journal for Infertility and Assisted Conception 19 (note).
Jackson E, 'UK Law and International Commercial Surrogacy: "The Very Antithesis of Sensible"' (2016) 4(3) Journal of Medical Law and Ethics 197.
Kuklin BH, 'The Justification for Protecting Reasonable Expectations' (2001) 29(3) Hofstra Law Review 863.
Kumari R, 'Surrogate Motherhood-Ethical or Commercial' (2010) Center for Social Research, 40.
Latourette AW, 'The Surrogate Mother Contract: In the Best Interests of Society?' (1990) 25(1) University of Richmond Law Review 53.
Laufer-Ukeles P, 'Mothering for Money: Regulating Commercial Intimacy' 2013 (88) Indiana Law Journal 1223.
Lewis BC, 'Due Date: Enforcing Surrogacy Promises in the Best Interest of the Child' (2013) 87(4) St. John's Law Review 899.
Margalit Y, 'In Defense of Surrogacy Agreements' (2014) 20 William & Mary Journal of Women and The Law 423.
Pierce-Gealy M, '"Are You My Mother?": Ohio's Crazy-Making Baby-Making Produces a New Definition of "Mother"' (1995) 28(3) Akron Law Review 535.
Purshouse C and Bracegirdle K, 'The Problem of Unenforceable Surrogacy Contracts: Can Unjust Enrichment Provide a Solution?' (2018) 26(4) Medical Law Review 5.
Schneider CE, 'Surrogate Motherhood from the Perspective of Family Law' (1990) 13 Harvard Journal of Law and Public Policy 125.
Schuck PH, 'Some Reflections on the Baby M Case' (1988) 76 Georgetown Law Journal 1793.
Scott ES, 'Surrogacy and The Politics of Commodification' (2009) 72 Journal of Law and Contemporary Problems 109, 110.
Whittaker A, 'From 'Mung Ming' to 'Baby Gammy': A Local History of Assisted Reproduction in Thailand' (2016) 2 Reproductive Biomedicine & Society Online 71.
Winfield PH, 'Public Policy in the English Common' (1928) 42(1) Harvard Law Review 76.

Yelpaala K, 'Restraining the Unruly Horse: The Use of Public Policy in Arbitration, Interstate and International' (1989) 2 Transnational Law 379.

Younger JT, 'What the Baby M Case Is Really All About' (1988) 6(2) Minnesota Journal of Law and Inequality 75.

Zalesne D, 'The Intersection of Contract Law, Reproductive Technology, and the Market: Families in the Age of ART' (2017) 51(2) University of Richmond Law Review 419.

Zegers-Hochschild F and others, 'The International Glossary on Infertility and Fertility Care, 2017' (2017) 32(9) Human Reproduction.

Online Sources

'Nigerian Couples Cautiously Turn to Surrogacy to Ease Fertility Woes' (New Vision 27 December 2018) <https://www.newvision.co.ug/new_vision/news/1491806/nigerian-couples-cautiously-surrogacy-ease-fertility-woes> accessed 27 October 2019.

'Tinubu's Daughter, Folasade Welcomes Second Surrogate Baby Girl' (PM News 25 October 2019) <https://www.pmnewsnigeria.com/2019/10/25/tinubus-daughter-folasade-welcomes-second-surrogate-baby-girl/ > accessed 27 October 2019.

Godwin A, 'Upsurge in Baby Factories, Sale of Infants Raises Concerns' The Guardian (Port Harcourt, 5 September 2020) <https://guardian.ng/news/upsurge-in-baby-factories-sale-of-infants-raises-concerns/> accessed 28 November 2021.

Grose J, 'The Sherri Shepherd Surrogacy Case Is a Mess. Prepare for More Like It' Slate (28 April 2015) <https://slate.com/human-interest/2015/04/sherri-shepherd-surrogacy-case-there-s-little-consensus-on-the-ethical-dimensions-of-surrogacy.html> accessed 28 November 2021.

Hamilton I, 'The Dirty Business of Baby Factories in Nigeria' The Organisation for World Peace (15 December 2020) <https://theowp.org/reports/the-dirty-business-of-baby-factories-in-nigeria/> accessed 28 November 2021.

Healthwise, 'Why We Carry Pregnancies for Fellow Women—Nigerian Surrogate Mothers' The Punch (26 December 2020) <https://healthwise.punchng.com/why-we-carry-pregnancies-for-fellow-women-nigerian-surrogate-mothers/ > accessed 28 November 2021.

Jabour B, 'Baby Gammy: Conflicting Reports about Baby Boy "Abandoned" in Thailand' The Guardian (Thailand, 4 August 2014) <https://www.theguardian.com/world/2014/aug/04/baby-gammy-conflicting-reports-about-baby-boy-abandoned-in-thailand> accessed 28 November 2021.

Lewak D, 'Sherri Shepherd Begged for a Family—Then She Abandoned us' Pagesix (13 March 2016) <https://pagesix.com/2016/03/13/sherri-shepherd-begged-for-a-child-and-then-abandoned-us/> accessed 28 November 2021.

Murdoch L and Howden S, 'Abandoned Baby Gammy Rushed to Hospital in Thailand' The Sydney Morning Herald (2 August 2014) <https://www.smh.com.au/national/abandoned-baby-gammy-rushed-to-hospital-in-thailand-20140801-zzj76.html> accessed 28 November 2021.

Pearlman J, 'Baby Gammy' was not Abandoned in Thailand, Court Rules' The Telegraph (Sydney, 14 April 2014) <https://www.telegraph.co.uk/news/2016/04/14/baby-gammy-was-not-abandoned-in-thailand-court-rules/#:~:text=A%20court%20in%20Australia%20has,keep%20his%20twin%20sister%20Pipah.> accessed 28 November 2021.

Zhang S, 'The Children of Sperm Donors Want to Change the Rules of Conception: Does Everyone Have a Right to Know Their Biological Parents? The Atlantic (15 October 2015) <https://www.theatlantic.com/science/archive/2021/10/do-we-have-right-know-our-biological-parents/620405/> accessed 28 November 2021.

Others

Stoll J, 'Surrogacy Arrangements and Legal Parenthood: Swedish Law in a Comparative Context' (PhD Thesis, Uppsala Universitet 2013).

The UN High Commissioner for Refugees (UNHCR), '2021 UNHCR, 'Best Interests Procedure Guidelines: Assessing and Determining the Best Interests of The Child' (2021).

CHAPTER 12

The Role of Data Collection in Developing Adequate Legal Mechanisms for the Practice of Assisted Reproductive Technologies in Sub-Saharan Africa

Bolanle Maryanne Oyekan

12.1 Part One

12.1.1 Introduction

Fertility is considered an integral part of womanhood especially in Africa where childbearing is essential to a complete family life. The consequences of undesired childlessness are particularly acute for women in Africa, where socio cultural values are built around fertility often leading to stigmatisation, isolation, disinheritance and neglect by close family units and

B. M. Oyekan (✉)
Graduate Studies, Faculty of Law, University of Ottawa, Ottawa, ON, Canada
e-mail: boyek050@uottawa.ca

O. S. Adelakun and E. Ndoni (eds.), *Reproductive Health and Assisted Reproductive Technologies In Sub-Saharan Africa*,
Sustainable Development Goals Series,
https://doi.org/10.1007/978-981-99-2411-0_12

the society.[1] An infertile woman is perceived to be abnormal, unfortunate or labelled as having lived a promiscuous and immoral life.

Assisted Human Reproduction ('AHR') is a term used interchangeably with Assisted Reproductive Technologies ('ART') in this chapter. While the former specifically refers to Assisted Reproduction in Human patients, the later emphasises the use of medical technologies for assisting humans in reproduction. Assisted Reproductive Technologies (ART) have been in use for over three decades as an intervention that has improved the lives of people suffering from various degrees of infertility and enabling them to bear their own offspring through medical technologies other than the traditional process of reproduction. This definition includes employing all procedures and treatments of in vitro handling of oocytes or sperms or embryos of human beings for the purpose of achieving a pregnancy. With the continuous advancements in ART, there have also been various issues on the ethical, legal, medical, socio cultural and religious challenges in the use of these technologies. Many scholars have focused on how these downsides affect men, women and children using these technologies or being born as a result of them. Some jurisdictions have taken a step ahead in monitoring and regulating these practices as much as they can as they evolve, however, some other jurisdictions have not been able to develop an approach to regulating the use of these technologies for various reasons.

Most African countries with emphasis on Nigeria, do not have a documented regulatory mechanism for ART to adequately assess and monitor practices and progress in the delivery of fertility care of ART especially using data collection as a tool. This chapter will thus highlight the urgency in recognising data collection and monitoring of ART outcomes as an important aspect in the regulatory framework for ART practices in Nigeria.

As the utilisation of ART has increased over the years, so has been the growing public concern in the quality of treatment received by women and its effect on the unborn child. In many African countries that have no regulations for ART practices, there has been the concern on the proliferation of ART clinics in urban settings by private fertility practitioners with no policy or regulatory guidance. While most of these concerns are valid, inadequate monitoring, collation and formal documentation

[1] William Ombelet and Jamie Onofre, 'IVF in Africa: What Is It All About?' [2019] 11 Facts, Views & Vision in ObGyn 65–76.

of ART outcomes is detrimental to influencing improvement in practices as it would be difficult to react to these concerns without the adequate evidence. Detailed knowledge of the prevalence of infertility, awareness of trends, geographical and demographic differences are very important for providers of fertility healthcare as well as policy makers in improving practices. This chapter has identified adequate data collection and monitoring of ART practices through dedicated ART registries as an important tool in influencing the need to regulate ART and why it should be an important aspect in a legal framework for ART.

This chapter is divided into four parts. Part one provides a background of ART and ethical issues arising from the practice of ART in fertility clinics highlighting the need for adequate monitoring of practices. In part two, an introduction of terms and an overview of how a public health surveillance method is suggested as a model for ART data collection in the context of this chapter. This will lead to unpacking ART data collection types and approaches. Part three refers to specific data collection registries and provides an overview of the approaches to data collection for ART. Part four discusses some identified problems in data collection and seeks to address and review the benefits and limitations of data collection to create a balance in its usefulness as a tool in a regulatory framework for ART practices. Finally, the recorded impact of data collection and how it has influenced regulatory development in countries where it is used is highlighted and suggestions on the need to incorporate data collection in a regulatory framework is provided. In conclusion, recommendations on how data collection for ART can be included in a regulatory framework would be provided and how it is an integral part of formulating adequate regulatory mechanisms for ART.

12.2 Part Two

12.2.1 Background

Assisted Human Reproduction (AHR) is an evolving and dynamic field in infertility healthcare and all interested stakeholders in this area of healthcare require accurate and current data to function efficiently. Accurate data collection in this context has been identified as an aspect of healthcare research which is a systematic inquiry intended to generate trustworthy evidence about issues in the field of healthcare and medicine.[2] In vitro fertilisation ('IVF') has been practised in Nigeria and many African countries for over 20 years,[3] though there is still no established regulatory framework to guide the practice and expansion of related technology.[4] IVF is in focus here as an Assisted Reproductive Technology because it is seen as the cornerstone of infertility management, and it is critical to supporting families in their desire to attain parenthood.[5] IVF as an ART treatment has demystified the harsh sentence of infertility on individuals that have reproductive challenges, but this is not devoid of its other consequences that border on social, ethical, and legal controversies to the lives of millions of individuals.[6] In response to statistics[7] and due to the high premium placed on childbearing in Africa, IVF and embryo transfer clinics? (IVF Clinics) are proliferating across countries in efforts to address the problem of infertility.[8] In Nigeria, the exact number of these clinics is not known because of constant proliferation,[9] yet there is no clear guidance on practices in these clinics. The gap created by the lack of regulation reflects a lack of standardisation of treatment protocols and an unrestricted use of discretion by fertility care practitioners regarding the healthcare provided to women in fertility centres creating a situation

[2] Vishnu Renjiht and others, 'Qualitative Methods in Health Care Research' [2021] 12 Int'l J Prev Med. <https://doi.org/10.4103/ijpvm.IJPVM_321_19> accessed 24 February 2022.

[3] Giwa Osagie 'Social and Ethical Aspects of Assisted Conception in Anglophone Sub-Saharan Africa, Medical, Ethical and Social Aspects of Assisted Reproduction', in E. Vayena and others, *Current Practices and Controversies in Assisted Reproduction Report of a WHO Meeting*, 20 (ISBN 92 4 159030 0: Geneva, 2002).

[4] Richard Ajayi and Dibosa-Osadolor, 'Stakeholder's Views on Ethical Issues in the Practice of In Vitro Fertilization and Embryo Transfer in Nigeria' [2011] 15(3) African J of Reprod. Health, 74.

[5] Laura Londra, Edward Wallach and Yulian Zhao, 'Assisted Reproduction: Ethical and Legal Issues' (2014) 19 Seminars in Fetal & Neonatal Medicine, 264.

[6] Ibid.

[7] Olalekan Adetoro and Ehigie Ebomoyi, 'The Prevalence of Infertility in a Rural Nigerian Community' [1991] 20(1) Afri. J of Med Sci, 23; In Nigeria, the First Test Tube Baby was delivered in 1989 at the Lagos University Teaching Hospital and since then, many IVF Clinics have been established.

[8] Patrick Okonta and others, 'Ethical Issues in the Practice of Assisted Reproductive Technologies in Nigeria: Empirical Data from Fertility Practitioners' [2018] 22(3) Afri J of Reprod Health, 54.

[9] Ibid., 52.

where the several contextual differences among the different countries where practices are adopted dominate treatments.[10] In Africa, only South Africa has legislated concerning ART to regulate the practice of AHR.[11]

Various ethical issues have been identified in the practice of ART in Nigeria which include but are not limited to embryo transfer resulting in multiple pregnancies and then multiple births, ovarian hyperstimulation in women, illegal sale of gametes, illegal surrogacy arrangements with underaged donors & surrogates, etc.[12] Empirical data generated by the Association for Fertility and Reproductive Health (AFRH), a non-partisan and non-governmental organisation in Nigeria at a stakeholder's conference,[13] identified several unethical issues which emphasises the urgent need for stakeholders[14] in developing countries to formulate cultural and context-specific guidelines to address these ethical dilemmas which would be adequately captured through recorded monitoring to reveal trends and areas that require urgent attention.[15] Through safety, quality assurance, and regulation of ART these ethical dilemmas would receive attention and progress the development of ART practices in the Nigeria.[16] In addition, several key factors affect IVF treatment rates, and this includes female age, previous failed IVF attempts, reduced ovarian reserve, duration of infertility, and the number of embryos replaced within the uterus amongst other factors. Due to the risks associated with treatments and the ethical concerns highlighted, there is an obvious gap in monitoring the outcome of treatments in fertility clinics which has proven that issue of recording outcomes for research or improvement of services requires the adequate attention it deserves. An ideal outcome measure in IVF incorporates clinical effectiveness, acceptability, and safety which should be reliable, valid,

[10] Ibid., 57.

[11] Joseph Fadare and Adebayo Adeniyi, 'Ethical Issues in Newer Assisted Reproductive Technologies: A View from Nigeria' [2015] 18 Niger J Clin Practice, 59. Parliament SA. National Health Act No. 61 of 2003 (Pretoria: Government Printers 2003).

[12] Ibid.

[13] Ijeoma Ezeome and others, 'Perception of Key Ethical Issues in Assisted Reproductive Technology (ART) by Providers and Clients in Nigeria' [2021] 13 International Journal of Women's Health 1033–1052.

[14] Ibid. Fertility Practitioners, Clients, Professional Organisation, Bioethicist, Government, etc.

[15] Joseph Fadare, 'Ethical Issues in New Assisted Reproductive Technologies', 57.

[16] Ibid., 59.

easy to generate and to understand.[17] It is obvious that the impact of ART on the society calls for adequate surveillance including vigilance of occurring adverse events in the face of evolving technology, hence the recording of activities in various countries through ART registries. These registries are embedded in established legal frameworks. The next part would provide definitions and explanations on terms used in this chapter and proceed to briefly review approaches adopted for ART data collection in ART registries in the United Kingdom, United States of America and South Africa.

12.2.2 Health Records

Health record keeping has been defined as a way to monitor, improve and report data on healthcare quality and safety. It is useful for assessment and evaluation studies to investigate social determinants of health, population health, practitioners' and patients' perceptions/attitudes towards a particular healthcare intervention and control of diseases outbreak.[18] I offer an opinion based on the definition of health record keeping which I have identified as to be slightly different from data collection, because while the former can be a mere administrative exercise the latter is a deliberate approach to using the health records to address health issues for research or policy improvement purposes.

12.2.3 Healthcare Research Methods

Healthcare research methods are evidence-based research techniques used in investigating various aspects of healthcare. Three principal approaches have been identified in healthcare research, viz, qualitative, quantitative and mixed methods approach.[19] While the quantitative approach uses mostly numeric data which is measured using statistical methods

[17] Hossam Abdalla and others, 'Is Meaningful Reporting of National IVF Outcome Data Possible? [2010] 25(1) Human Reprod., 9.

[18] Jeremy Leventhal and others, 'Designing a System for Patients Controlling Providers Access to their Electronic Health Records: Organizational and Technical Challenges' [2015] 30: S1 J of General Internal Medicine, 17.

[19] Renjith, Vishnu and others. 'Qualitative Methods in Health Care Research' [2021]) 12(20) Int'l J of Preventive Medicine, <https://doi.org/10.4103/ijpvm.IJPVM_321_19>.

to collate data and draw inferences, the qualitative method uses non-numeric data through recording, interpreting and analysing data with the goal of uncovering deeper meanings of human experiences and behaviour. A mixed approach adopts these two approaches. Qualitative research in the context of this chapter is grounded in the principles of bioethics, beneficence, non-maleficence, autonomy, and justice to ensure ethical issues in qualitative research are achieved when collecting data from human subjects that are vulnerable, maintaining the privacy of individuals and their families. In this light, the principles of bioethics,[20] although paramount for the protection of all parties involved are often difficult to reconcile in the context of relentless scientific advancement, increasing social demands, and unique legal frameworks.[21] The monitoring of ART practices is essential to improving infertility care and a mixed approach is ideal for consideration in developing a framework for data collection. This will ensure the inclusion of accurate and thorough reporting of the procedures and techniques used, as well as the documentation of reproductive outcomes that result from each type of ART procedure. The information whether quantitative or qualitative gathered through deliberate data collection constitutes the basis for improving practice guidelines and policies and serves as an important resource for counselling patients.[22]

12.2.4 ART Surveillance from a Public Health Surveillance Perspective

Another important aspect to consider is defining surveillance in the context of this discussion. ART Surveillance is defined as the continuous and systematic collection of health data needed for the analysis and interpretation of trends in ART medical care[23] including the safety of infertility

[20] Autonomy, Beneficence, Justice, and avoidance of maleficence (the pillars with which professional societies within the field of reproductive medicine have built recommendation guidelines).

[21] Laura Londe, 'Assisted Reproduction: Ethical and Legal Issues' (2014) 19, 264.

[22] Ibid., 265.

[23] Lisa Lee and Stephen Thacker, 'Public Health Surveillance and Knowing about Health in the Context of Growing Sources of Health Data' [2011] 14(6) Am J of Preventive Med 636–640. <https://doi.org/10.1016/j.amepre.2011.08.015> accessed 10 October 2021.

care participants. The reporting of health outcomes is viewed as beneficial for transparency, for improving outcomes, and for assisting patients in making informed decisions.[24] A public health surveillance approach is suggested here because infertility has been identified as a global health concern though its ranking is low in reproductive health agendas in Africa[25] which focus more on population-based estimates and are deficient in associated legal issues encompassing reporting of outcomes, government funding, public health research and generally dedicated data collection frameworks.

Despite Nigeria's strategic position in Africa, the healthcare space falls short of global standards as it is underserved in the availability of facilities, personnel and medical tools.[26] Provision of timely information through deliberate education and counselling is also not readily available especially for ART, hence adequate tracking techniques as used in public health sector to stem huge health insecurity, inequities and proper ethical conducts are lacking. Lisa Lee[27] rightly pointed out that data collection systems for health purposes, whether as disease reporting systems or risk factor assessments as is the case of ART remain a critical source of population-based information about key health conditions. In the case of women who are at the centre of reproduction, it is very important to recognise ART as an important aspect of the Reproductive Healthcare agenda and prioritise infertility care outcomes by monitoring trends and data collation employing qualitative and quantitative healthcare research methods with the aim of not only improving practices but also influencing policy decisions to standardise practices and stem unethical practices. In adopting a public health surveillance system approach as suggested in this chapter, the diagram reflects how health knowledge is achieved (Diagram 12.1):

[24] Hayden Homer, 'Reporting IVF Outcomes: The Devil is in the Detail' [2020] Aust NZ J Obstet Gynaecol, 11.

[25] Nathan Chimbatata and Chikondi Malimba 'Infertility in Sub-Saharan Africa: A Woman's Issue for How Long? A Qualitative Review of Literature' [2016] 4 Open Journal of Social Sciences, 96–102.

[26] Akinnagbe Orimisan and SAJ Obansa 'Health Care Financing in Nigeria: Prospects and Challenges' [2013] 4(1) Mediterranean Journal of Social Sciences, 221–236 ISSN 2039-9340.

[27] Ibid., 24.

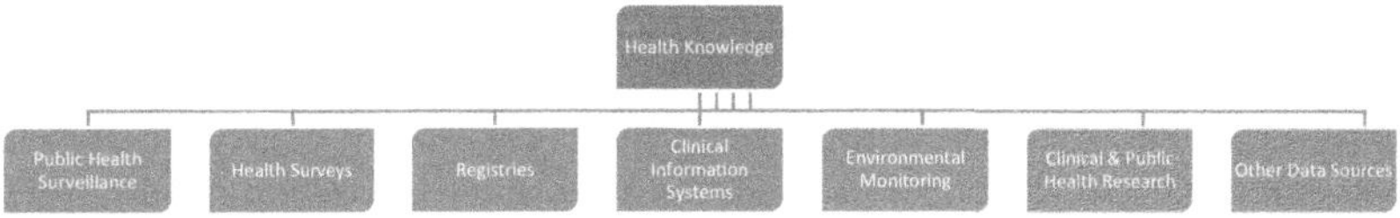

Diagram 12.1 Health knowledge chart[28]

From a public health surveillance perspective, recording multiple events about a health process over a period is vital to data collection. The information from varied data sources can then be incorporated into activities. Tracking of the data collected would be useful in understanding the effect of certain ART practices, for example, ovarian stimulation in some women leading to ovarian hyperstimulation syndrome which has fatal implications, and link such to health outcomes at individual or population levels, providing federal, state, or local agencies with important information for care practice prevention, detection, or control. While a public health approach to health surveillance is used as a tool in explaining how important data collection for monitoring ART outcomes for ART practices is, it is important to be clear that the importance of the right to keep one's health data privacy is an exercise of one's autonomy and very critical in clinical encounters such as ART. Issues on patient consent and confidentiality which also require clear attention specifically in healthcare in Nigeria and which is very important is not the focus in this chapter. From the chart above, Registries have been identified as a source of Health Knowledge and a vital part in surveillance.

12.2.5 Data Collection Approaches

From the foregoing, the importance of data collection in influencing ART practices and desired outcomes through data collected by ART data registries is clear. This is evidenced by existing Data registries in the various countries that have established them. The main approaches to ART Data collection in registries has been identified as Mandatory data

[28] Ibid., 637.

collection by established regulatory agencies and Voluntary data collection.[29] Mandatory data collection is a compulsory and usually statutory requirement for fertility clinics to submit data on specified treatment protocols with regards to compliance or otherwise within given time-frames. The data collected is usually reviewed and outcomes measured to determine improvement in treatments, trends in cases presented and the information are for ethical or clinical reference and drive policy development. Voluntary approach to data collection by ART data registries means fertility clinics or dedicated professional groups submit ART data under no compulsion. It is a flexible approach to data collection. The voluntary submission of data by fertility clinics is common in unregulated jurisdictions though it is not peculiar to these jurisdictions alone. Some regulated jurisdictions also adopt the voluntary approach to data collection. The process of monitoring and reporting ART can be challenging because of its revolutionary nature and continuous improvements in medicine, treatment, cost, national legislation and ethical debates which are not subject to continuous change.[30] For this reason, national, regional and global registries document and monitor ART activity, provide valuable, annual data of ART availability, utilisation, effectiveness and safety.[31] Many countries are now establishing national reporting systems, on which regional and world reporting systems rely on. Information is important in Health care and health professionals have the tendency of being relatively uninformed of how the laws by which they are bound to have developed, and of the range of legal arguments they may invoke to advance their purposes.[32]

[29] The United Kingdom and United States of America have through their regulatory agencies made collection of ART data mandatory. In Canada and through the regional ART Data Registry in Africa, ART data reporting by fertility centres is voluntary.

[30] Carmen Messerlian & Audrey Gaskins, 'Epidemiologic Approaches for Studying ART: Designs, Methods, Analysis and Interpretation' (2017) 4 Curr Epidemiol Rep, 124.Online.

[31] Silke Dyer and Fernando Zegers- Hochschild, 'Nobody Left Behind: The Role of Data Registries in Assisted Reproductive Technology' [2019] 4(1) Global Reprod. Health, 1.

[32] Rebecca Cook and others, 'Reproductive Health & Human Rights, Integrating Medicine, Ethics & Law' (Oxford University Press 2003).

12.2.6 Types of Data Registries

As stated above, three types of ART data registries have been identified: National, Regional or Global registries. National, regional, and global registries that document and monitor ART activity, provide valuable, annual data pertaining to ART availability, utilisation, effectiveness, and safety. Their most immediate value lies in creating visibility of these indicators by country, region, year and over time.[33] National data registries are created to monitor the use and effectiveness of ART within a country.[34] Regional data registries serve the same purpose but through a group of countries such as the African Network and Registry for Assisted Reproductive Technology (ANARA). The global registry is an international ART data registry that collates global reports from all available sources, such as National Data registries and Regional Data Registries to monitor trends and recommend policy directives in ART practice on a global level. The International Committee for Monitoring Assisted Reproductive Technology (ICMART) is the global data registry for ART, specific ART registries including the operations of the global registry are discussed later in this chapter.

12.2.7 Review of Specific ART Data Collection Registries

This section will review how ART Data registries operate in the North America (United States of America & Canada), Europe, Africa and a global ART registry (International Committee of highlighting the types of data collection and approaches to data collection.

12.2.7.1 United States of America

The United States of America (US) represents a mandatory approach to ART data collection. Data Registry in America originated from the need to collate data on congenital abnormalities in children and operated through the American Society for Reproductive Medicine (ASRM) and Society for Assisted Reproductive Technology (SART).[35] As the number of ART units increased in the US, unscrupulous practices developed due

[33] Silke Dyer, 'Nobody Left Behind' 1.

[34] Examples are United States of America, United Kingdom, Denmark etc.

[35] Dmitry Kissin and others, 'Monitoring Health Outcomes of Assisted Reproductive Technology' [2014] 371:1 N Engl. J Med, 91; Dmitry Kissin, 'States Monitoring ART

to lack of government regulation, and the concerns raised by this birthed to Fertility Clinic Success Rate and Certification Act (FCSRCA). Afterwards, the Centre for Disease Control and Prevention (CDC) in the US initiated data collection of ART procedures through the National Surveillance System('NASS').[36] Clinics that are members of the SART report their data to NASS through SART and clinics that are non-members can report to NASS directly.[37] The Fertility Clinic Success Rate and Certification Act (FCSRCA) releases the list of non-reporting clinics as stipulated by its law. All AHR units that are known to be in operation for any one year are meant to report their data to SART in compliance with FCSRCA.[38] This data is collated in an annual report. The US has one of the largest numbers of AHR units in the world and set explicit deadlines and guidelines for data submissions and explicit definitions for various criteria and terminology are required. The approach of the United States is the creation of an agency specifically for ART data collection under a statutory arrangement and make data collection and reporting mandatory for fertility clinics. It is important to note that the United States does not have a comprehensive law regulating ART like in Europe, instead some individual States have developed policies to monitor practices and there is a piecemeal approach to regulation through various government agencies,[39] yet there exists a national registry for ART data which has recorded success in its activities.

12.2.7.2 Europe

ART is regulated in the United Kingdom under a detailed legal mandate of the Human Fertilisation and Embryology Authority (HFEA) which licences fertility centres, collects and publishes detailed data on each type

(SMART) Collaborative: Data Collection, Linkage, Dissemination, and Use' [2013] 22(7) J of Women's Health, 571–580.

[36] Saswati Sunderan and others, 'ART Surveillance—United States, 2015' [2018] Morbidity & Morality Weekly Report: Surveillance Summary.

[37] Ibid., 35.

[38] United States. Fertility Clinic Success Rate and Certification Act of 1992: Public Law 102–493. US Statute Large. 1992 October 24; 106:3146–3152. PMID: 11660823.

[39] Lucy Frith and Eric Blyth, 'Assisted Reproductive Technology in the United States: Is more Regulation Needed?' [2014] 29:4 Reprod Biomed Online, 516–523, available online <https://doi.org/10.1016/j.rbmo.2014.06.018> .

of treatment[40] using a mandatory approach of data collection. The HFEA was set up as an Act of parliament to issue a code of practice and maintain a register of those receiving treatment and born because of treatment and composition.[41] By law, units that process and or store human gametes for use in treatment or research must be licenced by the HFEA.[42] Centres must document the procedures they carry out and be registered with HFEA. They must register patients and every treatment carried out as well.

In the rest of Europe, the National registry of all European countries is welcome to participate in data submission to the European IVF Monitoring Program (EIM) by principle. The legal obligation of single institutions offering ART services to report data to the authorities is very different depending on each country and as such the method of reporting varies widely.[43] The European Society of Human Reproduction and Embryology (ESHRE) is the data collection centre for the national registries. This represents a regional type of data collection for ART which has a wider coverage in terms of comparing practices in different countries. The EIM serves as a regional registry to which participating national registries submit data and this approach reveals the level of control a regional registry for ART data collection can have on individual participating registries or professional groups submitting data.

12.2.7.3 Canada

Canada operates a national registry for ART data through the Canadian Assisted Reproductive Technologies Register (CARTR) Plus which represents a national database, and the approach to reporting practices is voluntary.[44] Canada has a comprehensive law regulating ART through the Assisted Human Reproduction Act 2004 along with various regulations

[40] Jeffrey Keenan and others 'Assisted Reproduction Using Donated Embryos: Outcomes from Surveillance System in Six Countries' [2012] Human Reproduction, 78 <https://doi.org/10.1093/humrep/der459>Accessed 21 September 2021.

[41] Human Fertilization and Embryology Act 1990 c. 37. <Human Fertilization and Embryology Act 1990 (legislation.gov.uk)>.

[42] S. 11 HFEA.

[43] Christian De Geyter and others, '20 years of the European IVF Monitoring Consortium Registry: What Have We Learned? A Comparison with Registries from Two Other Regions' [2020] 35(12) Human Reprod., 2834.

[44] Jeffrey Keenan, 'Assisted Reproduction Using Donated Embryos' [2012] 748.

pursuant to the Act. However, the clinical practice of ART falls within the purview of the provincial governments by virtue of the health structure and system in Canada.[45] Despite this structure which leaves monitoring of practices to provincial governments, no Province has enacted a comprehensive regulatory framework for ART.[46] This has been attributed to the fact that most Assisted Reproductive services are delivered in private, for-profit clinics and are paid for out of pocket.[47] This strikes a chord in the structure partly and currently operable in Nigeria where there is no comprehensive regulation for ART practice and treatments are predominantly provided by private for profit and would be considered in the last part of this chapter with regard to the role data collection would play in a regulatory framework for ART in Nigeria.

12.2.7.4 Africa

The African Network and Registry for Assisted Reproductive Technology (ANARA) is a regional ART data registry and adopts a voluntary approach[48] to the collection of ART-related data from participating clinics in Africa. ANARA adopted the Latin American Registry of Assisted Reproduction under the umbrella of ICMART and focuses on creating harmony among people, overcoming barriers to data sharing, and developing capabilities among ART centres for data collection.[49] The voluntary approach of ANARA reflects a rising standard of ART in Africa. Some Nigerian fertility clinics submit reports to the regional registry on a voluntary basis[50] and data reported have been beneficial in monitoring both medical and non-medical practices, providing large and valuable research data and serving as a basis for comparison of practices in the continent with other climes.

[45] Martha Jackman, 'Constitutional Jurisdiction Over Health in Canada' [2000] 8 Health Law Journal, 1100.

[46] Vanessa Gruben, 'Regulating Reproduction', in Erdman and others (eds), Canadian Health Law and Policy (LexisNexis 2017) 424.

[47] Coleen Flood and others, 'Regulatory Failure: The Case of the Private-For-Profit IVF Sector'. in Lemmens and others (eds), Regulating Creation: The Law, Ethics and Policy of Assisted Human Reproduction (University of Toronto Press 2017) 14.

[48] Silke Dyer and others, 'ART in Africa: A 5-Year Trend Analysis from The African Network and Registry for Assisted Reproductive Technology' [2020] 41(4) RBMO, 605.

[49] Silke Dyer 'Nobody Left Behind' 2.

[50] Silke Dyer, 'ART in Africa' (Table 1) 607.

12.2.8 A Global Registry—International Committee for Monitoring Assisted Reproductive Technology

The International Committee for Monitoring Assisted Reproductive Technology (ICMART) is an overarching organisation, which is involved in collecting, analysing, and disseminating global ART data. The model for the collection of data of ART in a descending order is presently based on an international four-level reporting system[51] described in the diagram (Diagram 12.2):

The worldwide report on ART practices authored by ICMART[52] evaluates data to gain insight into ART practices and outcomes which demonstrated considerable disparities in live birth rates between regions in the world. Due to the kind of data collected ICMART can reveal improvement on certain parameters, decline in ART live birth rates. It is interesting to note the report on ART live births for the period 2008–2010 did not include the Middle East, large parts of Asia, and all of Africa. By 2014, the preliminary world report of ICMART showed a 9.6% increase in ART cycles worldwide. The major contributors were Japan, the United States of America, Spain, Russia, France, Germany, Italy, Australia, the United Kingdom, and Israel. Thirteen African countries also participated and provided reports with the African Network and Registry.[53] Nigeria was one of the African countries, but the data presented could not have been a full representation because only a few fertility care centres in Nigeria report voluntarily to ANARA as there is also yet to be a

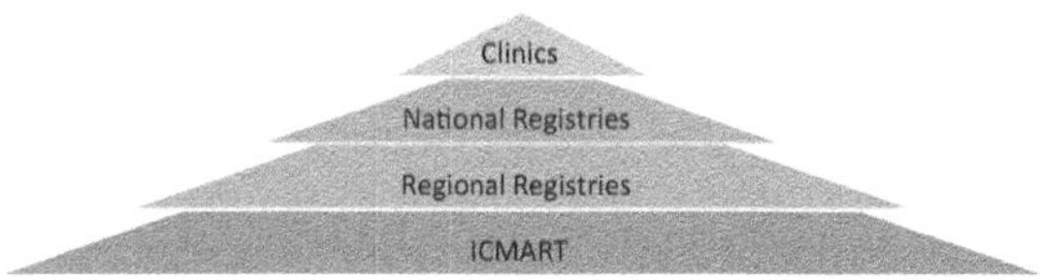

Diagram 12.2 ART data collection model

[51] Marc Germond and others, 'Core Data for Assisted Reproductive Technology Registers: Result of a Consensus Meeting' [2008] 17(6) Reprod. Biomed Online, 834.

[52] Silke Dyer, 'ART in Africa' 605. The report was for the period between 2008 and 2010.

[53] Benin, Cameroon, Egypt, Ghana, Ivory Coast, Mali, Mauritius, Morocco, Nigeria, Senegal, South Africa, Togo, and Tunisia.

comprehensive record for fertility centres practising ART.[54] The mode of collection at ICMART is that data is collected from regional or national registries or directly from individual clinics in a small number of countries where registers do not exist.

12.2.9 *Overview of Approaches to Data Collection*

Approaches to data collection have their inherent benefits and shortcomings. Generally, voluntary registries would potentially exhibit reporting biases as variations in clinical practices among clinics may lead to refraining from sharing relevant data. Lack of standardisation of practices in fertility care clinics brings about varied treatments especially concerning the transfer of embryos, cryopreservation standards and this may make reporting data uncomfortable for clinics that do not follow standard norms and policies for privacy reasons and fear of being branded. It is generally agreed that the preferred approach to data collection which ensures high-quality data validity and transparency is the mandatory approach with data collection at National levels. However, in countries where no governance of ART exists, the voluntary approach to data collection is deemed more convenient. Altogether, the validity of voluntary data collection registries has been called to question as some contributing centres do not feel comfortable sharing genuine data.[55]

12.3 Part Three

12.3.1 *ART Importance of Data Collection*

Firstly, Africa as a region has lagged in the establishment of National ART Data Registries[56] due to factors such as scantiness of scientific data, collaborations, government interests low fertility health literacy of patients and the public and most importantly clear regulations for ART practices, and this has epitomised the landscape of ART. Quality assurance has been identified to be the main target of collecting outcome data.[57]

[54] Silke Dyer, 'Nobody Left Behind' 2.

[55] Silke Dyer, 'Nobody Left Behind' [2019] 2.

[56] Ibid.

[57] Christian De Geyter and others, 'Data Collection Systems in ART Must Follow the Pace of Change in Clinical Practice' [2016] 31(10) Human Reprod. 2160.

To all stakeholders, both surveillance and vigilance in ART are crucial steps towards better quality control and full transparency.[58] The failure to report comprehensive data leads to underestimation of the risk of any treatment and the overestimation of its effectiveness.[59]

Secondly, the evolution of new reproductive technologies is another compelling and potential problem that informs ART data collection. Previously, treatment modalities uniformly consisted of straightforward series of events, starting with ovarian stimulation, and ending with a pregnancy test, and all this is traditionally reported within one year, however, cumulative outcome data of repeated cycles, even those including cryopreservation are now rarely available. Based on this, new approaches are required for data collection to achieve a complete catchment of information, long-term follow-up, and cumulative analysis over a prolonged time and across borders.[60]

Thirdly, reporting of ART outcomes, in theory, empowers prospective and current patients to make informed decisions about their treatment and choice of practitioners by providing accurate and transparent outcome data. This is intended to motivate fertility centres to practice high-quality evidence-based care.[61] The unintended consequences of this motivation may be that ART centre rankings may be the basis, but these rankings do not consistently consider important variables such as patient demographics or adverse clinical outcomes. Also, clinics advertise their success rates on websites sometimes in conflict, perhaps with professional guidelines intended to promote fair and meaningful data sharing without undue bias or deception.[62] It is documented that pregnancy and live birth rates have been indicated as the traditional metrics of ART success. Other factors that may be country and region-specific like access to adequate fertility treatments, costs, gendered, cultural and social issues may be

[58] Christian De Geyter, 'Assisted Reproductive Technology: Impact on Society and Need for Surveillance' [2019] 33 Best Practice & Research Clinical Endocrinology & Metabolism 1.

[59] Christian De Geyter, 'Data Collection Systems in ART' [2016] 2161.

[60] Ibid., 2161.

[61] Stephanie Gunderson and others, 'Public Reporting of IVF Outcomes Influences Medical Decision Making and Physician Training' [2020] 6(1) Fertility Research & Practice, 2.

[62] Ibid.

underplayed because they are not medically ascertained by medical professionals. Since ART practices affect different patient populations in varying ways, further research is needed to better define individual practices in different patient populations to aid patient choices.[63]

To this end, many countries have recognised the need for accurate and if possible, controlled data in their ART legal frameworks.[64] The relevance of data collection in monitoring practices and influencing regulatory development cannot be over emphasised. ART Data collection is beneficial and has its limitations which will be discussed below:

12.3.2 Benefits and Limitations of ART Data Registries: Important Considerations in a Regulatory Framework

12.3.2.1 Benefits of ART Data Collection

A major benefit of ART data collection would be to collate all data and analyse it to be able to identify trends that require regulatory attention. Fertility organisations or government bodies use registry data to inform guidelines or regulations. Information about the number of embryos transferred an upper age limit for women undergoing public treatment provides a good ground for regulatory influence in fertility practices.[65] Also, data registries provide large and valuable research data from which answers can be drawn to inform clinical and laboratory practices,[66] which would aid context-specific type of data as each country is different and has its peculiar experiences. These recorded outcomes highlight areas that require the needed attention in the kind of data collected and how such data would influence regulation. Another benefit is that national, regional, and global benchmarks are made available against which individual centres and countries can compare themselves. The benefits of routinely collected data include the coverage of populations of data that can be used to link other data sources. The establishment of large structured and integrated nationwide data sources tailored to respond to both research as well as

[63] Vitaly Kushinir and others, 'Systematic Review of Worldwide Trends in Assisted Reproductive Technology' [2017]15 Reprod. Biol Endocrinology, 7.

[64] Christian De Geyter, 'ART Systems: Impact on Society' [2019] 5.

[65] Silke Dyer, 'Nobody Left Behind' [2019] 1.

[66] Ibid., 2.

regulatory requirements is necessary to provide clinically useful information, and would make them more accessible at regional, national and international levels.[67]

12.3.2.2 Limitations

The limitations registries face in reporting data include; racial-ethnic and economic disparities in access to diagnosis and treatment which are difficult to address and may lead to underestimating the burden of infertility in minorities, especially given the huge disparities in underlying factors.[68] Typical example would be socio-economic disparities with respect to affordability of treatments which would favour specific groups and also accessibility of services in rural and urban areas in Nigeria. A framework that recognises differences and inequities presented in healthcare would be beneficial to address this limitation.

A single all-encompassing outcome runs the risk of creating league tables which could have unintended consequences as clinics may seek to gain superiority over one another.[69] Conventionally, all outcome measures include a numerator that represents the primary clinical parameter for success (e.g., live birth) and a denominator that defines the clinical context in which the outcome is measured, (e.g., IVF treatment cycle). The current private sector-driven approach to fertility healthcare delivery in Nigeria would typically favour clinics if success rates were the focus in ART data collection. As it is, there is no standardisation of practices and no clear regulatory pathway or consequences for unethical practices asides general medical/clinical intervention from professional associations. This limitation would be addressed if other important indicators are factored in data collection especially parameters on the ART process from reproductive material harvesting to pregnancy and eventual birth of children. Traditionally and for convenience IVF outcomes are presented as live birth per cycle of treatment initiated. Although live birth per woman is desirable, the need to have a time horizon for annual

[67] Salvatore Crisafulli and others, 'Role of Healthcare Databases and Registries for Surveillance of Orphan Drugs in the Real-World Setting: The Italian Case Study' [2019] 18(6) Expert Opinion on Drug Safety, 497.

[68] Maurizo Macaluso, 'A Public Health Focus on Infertility Prevention, Detection and Management' [2010] 93(1) Fertility & Sterility, 16.

[69] Hayden Homer, 'Reporting IVF Outcomes: The Devil Is in the Detail' [2020] Aust NZ J Obstet Gynaecol, 11.

reports from National datasets means that live birth per treatment cycle is the commonly chosen outcome published by most registries.[70] This can be very misleading as it does not consider the possibility of under-reporting cycle cancellations, differences in case-mix (such as potential poor responders or patients with repeated IVF failures).[71]

There is no denying the fact that the growing complexity of the practice of ART and its quest to improve success rates are forcing ever more significant alterations in the reporting of outcomes.[72] This has been interpreted to mean that the well-intentioned focus on consumer friendliness may fall prey to information overload and potential misinterpretation. There is a lack of infrastructure for standardised reporting on many public health issues and a need for cultural and social sensitivity when such data are gathered.[73] Additionally, the design of surveillance systems can be limited when existing policies assume a focus that is too narrow such that important aspects or consequences of policy interventions are missed.[74] The lack of global consensus regarding crucial unified outcome measures renders data reported by different registries difficult to compare due to reasons such as huge differences in cost of treatment, access to care, characteristics of patients treated and duration of infertility just to mention a few.[75]

[70] Hossam Abdalla, 'Is Meaningful Reporting of National IVF Outcome Data Possible?' [2010] 9.

[71] Ibid.

[72] Stan Williams and others, 'Public Reporting of Assisted Reproductive Technology Outcomes: Past, Present, and Future' [2015] Am J Obs & Gyn, 157.

[73] Sari Tudiver and others, 'Women's Surveillance: Implications for Policy' [2004] 4(31) BMC Women's Health, 2.

[74] Ibid.

[75] Bart Fauser, 'Towards the Global Coverage of a Unified Registry of IVF Outcomes' [2019] 38(2) Reprod. Biomed, 133.

12.4 Part Four

12.4.1 Influence of ART Data Collection in Regulatory Development

In recent times, a series of scientific and medical advances have all but deconstructed ART practice patterns thereby demanding that current reporting platforms be reconsidered for their continued ability to afford stakeholders with reasonable estimates of specific fertility treatments.[76] Also, in the past few years and at variable intervals, recommended limits for the numbers of embryo transfers that lead to multiple pregnancies and its following consequences have been issued based on identifiable data. In the US, stratified by the treatment category and the woman's age, both the Centre for Disease Control and Prevention (CDC) and the Society for Assisted Reproductive Technology (SART) under the relevant statute of the Fertility Clinic Success Rate and Certification Act[77] reports take great care to highlight the nationwide and clinic-specific embryo implantation rates along with pregnancy and live birth rates per cycle and transfer.[78]

It is important in this chapter to mention the major achievements of ANARA which is the existing framework for ART data collection in Africa. Until ANARA, data had largely been lacking because, for a quarter of a century, Africa had been behind other world regions that established ART registries to monitor trends and outcomes of ART and to report on indicators annually.[79] ART data collection has positively allowed the comparison of practices to generate clinical approaches to treatments in jurisdictions of the US and Europe (through EIM) to expand reporting range to include clinical outcomes of controlled ovarian hyperstimulation and timed intrauterine insemination as a significant driver of iatrogenic multiple births in need of enhanced surveillance and oversight.[80] Albeit in a subtle way, data collection is unifying practices and closing up wide disparities in access to ART. To be relevant to policy, registries seek

[76] Stan Williams, 'Public Reporting of ART' [2015], 157.

[77] FCSRCA.

[78] Stan Williams, 'Public Reporting of ART' [2015], 157.

[79] Silke Dyer and Thinus Kruger, 'Assisted Reproductive Technology in South Africa: First Results Generated from the South African Register of Assisted Reproductive Techniques' [2012] 102(3) SAMJ, 167.

[80] Aniket Kulkami and others, 'Fertility Treatments and Multiple Births in the United States' [2013] 369 N Engl J Med, 2218–2225.

to capture a range of data about the context of health behaviours and the interplay between the social and biological determinants of health including sex and gender differences.[81] From ICMART data, a negative association between gender inequality and ART utilisation has recently been shown; the greater the gender equality, the lower the ART utilisation.[82] Lastly, the rapid expansion of ART services in Nigeria has stimulated public interest in the need to address related ethical issues and the institutionalisation of regulatory guidelines to regulate the practice of ART in Nigeria, in other to protect patients' rights and safety.[83] This can only be fostered by adequate monitoring through data collection and surveillance.

12.4.2 How Can ART Data Be Incorporated into a Regulatory Framework to Influence the Development of Appropriate Legal Mechanisms in Nigeria?

Generally, ART practices in Nigeria are operable under the general principles in the law of contract, torts and family law as there is yet to be any specific regulation established to govern this field. This opens stakeholders to the unwieldy application of these general principles to issues that are specific to the healthcare activities and resulting issues of patients and children conceived or born through ART practices. The patient is thus subject to agreements made between themselves and their medical practitioner. There have been various discussions by scholars on developing adequate legal framework for ART practices in Nigeria and though this has received attention by the legislature through proposed bills,[84] there is still no comprehensive regulation for ART practices. This chapter has highlighted

[81] Sari Tudiver, 'Women's Surveillance: Implications for Policy' [2004] 1.

[82] Georgina Chambers and others, 'Gender Inequality and Utilization of ART: An International Analysis' [2018] 33(1) Hum Reprod, 65.

[83] Kehinde Bamgbopa and Patrick Okonta, 'Public Perceptions on Ethics in the Practice of ART in Nigeria [2018] 3(3) Global Reprod Health, 13.

[84] 'A Bill for an Act for the Regulations of In-vitro Fertilization, to prohibit certain practices in connection with IVF, to establish and IVF Authority to make provision in respect of children born of IVF process and for connected purposes (2017) (SB 127 and 'A Bill for an Act to provide for the Regulation and Supervision of Assisted Reproductive Technology and for matters connected therewith, 2017 (SB 325)—Both bills were read for the second time on the floor of the Senate in Nigeria and are still awaiting a third reading that will pass it into law.

the importance of data collection through the various approaches and methods of ART data collection at National, Regional and Global levels to emphasise how information gathering on ethical practices affect all the stakeholders in a fertility treatment and how the recording of outcomes would help in collating trends that would influence regulatory intervention. A good example is the role data collection has framed embryo transfer practices in various jurisdictions in respect with its effect on multiple pregnancies and births. In arguing for a Data collection approach using a public health perspective, much can be derived from existing types and approaches to data collection in ART registries discussed earlier in this chapter.

From a Nigerian context-specific perspective it is suggested that the legal framework for ART should make provisions for a National ART Data registry. The goal of the National Registry is to provide information to stakeholders, e.g., couples, other clinics, professionals, policy makers and global or regional registries, research purposes to follow up on ART treatments, evaluation of treatment outcomes for improvement in healthcare provision using core data sets that contain information that is needed in a manner that it can be usefully analysed. This National ART registry would act as a collation centre in Nigeria and data can then be provided to ANARA.

The approach for data collection should be mandatory for all practicing fertility centres both in the private and public sectors incorporating adequate feedback and audit mechanisms for improving treatment outcomes and ensuring practices follow laid down ethical procedures. There should also be a register of participating clinics to keep track of practices and ensure proper monitoring. Conditions bordering on facilities, ethical healthcare commitments and data collation centres within such clinics should also be stipulated.

The model suggested for the National ART data registry would require the establishment of regulatory bodies from existing National Health Authorities which would be dedicated to ART data collection. The data collected should be detailed incorporating relevant parameters such as clinical practices, medical, social, economic data relevant to policy which capture data about the context of reproductive health behaviours and their interplay between social and biological determinants of health including gender differences. The framework should provide detailed guidance in the type of data collected and should include both general population-based estimates and other indicators in addition to types of infertility issues and how they are managed. Access to treatment, utilisation of ART and burden of funding treatments is suggested as important information to be collected by the ART registry to create a balance in women accessing infertility services in a bid to edging healthcare disparities/inequities.

With respect to fertility centres, it is important to take learning from current trends where publishing of data based on success rates provides the perception of adequate care. It is important to note that part of the goal of data collection is to enable an evaluation of treatment, clearly data recorded and the way it is recorded influences the final analysis of success levels.

12.5 Part Five

12.5.1 Conclusion

The time has come to urgently address the fertility provision gap in developing countries by incorporating simplified and cost-effective Assisted Reproductive Technology programs to serve as valid treatment protocols when other alternatives and preventive measures have failed.[85] Data on the outcomes of such simplified and less expensive approaches must however be continually monitored and analysed to measure cost-effectiveness and benefits.[86] It is advocated that National ART data registries would effective and would discourage unwieldy collation and better monitoring by professional associations or government institutions, and also because of the diversity in healthcare structures. Incorporating ART data collection through national registries in the regulatory framework for ART will make the regional structure in ANARA more effective just like the EIM in Europe, as there is good reason to believe that the ANARA regional registry will ultimately help to reduce the burden of infertility in Africa.[87]

[85] Alfred Murage and others, 'Assisted Reproductive Services Provision in a Developing Country: Time to Act' [2011] 96(4) Fertility & Sterility, 967.

[86] Ibid., 967.

[87] Silke Dyer, 'Nobody Left Behind' [2019] 2.

Bibliography

Books

Crawford S and others, ART Surveillance: Who, What, When and How? (4 edn, Cambridge University Press 2019)

Salam H, The Evidence-Based Practice of Assisted Reproduction. In Orit Taubman Ben-ari (ed), Pathways and Barriers to Parenthood-Existential Concerns Regarding Fertility, Pregnancy and Early Parenthood (Springer Publishers: Switzerland 2019) 152

Toner J and others, ART Surveillance in North America. In Dmitry K and others (eds), Assisted Reproductive Technology Surveillance (Cambridge University Press: United Kingdom 2019) 172

Wager K and others, Health Care Information Systems—A Practical Approach to Healthcare Management (Jossey Bass Publishers: United States 2017)

Journal Articles

Abbasi M and others, 'The Development of a Minimum Data Set for an Infertility Registry' [2018] 15(1) Perspectives in Health Information Management 1.

Anderson R, 'The Collection, Linking and Use of Data in Biomedical Research and Healthcare: Ethical Issues' [2015] 1(1) Nuffield Council of Bioethics <https://doi.org/10.17863/CAM.31760> accessed 12 December 2021

Benchimol E and others, 'Development and Use of Reporting Guidelines for Assessing the Quality of Validation Studies of Health Administrative Data' [2011] 64(8) Journal of Clinical Epidemiology 821–829

Bernstein A and Sweetney M, 'Public Health Surveillance Data: Legal, Policy, Ethical, Regulatory & Practical Issues' [2012] 61(1) MMWR 30

De Geyter C and others, 'Assisted Reproductive Technology: Impact on Society and Need for Surveillance [2019] 33(1) Best Practice & Research Clinical Endocrinology & Metabolism 3–8

———, 'Data Collection Systems in ART Must Follow the Pace of Change in Clinical Practice' [2016] 31(10) Human Reproduction 2160–2163

———, '20 Years of the European IVF Monitoring Consortium Registry: What Have We Learned? A Comparison with Registries from Two Other Regions' [2020] 35(12) Human Reproduction 2832

De Mouzon J and others, 'Establishing a National In Vitro Fertilization Registry: Methodological Problems & Analysis of Success Rates' [1993] 12(1) Statistics in Medicine 39–50

De Mouzon J, 'International Committee for Monitoring Assisted Reproductive Technologies World Report on Assisted Reproductive Technology 2012' [2020] 35(8) Human Reproduction 1900–1913

Gunderson S and others, 'Public reporting of IVF Outcomes Influences Medical Decision Making and Physician Training' [2020] 6(1) Fertility Research & Practice 1–6

Jain T and others, '30 years of Data: Impact of the United States in In-Vitro Fertilization Data Registry on Advancing Fertility Care' [2019] 111(3) Fertility and Sterility 2832

Kissin D and others, 'States Monitoring ART (SMART) Collaborative: Data Collection, Linkage, Dissemination and Use' [2013] 22(7) Journal of Women's Health 571–580

Kruse C and others, 'The Use of Electronic Health Records to Support Population Health: A Systematic Review of the Literature' [2018] 42(11) Journal of Medical Systems 1–16

Kushinir V and others, 'Systematic Review of Worldwide Trends in Assisted Reproductive Technology' [2017] 15(1) Reproductive Biology & Endocrinology 1–9

Lancaster P and others, 'Registers of IVF and Assisted Conception' [1996] 11(4) Human Reproduction <https://doi.org/10.1093/humrep/11.suppl_4.89> accessed 12 November 2021

Lee L and Thacker S, 'Public Health Surveillance and Knowing About Health in the Context of Growing Sources of Health Data' [2011] 41(6) American Journal of Preventive Medicine 636–640

Luceno F, 'Comparison of IVF Cycles Reported in a Voluntary ART Registry with a Mandatory Registry in Spain' [2010] 25(12) Human Reproduction <https://doi.org/10.1093/humrep/deq267> accessed 15 October 2021

Menizibeya W, 'The Nigerian Healthcare System: Need for Integrating Adequate Medical Intelligence and Surveillance Systems' [2011] 3(4) Journal of Pharmacy & Bio allied Sciences 470

Nygren K, 'International Registries of Assisted Reproductive Technologies'. In Vayena and others (eds), Report of a Meeting on Medical, Ethical & Social Aspects of Assisted Reproduction (World Health Organization 2002) 377.

Sadeghi M, 'The 40th Anniversary of IVF: Has ART's Success Reached its Peak?' [2018] 19(2) Journal of Reproduction and Fertility 16

Schmidt F, 'Demographic and Medical Consequences of the Postponement of Parenthood' [2012] 18(1) Human Reproduction, ESHRE Reproduction and Society Task Force 29

Silke D and others, 'ART in Africa: A 5-Year Trend Analysis from the African Network and Registry for Assisted Reproductive Technology' [2020] 41(4) RBMO, 604

St Louis M and Thacker S, 'Global Health Surveillance' [2012] 61(1) MMWR 15

Sunderan S, 'ART Surveillance- United States, 2015' [2018] 1(1) Morbidity and Morality Weekly Report: Surveillance Summary

Wyns C, 'For the European IVF Monitoring Consortium for the European Society of Human Reproduction and Embryology (ESHRE) ART in Europe 2016: Results generated from European Registries' [2020] 1(1) Human Reproduction 2832

Zahmatkeshan M and others, 'ART Registries—Characteristics and Experiences: A Comparative Study' [2019] 8(3) Journal of Family Medicine and Primary Care 449

Index

O. S. Adelakun and E. Ndoni (eds.), *Reproductive Health and Assisted Reproductive Technologies In Sub-Saharan Africa*, Sustainable Development Goals Series, https://doi.org/10.1007/978-981-99-2411-0

The manufacturer's authorised representative in the EU is Springer Nature Customer Service Centre GmbH, Europaplatz 3, 69115 Heidelberg, Germany. If you have any concerns regarding our products, please contact ProductSafety@springernature.com

Printed and bound by CPI Group (UK) Ltd, Croydon, CR0 4YY
30/09/2026
02225311-0013